Paul Andreu, Architect

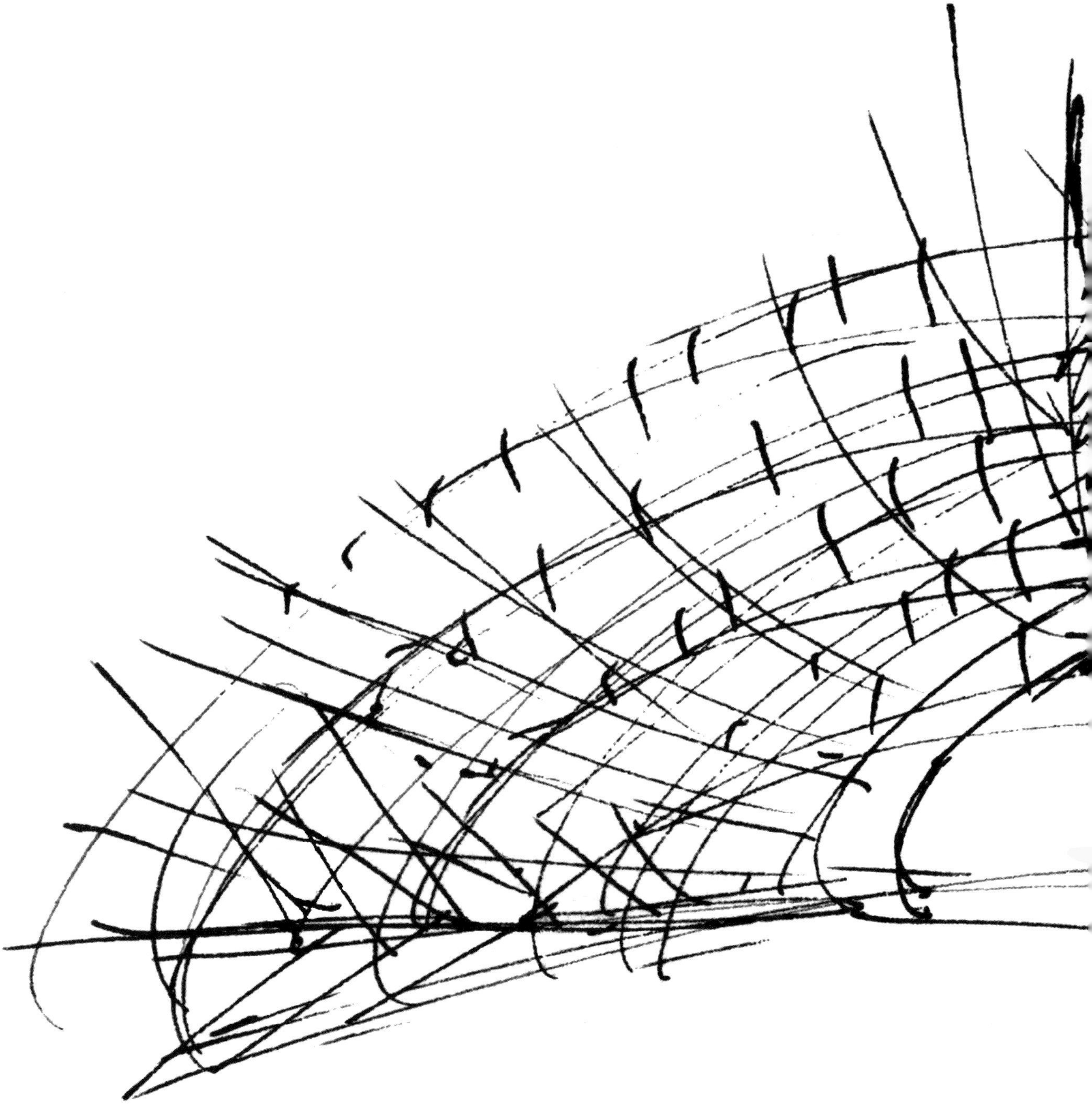

Paul Andreu, Architect

Philip Jodidio

With a Preface by Adrian Frutiger

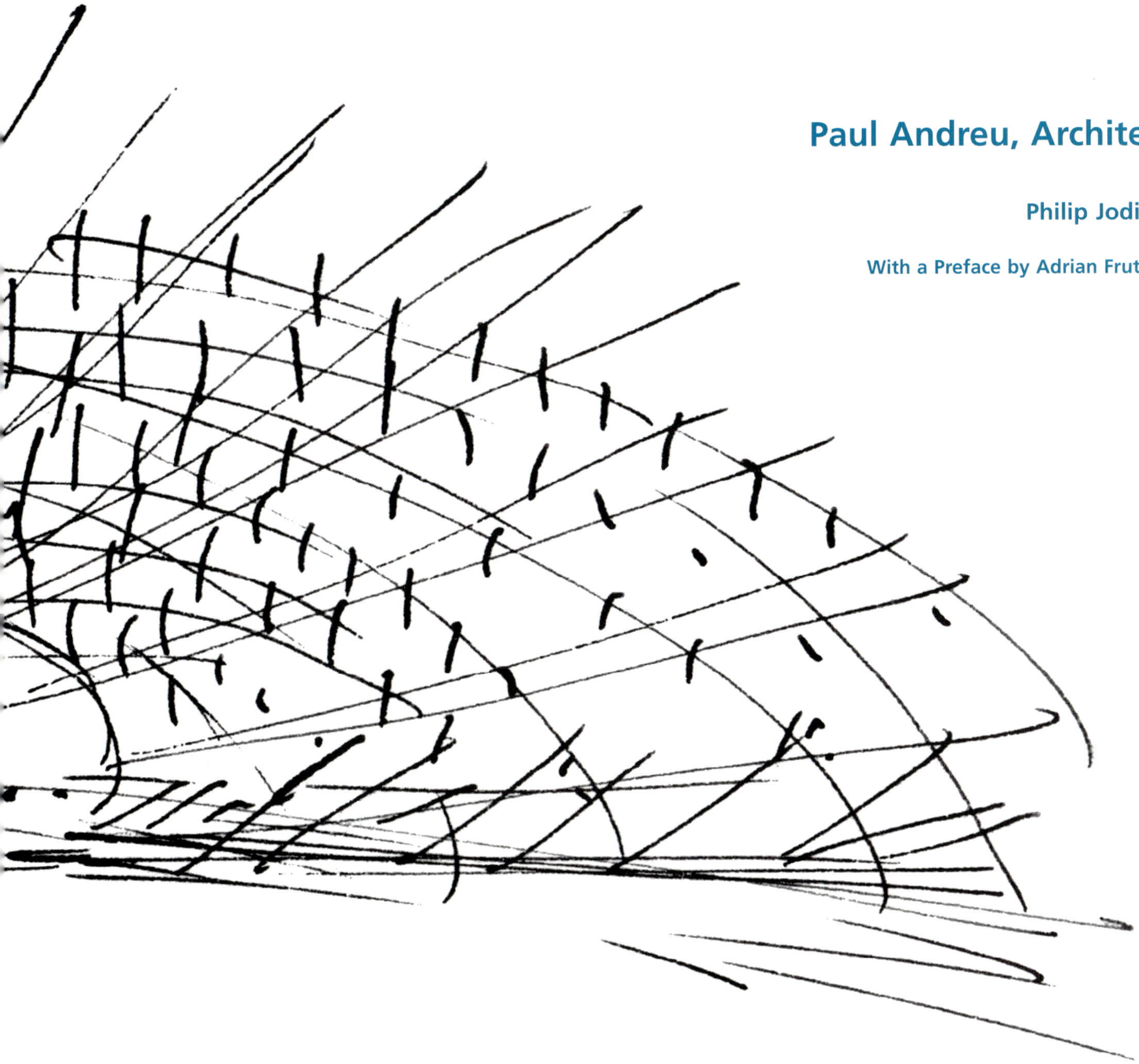

BIRKHÄUSER – Publishers for Architecture
Basel · Berlin · Boston

Layout and cover design:
Sans Studio, Paris

Coordination and research for the office of Paul Andreu:
Patricia Casse, Paris

Translation of the preface by Adrian Frutiger:
Michael Robinson, London

Fonts: Frutiger Light / Frutiger Roman / Frutiger Bold
Paper: Zanders Mega-Matt 150 g/m²
Photolithography: BSMD, Paris
Printing and Binding: fgb Freiburger Graphische Betriebe

A CIP catalogue record for this book is available from the Library of Congress, Washington D.C., USA

Bibliographic information published by Die Deutsche Bibliothek
Die Deutsche Bibliothek lists this publication in the Deutsche Nationalbibliografie;
detailed bibliographic data is available in the Internet at <http://dnb.ddb.de>.

Part of Springer Science + Business Media
Printed on acid-free paper produced from chlorine-free pulp. TCF ∞
Printed in Germany
ISBN 3-7643-7010-6

www.birkhauser.ch
9 8 7 6 5 4 3 2 1

Contents

Preface by Adrian Frutiger

A Building, a Typeface

Architecture and lettering have been related formally since ancient times. Their form mirrors the intellectual and cultural life of every epoch. And yet the two are seen as distinct because buildings have three dimensions and printed pages two planes. It was conversations about such simple and yet serious topics that sparked the friendship between Paul Andreu and me.

We first met in summer 1970. Paul Andreu told me he was looking for a qualified colleague to work with him on a complete signing system for the Roissy airport. He knew my name because of the success of the "Univers" font. I was delighted to accept his offer. I realized even while I was on my way home that Univers wouldn't do for this particular purpose. The Univers family (with 21 variants) is built up on a closed chain grid. Univers is based on a closed curve, and the letters fit together like the links of a chain. The reader's eye glides over it, taking in words, indeed whole sentences, at a glance. My mind was looking to establish rules for legibility in new conditions. Absorbing visual information from signs requires open, easily recognizable characters. Signs and signals giving directions over a distance in crowded passenger areas have to meet the same criteria. Letters and figures have to be recognizable from any angle in a flash, e.g. diagonally from below, distorted - when walking quickly through the space.

So I was faced with a completely new task. We had to design a sans-serif font that would be appropriate to these new requirements. The letter S, with very open internal forms, emerged as a basis. The other letters and figures followed. We set up a fictitious sign, and flaws emerged when we tried looking at it. All the basic needs for a "signal font" were in place after ten days' intensive work. Paul Andreu had explained the nature of the task to me. Bilingual signs: French in black on white, English white lettering on a dark yellow background. We made a sign:

Départ Porte S-25 — Departure Gate S-25 (on a yellow background)

I went to see Paul Andreu with this sign. I simply explained that Univers was too round and closed for a signal font. This was a new font, with instantly comprehensible figures and letters. I saw his eyes light up, he just said: "A new alphabet for the airport!" That was the start of an association that was to last for five years.

There were about ten people involved in our working group: Paul Andreu, his colleagues, architects and technicians, P. Motte, the interior designer and us for the signing. We met twice or three times a month. The way Paul Andreu led the discussions quickly revealed that he'd studied both architecture and building engineering. This double training meant he could intervene positively in the

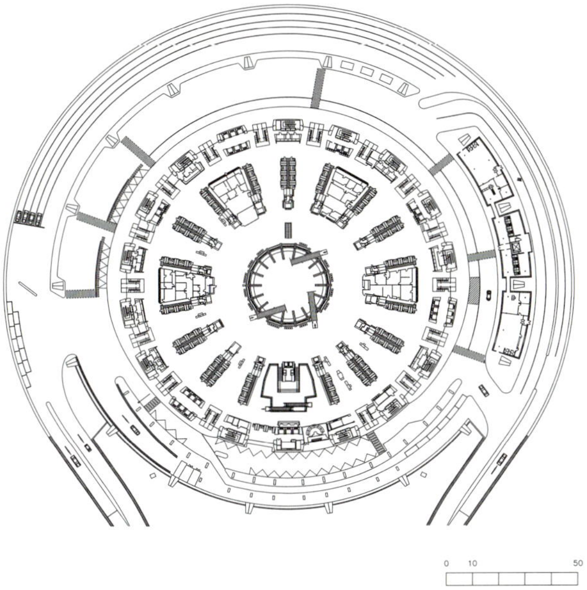

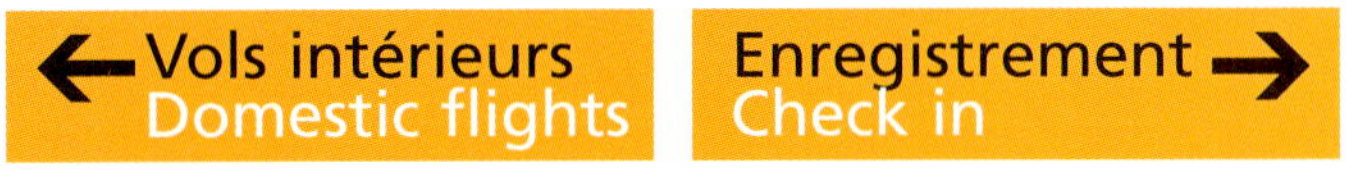

Paul Andreu confirms that Adrian Frutiger was inspired by the round form of Terminal 1 when he conceived the typography for the airport. Above, a drawing by Andreu and two of the Terminal 1 signs designed by Frutiger.

This book is typeset in Frutiger Light, Frutiger Roman and Frutiger Bold

discussions. The signs were discussed as well. I explained the typographical structure: lines of lettering consisting of cap height, ascenders, descenders, the distance between the lines, the space above and below and the margins. All these ideas were new to my architecture colleagues, even though it was actually just architecture in two dimensions.

We often went on chatting after the discussions. We moved on from architecture and typography to more general considerations, indeed convictions, about being human. What is my responsibility to the environment? I remember him saying something along these lines: "The essential thing is the built work. The meaning of an architect's profession is service to the building for which he is responsible." I can say the same thing about fonts. These are tools serving writer and reader. A typeface is good if readers don't notice it.

Access from central Paris to Charles-de-Gaulle Airport is by a direct rail link. The station building is beautifully constructed: the roof, supported by slender columns, is almost like a flat cathedral, perforated by wide skylights. The railway runs right down at the bottom. The whole thing is built in fine fair-faced concrete. Paul Andreu wanted to stop the walls of the sunken railway being festooned with posters, as the Métro stations are. There is a French law stating that no poster can be put up if a wall has a work of art on it. Paul Andreu asked me to suggest a lively design for the walls. I started throwing ideas down - and then throwing them out. One day I had a vision: a five giant fingers, scratching symbolic signs in the concrete. I started sketching feverishly: large, symbolic drawings built up into a band, each sign a kind of symbol, barely recognizable. The timber shuttering was made up of tall panels with a ventilation aperture at the top. This constant rhythm produced something like a musical variation. The series of signs developed from this. A kind of Noah's Ark flowed into a fish shape, and mathematical sign-shapes alternated with kinds of snake or fish. Viewers start to see a figure, but then the idea slips away from them.

I finished my design two or three weeks later. I showed Paul Andreu the whole thing, the sketches and the concrete experiment. He accepted this strange "work of art."

This piece of work was the last thing I had to do for Charles-de-Gaulle Airport. Other projects were waiting for me. Linotype later bought the Roissy alphabet. We built it up into a font family named after me.

Paul Andreu and I met up many more times to look at things or talk. Friendships this deep last for ever.

Paul Andreu is surely one of the most influential architects of his generation. Given the nature of his work, concentrated on airports, millions of travelers across the world experience his designs each year without necessarily knowing the architect's name. Today, he is bringing his pragmatic sense of combined beauty and functionality to significant public buildings like the new Beijing National Opera. No living French architect has straddled the globe in this fashion and the time has surely come to recognize the importance of the work of Paul Andreu.

From Darkness into Light
The Architecture of Paul Andreu

The rapport between creativity and national identity is often debated inconclusively. Does an artist or an architect really include something of their own country in their work? This question is undoubtedly not precise enough. Multiple factors influence design, for example education and the attitude of the creator. The case of Japanese architects like Tadao Ando who only grudgingly admit that there are numerous national characteristics in their work comes to mind. Indeed, at a certain level of international notoriety, an architect becomes more a man or woman of the world than a local figure. Great architecture must surely reach beyond national boundaries to express emotions and needs that are shared across civilizations. And yet every architect has his point of departure, his formative experience. The case of Paul Andreu is a fascinating one because he is very much a product of the French system, and yet he has succeeded in building around the globe. Is there something "French" about his work, some quality that may be unique to his background?
Paul Andreu was born on July 10, 1938 in Caudéran in the Gironde region of France. He obtained diplomas from the École Polytechnique (1961), the École Nationale des Ponts et Chaussées (1963, as an engineer) and as an architect from the École des Beaux Arts in Paris (1968). This curriculum vitae is particularly impressive if one knows the French educational system. Architect-engineers are a rare breed, but very few Frenchmen hold diplomas from such prestigious schools as Polytechnique, Ponts et Chaussées and the Beaux-Arts. Quite obviously Andreu is not of the breed of self-taught architects that seem to fascinate the public. Indeed he reacts testily to those who may not understand the nature of his educational background. "Sometimes the critics make me laugh," he says, "for example the fellow who wrote, 'He doesn't have an architect's diploma, he is just an engineer.' Well, I'm sorry if Wright, Le Corbusier and Ando didn't get their diplomas and I did, then I must be the fool." As Chief Architect of the Aéroports de Paris he has been responsible not only for the development of Charles-de-Gaulle (Roissy) Airport, but also for the development of more than fifty other airports around the world such as those of Jakarta (Soekarno-Hatta Airport, 1977-85), Abu Dhabi or Shanghai (Shanghai Pudong Airport, 1996-99). Andreu has also worked on other large-scale projects such as the terminal for the Channel Tunnel (French Terminal, Calais, 1986-93) and currently

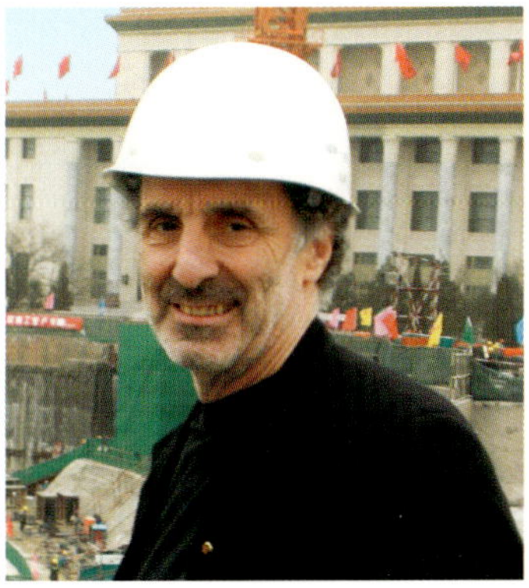

A portrait of Paul Andreu taken on one of his many visits to a work site.

the Beijing Opera House (The National Grand Theater, 1999-2005).
Airport design is indeed a very special branch of architecture and few individuals really make a significant mark of their own in such large-scale and diverse projects. Rather large, anonymous firms are often responsible for mediocre designs that are more of a burden to travelers than a pleasure. Associated with the Aéroports de Paris organization, Andreu has presided over the destiny of Roissy Charles-de-Gaulle Airport for almost forty years. In itself this would have sufficed to put him in the company of major world architects, but he has gone much further. Though a statistical approach is of little interest in this case, it can be asked if any one architect has built structures seen by more people in the world than Paul Andreu. Tens of millions of voyagers move through his airports, most of them never having heard of the designer, but that is also not the point. By mastering the art of airport design, and moving beyond the complex practical considerations to the realm of architectural creativity, he has done more than most to make airline travel on a planetary scale conceivable. Working with budgetary constraints that would have hampered lesser designers, Andreu has made Roissy and other airports pleasant, light-filled experiences. Naturally an evolving pattern of greater and greater security needs has somewhat altered even his most successful terminals, but the fact remains that in a structure like Roissy Terminal 2 F, the voyager has an experience of a kind of modern architecture that serves and uplifts.
Does Andreu then have something very particularly French about him? A pragmatism and a humor that goes with a broad cultural background undoubtedly. He also has a humility which is somewhat rarer amongst the elite of the French cultural establishment, and that may be one of the secrets to his worldwide success. Paul Andreu questions himself and those around him, he seeks and finds responses. In this sense, he may be an example of what is best in France. Formed by its excellent "grandes écoles" that train only the brightest students, he brings an inquisitive character and an ability to doubt to his work. Both Polytechnique and Ponts et Chaussées go beyond teaching technical subjects and actually form the student's way of thinking. As an engineer, Andreu surely approaches his buildings in a different way than a "pure" architect. Indeed, the interview he granted for this book is revealing in that respect. His method is not one of simple esthetics applied to an underlying structure that is repetitive or unimaginative. He looks within and makes esthetics obey a rigorous reasoning that may well be a fruit of his origins and education.

Paul Andreu's experience as an architect is indeed unique, having been based so strongly in the area of airports. More than specifically French characteristics, it appears that his work can be identified through a series of conditions and concepts that are either the result of his ongoing work, a matter of choice or fundamental questions related to his education and background as an engineer-architect. As he says, questions of style may be more for the domain of the critics than for architects themselves. Though he rejects the idea that he has a "style" his creative life has led him to a number of conclusions and somewhat atypical solutions that form a whole, that can be observed not only in his airports, but also in his more recent work on museums or cultural facilities. There is something of the demiurge in Paul Andreu, as there often is in an architect, but he has managed to build on such a scale that this tendency is exacerbated or accentuated more than it is amongst many of his colleagues. He has had the opportunity to create his own universes, with the powerful backing of the Aéroports de Paris, and that desire to make almost self-sufficient entities carries forward even into his newer, more urban projects. Paul Andreu's designs are more closed shells opening out into the light than they are fundamentally permeable. Often womb-like but clearly destined to vast in and out flows, they are specific to his personality and to his experience. In this, Paul Andreu's case is unique and fascinating. His route would not be one that others could easily follow, but examining his path is nonetheless an instructive activity in the context of the differing solutions proposed by contemporary architects for the needs of modern society.

The Master of Roissy

Paul Andreu began working for the Aéroports de Paris in 1965, but it was in 1967 when work began on the new airport at Roissy that he came to play a more prominent role. His own description of his role in the design of Charles-de-Gaulle Airport is very instructive for understanding his method, even beyond the area of airport design. It might be imagined for example that the number of practical constraints in airport construction ranging from transport interface (car, rail, bus etc.) to security to baggage handling and traffic would severely restrict the possible creativity of the architect. On this point, Andreu says, "I don't think that the technical constraints in an airport are any more invasive than in a hospital for example. Two things are important in airport design – having a good deal of experience and knowing the program. That is where the architecture comes in. Funnily enough knowing nothing and knowing a great deal can both be stimulating. What is really bad is knowing just a little. It holds you back, you can't invent in that situation." Nonetheless it could be imagined that in a project as complex as Roissy the degree of personal intervention of any one person, be he the Chief Architect as was Andreu's case would be limited. Andreu replies, "There is not a building I have worked on in which I have not had a determining influence. And it is not just because I make choices, it is also because I draw myself. Some very lucid architects are able

A picture taken in about 1996 of the Charles-de-Gaulle Airport, Terminal 2 F, when work was advancing on the shell of the central volume of the structure. Paul Andreu is visible with his back turned in a black shirt.

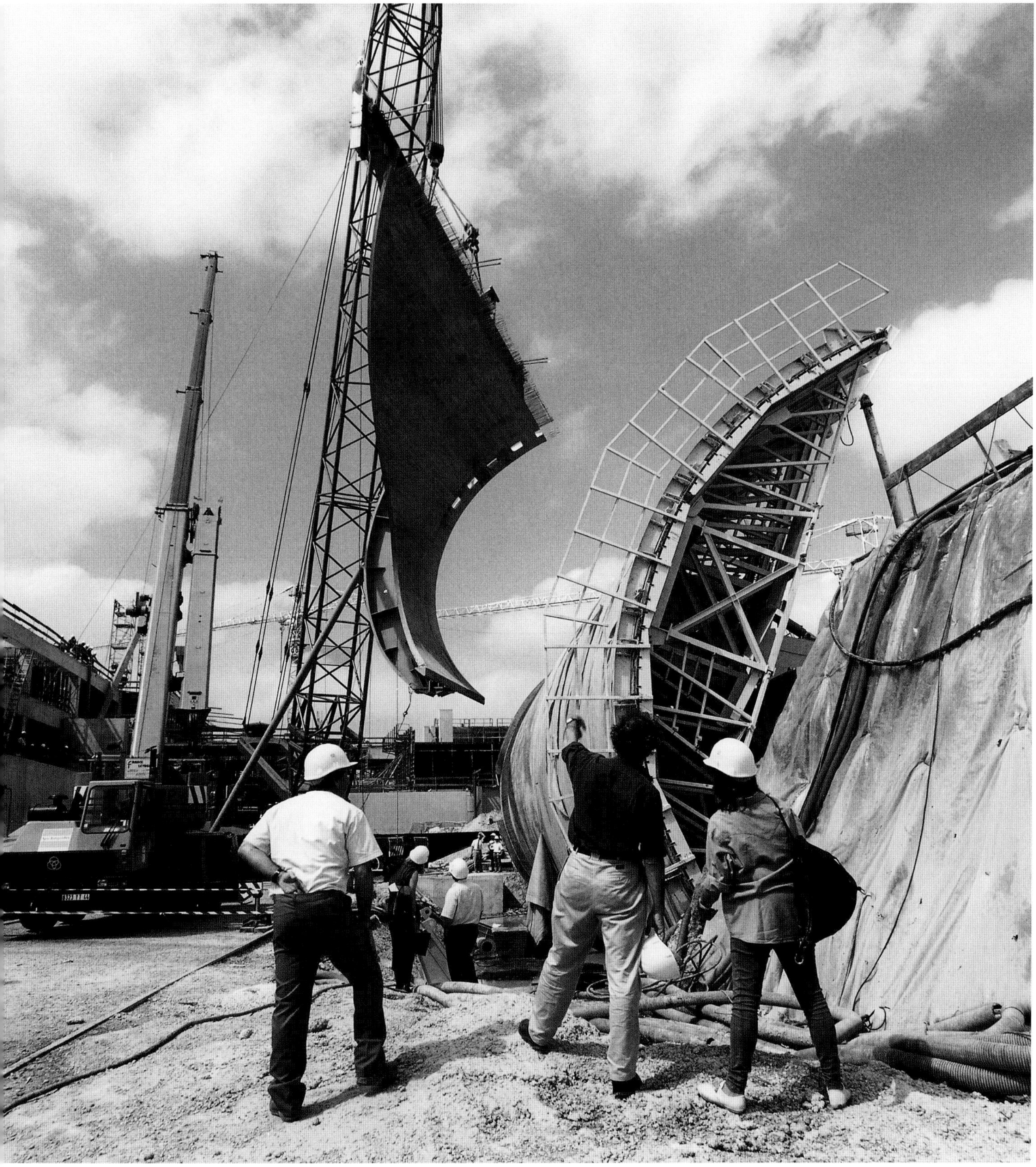

to pick between a few alternatives, but frequently they don't draw themselves … they give general orientations. Some people can do that, but I absolutely can't. I am incapable of choosing one alternative if I have not myself gone through the process of trying to find my own solution. I can certainly opt for somebody else's idea, but I have to have my own concept. In 95 percent of my buildings the parti is my own. At the same time, I need strong people around me. You can't go from a drawing to something that actually works without help."

One interesting aspect of Andreu's work is clearly his training as an engineer. Watching him draw or seeing his attention to detail can give the impression that he is very technically oriented. "I am interested in the technical aspects of architecture of course," he says, "but I rarely can dissociate the two. When I work on a project, I find that there is often an early period dominated by a kind of euphoria, an optimism if you will. Usually, I seek to inspire myself from something I did before, but then there comes the time when it becomes obvious that that won't work." Andreu's admission that he refers back to his own earlier solutions might well be an indication of a lack of inspiration, an idea that he forcefully rejects. "An original idea is never the product of pure methodological analysis," he says. "It is necessary to have already done something to be able to arrive at what I would call a frontier of dissatisfaction, an impossibility. A new idea is always a product of dissatisfaction, and not of some kind of abstract organized reasoning." It may not always be possible to identify the specific elements in Andreu's architecture that are linked to his engineer's background, but there are always great openings, vaults, domes or other indications that technology has been stretched to its rational limits in his buildings.

The idea of dissatisfaction seems deep-seated in Paul Andreu himself. There is a kind of melancholy in his way of being that could show that he has been frustrated by his own inability to create in a certain way. "I have neither regrets nor remorse about what I have done, and yet I am self-critical," he says. "When I was young, I couldn't stand walking through my own projects. I was like a stage director who doesn't go to his own plays. I love a work site because you can still intervene in some ways, but with a completed building, you can't." Having reached an obvious professional maturity, Paul Andreu no longer seems to have the same reticence about his own work. "I have come to grips with the idea of perfection," he explains. "I know that things can never really be perfect. I have also concluded that actively pursuing perfection can lead to a drying up of the substance of architecture. There is a way of seeking perfection that empties architecture of its meaning and feeling. Today, I understand that there is something fundamentally interesting in imperfection." The carefully crafted

Charles-de-Gaulle Airport Terminal 1 as seen from the runway side. Although the building is in fact quite massive, from even a slight distance, its low-lying volume gives it a less imposing presence than might be expected.

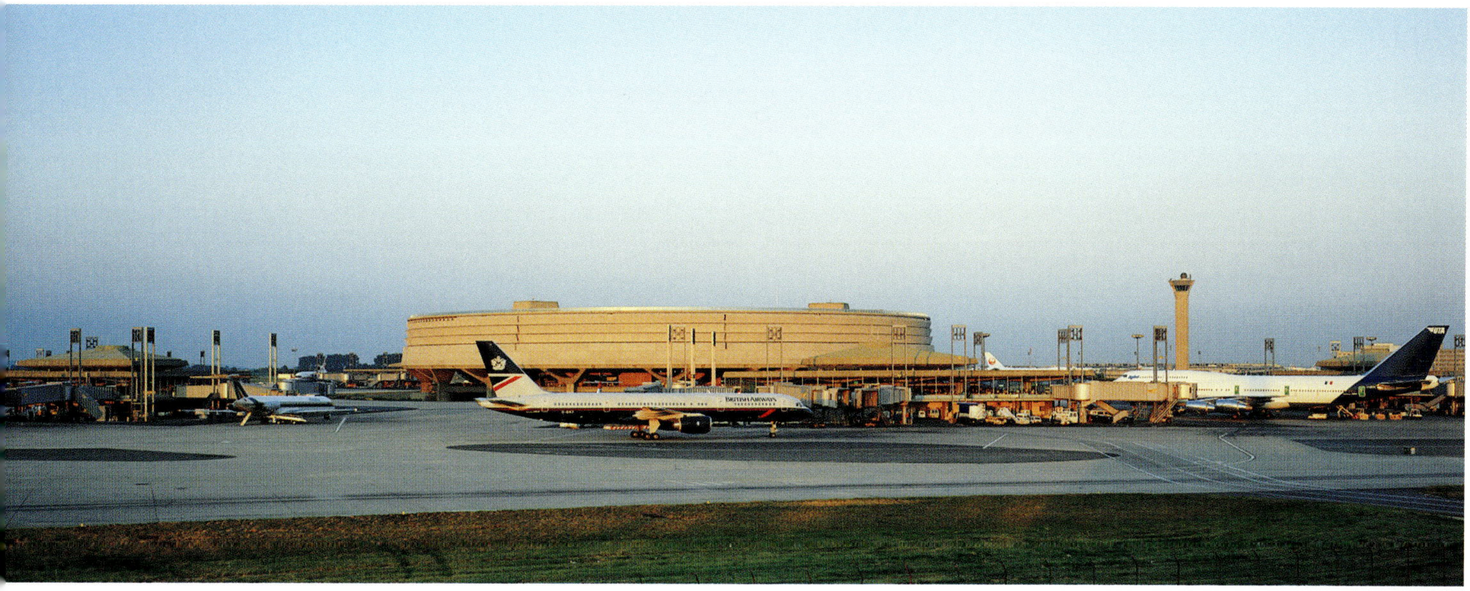

buildings of Paul Andreu may not reveal obvious flaws, but his explanation goes a long way to revealing what separates him from less creative architects. "Imagine a big concrete panel," he says. "Sometimes there is a flaw, something that the people who worked on it just did not see or predict. But that flaw can have great interest. Think of the stones that the Chinese have long collected because they evoke an imaginary scene. It may be imperfections in the stones that make people dream. But that happens precisely because nobody planned it that way. You can't plan imperfections, it would be a bit like planning naiveté, but imperfections are what gives life."

One of the obvious strong points of the architecture of Paul Andreu has been his ability to imagine the future development of airports or other facilities. Roissy is the most obvious case in point, with its successive phases. And yet there is a troubling dissimilarity between the round, fortress-like concrete volume and the more open glass, steel and concrete designs of Roissy 2. Why was there less continuity here than might have been imagined? Paul Andreu explains the change and some of the underlying forces that dictate airport architecture. "The reasons for the differences between Roissy 1 and Roissy 2 are clear," he says. "From the very first, Roissy was destined to be a modular airport that could be expanded. At the time, in the late 1960's, we couldn't imagine creating a terminal that could handle more than six million passengers a year. That was the capacity at the time of Orly Sud. So in the original plans we conceived of five identical, round terminals, each handling six million passengers. Afterwards, we thought it would be time to create another airport elsewhere. But the situation evolved, even as we were designing Roissy 1. We thought, for example that very large supersonic aircraft would be available soon. And we realized a little late that six million passengers wasn't enough – Roissy 1 had to be increased to a capacity of eight or nine million. It is essential too to realize that the client is important in these situations. Air France did not have an obvious financial interest in leaving Orly at the time, when Roissy 1 got underway, but for Roissy 2, they did, and they decided that they didn't like the idea of identical round terminals. This occurred at the time of the first oil crisis, when Roissy 2 was being conceived. And things

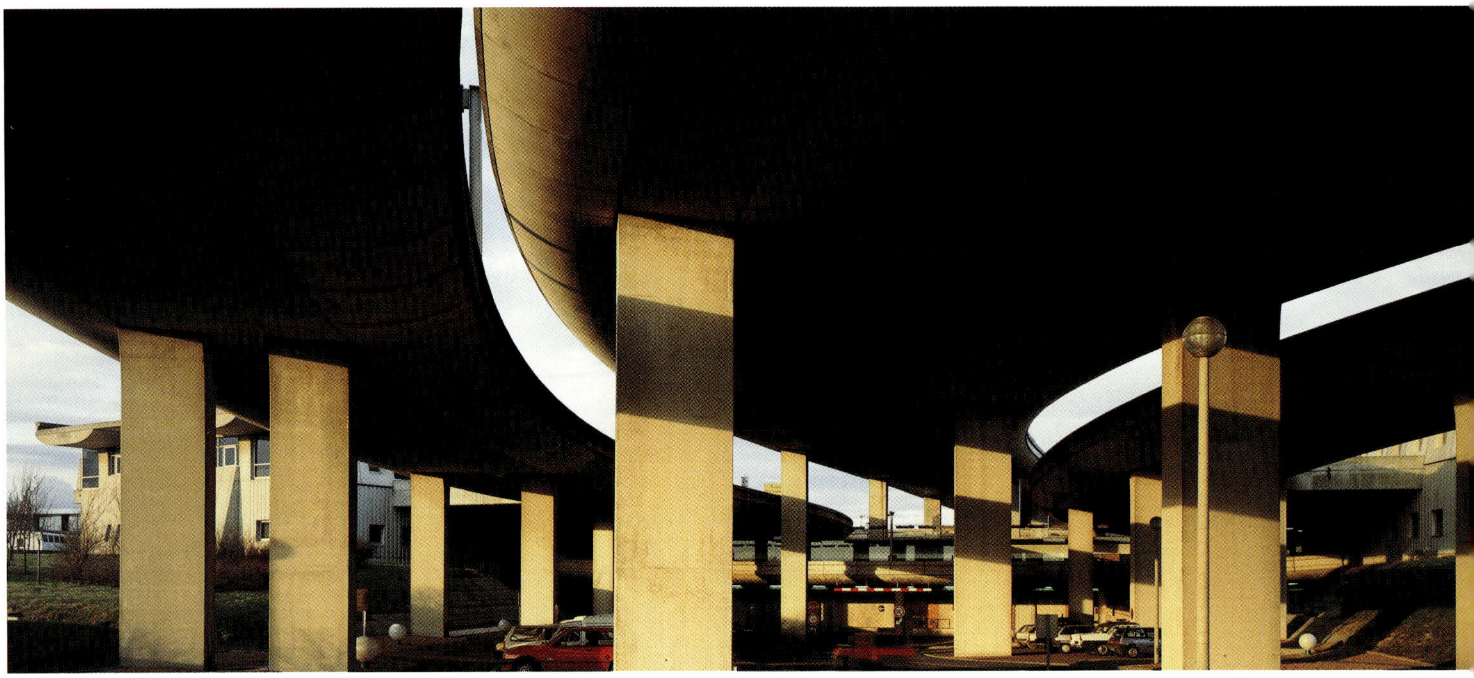

had to be inexpensive ..." Still the radical stylistic change between the two parts of the airport is not clear. Why was the round form abandoned? "Because it was stilted," says Andreu. "You could handle up to ten million, and then what? Another one three or four kilometers away? And then what do you do with traffic between terminals? Roissy 1 was crystalline, fixed in space and time. Roissy 2 was conceived more in a pattern of arborescence-programmed growth. Transit passengers had become an important issue between the dates of the two terminals."

One rather striking element about Roissy and indeed some of Andreu's other airports, is the looping road system whose logic is not at once readily apparent. Today, the hotels that populate the immediate areas around the airport are not all readily accessible. Andreu says that he was very much involved in the process of the road design, but did not always agree with what developed with time. "What we really needed," says Andreu, "is two separate road systems – one for the terminals and another for ancillary buildings like the hotels. Once people started making exceptions to that rule, things got less and less rational." Indeed access roads play a significant role in Andreu's reasoning. "The issue of complexity arises in the case of Roissy 1," he says, "because so many roads are inside the main volume. Roissy 2 changes this idea completely, the roads are outside and the architecture is lighter and brighter." Andreu's remark about compromises in road design, implying that decisions other than his own may have created undue complexity, again raises the issue of just how much influence one man can have on such a vast enterprise. It would seem clear that the opportunities for unfortunate compromise increase in proportion to the size of the project. "When one speaks in terms of architectural units," says Andreu, "it sounds suspiciously like arithmetic. It isn't some kind of theoretical calculation that dictates what happens, it is the systems themselves. All living organisms have an infinite desire to reproduce and a capacity to adapt to

Charles-de-Gaulle Airport, Terminal 2 A as seen from the looping access road system.

circumstances. Rigidity leads to death. Modernism was a sort of mad vision, in the image of Le Corbusier's Plan Voisin that would have reshaped Paris. This was the result of a love of mathematically oriented planning. In Roissy 2, there was a persistence in certain forms and ideas, but there is also a capacity to adapt the structures to new circumstances. One of the main virtues of Roissy 2 was that we decided to clearly separate areas under construction from active terminals. This decision was born out of our observation of some permanent work sites like La Défense. Our capacity to enlarge Roissy 2 in an efficient, coherent matter was largely a question of road design. Instead of an apparently logical straight road that cuts through the heart of an airport like the one in Dallas-Fort Worth, we made a succession of looping roads. When we wanted to add a high-speed rail station to Terminal 2 F, we were able to do it because of this capacity to route traffic around work sites." Andreu admits that he attempted in the 1990's to rectify some of the undue complexity that crept into the Roissy road plan but that questions of cost and incomprehension made him give up. "Were the occupation of land is concerned," he says, "some people just can't understand that users have difficulty with roads or structures that are drawn up by such clever minds." Andreu touches in passing here on the issue of French engineering and its frequent incapacity to propose solutions that are readily usable. Andreu's own engineering bias was undoubtedly tempered by his architectural background, but also by his humanism. It could be noted in passing however that he is at once critical of the complexity of the road systems of Roissy and thoroughly defensive of them, suggesting that looping roads were really what made the whole thing possible. There is also a question of proportion in the reaction of architects and engineers to the needs of the public. As Andreu says, sometimes the designers just can't understand that the public does not use systems as they were intended to be used. Paul Andreu is critical of the straight access road of Dallas-Fort Worth Airport for example because it was not the most practical solution for expansions undertaken after the original design was completed. And yet, what might the opinion of the users be? That they are inconvenienced by construction? Surely, but they might also find that a straight road is easier to understand on the whole than looping overpasses and tunnels. Paul Andreu seems to grasp the significance of this issue and to balance the degree of practicality from a builder's point of view with that of the ultimate user in a fair way. He does seem a bit ill at ease on this point however.

From Roissy 1 to Roissy 2

At first glance it would appear that aside from form and materials, another difference between Roissy 1 and 2 is the increased luminosity of the newer terminals. "In Roissy 1," says Andreu, "the main body of the structure is opaque, but the traveler moves toward the light at the center of the structure. Actually there is a similar phenomena in Roissy 2, because you move from relative darkness in the main terminal toward more light near the aircraft boarding areas. I really didn't have any theoretical basis for making whatever change there is here. It is true that Roissy 2 was immediately more transparent than Roissy 1. We wanted passengers to be able to see the aircraft from the road. The 2 F terminal may balance the opacity of the early structure with the lightness and transparency of the first parts of terminal 2."

Although Paul Andreu speaks readily here of his experience at Roissy, his vocabulary and his process were very much the same in other cases. But can it be said that he has a personal style? "No," he answers. "The idea of style is an empty one for any self-respecting creator. It is critics and historians who should talk about style, because they have a need to arrange things in neat schools or trends. Architects who use style as a way to get well-known aren't even worthy of being called creators." And what does Andreu think of a strong geometrically based architecture like that of Tadao Ando. Does Ando have a style? "No," says Andreu, "it is his work. It is a constraint that he voluntarily puts on his own work." Andreu may appear to inspire himself from certain forms of nature, even female anatomy for example, but he says, "I design a lot of curved buildings, I don't know why, I don't have a theory. I like women, but it isn't when I look at a woman that I am inspired to design a building. What is interesting is seeing that nature respects certain forms." In this remark lies another key to understanding the work of Paul Andreu. To an observer, it might seem that even such geometric designs as that of Roissy 1 have an anatomical or anthropomorphic source of inspiration. Andreu explicitly denies being inspired in such a direct way, but he does say, "I am interested in a lot of things, but I am not capable of the kind of marvel expressed by the self-taught. I am fascinated by the forms of nature, but that is not what inspires the forms of my architecture." Insistent in a curiously irritated way on the significance of his own education, Andreu does nonetheless use "natural" forms like the vortex in some of his work.

It should also be pointed out that Andreu's curiosity and broad culture inform his work and make it richer in an interesting way. In the process of designing Roissy 1, he came across Adrian Frutiger of Switzerland. Born in Unterseen in 1928, Frutiger is a graphic designer, typographer and type designer, associated with Deberny & Peignot, Bauer and Linotype. Frutiger's greatest accomplishment was the design of the extremely successful typeface family, Univers. It was introduced in 1957 both for photo and hot metal composition and almost every typesetting system in the world licensed it for use. Frutiger created an ingenious numbering system

A picture taken in 2003 of the waiting lounge of Charles-de-Gaulle Airport Terminal 2 E, the most recently completed extension of the facility. The architect collaborated with the designers of the furniture in this light-filled tubular volume.

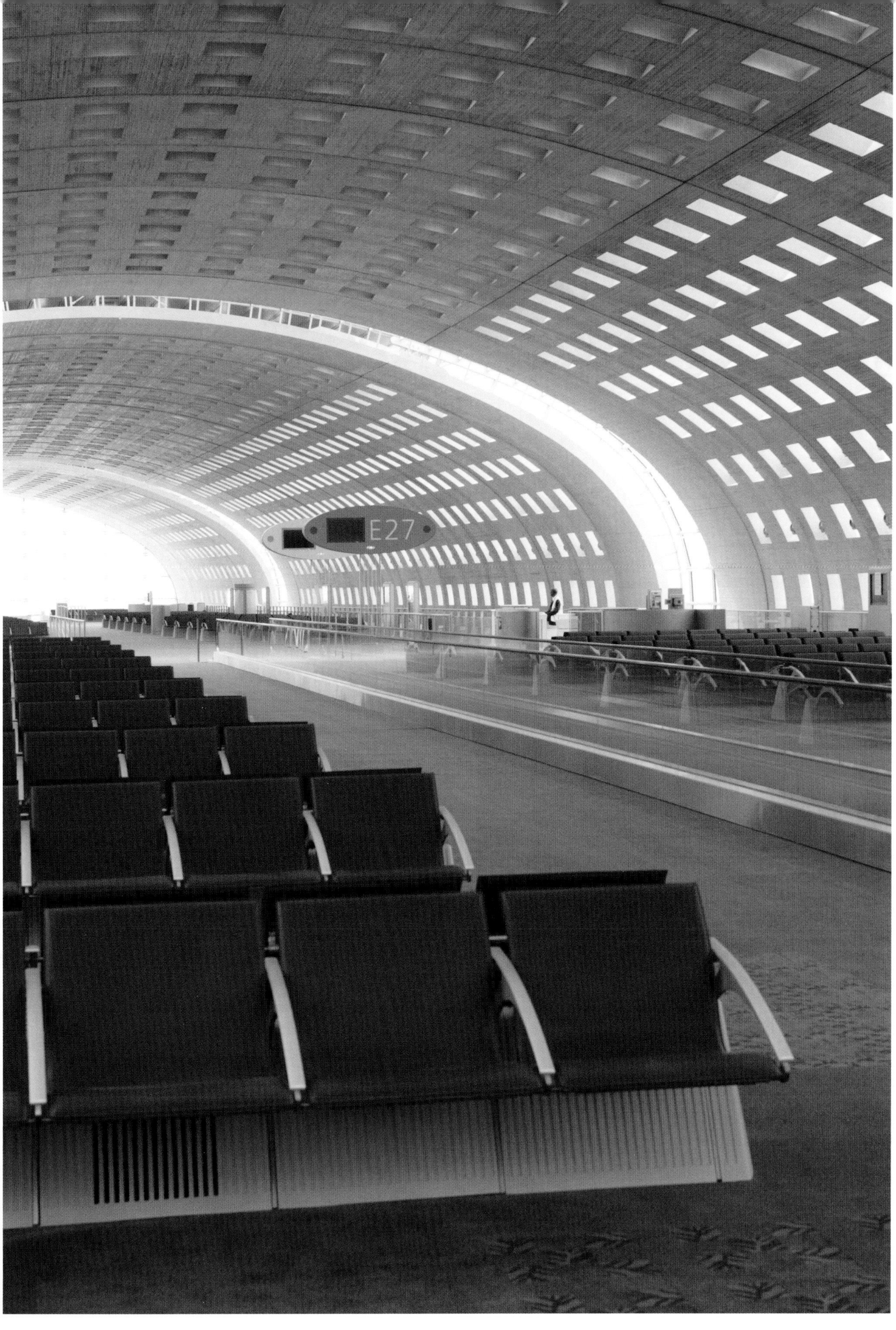
E27

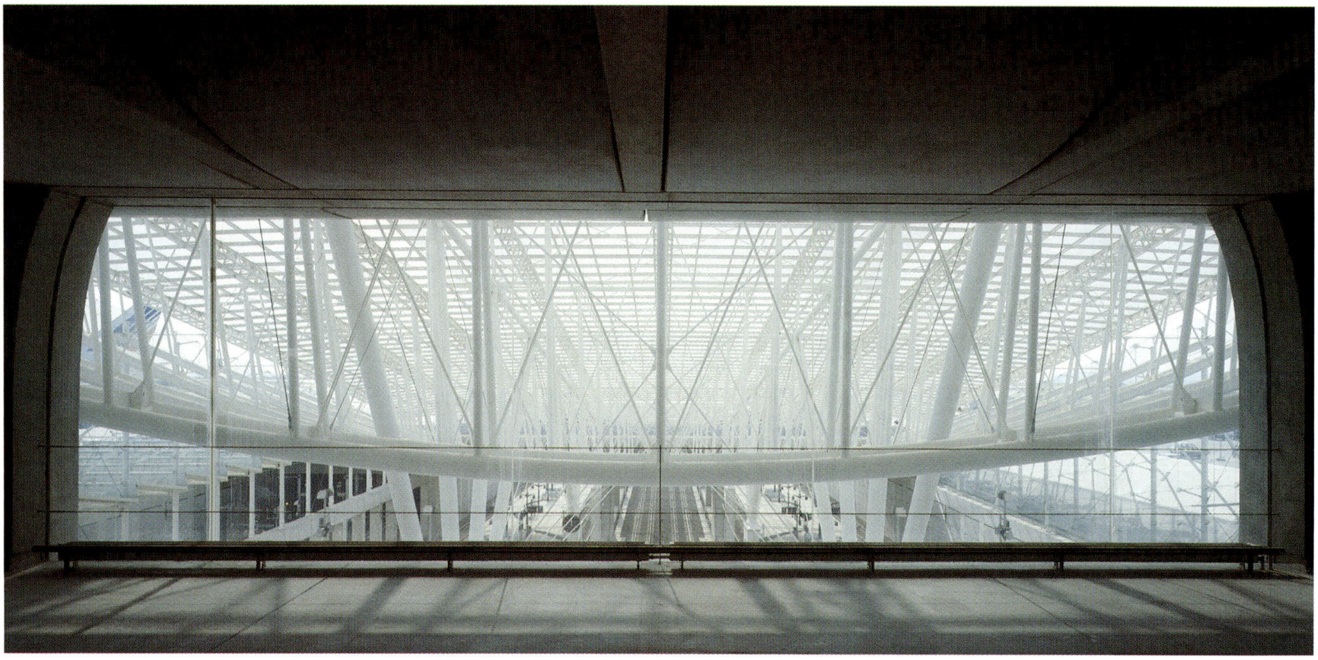

to indicate weight and width in the twenty-one variants of the Univers family. During the past four decades Adrian Frutiger probably did more work on sign alphabets than any other designer. He created signs for Gaz de France, Electricité de France, and at the behest of Paul Andreu, for the Charles-de-Gaulle Airport. Andreu engaged in a fascinating dialogue with Frutiger and from their conversations a family of typography emerged, first under the name of Roissy and then later Frutiger/Roissy for Linotype (1976), and finally simply Frutiger. This book is in fact set in Frutiger typography. With an open mind and an ability to listen, Paul Andreu plunged with Frutiger into the little-known complexities of typography and emerged with signage that truly reflected the spirit of the architecture. Again, the power and position of Aéroports de Paris as a virtual monopoly on airport construction in France permitted Andreu to get intimately involved with almost every phase of the design, but it is a rare architect who presides over the creation of a family of typography for one of his projects.

The issue of style in Paul Andreu's work, almost like that of French influences is difficult to resolve, but he has his own clear opinion about how he works. "The appearance of building is a result of a method," he continues. "I very rarely repeat esthetic elements in any conscious way, but I know that there are significant 'cross-fertilizations' in what I do. There are construction details that resemble each other from project to project; I guess you could say that I just let my hand do its work." Andreu's frequent reference to drawing as though a sketch were the only way to create architecture extends to a dislike for the machine. "I could never look for solutions with a machine because the machine does not allow the hand to express itself properly. A machine doesn't make mistakes. I can't imagine how you could introduce the kind of 'happy' mistake that is so important for living architecture. What I will never accept is to sketch a shape and then hand it over to an engineer to make sure it can stand up on its own. I don't want to make some kind of a sculpture," he says, in a barely veiled reference to the work of Frank Gehry amongst others.

A view from a passageway down into the glazed areas of the TGV Station at Roissy designed by Paul Andreu in collaboration with the SNCF and the architect Jean-Marie Duthilleul of the Agence des Gares.

From Roissy 2F to the Rest of the World

Paul Andreu's work on airports all over the world made him familiar with varied work methods. With this knowledge and being used to traveling widely, he began, especially in the 1990's to move into another realm of design. This shift happens to coincide with the design and construction of Roissy 2 F (1988-98). With the arching roof of the boarding peninsulas and the glazed waiting rooms at the tip of each peninsula, Andreu reached a kind of perfection that had not exactly eluded him in previous work, but which here came to its logical conclusion. He had taken on one of the largest and most complex ongoing construction projects in the world and mastered it. This might be enough to complete the resume of most architects, but for Paul Andreu, it has been more a point of departure, or the signal of a new beginning. With the studies for Kansai Airport, he had become familiar with the arcane world of Japanese construction. He in fact obtained a license to practice as an architect in Japan, an almost unheard of accomplishment for a Westerner. This was in 1990, just prior to his work on the Osaka Maritime Museum (1993-2000). Breaking out of the airport mold became one of his major preoccupations but much of his experience was useful in the case of the Museum in Osaka. Located just across the Bay from the massive Kansai project, there are obvious circumstantial links between the two designs, but the fact that the Museum is approached through a tunnel that brings visitors under a great glass dome is also reminiscent of some of his terminals. Movement from darkness into light is a constant in his work and in such projects as Roissy Terminal, tunnels are the preferred method of transition from one world into another. By no means static, Paul Andreu's designs are actually about movement in a more direct and real sense than most other contemporary architecture. Perhaps it is because he has served an industry of movement, but this also appears to be a part of his own method and doctrine. The architect brings the visitor from the darkness into the light. This is a metaphor for travel and indeed for life itself. The great glass dome of Osaka is first and foremost a technical achievement in this land of the trembling earth. Using knowledge garnered at Kansai and elsewhere, Andreu conceived a radical plan that was firmly based in the realm of what engineering can make possible. Seeing the dome arrive on its barge and be lifted into place by an enormous crane, the excitement and risk inherent in this architect's work became clear. No number of denials that nature informs and guides his work will suffice to convince the attentive spectator that this is not more than an architecture of superficial esthetics. Andreu's architecture works, it fulfills its functions, and it goes beyond the needs of the client to address itself directly to the visitor. Osaka is a case of engineering, architecture and local techniques mastered. What Andreu calls "cross-fertilization" from and to his own work is obvious here, be it in the early tunnels at Charles-de-Gaulle or in the upcoming underwater approach to the Beijing National Grand Theater. As he explains himself, he thinks first of one of his own solutions and arrives only gradually at the conclusion that he must go further. Tunnels and passageways from dark to light are like the pedimenti that appear in a painter's canvas, reminiscences of other ideas, starting points. Obviously in a case like Osaka, Andreu owes a great debt to Buckminster Fuller who pioneered the design of geodesic domes. This may thus not be the most original design but it is a dramatic one in a "new" place, reclaimed land in the Bay of Osaka.

Paul Andreu has taken on the design and construction of very large buildings in China with a gusto that certainly proves he has wanted to go beyond airport design. Though he did create the Shanghai Pudong Airport, his most visible and controversial building has been the Beijing National Grand Theater. In 1997, the Chinese government revived an idea of creating a national opera house that dated back to the 1950's. In an invitation and open competition organized in 1998, Andreu was selected over dozens of other entries, half of which were from Chinese architects. His enormous oval titanium outer shell with a central glass structure in the shape of a curtain surprised Chinese architects who feared that the government would opt for too conservative a plan. Andreu's design made them feel that this Western architect had gone too far, especially in a highly sensitive cultural district. The truth be told, Tien An Men is one of the most impressive squares in the world, but mainly because of its enormous proportions. Its only distinguished architecture is the Qing gate to the Forbidden City, with its famous portrait of Chairman Mao. At the other end of the Square, lies the embalmed body of the Great Helmsman himself in a squat mausoleum. The Great Hall of the People and a museum of history occupy the remaining two sides of the square. Neither of these structures, though grand in their proportions can be called good architecture. They are Stalinist reminders of a past that might be better forgotten. Andreu's site is directly behind the Great Hall of the People and he has chosen to break radically with any sign of a relationship to Chinese tradition. As he says, in response to virulent attacks in the Chinese and international press, "They said that I have no culture. I never pretended to be a specialist of Chinese culture ..." When he speaks of the upturned roofs of the Forbidden City and points out that his great titanium shell turns down, he is not at his most convincing. The National Grand Theater is an object unto itself, as its location in a great artificial pond makes abundantly clear. Andreu also seeks through the use of an approach tunnel to make visitors leave the everyday world behind to approach the magic of opera. This is, in a sense, a gesture of closing his

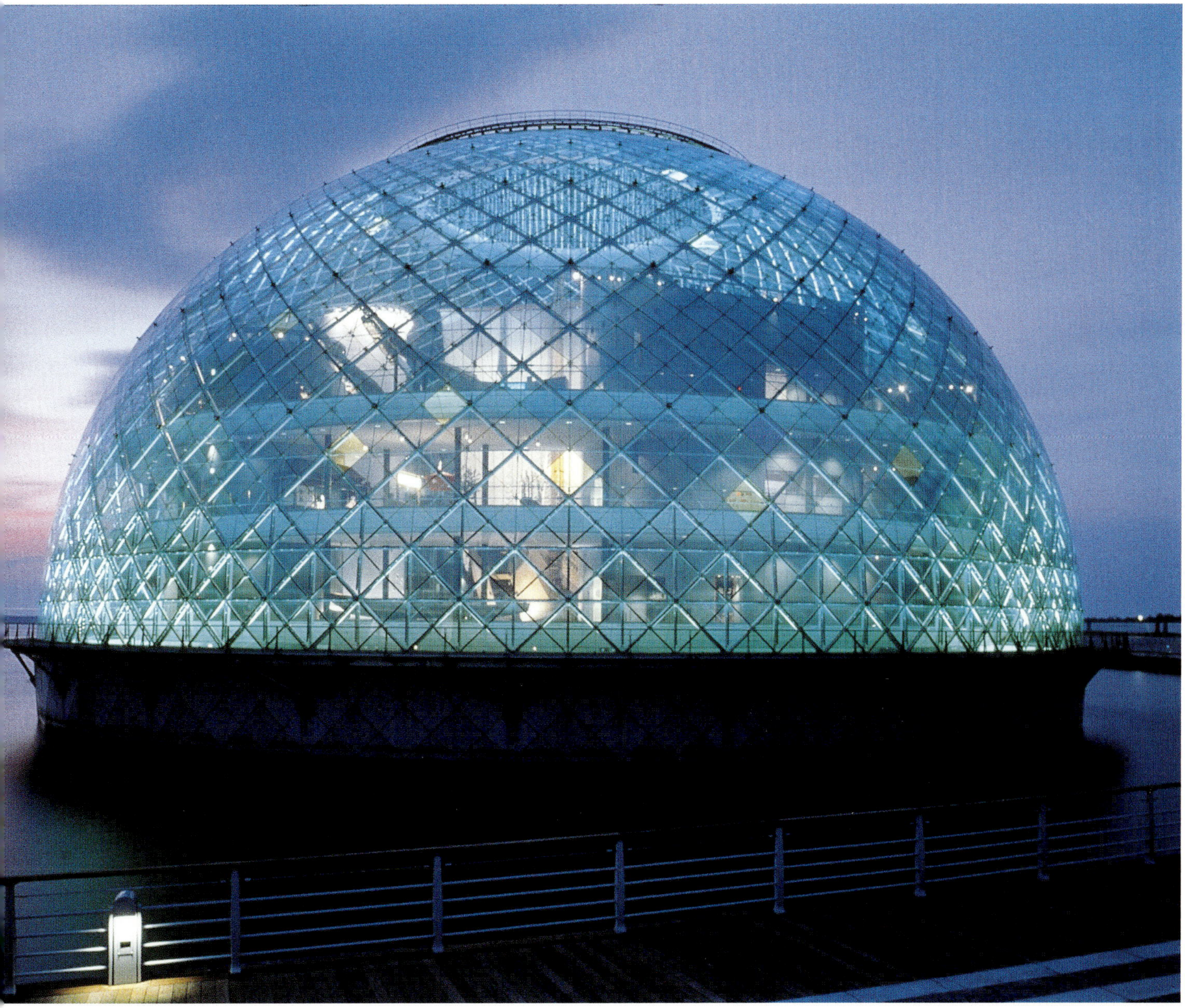

The Osaka Maritime Museum whose essential form is that of a geodesic dome, sits in the Bay of Osaka at nightfall, glowing from within.

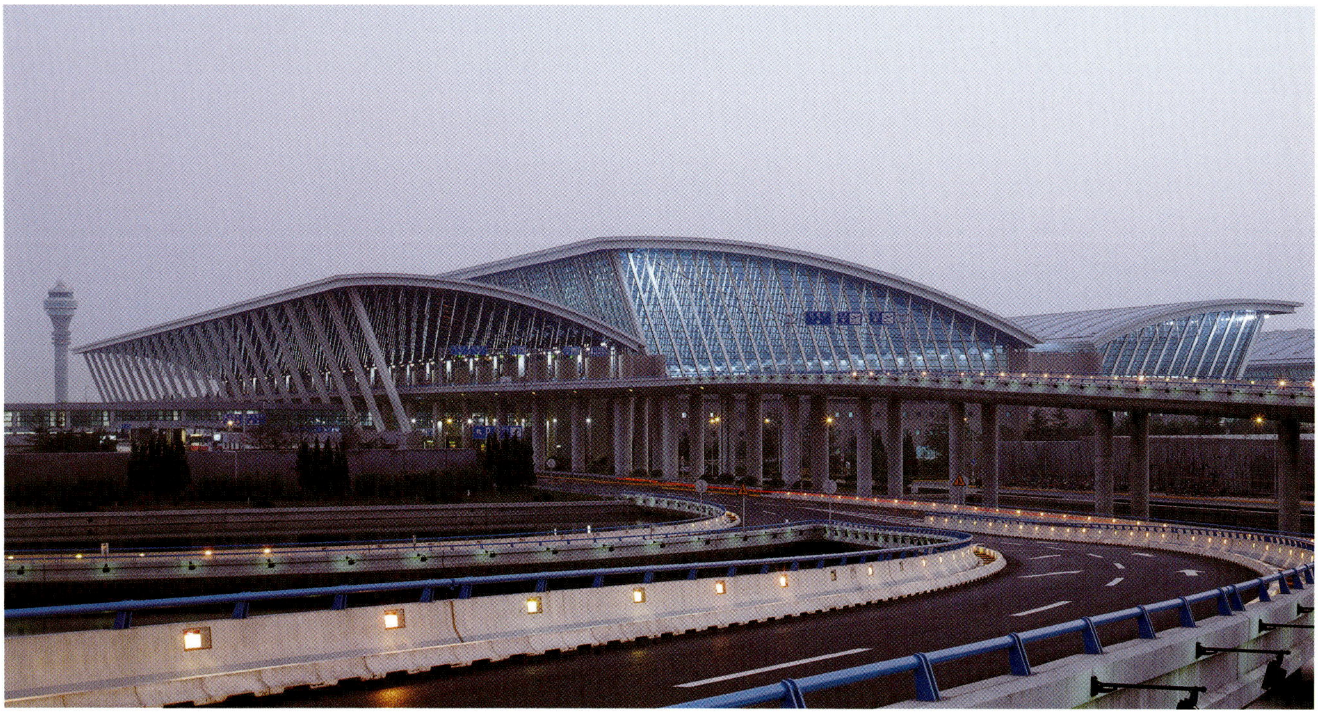

architecture to its environment. Enter here and you are in another world, he seems to say. That goal could be laudable in the purely operatic context, but there are other issues at play. What will the future of Beijing which had its own traditions that are being rapidly swept away by modernization, be in architectural terms. It may not be up to Paul Andreu or other visiting foreign architects to create a new Chinese style, but they ignore the vast history of China at their own peril.

The Chinese Puzzle

It is true that other considerable figures of the world of architecture have tried their hands at developing a new way of designing in Beijing. No less than I.M. Pei took on the challenge nearby with his new headquarters for the Bank of China. This very large structure (173,000 square meters) is actually the work of Pei Partnership – the two sons of I.M. Pei, Chien Chung Pei and Li Chung Pei were the Partners in charge of the project. Rising up to 15 floors above grade, the structure includes a spectacular 45-meter high, 3,000 square meter atrium. The atrium garden is decorated with 40 tons of rock from the Stone Forest in Yunan Province and bamboo trees from Hangzhou that rise to a height of almost 20 meters. A 2,000 seat auditorium, 97,000 square meters of office space and 13,500 square meters of leasable tenant space, give an idea of the sheer scale of the structure. The materials used are buff-colored Italian travertine with honed finish for the facades, and Chinese gray granites for the exterior paving. In the public interiors and banking halls, Italian travertine, gray granite and marble floors and walls with natural anodized aluminum ceiling panels were used. The very density of the program on the 13,000 square meter site made it difficult to avoid giving a massive profile to the Headquarters, but the quality of the design and finishing given by the Pei family, in particular for the atrium and banking halls manages to reconcile the client's requirements with a true concern for architectural excellence.

A picture of Shanghai Pudong Airport taken in 1999 showing the approach road and the asymmetrical wing-like volumes of the terminal structure.

Following pages:
The National Grand Theater of China, to be completed in 2005.

It would appear that the Pei family, who are of course of Chinese origin have sought more actively than Paul Andreu to give "Chinese characteristics" to their brand of modernity. There is no rock from Yunan province in Paul Andreu's plan although he intends to ask Pei's friend the painter Zao Wu Ki to participate in the decoration of the Theater. Pei's Bank of China is a rather heavy structure that may not be an example of his best work. Of course the program, with its high-density requirements determined much of the design. Andreu's project is not subject to such requirements of density and as a major cultural facility, is given over by nature more to public space and spectacular design. Nor indeed may it provide clues as to the direction of future Chinese modern architecture. That said, it is a thirst for structures that are at the level of the best work in the West that has prodded the Chinese to seek out or to select such architects as Paul Andreu. Upturned roofs would not have quenched the Chinese thirst for a significant place in the modern world. It is no accident that Paul Andreu's project was selected. This is an example of current Western contemporary architecture that will surely serve its function well. It is another matter to say that something more inventive and influential might well have taken its place. The titanium turtle-shell design is reminiscent of a number of other recent structures built outside of China. Though it is not certain that Beijing's dusty environment will treat this surface well that is not a significant argument against the Andreu design. The question of national identity in design in general comes back here in an interesting way. The question of Chinese identity is pertinent, but this is no more a "French" structure than it is a Chinese one. Andreu's French qualities are a rationalization of large-scale design and construction that also clearly suited the needs of contemporary China. This design is big (because the program called for a large facility) but it is also intelligently designed ... truly made to be built and not just an esthetic daydream. From the practical to the esthetic, Paul Andreu's reasoning follows a very similar path to what has been seen in his airport work. Get the job done, do it well and make it attractive, in that order.

"What I look for in every project," Paul Andreu has written, "is its internal coherence and its intelligibility, but at the same time, its relation to what surrounds it. Each project seems to me to be a closed and complete world, at the same time as it is a part of a larger whole, which is to say its physical location, its site, and in a more general way the environment. The whole that I imagine is very often an entity that exists only in my mind ... a mental reconstruction of a disparate group of elements. That is why I often think of my projects as elements that are detached from the broken up body of the city." Beijing faces a formidable task in finding any coherency in an explosion of new

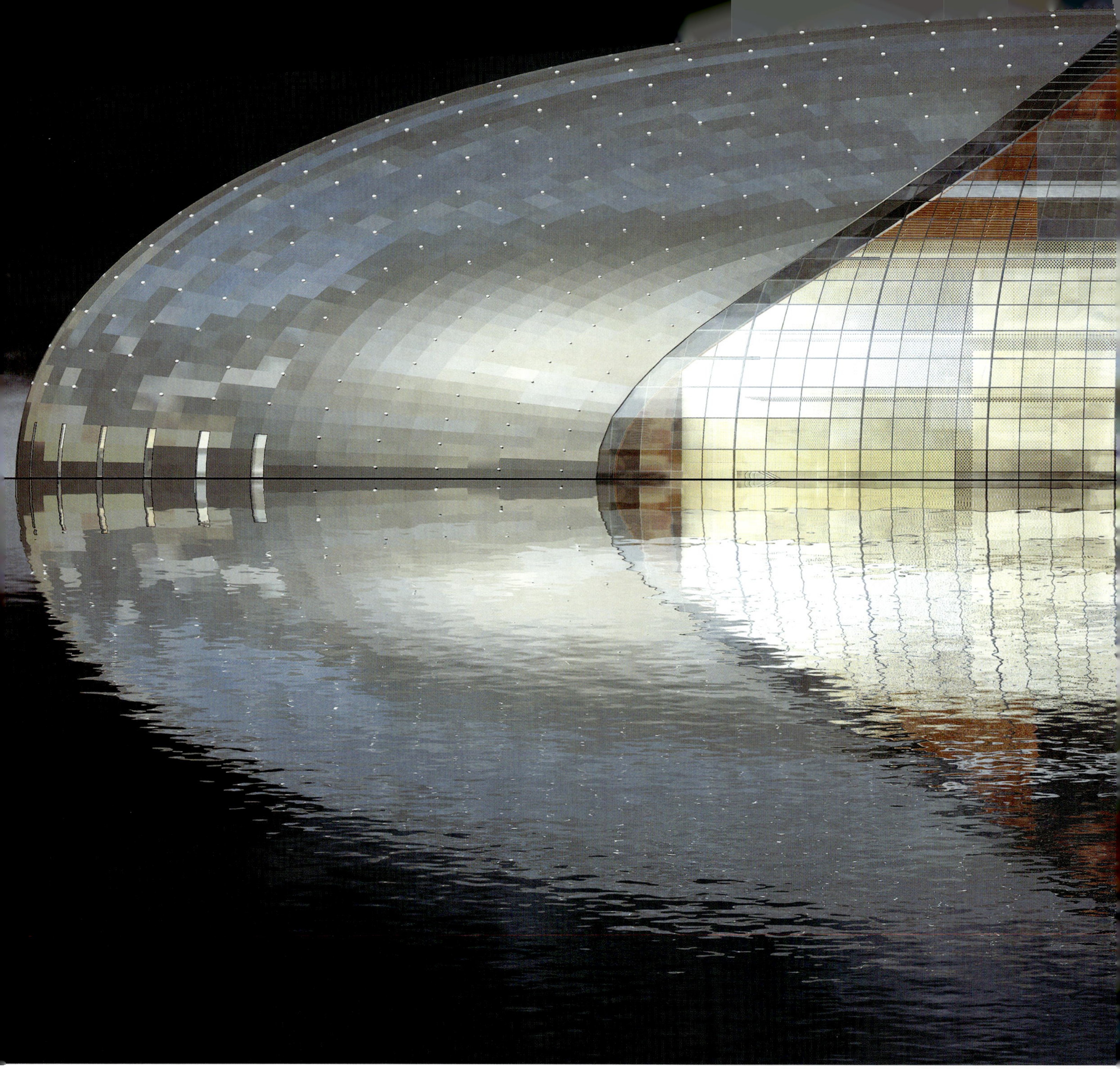

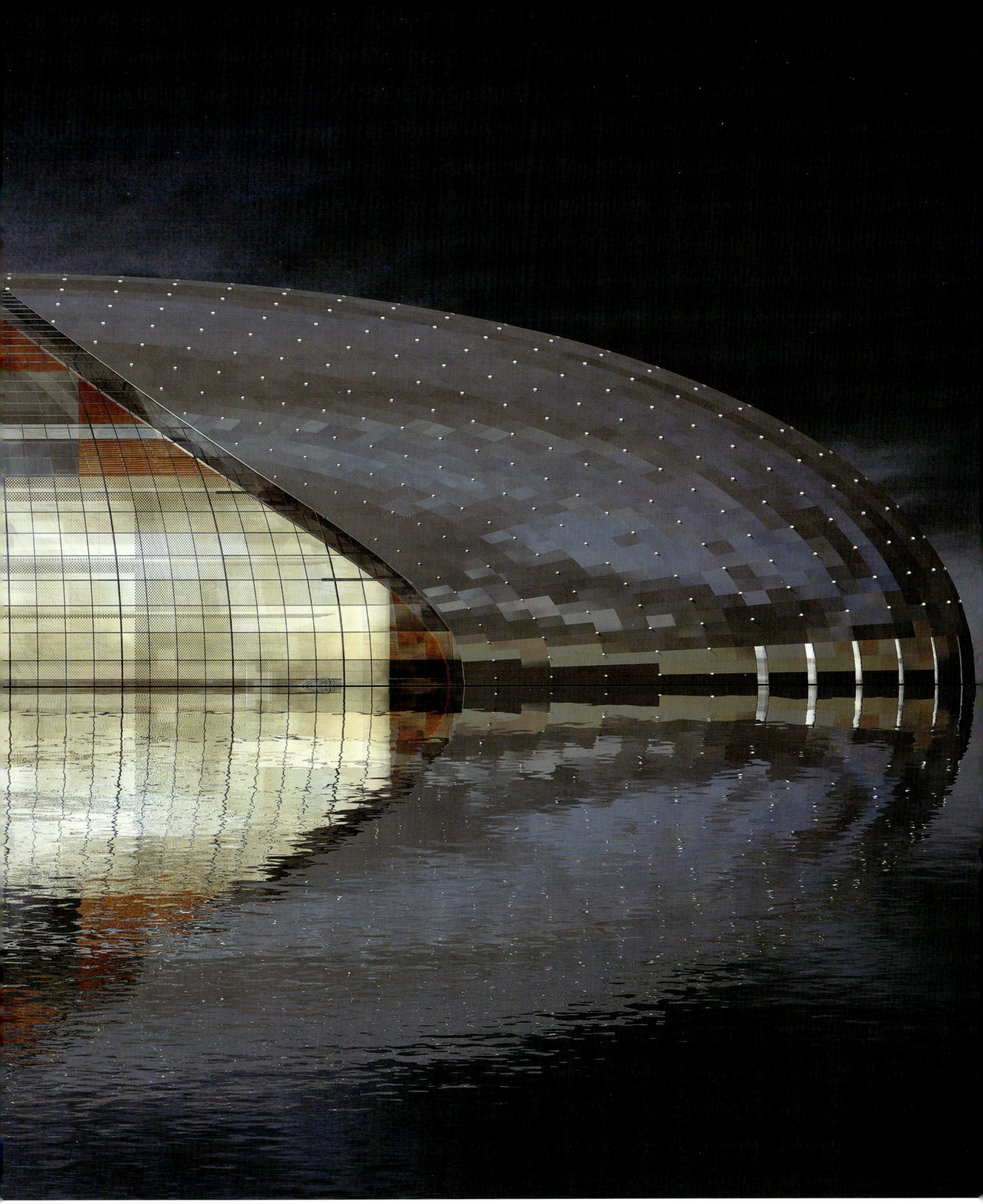

construction. Andreu's peaceful island shell may not help the Chinese capital to regain a lost intelligibility, but is it not, in a sense a modern-day version of the Forbidden City … a closed volume in a carefully circumscribed site. Today's Forbidden City, like Andreu's new Theater is open to the public, but both remain, in architectural terms, sealed entities. It should be noted that this checkerboard type of constitution is deeply rooted in Chinese thinking about the city. Beijing, despite its complexities past and present, follows a much more orthogonal plan for example than any Japanese city with the possible exception of Kyoto (which was based on Chinese designs). With its park and surrounding pond, the Grand National Theater is surely more inviting than Pei's massive Bank of China, but the orthogonal plan calls either for closed volumes or open spaces. Andreu's Theater is something of both, and it introduces curves that are not typical of Chinese architecture either.

At a certain time, an American architect sought to convince the Chinese of the inherent virtues of a major city that relied on bicycle transport far more than automobiles. Less pollution, less congestion … and he was told in no uncertain terms that for this rising economy, bicycles were a more a symbol of a backward economy than they were away to avoid the plagues of the West. What China and other developing countries want is not a lesson from Westerners about the ills they must avoid. Their urgent desire is to be modern, with all that implies in the way of discomfort and economic growth. In this context, Andreu's project is a fully comprehensible choice, it is a symbol of modernity that may have its faults, but which is close to the Chinese desire to leapfrog their economy into the ranks of the leading countries. Gone, the ramshackle but charming residential streets that used to surround the Forbidden City. On a massive scale like that introduced by the Communist regime at its outset, here is a brand new symbol of culture and mastery of the tools of the modern world.

A similar analysis could be applied to the Osaka Maritime Museum that bears no identifiable relationship to Japanese architecture whatsoever. As a more modern nation than China, Japan has of course gone much further into the use of Western forms and architecture. Japan is also a place where odd-shaped buildings have long been accepted. There is no desperate search for a Japanese way of doing things here, and the Japanese would hardly call on a French architect to identify a new way for them. This is a matter of internal debate in the indigenous architectural community. Foreign architects bring a certain amount of cachet to their realizations and thus may attract more visitors than "ordinary" designs. Again, nothing could be further than a glass dome from Japanese architecture, if only because a real mastery of glass in a seismic environment

A view of the Guangzhou Gymnasium taken from neighboring Baiyun hills and looking toward the vast city, formerly known as Canton. The three oblong domed structures glow from within at night.

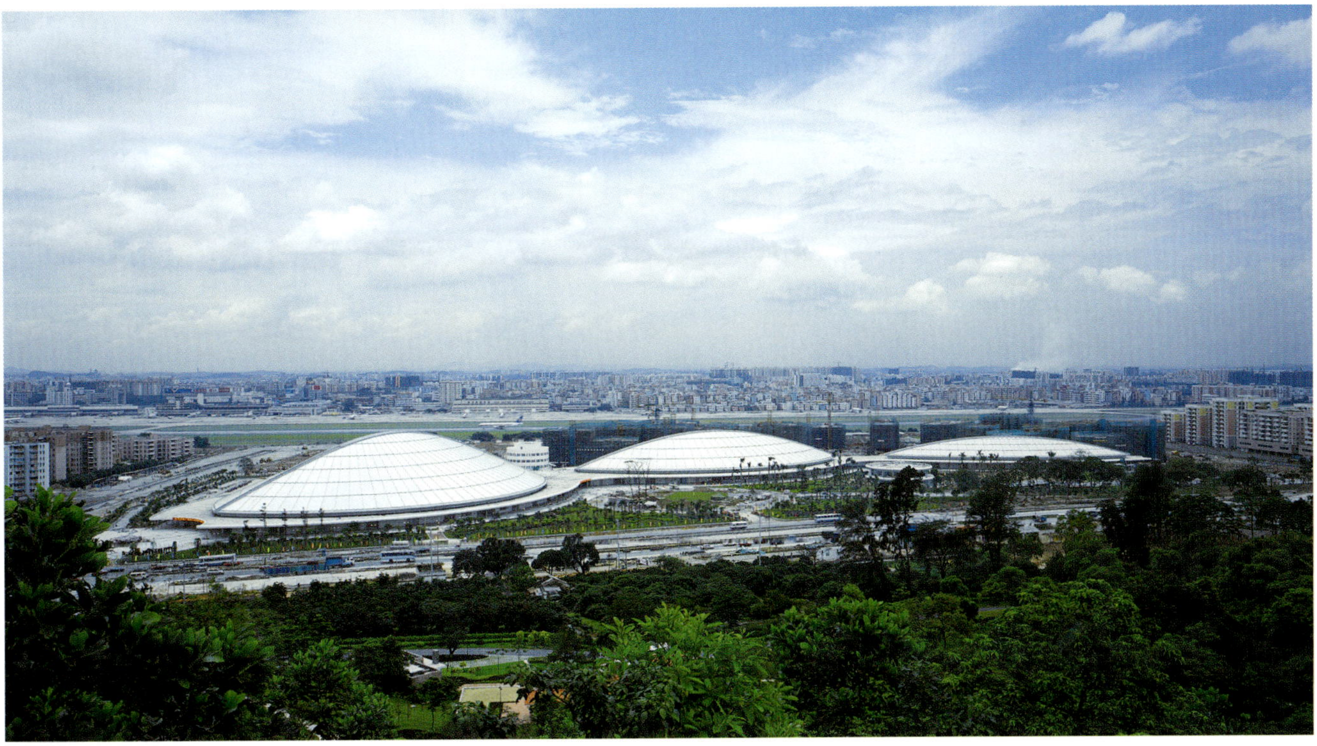

is a relatively recent accomplishment. Rafael Viñoly's Tokyo Cultural Forum (1990-95) on the site of the former Tokyo City Hall is another Western contemplation on the idea of crystalline fragility in the face of an unstable earth. Rafael Viñoly is also coincidentally one of the very few Westerners along with Andreu, to have obtained certification to work in Japan as an architect.

Orthodox Modernism often bred structures that rejected their environment in an almost militant way. This was the tabula rasa of a Walter Gropius. Andreu does not specifically reject all that surrounds his buildings, but neither does he seek to reflect and improve upon those surroundings. Modernist designs often sat on top of the earth in a kind of fragile equilibrium. Andreu does not fear to dig into the ground or to sit his buildings in basins, as he has done in both Osaka and Beijing. Although he was the planning mastermind of Kansai Airport and not its architect, it can be noted that the huge curving arc of a building imagined by Piano was conceived a part of huge circle, whose main volume would be underground. Tunnels and passageways leading to the light are a fixation of his, but so too is the freestanding volume first seen in Roissy Terminal 1. Intended for a vast flow of in and out traffic, Roissy 1 is nonetheless a closed object in appearance. This is the case of the Osaka Maritime Museum and the Beijing Opera too. Roissy 2 displays more transparent features, but with the terminal arcs facing each other, enclosing central parking areas, it too has something of the closed shell concept that recurs frequently in Andreu's work.

Paul Andreu has had the fortune or the desire to work on projects on a massive scale, like Roissy and other airports. These are a form of urbanism, but they are also, frequently, a collection of discreet forms intended to function together. The closed entity that offers a passage to light is

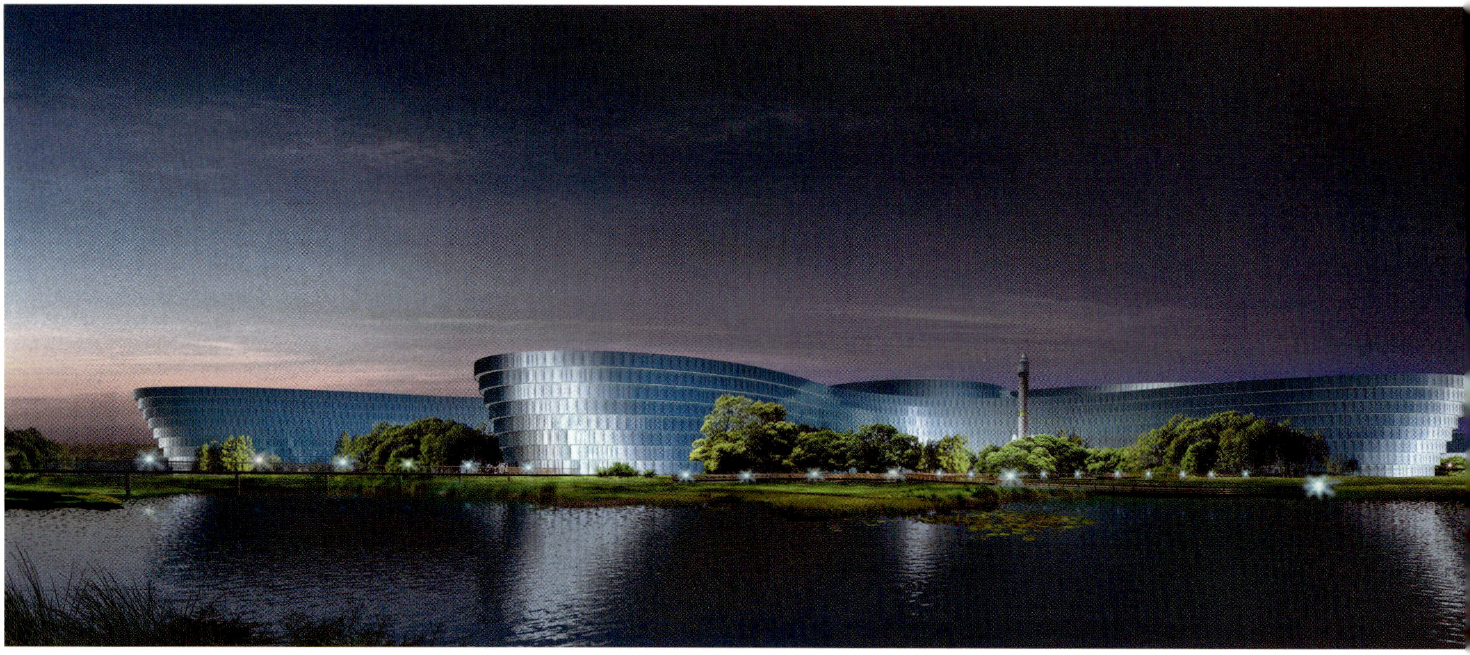

a preoccupation that takes on almost Freudian connotations in his work … the womb, birth and flight. The idea of flight is either literal in the case of an airport or figurative in the case of an opera house or a museum … a flight of fancy, a flight of the imagination. And whatever the shape or function, Andreu maintains a steady mastery of the technicalities of construction. He uses his engineering background to find innovative and yet efficient solutions to give space something of the nobility that it might otherwise not have. As his own words testify, Andreu might reject the idea of a fundamentally anthropomorphic inspiration. He would seek rather to explain why there may be apparent similarities between the forms and functions of nature and those found in his own architecture. The idea of a womb and a coming into the light need not actually be explained so graphically – these are images that testify to recurring elements in Paul Andreu's architecture and not necessarily to his way of thinking about buildings. He likes the contrast of light and dark, he avows a tendency to move from one to the other in much of his work. No more is needed to prove a point. The greatest architecture has inscribed in its forms and proportions the image of its creator. Architecture cannot ignore that the body is its beginning and its end, it is there to serve and to function in an efficient way. These are the needs that Andreu's work tends to serve, and in that he does attain the status of a major architect, in particular because so many millions must follow the path he has drawn from darkness into light.

Architecture Formed by Light

Speaking in broad terms about his recent work, Paul Andreu has stated, "Another fundamental idea of my work is that architecture always leaves the hands of its creator as an incomplete idea. It has to be submitted to the elements, to light, wind and water in order to be complete. This is an idea that has amplified itself progressively as my career has gone forward. Perhaps the point of origin is the central open space of the Roissy 1 Terminal, open to light, water and the unpredictable movement of travelers through the glass walkways. My most recent work has more fully integrated the

The Guangzhou Science Center also located in Guangzhou and slated for completion proposal. In this virtual image, water and the natural setting blend with the lobed design to create a harmonious complex.

fragile and fugitive traces of light that complete the architecture in ever changing ways." Paul Andreu cites the Roissy 2 E and F in this context, as well as the Maritime Museum of Osaka and the Canton sports facility. "Lightness and transparency are qualities that fascinate me in architecture," he continues. "I apply a great amount of effort to the rigor and 'truth' of the design so that these qualities can be freely expressed in the finished work. What is most important to me finally, is space itself, its structure, its limits, and the ways in which it struggles against light and melts into it. This," concludes Paul Andreu, "is why I have always tried to avoid closing myself into the inherent limitations of a style, or an attitude: each project brings forth a specific reaction, although I hope that I have gained in the process and that each new work draws on what went before in order to profit from the past."

Located in Shanghai, Paul Andreu's Oriental Art Center is a large facility that further demonstrates his commitment to China and to escaping the realm of airport design. It houses a Philharmonic Concert Hall, Lyric Theater and a Chamber Music Hall. With its closed volumes, the Shanghai facility is not fundamentally unlike many of Andreu's other projects, and even specifically recalls the volume of the most recent extension of the Nice-Côte d'Azur Airport. The volumes, he says, "house and protect" cultural activities, "as one might protect a place that is precious and fragile."

The Andreu Method

If Paul Andreu has a method, it consists in first looking carefully at the technical requirements and planned function of a facility. From there, consciously or unconsciously he looks back into his own experience to see what solutions can be applied to a new situation. He says that he rejects specific adaptations of an existing form, and yet the functional patterns of airports for example give him a basis that is even stronger than his own penchant for given solutions. Traffic, security, access or baggage are facets of a kind of function he knows well. This then is the grid of his thought – the ways in which a structure or complex has to work. From there he has consistently sought intelligent engineering solutions that also bring light and space to the ultimate beneficiaries of his work – the travelers or visitors he serves once the client has had his say. Perhaps his form of applied logic prevents him from fully breaking out of a mold, but then he specifically rejects the kind of sculptural architecture devised by such figures as Frank Gehry. Paul Andreu does not reject the idea of the architect as artist, but he clearly feels that the capriciousness of some artists has no place in serious construction. Like artists, Andreu feels that his work is the result of a personal engagement leading to a challenge to the established order. He feels that a building can indeed be a work of art, albeit a useful work unlike most paintings or sculptures for example. He is an architect and an engineer, a craftsman of solutions who has mastered the large scale better than almost any other figure of his generation. It cannot be stated enough that through his airports in particular, Paul Andreu has touched so many millions of people that almost no other architect could claim with reason to have influenced more people's lives. This is all the more true because the unique structure of Aéroports de Paris gave him a personal authority which is usually much more diluted in other countries amongst teams of architects and designers.

His own persistence and steadiness should also be cited as undeniable qualities. Carrying forward a project like Roissy Airport over a period of forty years requires a consistency and an application that escapes many lesser figures. And yet few people outside of the architectural profession really know of the work of Paul Andreu. He is far less well known than a Frank Gehry, while it is clear that his work has been seen by hundreds of times more people than any Gehry work including the Guggenheim Bilbao. Paul Andreu is not a creator of the brilliantly fashionable, and the most extreme controversy he has engendered, in Beijing, is the product more of local sensitivities and French in-fighting than it is of a truly radical design. Beijing is one of the only examples of his work where Andreu has been faced with the daunting problems of an historic and culturally significant environment. His closed bubbles, even that of Osaka are usually set in the periphery of great cities, on formerly empty land. This too is a very specific aspect of his work. When given the opportunity to build in Beijing, he chose a closed shape, which surely will admit light, but which is nonetheless a sealed shell. Very few architects have built so prolifically in such circumstances of relative isolation. Of course Roissy is a veritable web of interconnecting roads, runways and rail lines, but it grew nonetheless out of an empty field. Andreu's buildings are nodes of activity that interact with their environment but do not fundamentally become part of it.

His appreciation of light may indeed be inspired by the Japanese attitude to this manifestation of nature. For Ando and many others, closed forms that exclude a chaotic urban environment are a frequent device. When they conceive of a building however, they are careful to bring daylight in, as a direct manifestation of nature. Nature is within if the light falls in and moves through a building. Andreu, though he does not avow a specifically Japanese influence in this aspect of his work seems to treat nature in a similar way. In one more specific case of interaction with nature, his Jakarta airport, he sought to recreate an idealized and greatly enlarged Indonesian village, with its typical local vegetation. This was not so much a veritable interaction with nature as it was yet another creation of an architecturally isolated world. Paul Andreu's buildings are most typically

In Paul Andreu's CBD Core proposal for the new business district of the Chinese capital, two towers, respectively 300 and 250 meters in height rise above the central square made up of a circle inscribed in a square.

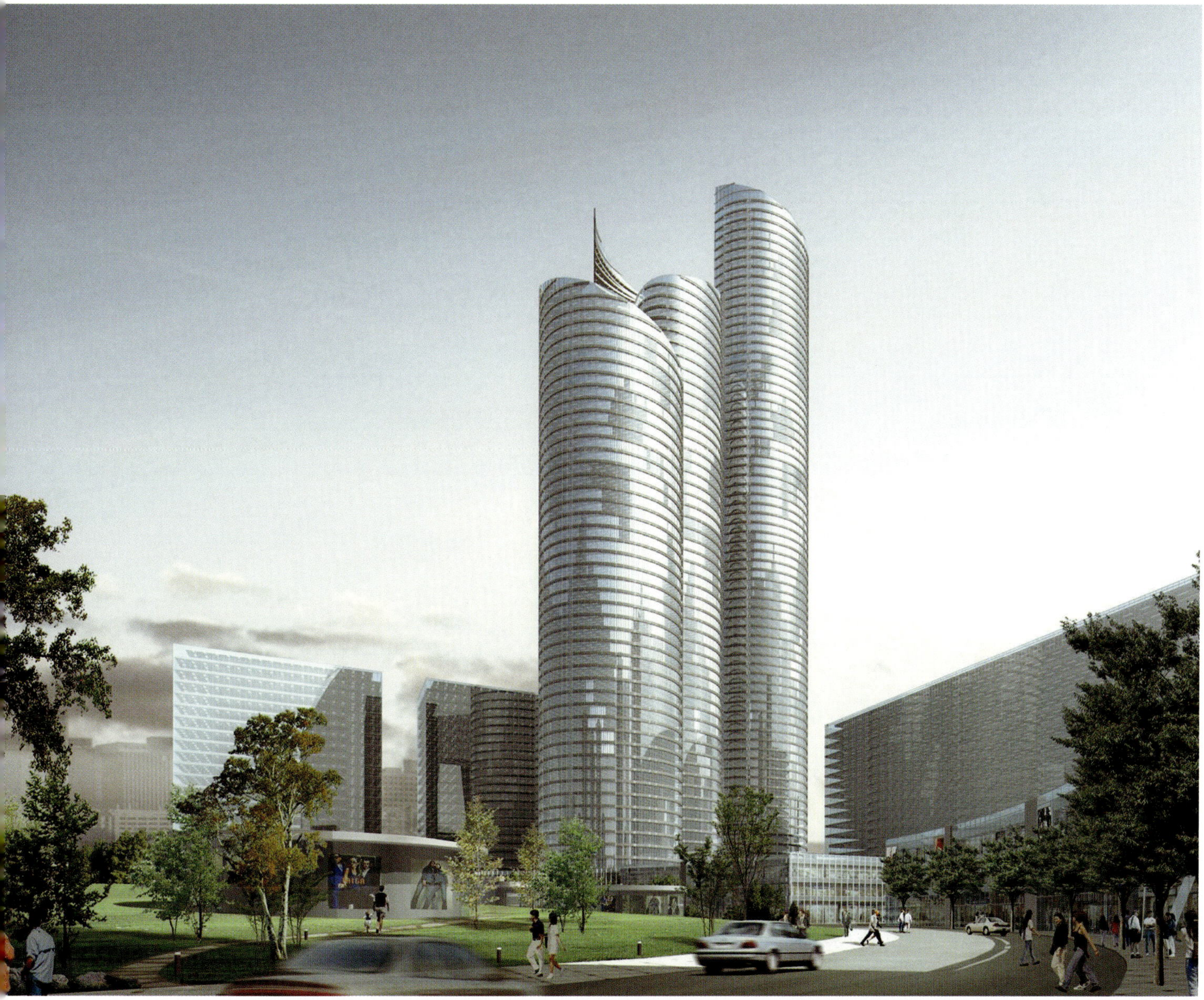

worlds unto themselves, ideal places where everything functions perfectly and where travelers go on their way feeling uplifted and well cared for. This in itself is a substantial accomplishment, but the fact remains that by the very nature of his professional activities, Paul Andreu is an architect apart, one who, not unlike a minor deity, creates his own universe over and over again. This may well be the very definition of the role of the architect, one that modern urban environments and economic realities rarely allow to be fulfilled. In the dreams, drawings and buildings of Paul Andreu, a man has created worlds of his own where millions move and live. Of course he has counted on the help of others, but much more than others of his generation, he has left his own imprint on a vast territory, at the periphery of great cities, where nothing stood before he came.

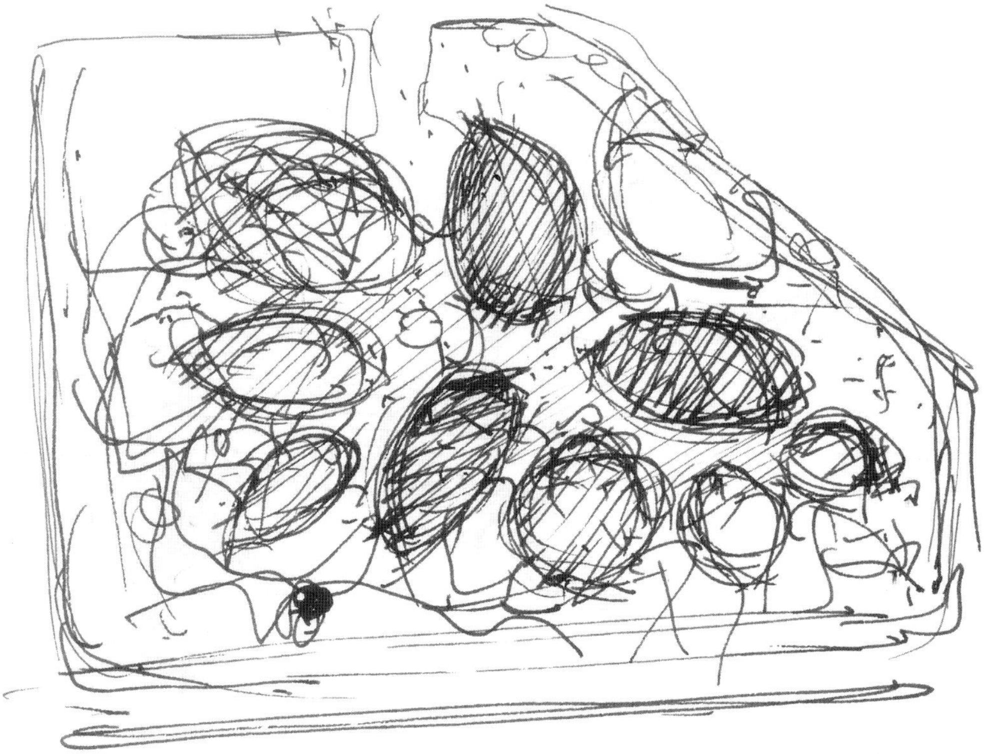

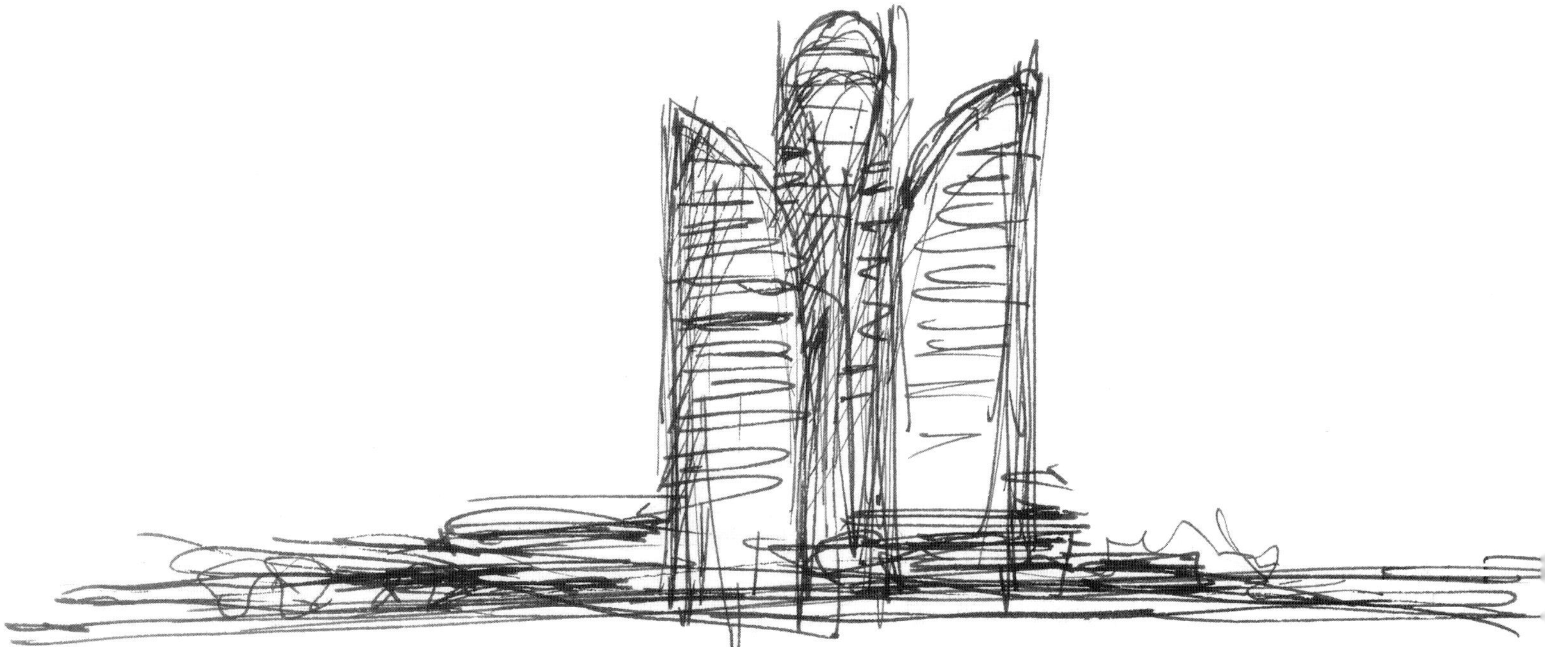

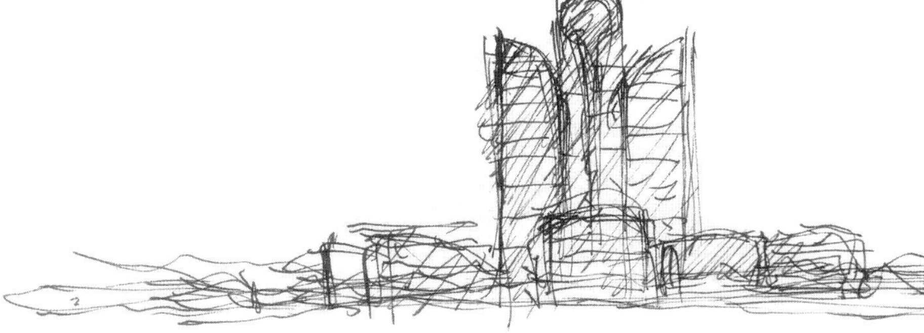

24.01.02.

23 Projects from 1967 to 2005

Terminal 1 of Charles-de-Gaulle Airport was in many ways the most significant or seminal of Paul Andreu's projects. Not only did work on the airport form a good part of his career, but it also opened doors to work in the rest of the world.

Charles-de-Gaulle Airport - Terminal 1 **Paris**

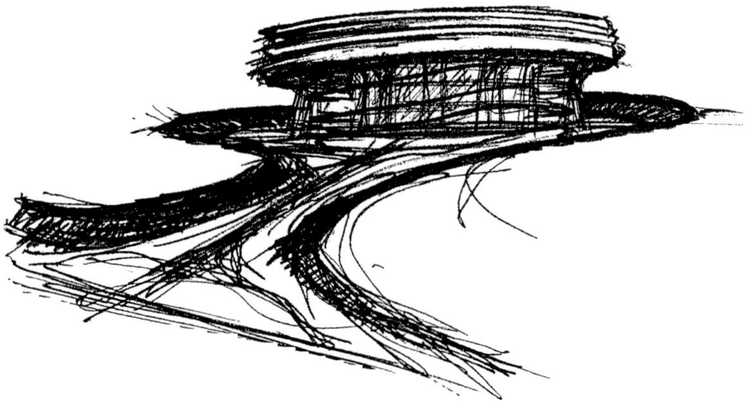

Country: France
Use: Airport
Start of project: 1967
Completion: 1974
Surface of central building: 195,000 m^2
Capacity: 9.6 million passengers per year

Put into service in March 1974, this terminal was intended to handle nine million passengers a year. Its overall size including the central building and the boarding "satellites" is 248,000 square meters. The round shape of the 190-meter diameter main structure was dictated by the desire to shorten the distances that passengers have to cross between their arrival by car or bus, and the aircraft. The 51 boarding gates are arrayed around this hub in the seven trapezoidal satellites. Slightly more distant locations reached by bus permit a further 21 aircraft to load or unload at Terminal 1. In an unusual configuration parking space for 3,800 cars is provided for on the seventh, eighth and ninth levels above the departures, transfers and arrivals floors.

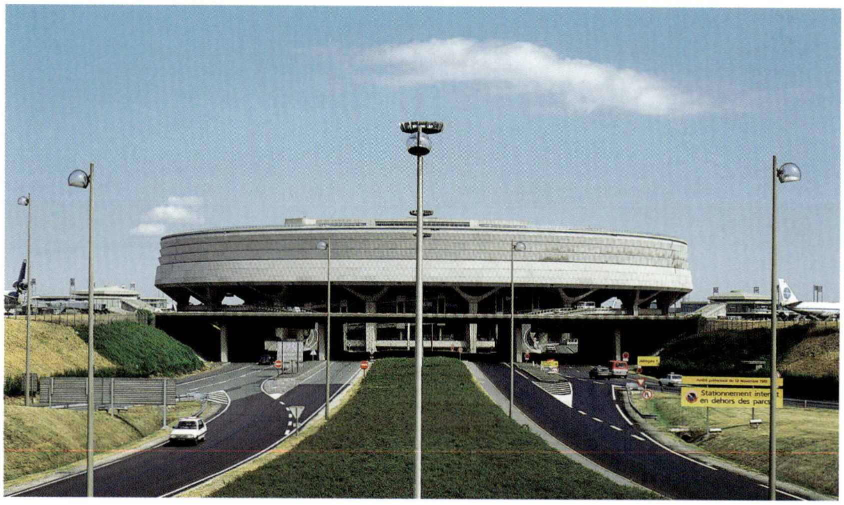

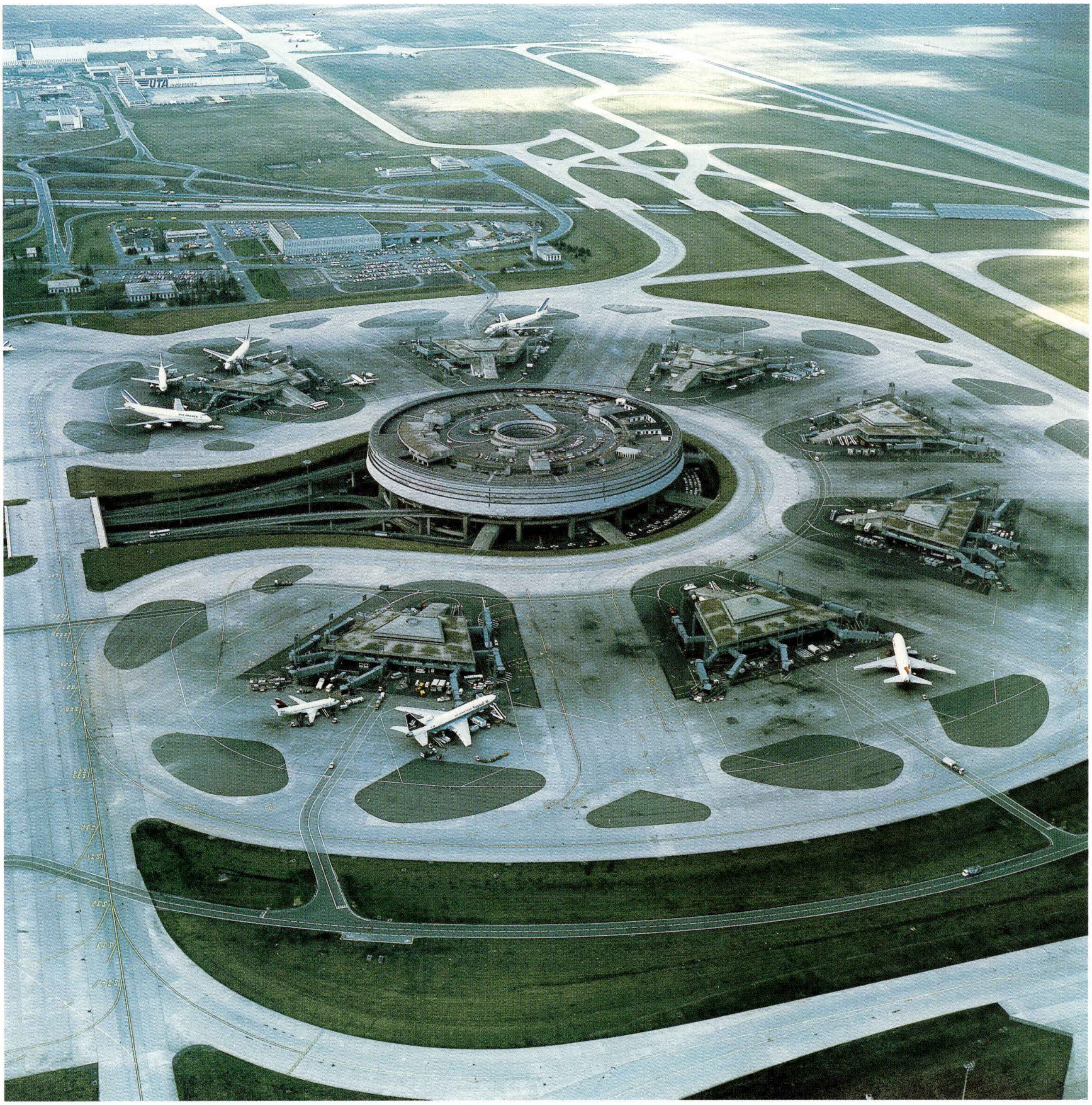

A sketch by Paul Andreu and a ground level photo demonstrate the dynamic nature of the design of Terminal 1. Automobile traffic enters the structure directly. Above, an aerial view shows the radiating pattern of the aircraft docking points around the central disk.

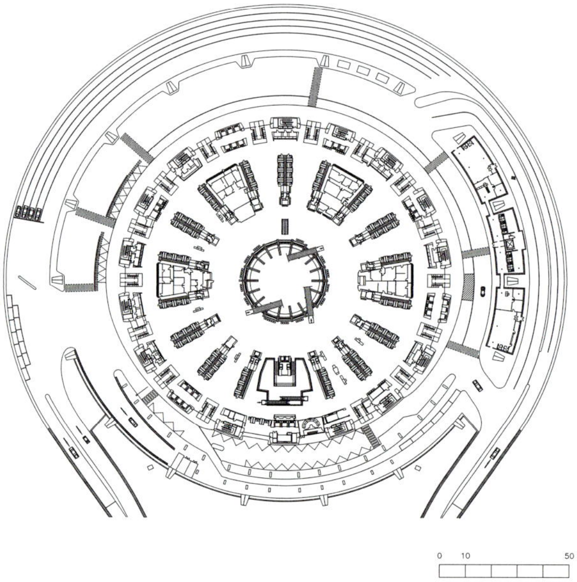

Especially before hotels and other structures had been built in the areas around Terminal 1, it stood out on these rolling agricultural lands like a curious fortress, obviously modern because of its materials, but also medieval in its solidity. Others have chosen to see in Terminal 1 a kind of huge flying saucer, landed from sometime in the future on the outskirts of Paris. Today it is difficult to convey the extent to which Terminal 1 was received as an esthetic and architectural surprise. That its shape should have been so completely dictated by the constraints of engineering and practicality only serves to underline its fundamental legitimacy. Though his esthetic impulses surely play a large role in the space that traveler's experience, Andreu was also acting as the skilful interpreter of the myriad requirements of the airport in the late twentieth century.

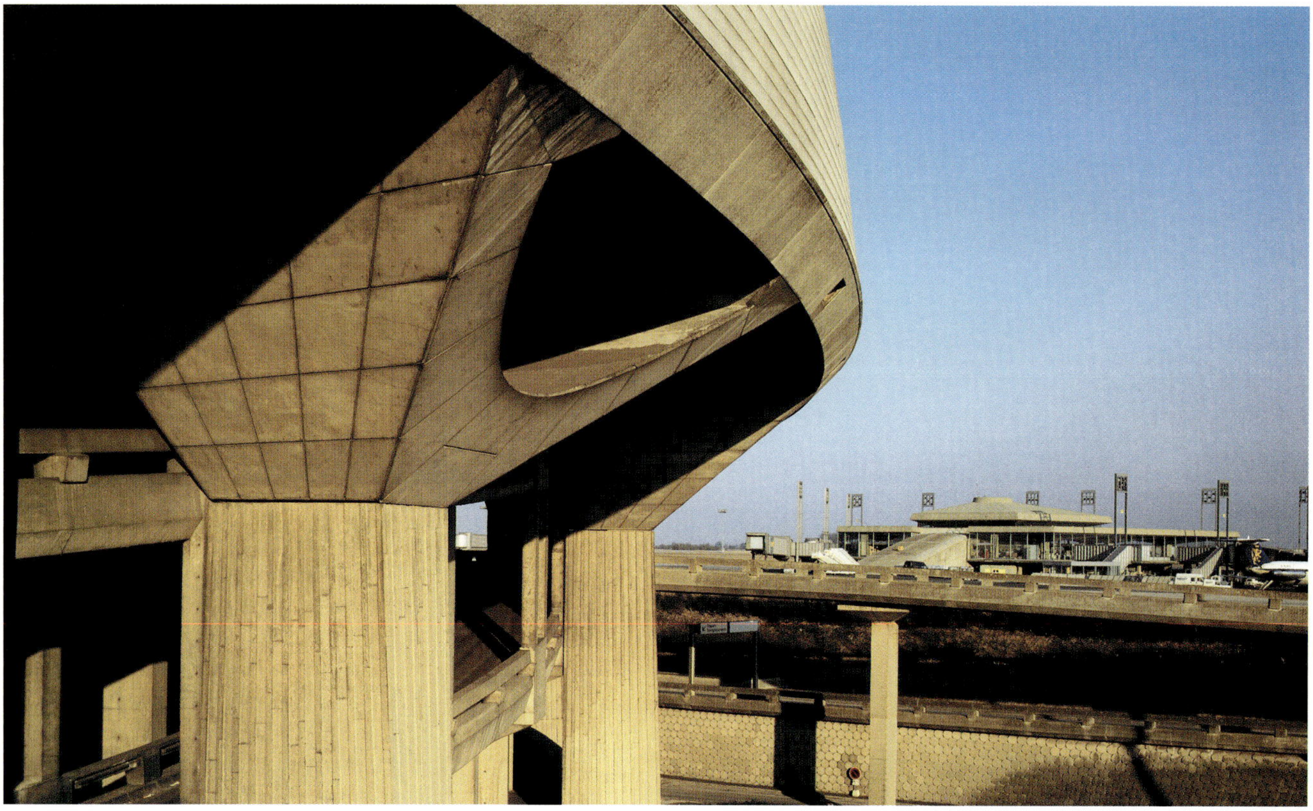

Elevated roads are a frequent element of Andreu's airport design. A floor plan of Terminal 1 again shows how the outer circle has been used to order the inner workings of the travelers' space. Below, a view of the control tower which confirms the strict simplicity of the architect's design.

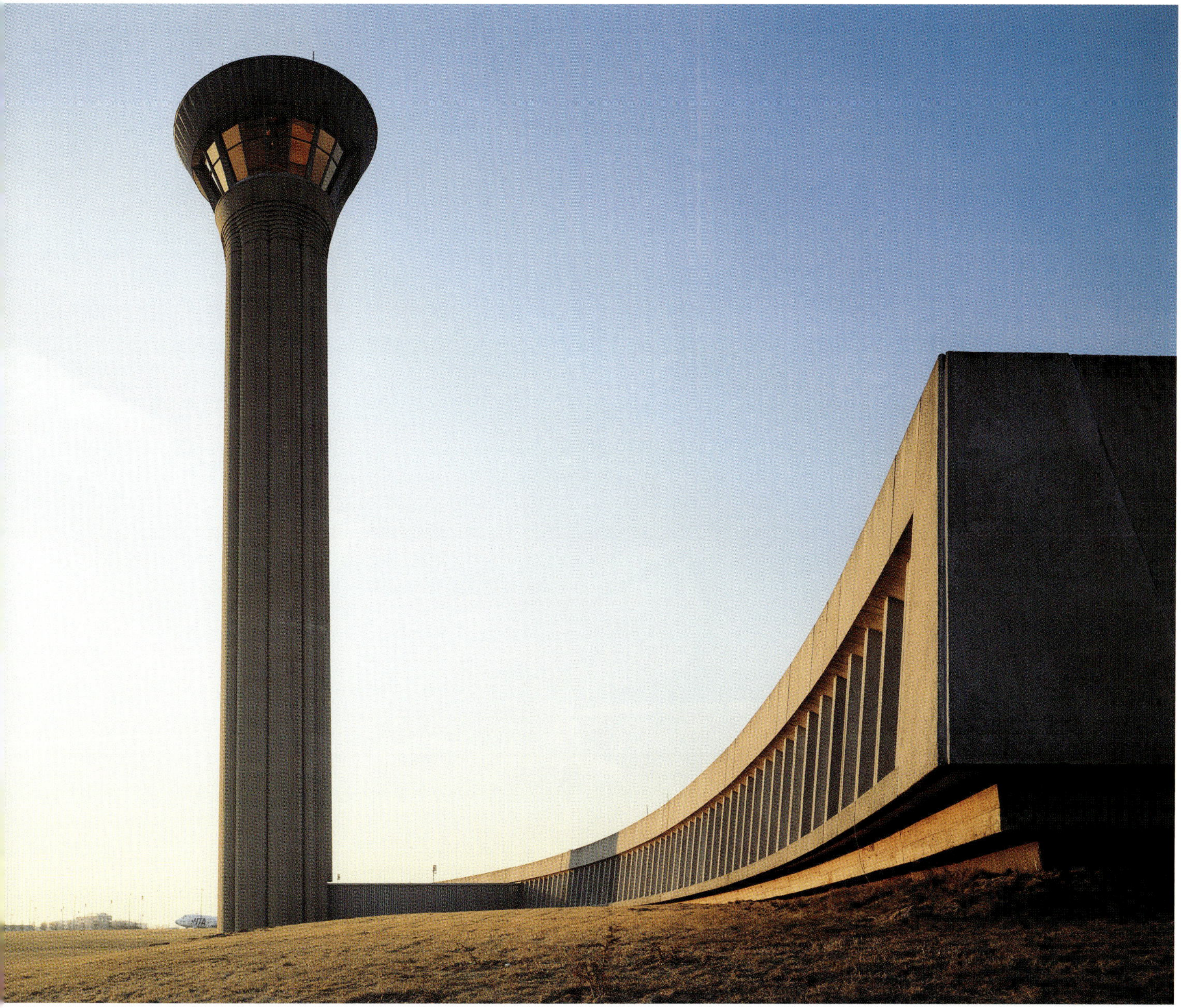

Whether in drawings or in photos, the heart of Terminal 1 belies the strong simplicity of the external mega-structure. The inner courtyard, also round is criss-crossed by moving walkways that hang over a (round) fountain. This Piranesian vision of space gave rise to the most famous photos of Terminal 1.

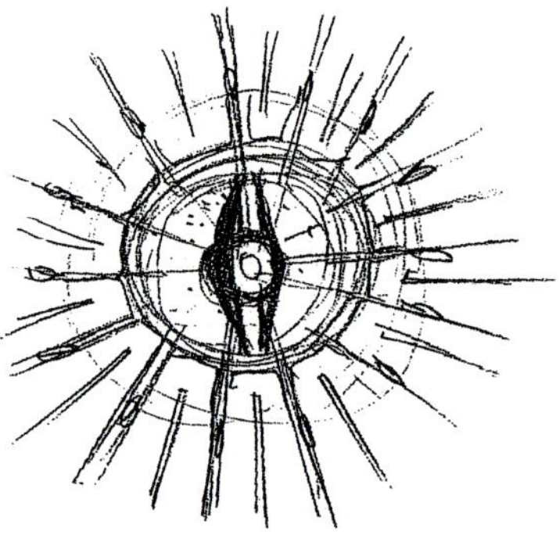

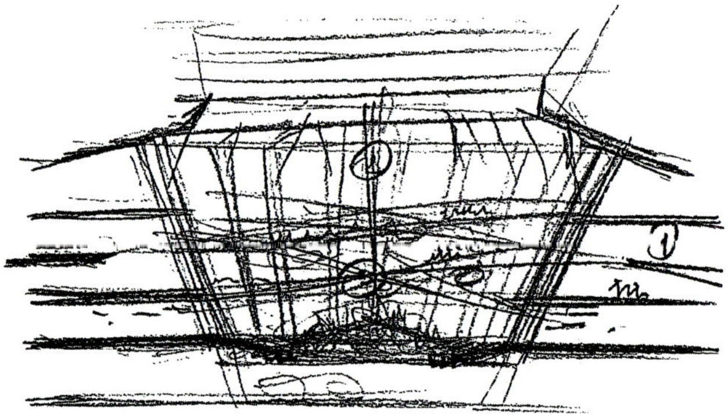

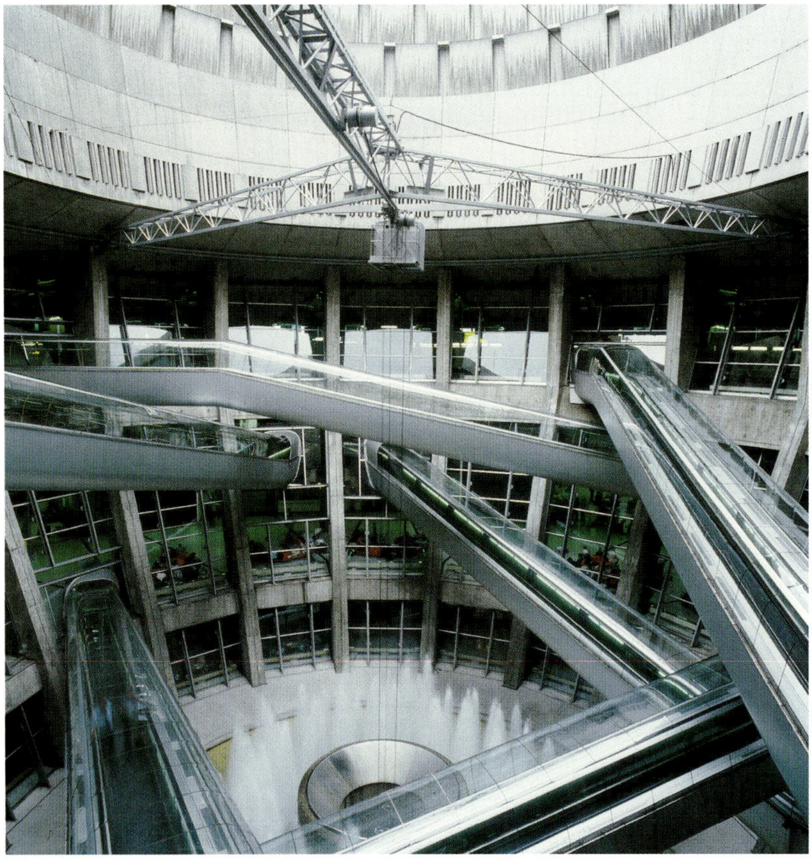

One of the most stunning architectural features of Terminal 1 is its nearly empty central core, crossed by six moving walkways that allow passengers to go from one level to another. The core, with a central fountain serves to bring light into the heart of what appears to be the closed cylindrical shape of the terminal as seen from the outside. Visually, from the moment it is first approached, Terminal 1 gives an impression of continual movement. Taxiing aircraft, moving cars, and then passengers on foot animate every aspect of the facility, and the vision of travelers gliding through the glass tubes that crisscross the core is a particularly strong reminder that this solid form is in fact a vortex, a point of departure or arrival from the rest of the world. Despite its solidly geometric basis, Terminal 1, with its spiraling roads and tubular, suspended walkways, has something Piranesian about it, something that one might liken as much to baroque or mannerist forms as to a pure modernism. Working with a circle at the origin of the project, Andreu widens his

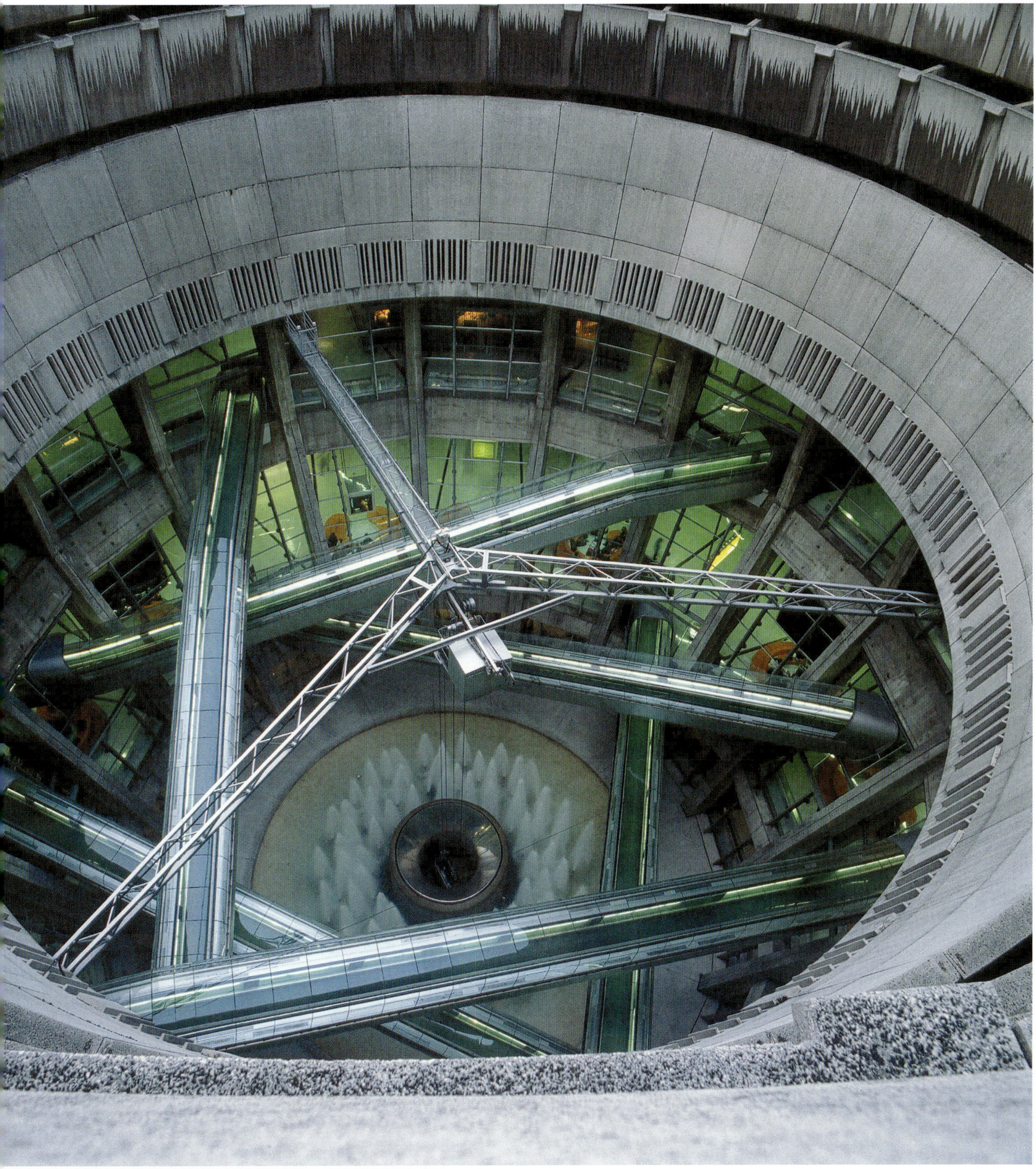

The relative austerity of Terminal 1's exterior is contrasted by its bright, and often colorfully furnished interior spaces. Wide bay windows admit ample natural light and give views either to the inner courtyard (right) or back to the main terminal from the boarding zones (right page). A section of the main structure reveals a spiral design that animates the space and facilitates overall movement.

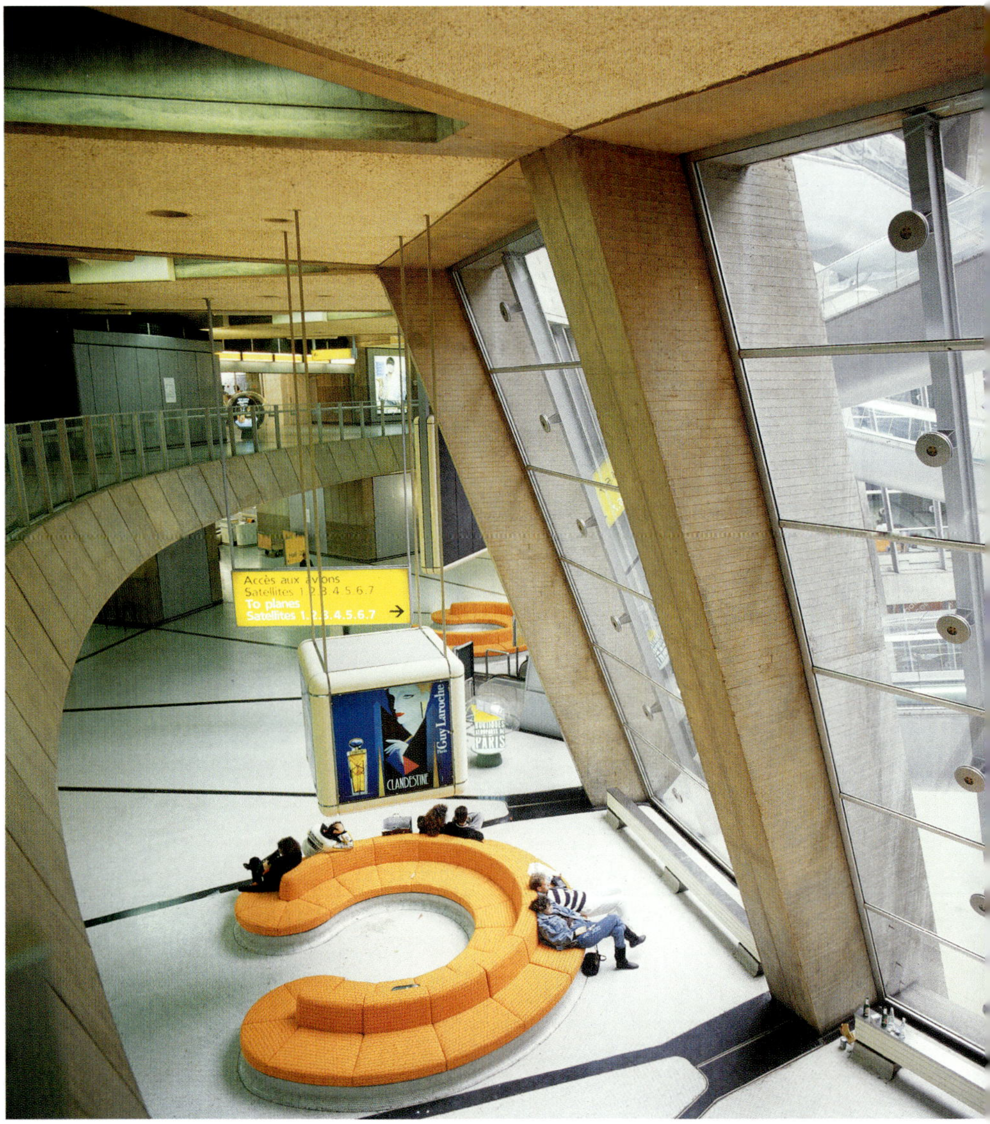

pattern into what can be interpreted either as a spiraling vortex, or to an anthropomorphic shape more basic still – that of a female sex, the ultimate point of departure of life.

Paul Andreu was interested in every aspect of the development of the Roissy project. He went so far as to collaborate with Adrian Frutiger who developed the graphic designs for the signage of the new airport. It might be considered unusual that an architect would have such a wide degree of control on a project of this nature. Indeed, the centralized control of airport design through the Aéroports de Paris, Andreu's

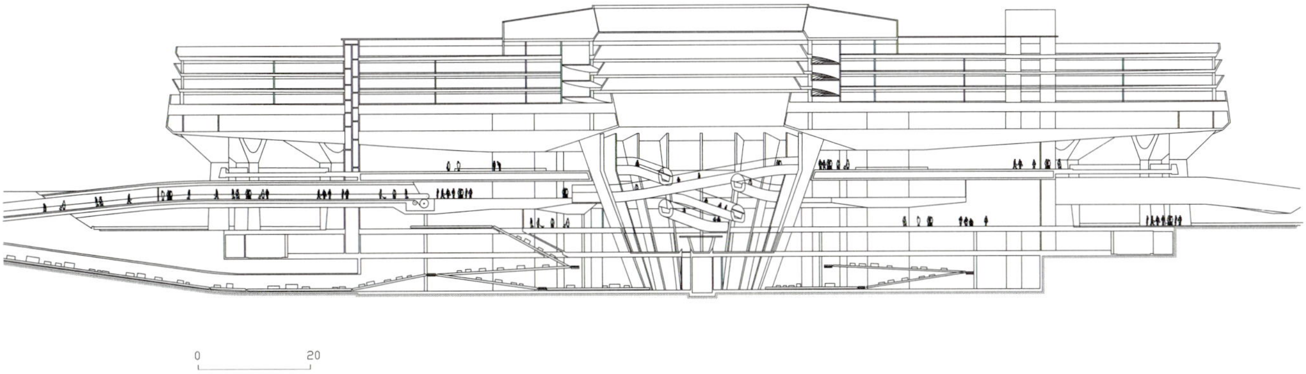
0
20

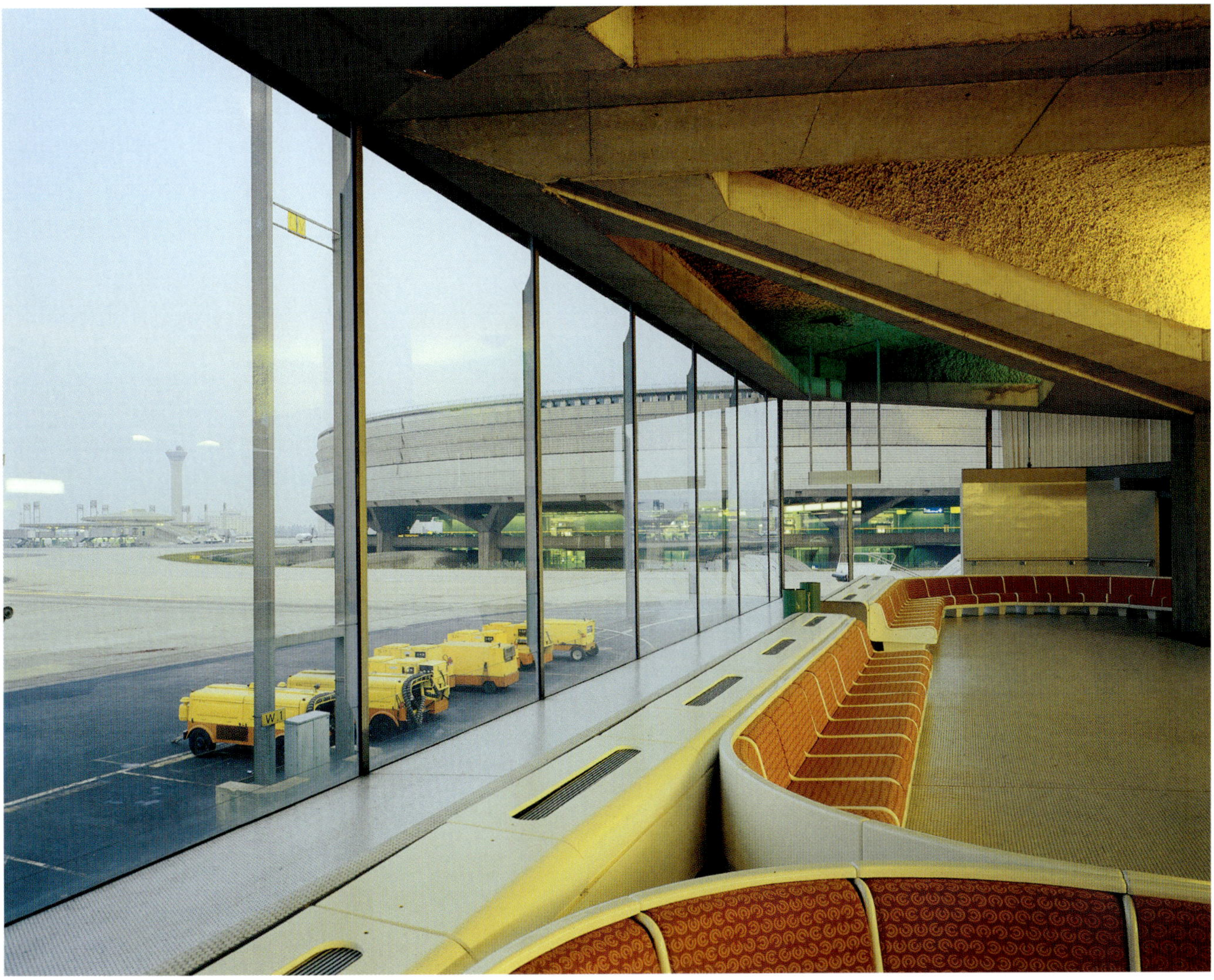

Andreu contrasts inner darkness with the light he associates most clearly with departure zones. Movement through Terminal 1 frequently offers views on other travelers or the ongoing activity of the airport. Travelers animate the space and in a sense unconsciously entertain each other.

employer made this type of involvement possible. In other countries, where the involvement of government organizations is lesser, a greater division of responsibility might well have been imposed, if only for purely commercial reasons. Here the architect-engineer has had the opportunity to truly be at the origin of one of the great airports in the world. Its architecture, but also its engineering and its essential relationship to the functioning of a modern airport, are all within the purview of Paul Andreu. This is very much his design, no matter how large the group of analysts, designers or engineers was.

The architect clearly plays on light and dark in his design. Ticketing counters in the outer circle of the complex are essentially served by artificial light, but when the visitor heads toward customs, he crosses the central void, exposed to strong daylight. From there, the path to the aircraft is also punctuated by an alternance of dark (in the tunnels leading to the satellites) and light (in the boarding areas themselves). This facility is also a product of French engineering, with all that implies in the way of brilliance and circumlocution. The vortex of Terminal 1 is the active node of the master plan for Roissy airport – a 3,000-hectare plot of farmland next to the A1 highway leading into Paris from the North. As Paul Andreu says clearly, Terminal 1 was the "the basis itself, the origin" of what was to come in his future work on the Charles-de-Gaulle Airport.

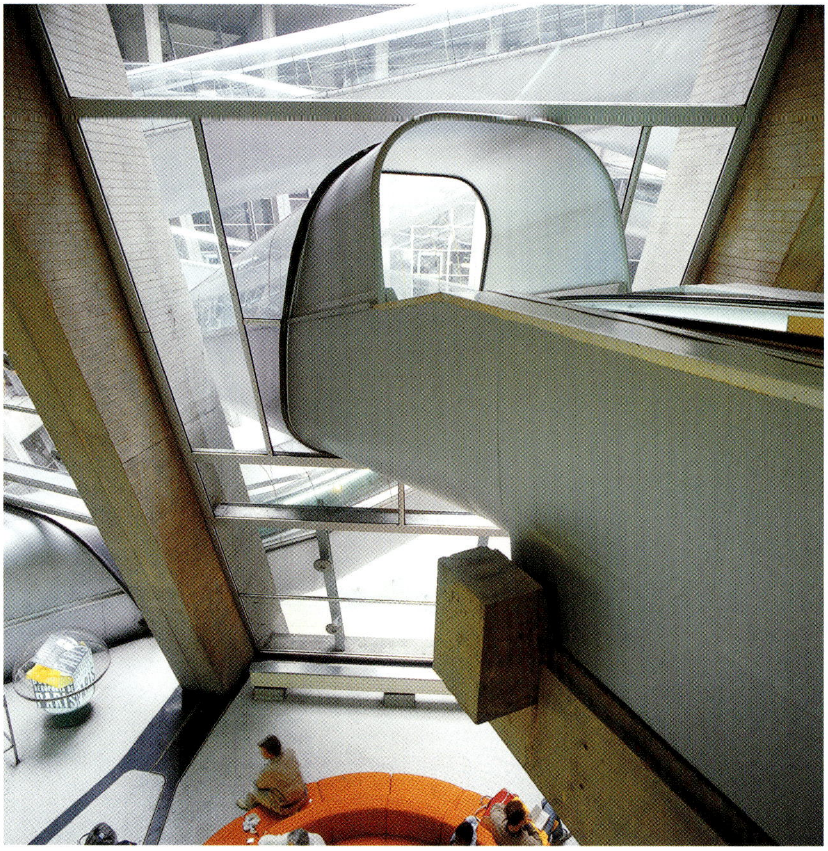

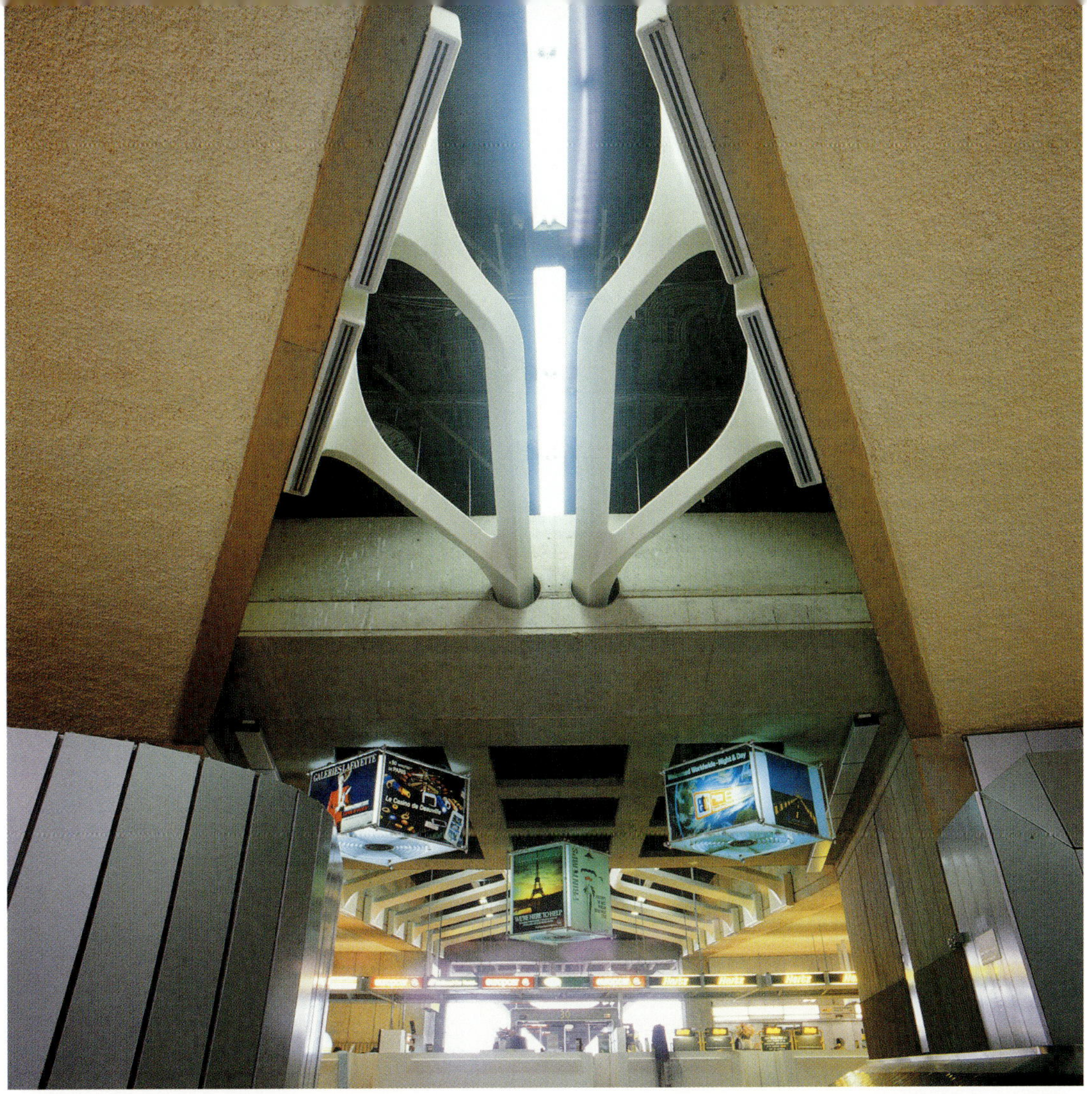
GALERIES LAFAYETTE

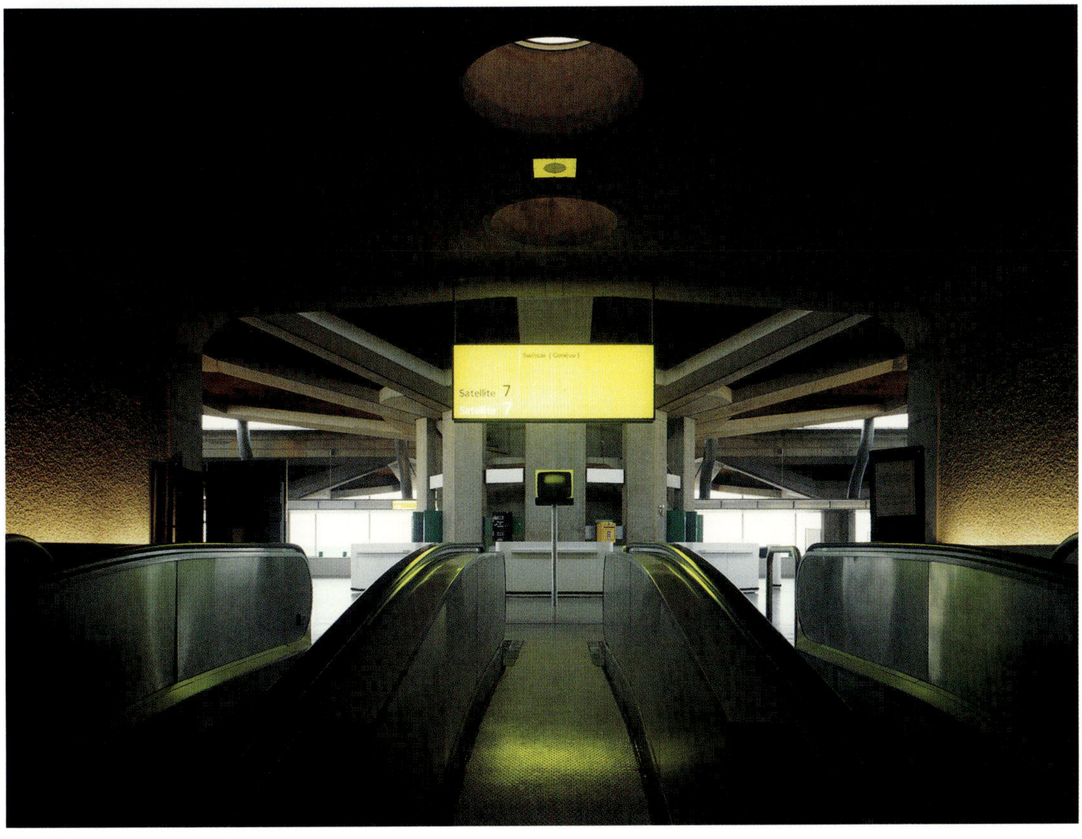
Satellite 7
Satellite 7

Renovation **2003-2005**

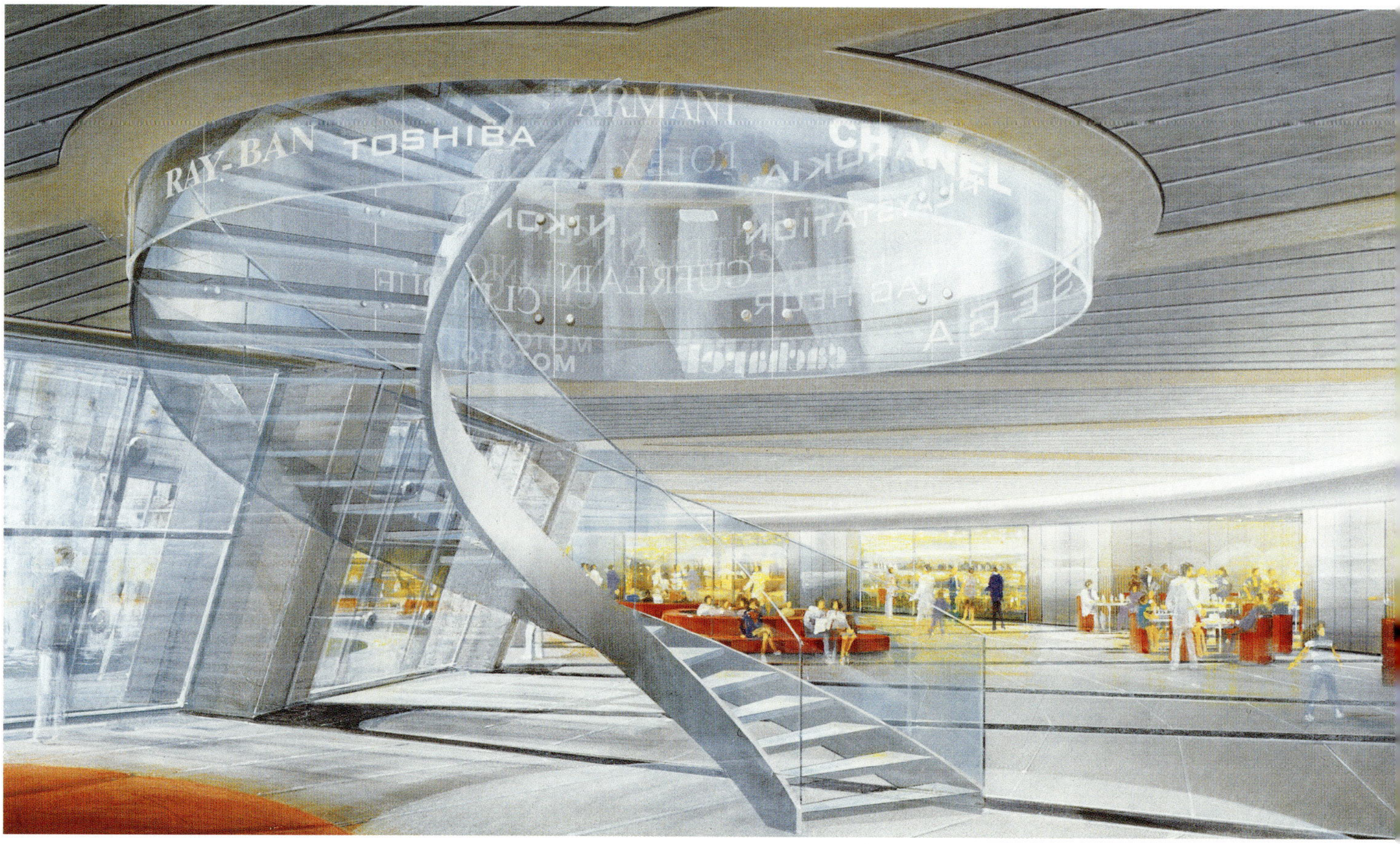

More than a quarter century after its opening, handling some 13 million passengers a year, and no less than 60 airlines, Terminal 1 reached a state when a renovation had to be considered. Paul Andreu undertook this work as one of his last tasks at the Aéroports de Paris, seeking not only to give a new, brighter appearance to the space, but also to take into account the numerous evolutions in airline traffic that have occurred since Terminal 1 was conceived. Heightened security needs and the installation of a new automatic transport system linking Terminals 1 and 2 necessitated changes in the layout of the facility, handled by Paul Andreu with his usual efficiency and sense of airport aesthetics and function.

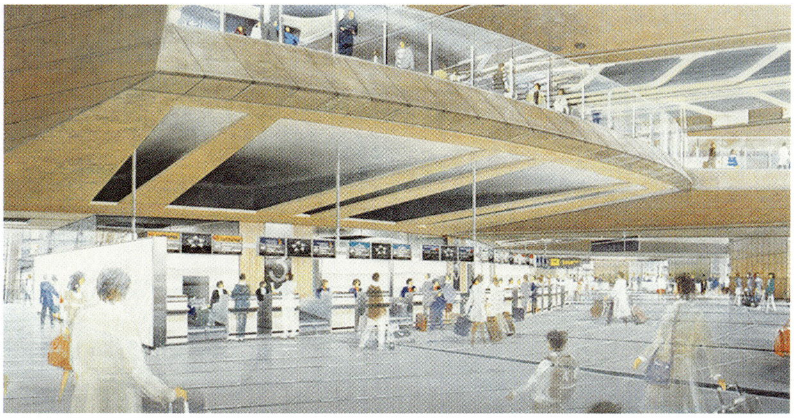

The new automatic transport system arrives at the level of the boutiques, increasing the need for open passenger movement from the boutique level to that of the departures. A new, open spiral staircase is symbolic of the architect's increased interest in transparency and light-filled spaces.

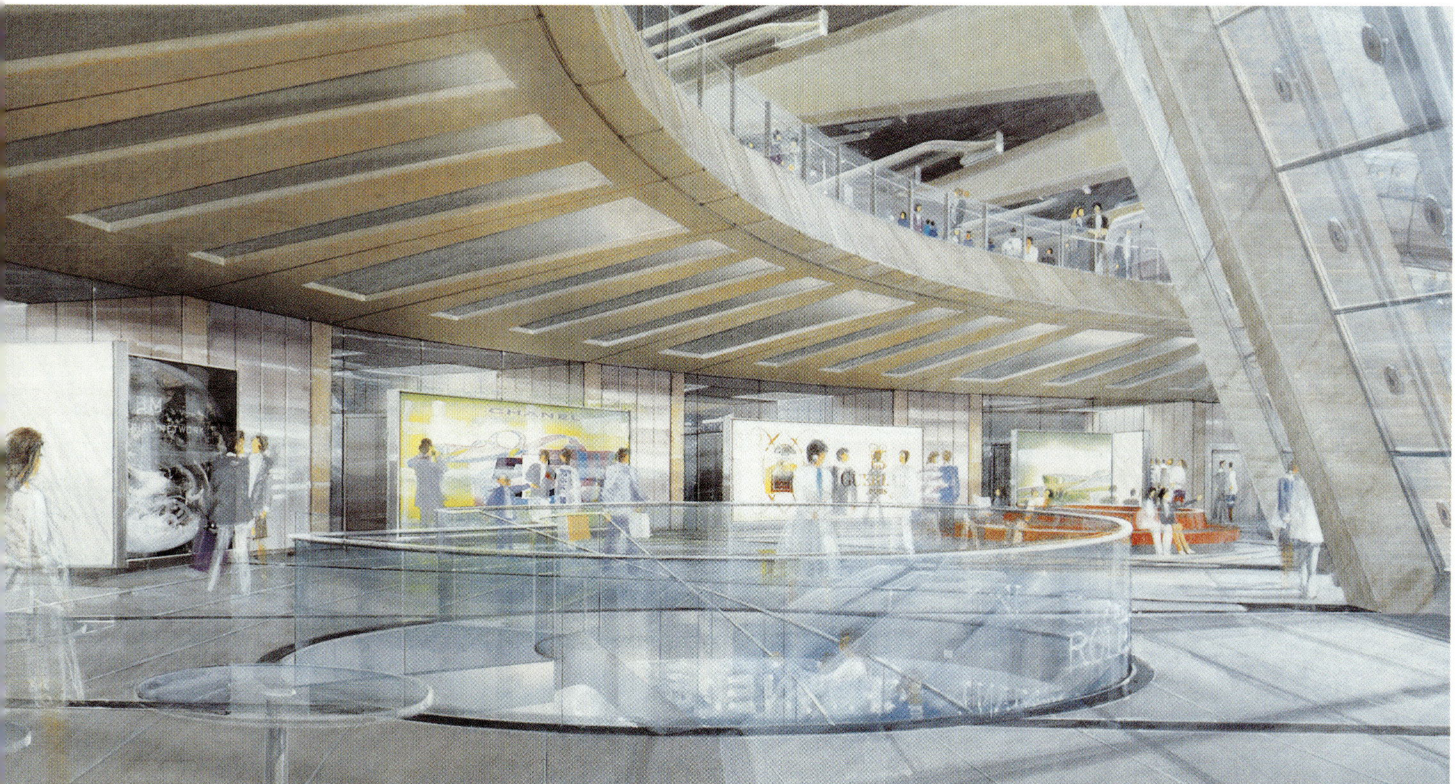

Terminal 2 represented a radical architectural departure from Terminal 1. Not only was the open shape of the structures quite different from the closed disk of the original airport, but Andreu's concept of efficient airport enlargement was born of his strategy here.

46 ## Charles-de-Gaulle Airport - Terminal 2 - A and B **Paris**

Country: France
Use: Airport
Start of project: 1972
Completion: 1981/1982
Surface: c. 50,000 m² each
Capacity: 10 million passengers per year (2 B: 6M, 2 A: 4M)

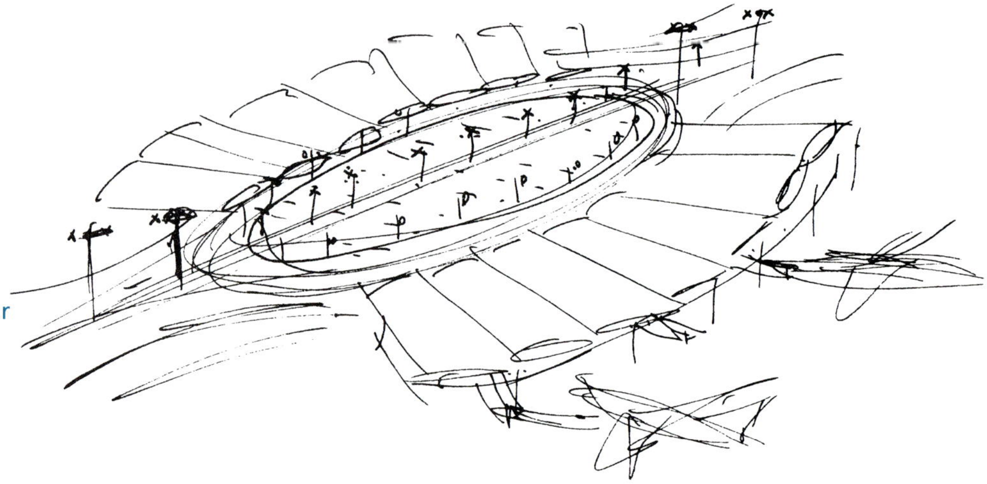

The work on Terminal 2 began two years before the completion of Terminal 1, and its first two elements became operational respectively in 1981 and 1982. At an area of 50,300 square meters, Hall A was intended for a traffic flow of 4 million passengers a year. It's nearly identical cousin, Hall B measures 50,000 square meters and handles 6 million travelers. 3,680 parking spots, and 112 check-in counters form the necessary infrastructure for this volume of clients. One of the very interesting aspects of this project is that it was from the outset designed as part of a modular system, destined to be enlarged as demand increased. Further, the disposition of the elements of the composition permitted one hall to function even as the other was under construction. Clearly, the fact that Roissy was situated in former agricultural land made this kind of planning feasible, but accomplishing it with the degree of efficiency obtained was no small feat. Essential to this success was a mastery not only of the architectural and engineering problems involved, but also of the road system serving the whole airport and more specifically the new zones.

Rather than the round shape chosen for Terminal 1, Andreu opted here for long, narrow structures, allowing a transition from taxi to aircraft in a space of less than 60 meters. The shell roofing system clearly indicated the direction of movement of travelers, but this is already apparent from the essential transparency of the buildings. The planes are visible

From the strictly circular plan of Terminal 1, which was difficult to link to new structures, Andreu moved to an oblong plan that might be likened to an eye in its form. The main advantage of this layout is that it became possible to link one terminal to the next and to carry out construction work on new areas without disturbing the functions of the existing facilities.

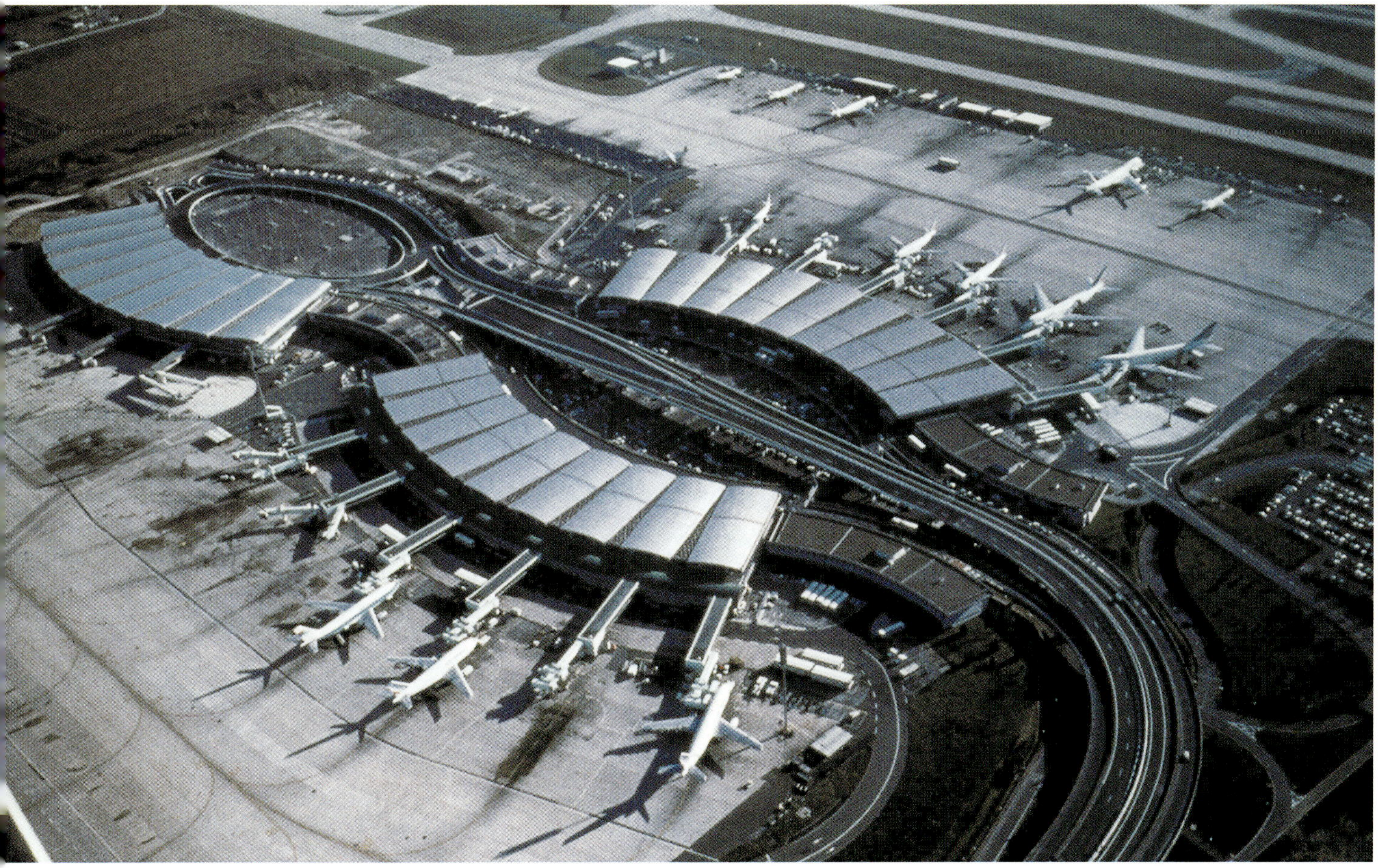

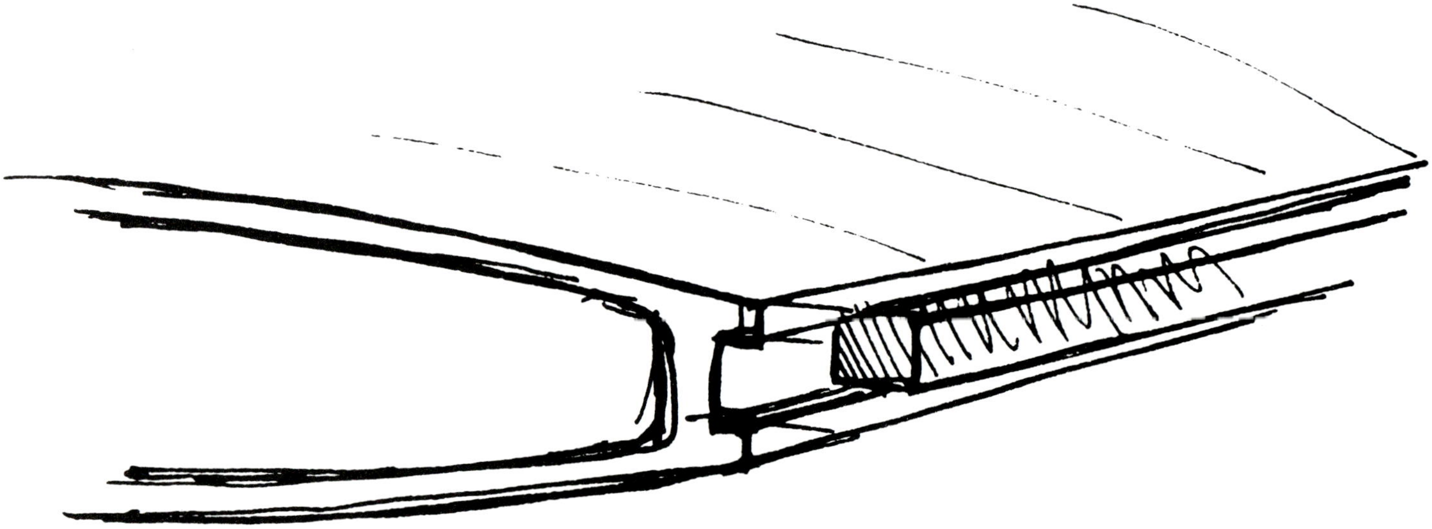

The successive roof shells of Terminal 2 A and B link to each other and also echo the ocular form of the overall plan. Andreu masters the use of different levels for arrivals, departures and parking. In the case of Terminal 2 A and B, the central islands are in fact densely used parking areas. Despite a regular repetition of the roof theme, the curve of the terminal buildings gives them an animated aspect that would have been missing had they been arrayed in a straight line.

practically from the entrance doors on the street side. In a way, Andreu has alternated here, from the external opacity of Terminal 1, to a considerably more open and "friendly" appearance. Still sheltered in the outstretched arms of the two halls, the traveler here does not have the same sense of entering a huge flying saucer bound for another planet. Less exotic and more "pedestrian" air travel had evolved between the dates of Terminal 1 and the beginnings of Terminal 2. And yet, in both instances, Andreu's work served to make the experience of waiting or movement agreeable, never allowing himself to make the kind of anonymous spaces that came to dominate rail travel for example. For Andreu, Terminal 2, Halls A and B, mark "an effort to create

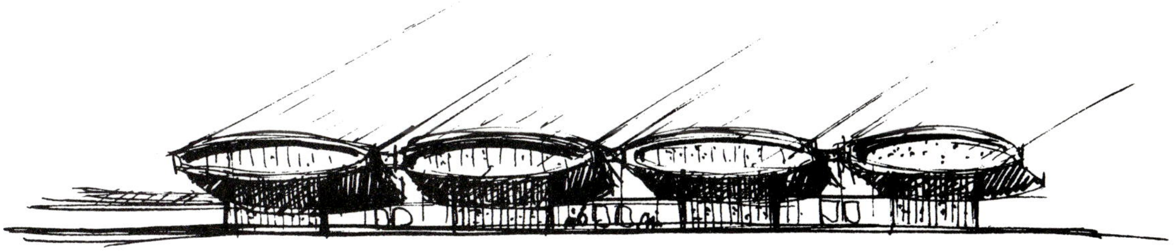

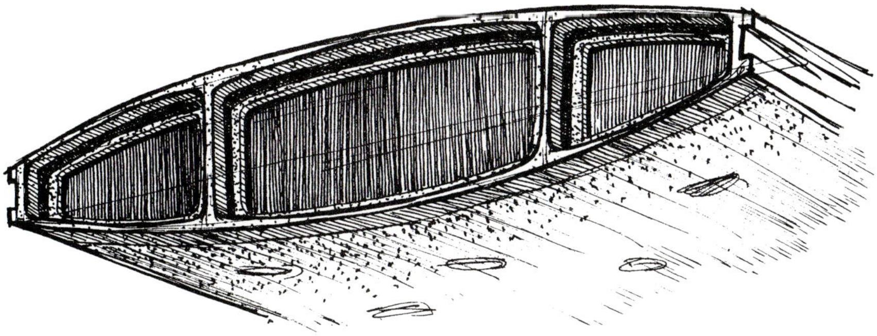

a repetitive, open structure."
Again, a view of the plans for Terminal 2 may allow for an anthropomorphic interpretation of the design. The elongated oval opening for car parking might bring to mind the shape of an eye, and the undulated repetition of the roofing of the two halls is not without some reference to eye lashes. This essentially elliptical design is repeated in the succession of coffers supporting the roof. Visible from both the runway side and the automobile access areas, these elliptical forms support the roof and simultaneously allow the technical systems to be hidden and acceded to from above without disturbing passenger

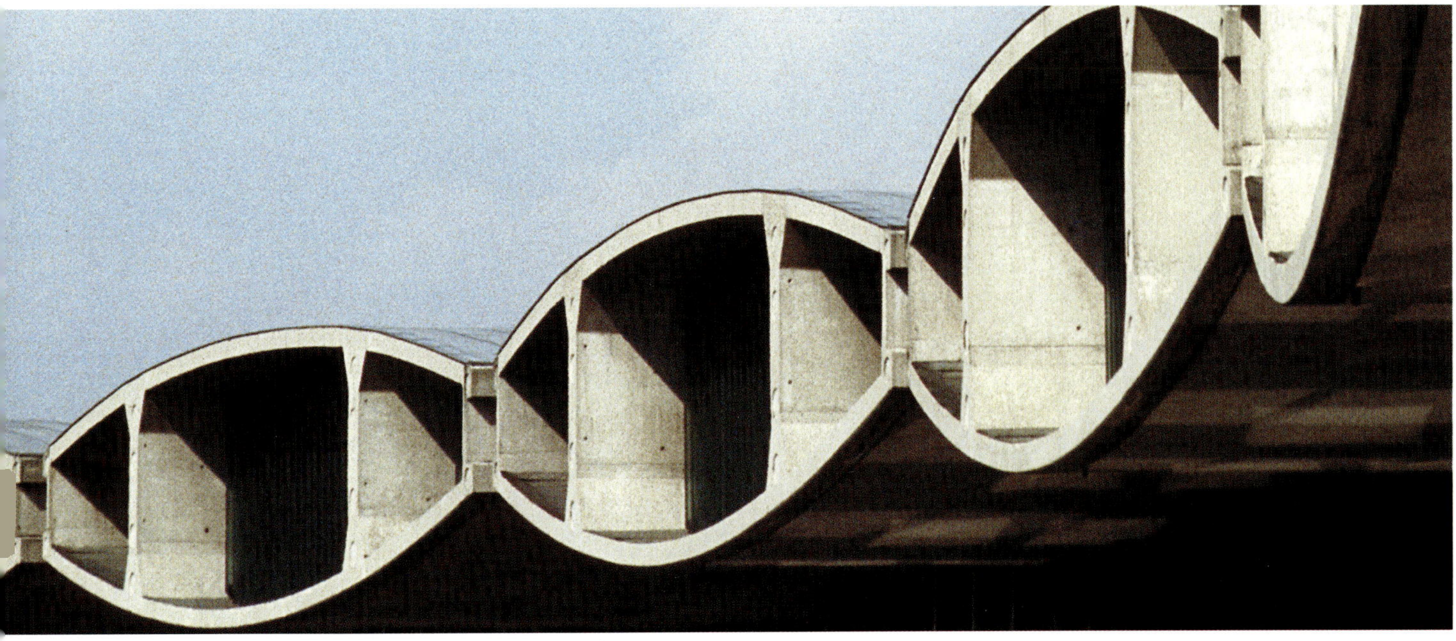

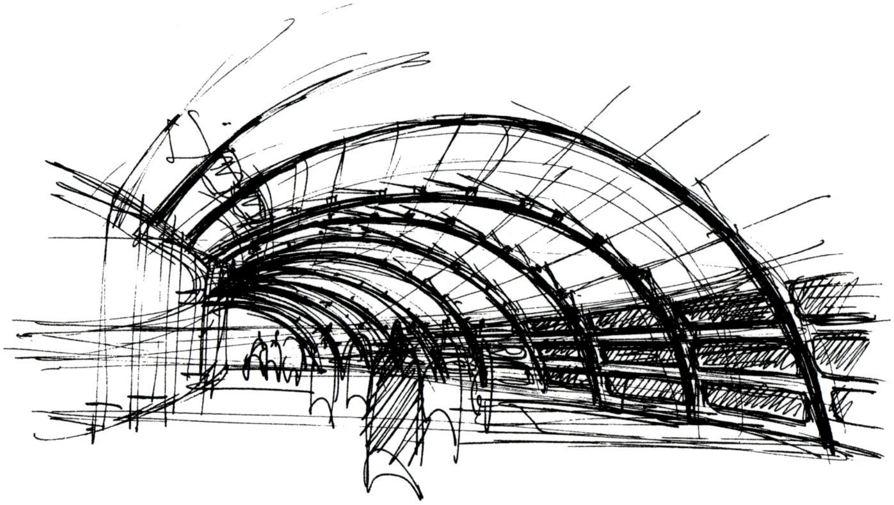

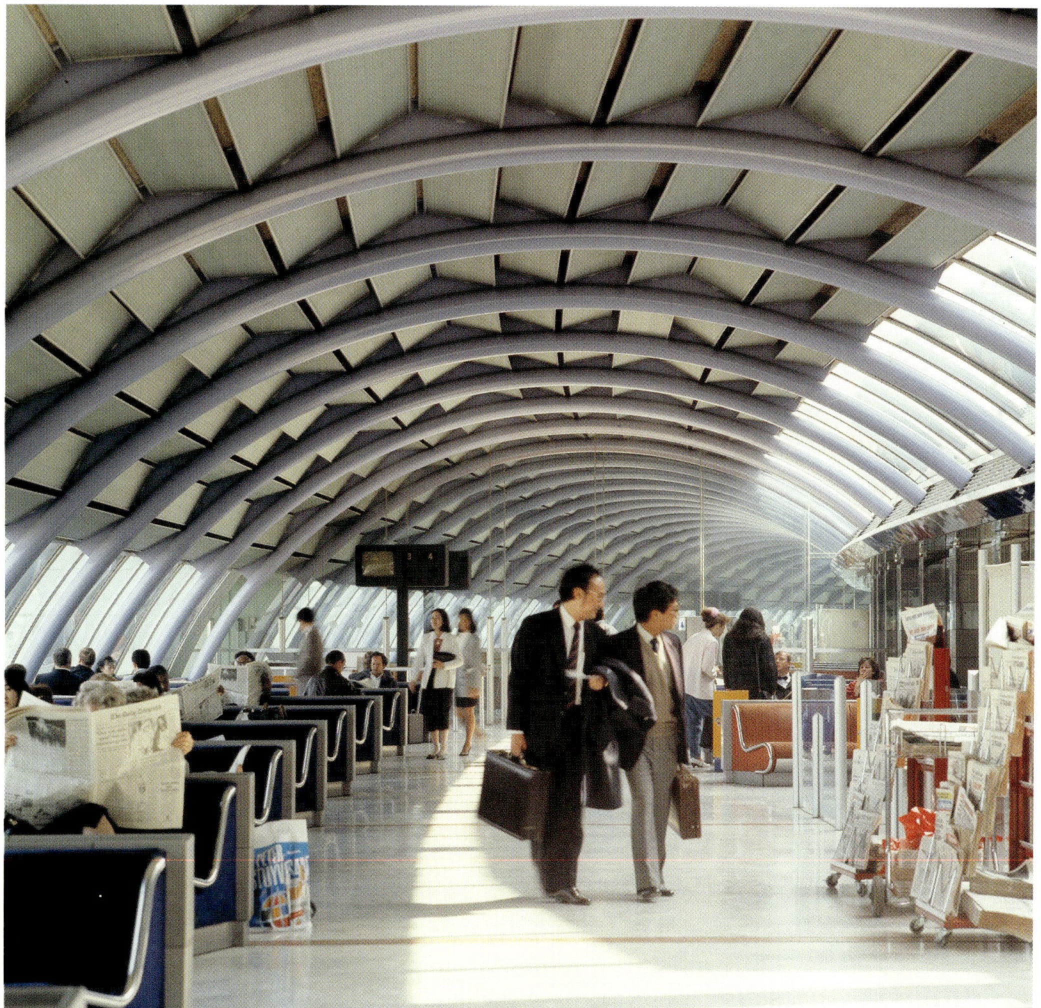

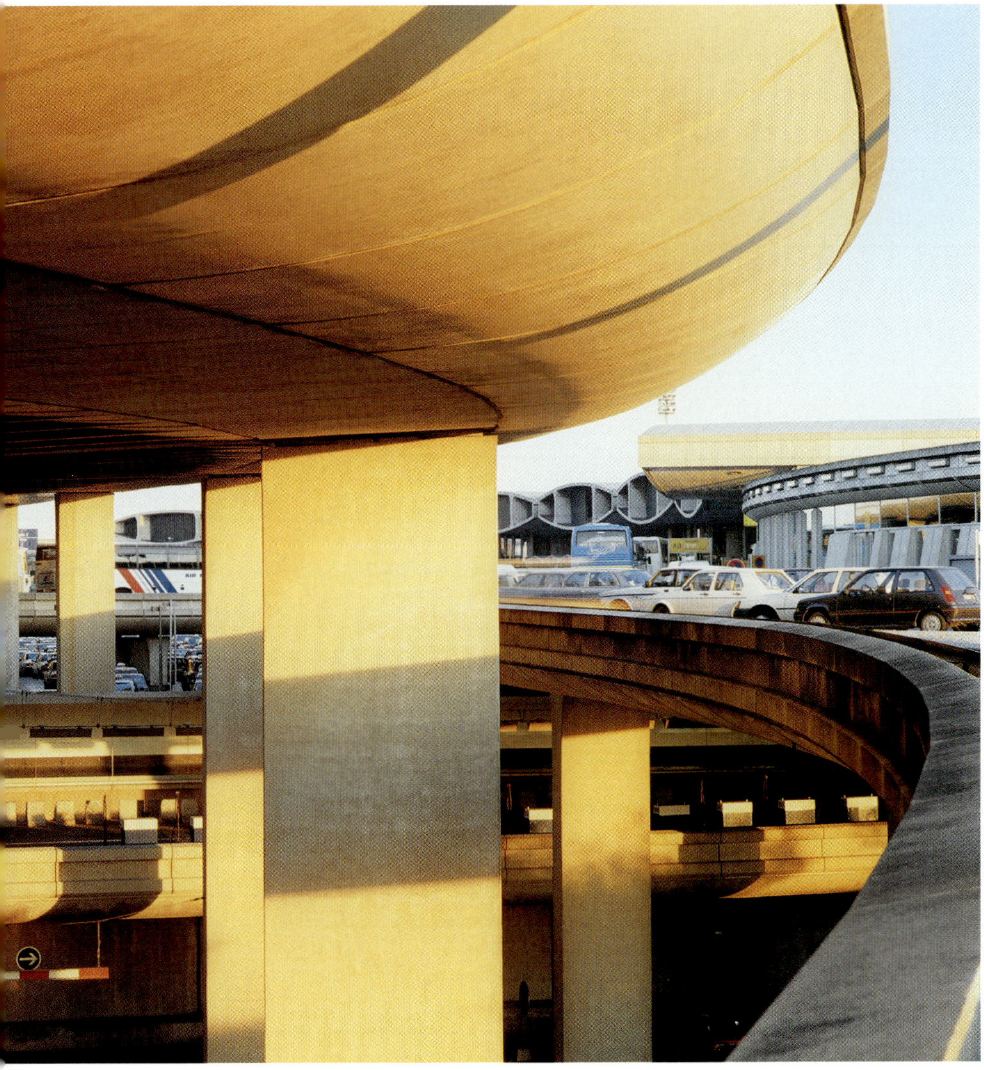

Curves of various types characterize the spaces, both interior and exterior. Whether it be inside the terminals where a partially open shell offers protection from the sun and views to the exterior, or outside where elevated roads assume a similar inverted shell design. These views emphasize that Andreu thinks not only of the architecture of the buildings, but also of the access roads and passenger flow, essential characteristics of modern airports.

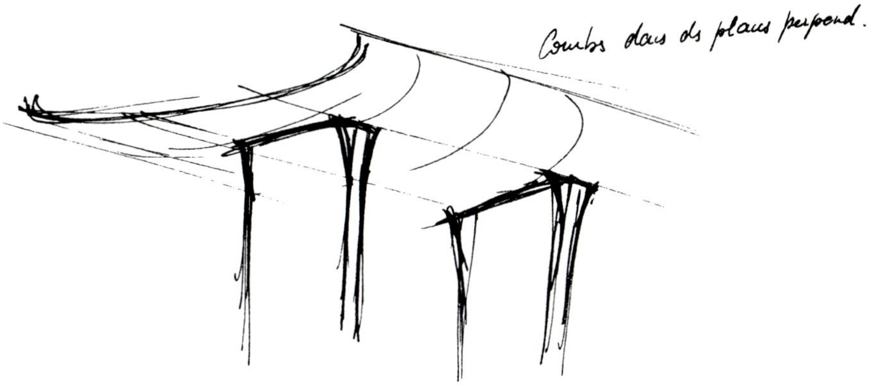

movement. A more basic interpretation of the elliptical with its axial flow might again evoke the female sex. This is not to say that Andreu is consciously adapting an anthropomorphic scheme. Rather the shapes of nature, and the human body in particular have long informed architectural designs for reasons of simplicity, commodity and fundamental familiarity. A purely modernist scheme might well have straightened roads, and left fewer curves in this architecture. Andreu's approach to modernity is suffused with a sense of deep practicality, both in engineering terms and vis-à-vis the user. Whether the form of what the painter Gustave Courbet called "The Origin of the World" was directly present in Paul Andreu's mind when he designed Terminal 2 or not is hardly an issue. There is an undeniable drive here to make things work and to make them agreeable to the traveler.
That Andreu's architecture might at its best evoke the human body is neither surprising nor contrary to the most contemporary definitions of efficiency.

Satellite A **1996-1999**

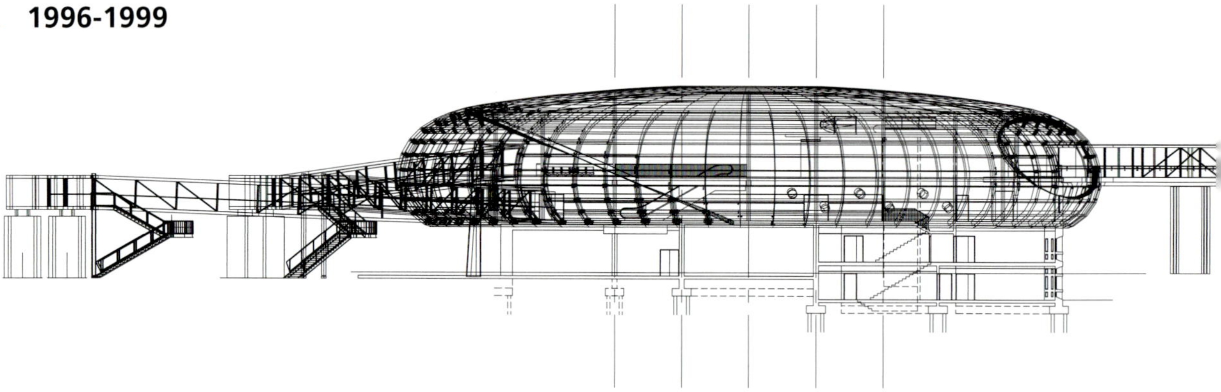

Although it has a round form that might recall the earlier Terminal 1 building, Satellite A is different from its predecessor in almost every other aspect. Its metallic, open design is almost the reverse of the externally closed concrete volume of the first structure. There is something of the "flying saucer" in this design but it is sleek enough not to appear dated. Light is a visibly significant element in the design "making its functions easy to grasp," according to the architect. This light is brought in in good part by two large oblong openings located where the loading bridges and connecting passageway are connected to the building. Although Paul Andreu manages to create a smooth transition from Terminal 2 A to Satellite A, it is obvious that his thinking has evolved since the earlier structures were designed. Clarity and lightness are the themes here in a structure where it goes almost without saying that the architect has fully mastered the technical complexities of passenger movement and airport design. The shell is 56 meters in diameter and rises to a maximum height of 11 meters. Three wide-bodied aircraft can dock simultaneously at the facility, where deplaning occurs on the first floor above ground and boarding lounges are located on the second floor. The curved exterior of the Satellite is clad in flat glass and aluminum panels with a concrete and steel support structure. Measuring 6,371 square meters, Satellite A was designed to handle 900,000 passengers a year.

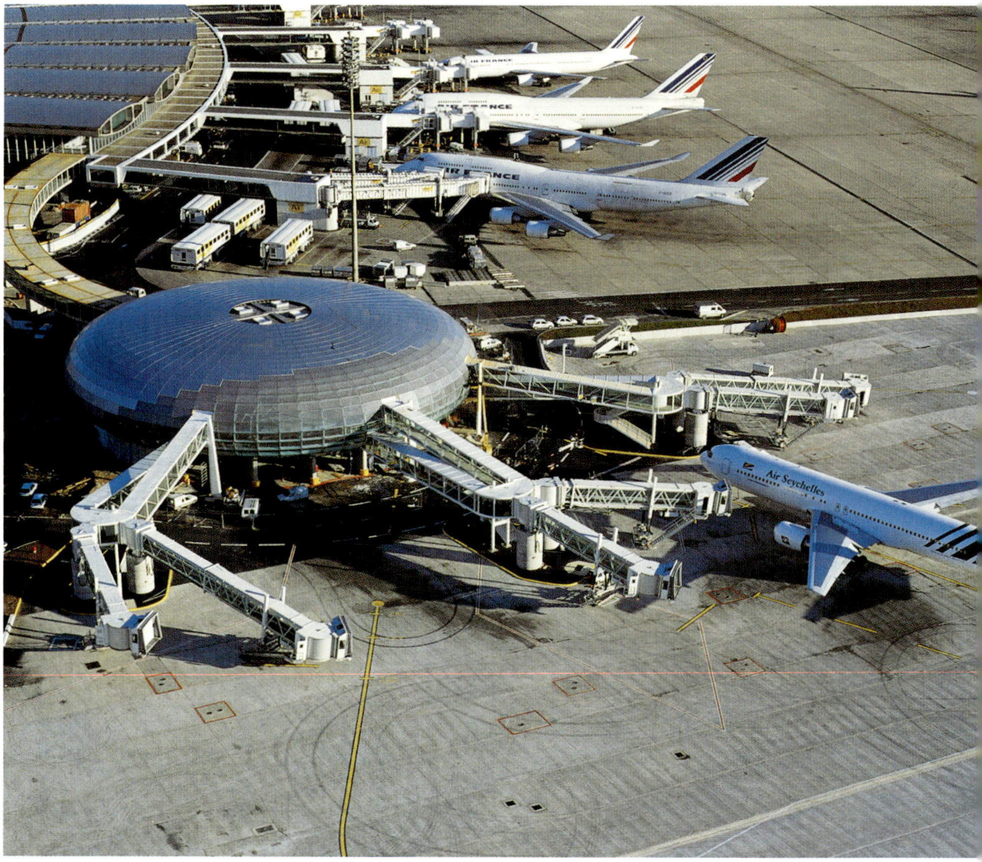

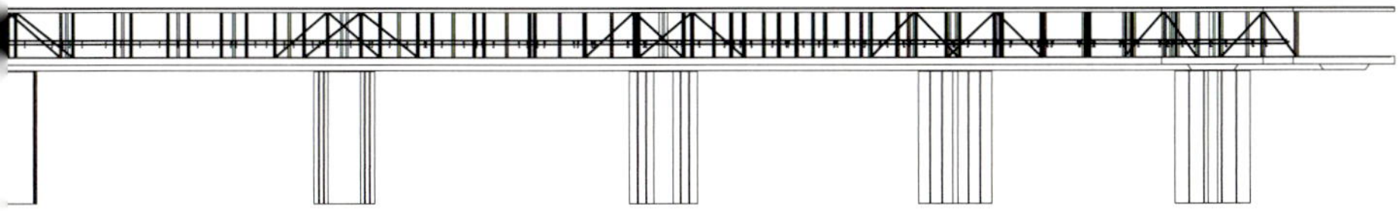

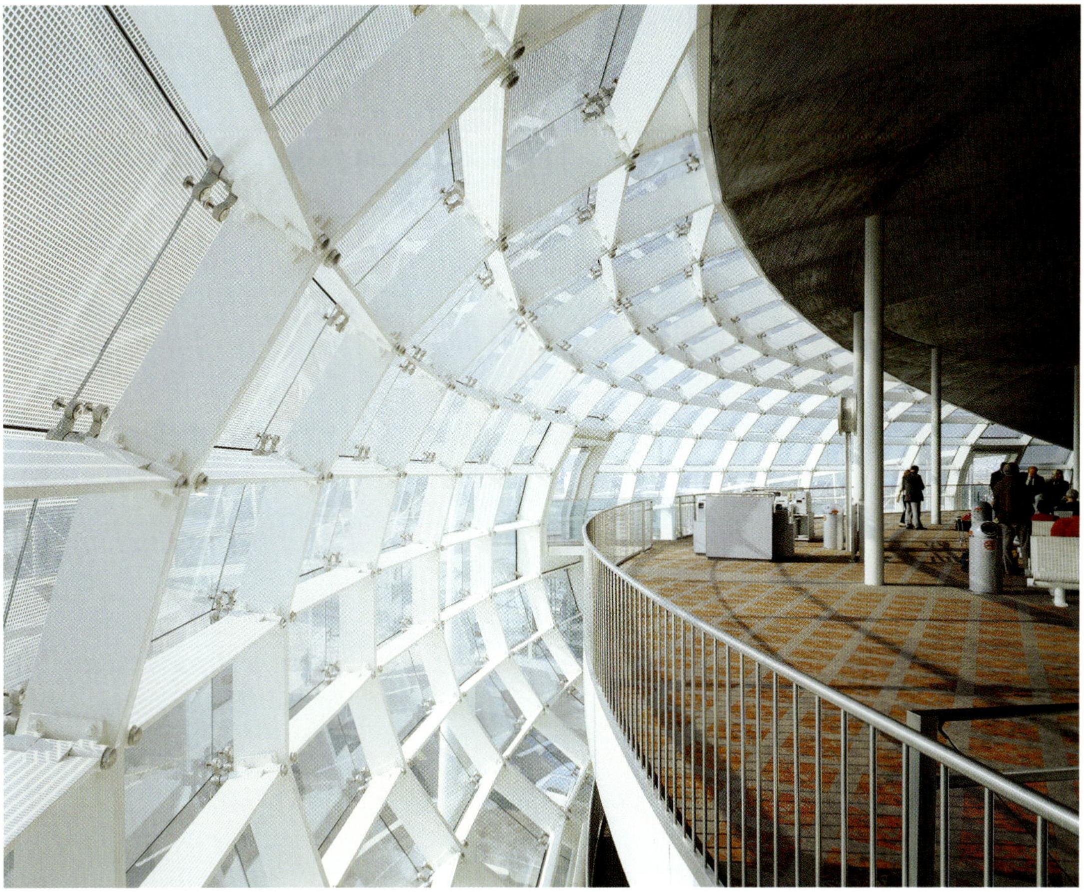

Much more recent than the structure to which it is attached, Satellite A nonetheless again makes use of the partially open shell seen in the early phases of the development of Terminal 2. Despite its smooth outer skin, Satellite A is a very technical structure as the drawing above shows.

Combining an arc and a circle in his plan for the Abu Dhabi Airport, Paul Andreu as usual is attentive to the succession of spaces the traveler passes through on his way from ground transport to the aircraft. Despite the smaller scale of this airport as compared for example to Charles-de-Gaulle, the architect nonetheless calls on the kinds of sweeping curves seen in his other work.

Abu Dhabi Airport **Abu Dhabi**

Country: United Arab Emirates
Use: Airport
Start of project: 1975
Completion: 1982
Surface of central building: 45,000 m^2
Capacity: 3.1 million passengers per year

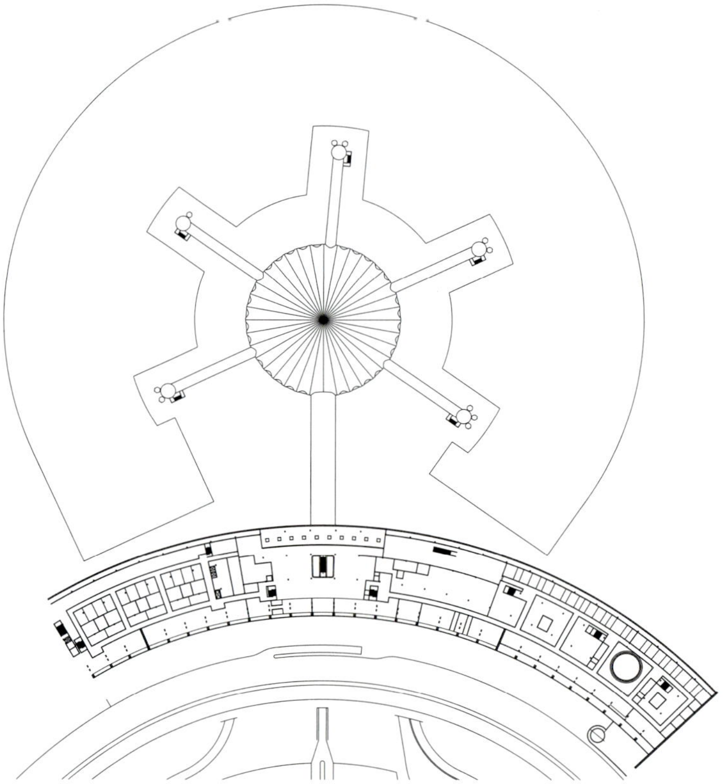

Obviously conceived on a smaller scale than the Paris airport structures, the Abu Dhabi Airport was inaugurated in 1982. Intended for 3.1 million passengers per year, the design includes 45,000 square meters for the main building and 7,100 square meters for the satellite. There were 28 check-in counters and 1,600 parking spots included in the scheme. In a way, the plan of this airport could be likened to a fusion between Roissy's Terminal 1 and Terminal 2. The main building in Abu Dhabi is a broad curve, while the satellite is circular. Andreu compares the design of the satellite to that of a "shell" or a cave – gray on the outside and colorful within. Using a gamut of geometric forms, torus, and warped hexagons, the architect again creates a sense of movement, and in this instance a protection from the harsh Middle Eastern sun. A blue to green transition in the patterns for the interior

A plan of the airport on the left-hand page demonstrates the fundamental simplicity of the design, while, below, a drawing gives an idea of the view of an arriving or departing passenger on board an aircraft.

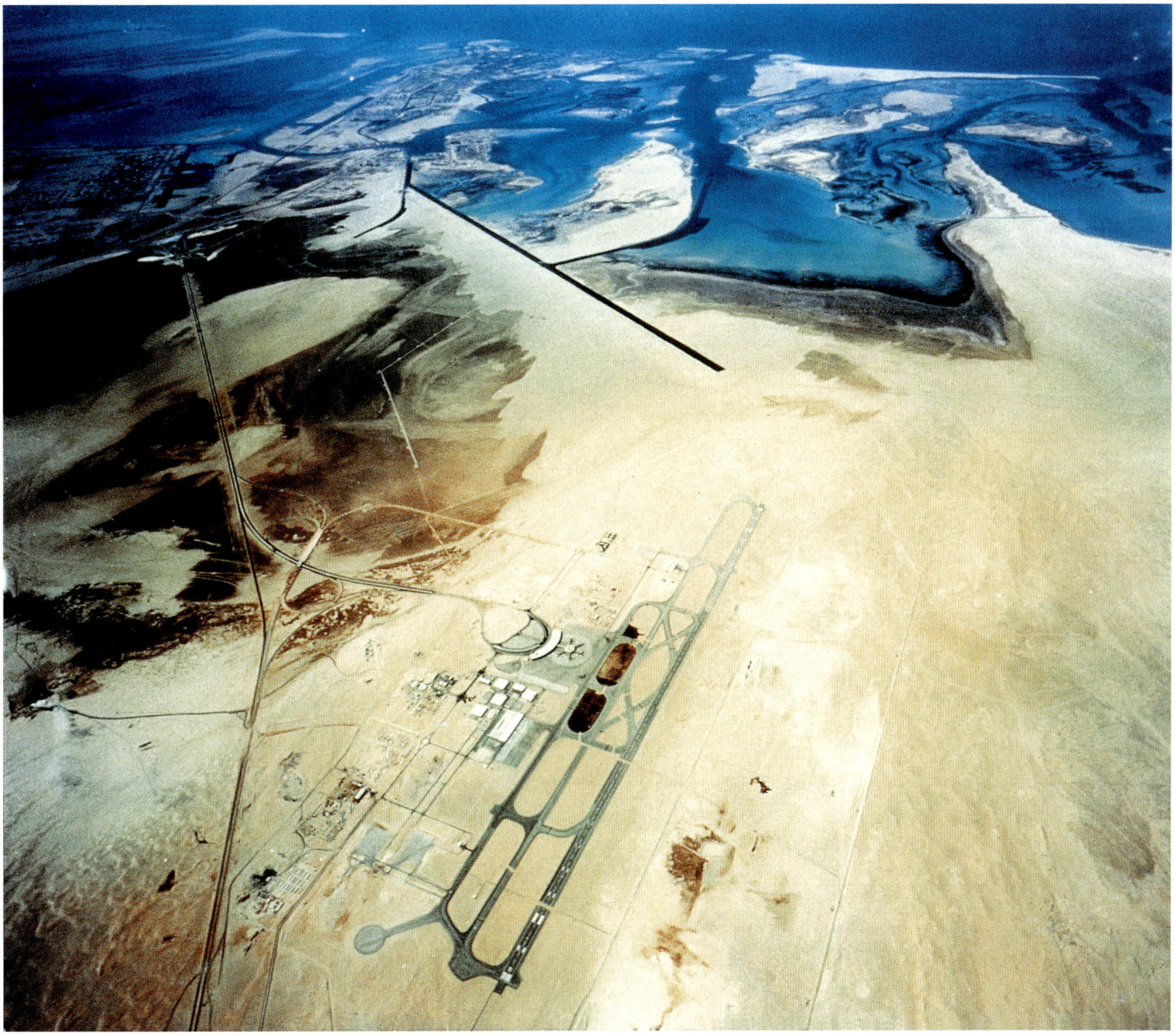

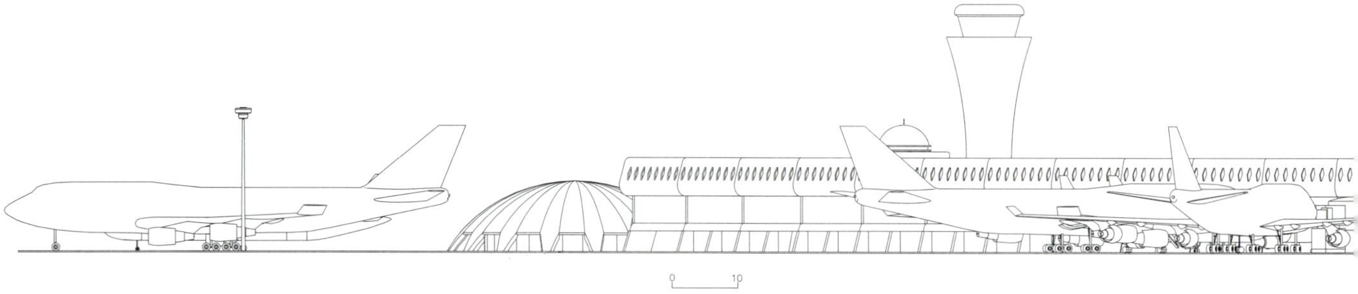

tiles produces what he calls a "moving fountain of color." Paul Andreu today remembers this design as being the first time he had used color, a fact that does underline the relatively gray color schemes of Roissy. An element of what one might be tempted to call "local color" also because of the tent-like configuration of the satellite, is not sufficiently emphasized to give a "post-modern" feeling to the space, and yet perhaps because of the tiling, the interiors of the building are somewhat "dated" in their appearance as seen today.

Like Terminal 2, this facility was also designed with the possibility of future expansion very much in mind. The future

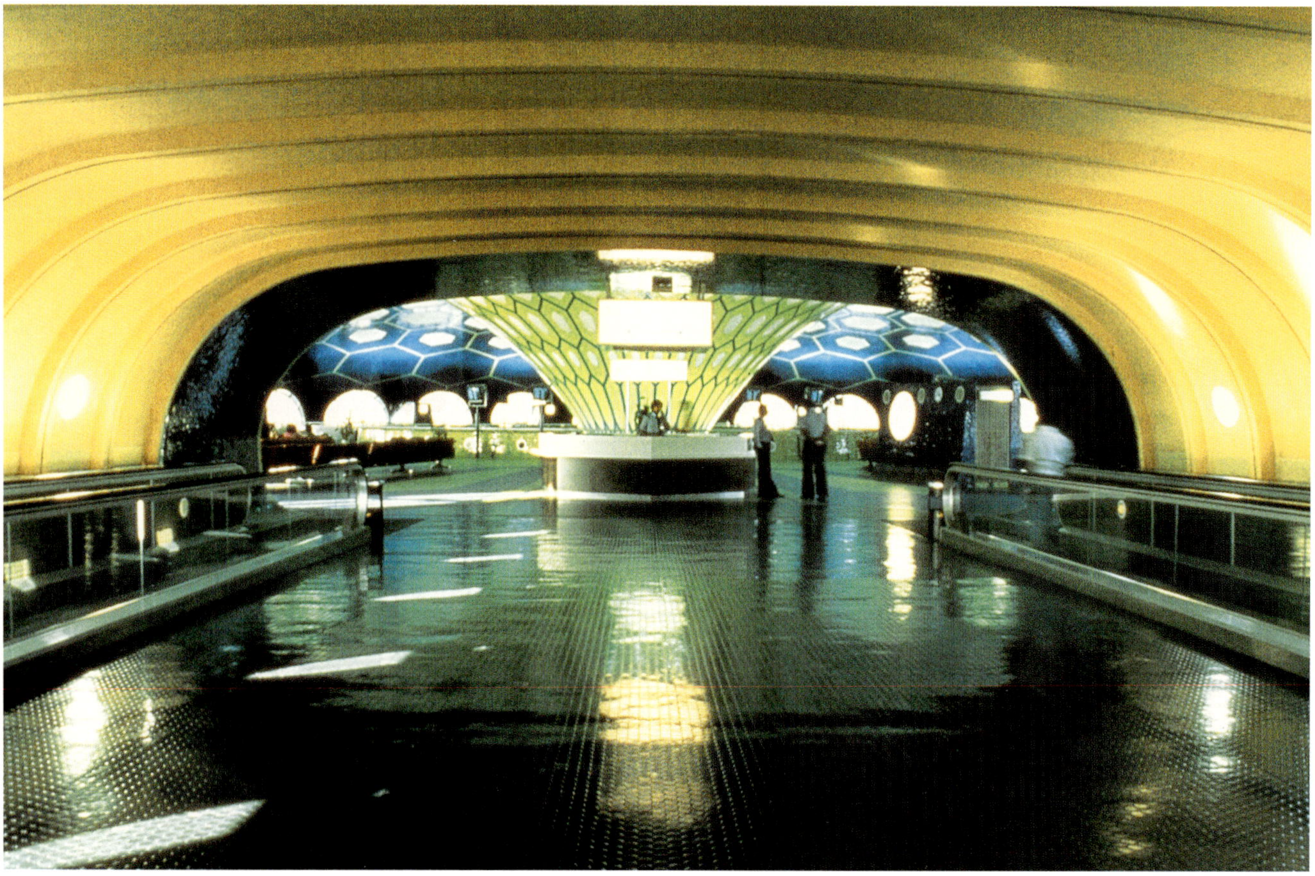

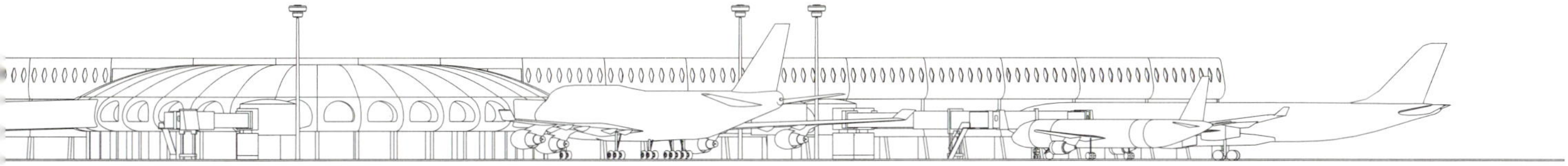

A subtle use of geometric decorative patterns often found in Islamic art and a design that shelters from the harsh sun are indications of the architect's adaptation to local circumstances in this terminal.

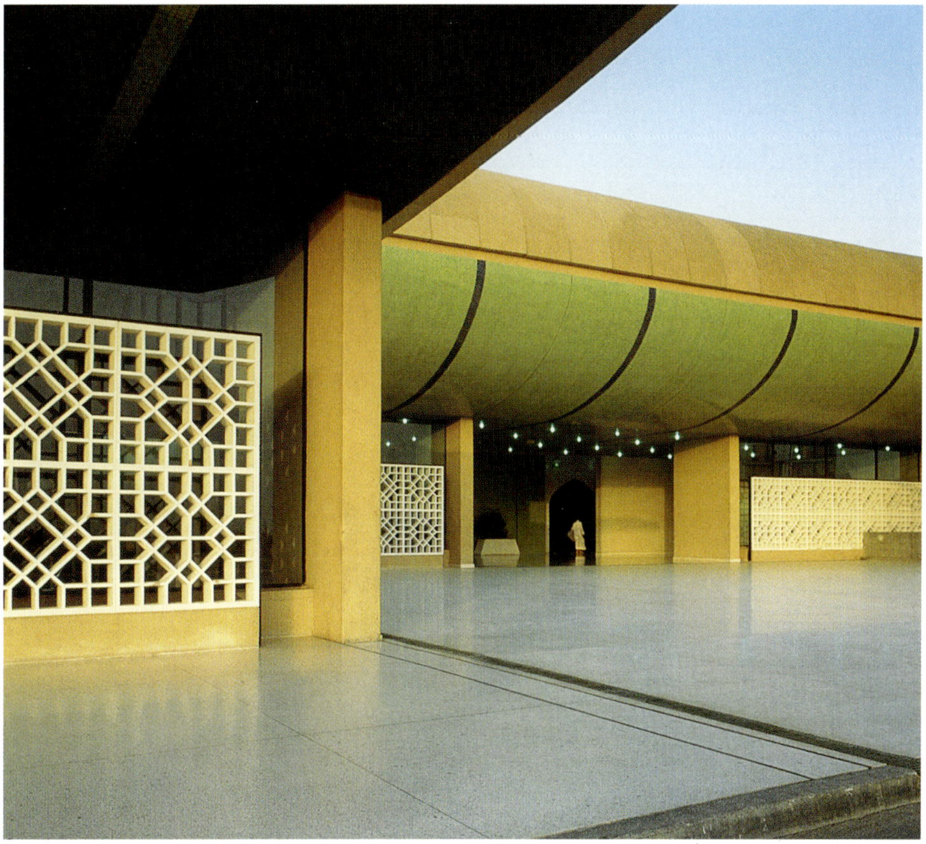

addition of new elements on the convex or runway side of the main building was provided for in the original plan, as was a doubling of terminal activities through zones earmarked for that purpose. The overall plan of the complex is interesting too because of its fundamental asymmetry. The focal point where the satellite connects to the main building reaches the arc of that structure not at the middle as one might expect but off to one side. So too, the parking zones do not form a regular geometric shape, but are more amoebic and off-center in their outline.

The function of the single satellite here is somewhat different than the multiple extensions of Terminal 1. Check-in and baggage delivery for local passengers are concentrated in the main building in Abu

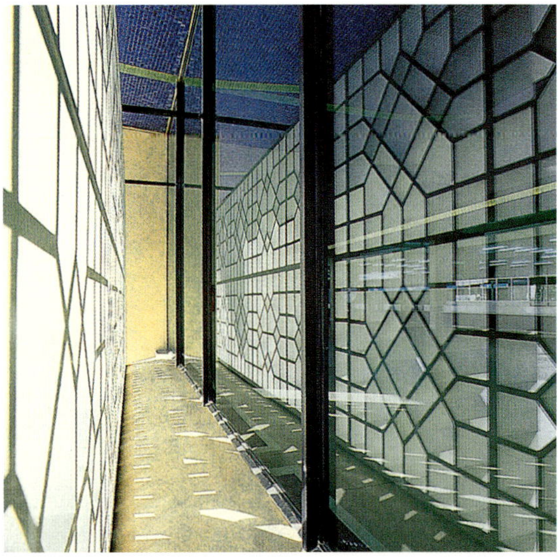

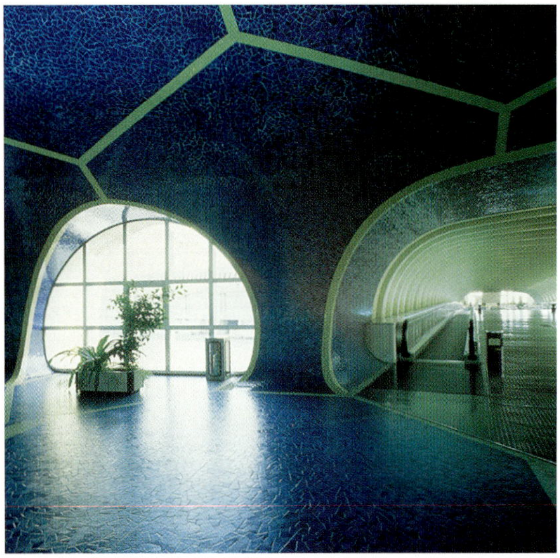

Comparable to a mushroom or a maelstrom, the boarding zone again makes use of Islamic decorative patterns in an oblique way, here bringing to mind certain ceramics for example, but not necessarily indulging in any quotation of existing Middle Eastern architecture. Light and dark are even more strongly contrasted here than in cloudy northern Europe.

Dhabi while arrivals, departures, and above all, transit are located in the round satellite. Andreu compares this transit space to "an umbilical point, a discontinuity in space in the mathematical sense." Both here and in the cascading tiled interior of the main building, the notion of a vortex is again evoked – a point of departure or arrival, a point of waiting or "discontinuity." The cave-like references in Abu-Dhabi are clearly related to the harsh sun and heat of the environment, but from womb to "umbilical point," the attentive visitor will have noticed the parallels drawn between travel by air and travel through life. Again, this kind of interpretation has little direct bearing on an appreciation of Paul Andreu's mastery of the science of moving people efficiently from one type of transport to another. The airport generates a very particular set of requirements that Andreu mastered from the first, in part with the help of his collaborators from the Aéroports de Paris organization. Once the basic requirements are met, then a more "philosophical" or esthetic element can enter into the equation. Andreu chooses to make the esthetics an integral part of the location but also the function of the facility. There can be little quarreling with his oblique references to birth as seen in Abu Dhabi and elsewhere, but it is significant that such thoughts in no way contradict or interfere with the usefulness of the airport. Rather, there is a philosophical harmony that emerges in his interpretation of the voyage of life.

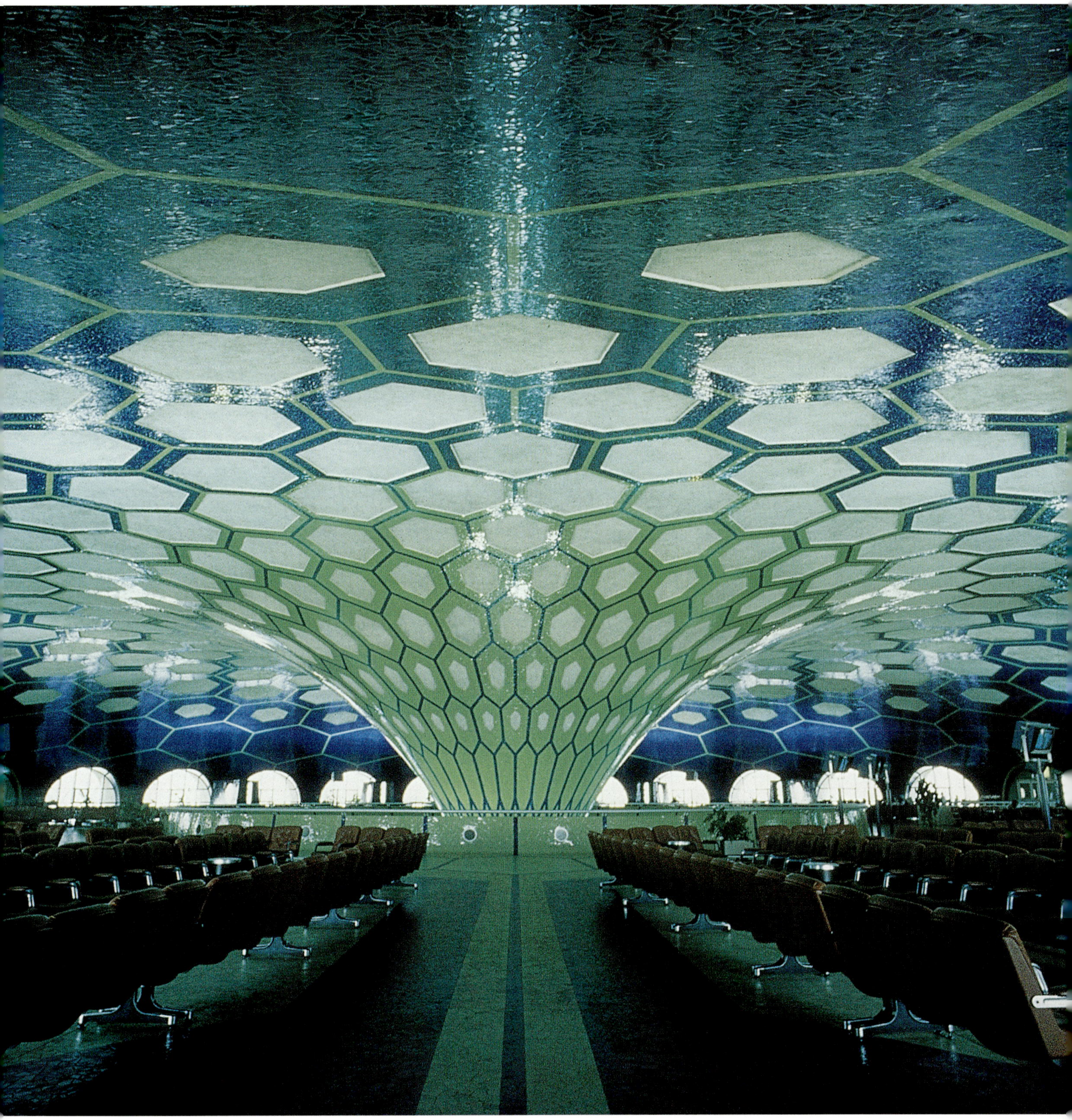

Abu Dhabi Airport

Module 2 1997-2004

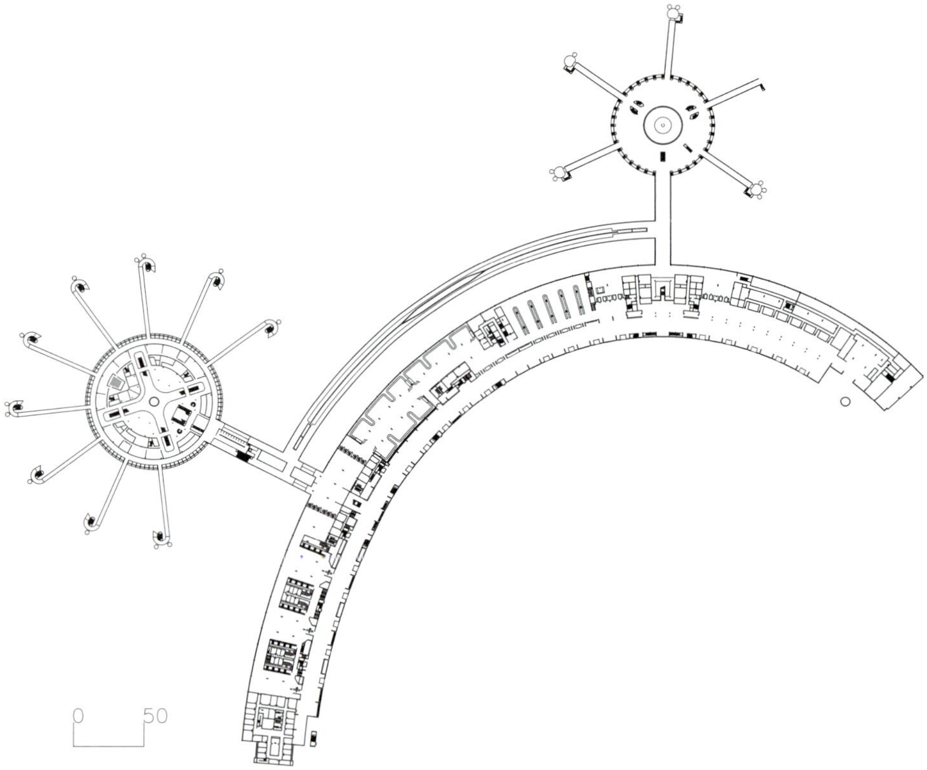

Like a successful movie that spawns second versions, Andreu's airport projects have on occasion engendered sequels. This is the case of Abu Dhabi where the French architect has undertaken a second module for the airport he designed and built in 1985-92. The new terminal is intended for an annual traffic of 3.5 million passengers and includes a 42,410 square meter terminal with a 17,000 square meter satellite. 45 check-in counters serve eleven stands for aircraft in contact with the Terminal and seven remote stands. The architect apparently uses the same family of shapes as he employed in the original airport, but here he enlarges the diameter of the new satellite to 101 meters. The vaulted form of the satellite is designed around 100 steel tube supports 25 centimeters in diameter. Andreu graduates the transparencies of the surfaces of his structure, going from transparency at eye level to a deep blue and a green at the top of the vault. The program calls for 4,000 square meters of boutique space,

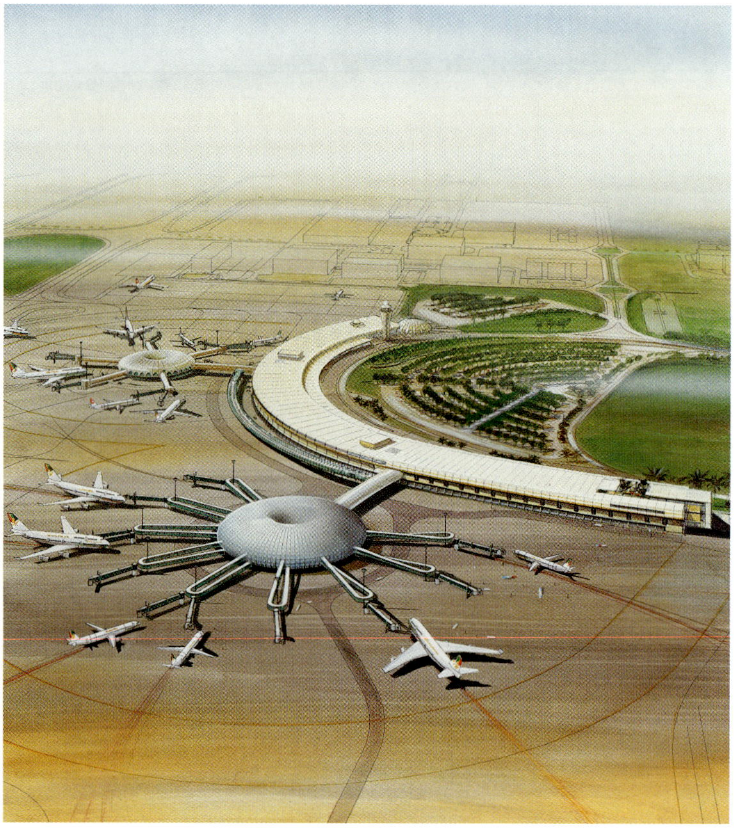

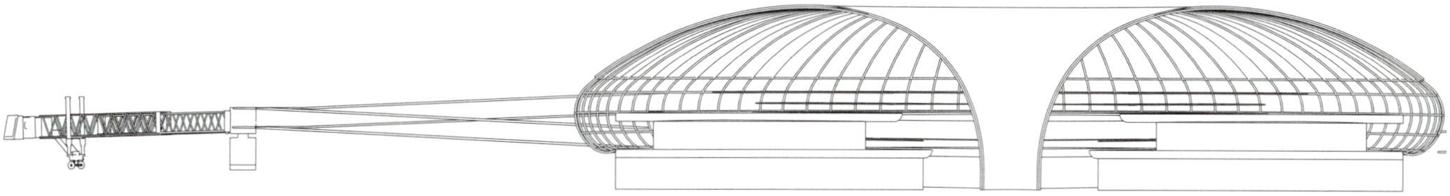

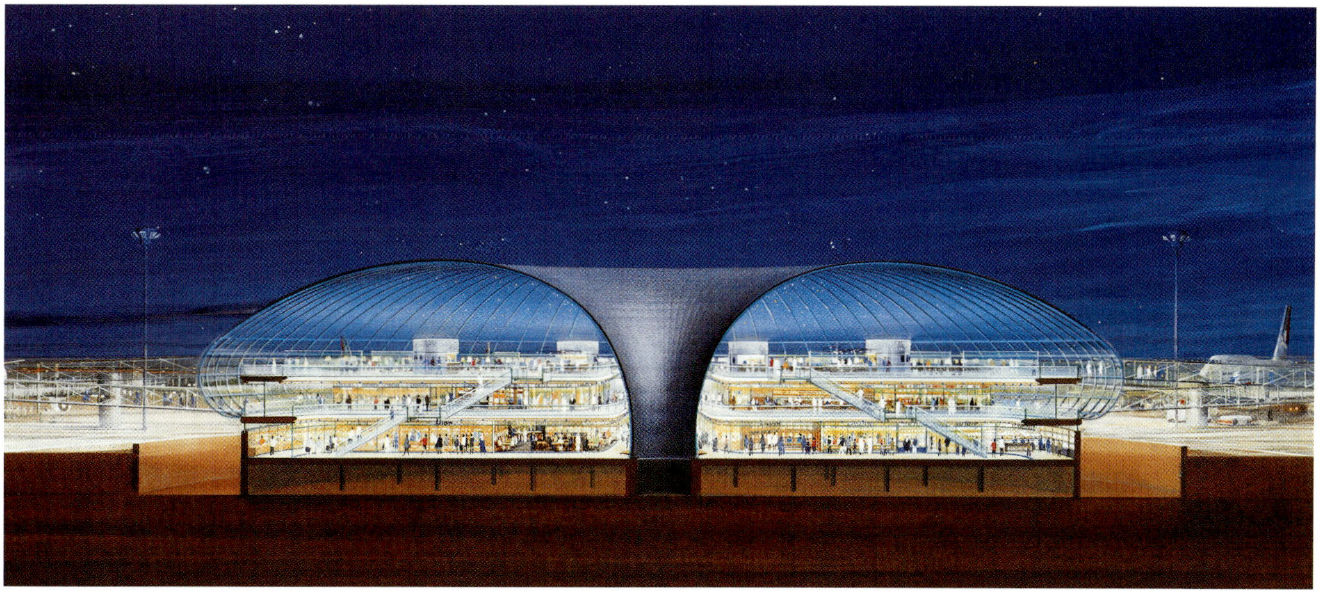

By adding a second mushroom-shaped boarding structure, Andreu shows how adaptable his architecture is in the face of rising passenger volumes. Though his decorative enthusiasm appears to have been tempered somewhat with the passage of time, the architect nonetheless insists on creating a visual similarity between the early terminal and this new addition.

in a typical arrangement in Persian Gulf airports. Like a fountain, or to go back to the imagery of Charles-de-Gaulle Terminal 1, a vortex that converges where the shopping arcade "streets" meet, one might say that the roof is the message. Andreu likens this overarching roof to a "starry desert night." As has been the case from the outset, Paul Andreu often has recourse to architectural imagery linked to birth and death, to departures and life. This is a natural association in the case of travel, but one that has rarely if ever been made in airport design. Plans call for future expansion of Abu Dhabi airport with a new terminal structure to be built along the loop of the access road. Here as elsewhere, Paul Andreu has not only been able to link past and present mutations of his own airports, but also to plan carefully for easy expansion in the future. Compared to most contemporary architecture that takes users needs into account less than might be hoped, Andreu's efficient, user-friendly designs are also crafted to make the task of the controlling authorities easier when it comes to day-to-day operations or to consecutive expansions. Calling on the same round form as he used in the original Charles-de-Gaulle building and indeed in Abu Dhabi itself, Andreu retains an interest in basic geometries while also mastering the complexities of traffic and baggage movement in a modern airport.

The airport of Jakarta has a distinctly "local" flavor about it, even if it maintains the high levels of efficiency and modernity associated with Andreu's architecture. Rarely did he come so close to a "post-modern" design.

Jakarta International Airport Soekarno-Hatta Jakarta

Country: Indonesia
Use: Airport
Start of project: 1977
Completion: 1985
Surface: 285,000 m^2
Capacity: 23 million passengers per year

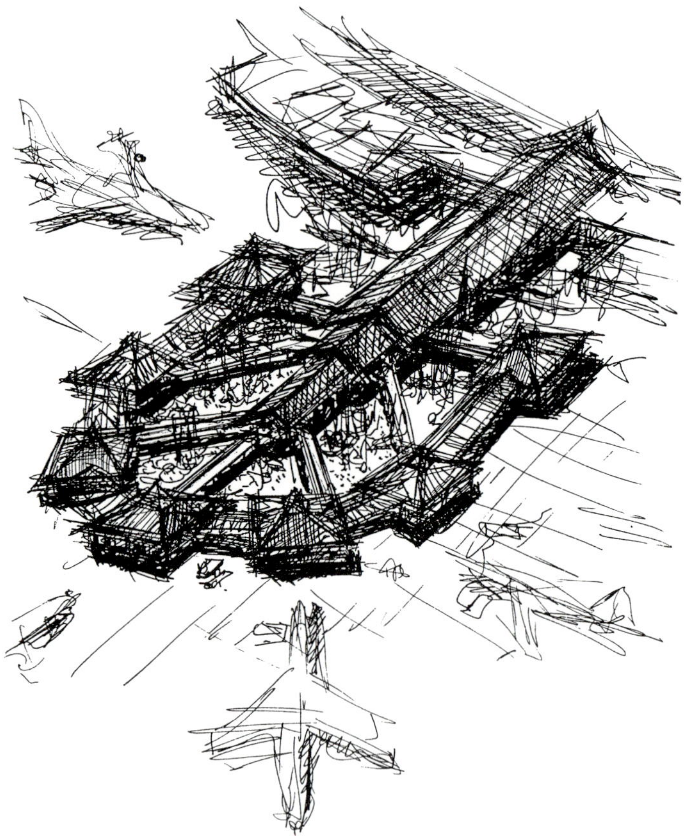

With a planned annual traffic of 23 million passengers (for the two terminals), the Jakarta Airport is a much larger facility than that of Abu Dhabi. Designed to handle 48 aircraft in direct contact with the airport, the terminals include a total area of 285,000 square meters with a further 87,000 square meters given over to garden space. This may be the project where Paul Andreu came closest to a "post-modern" attitude, modeling his design on that of an Indonesian village: "a cluster of small houses with red tile roofs set amid trees between large stretches of rice fields." He makes a great deal of the integration of the red tiled roof pavilions with the natural setting, much as Indonesian architecture does, it is true, allow for a direct contact with the environment.

Again intended to facilitate future expansion, Andreu's design for Jakarta makes some reference to Indonesian village architecture, while maintaining the high level of functional efficiency for which he has become justifiably famous.

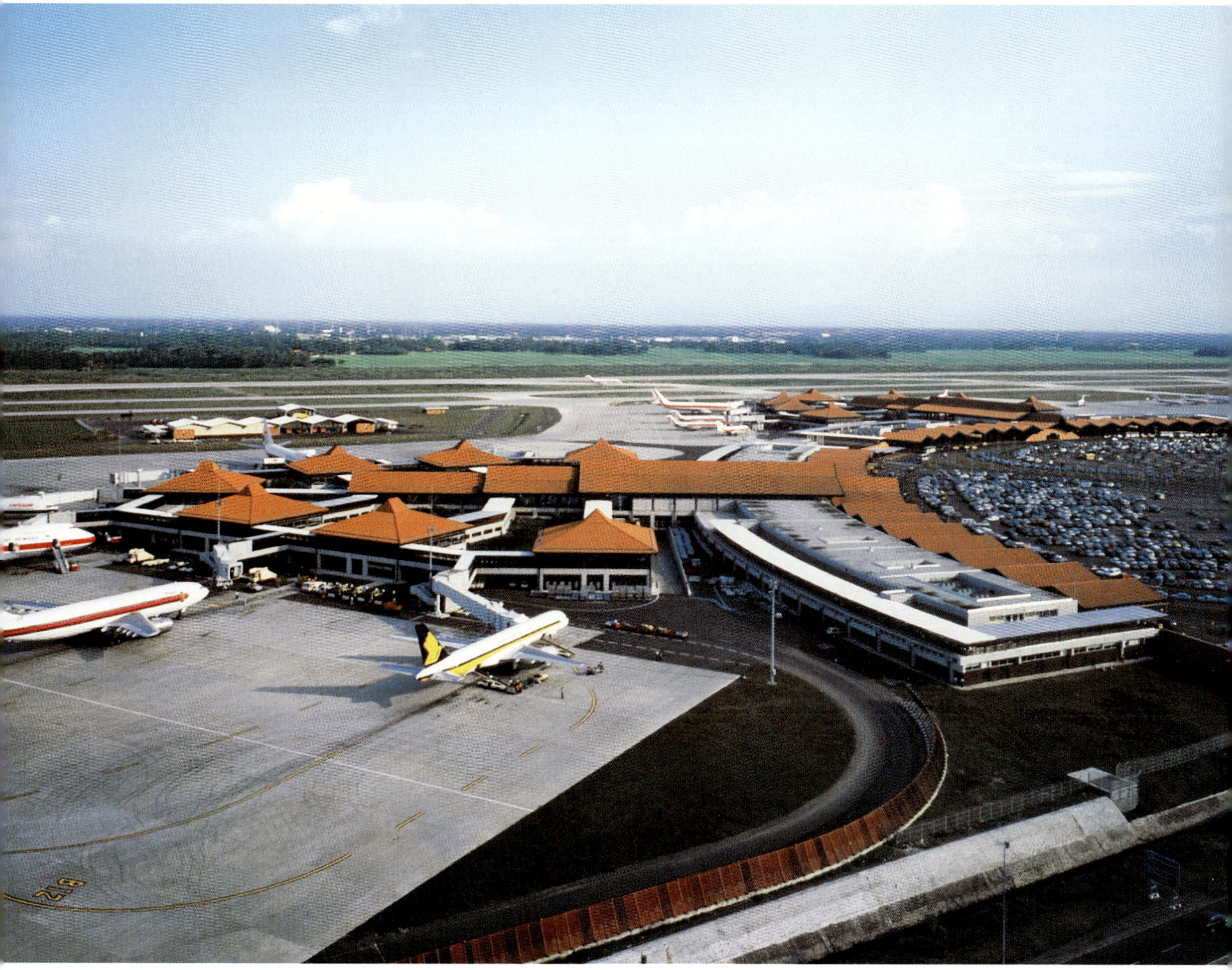

Jakarta Soekarno-Hatta Airport

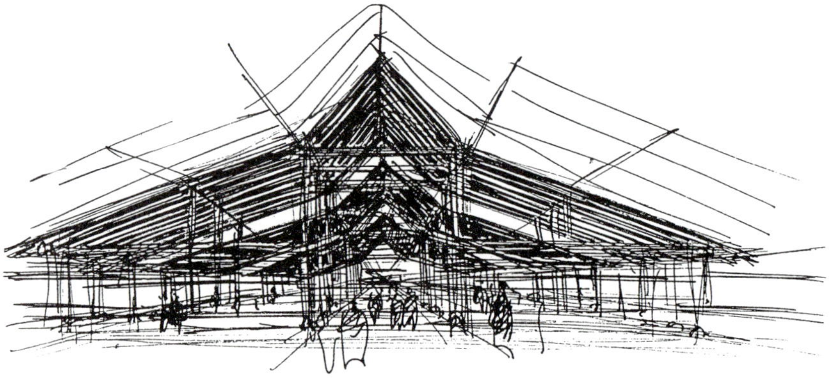

Winner of an Aga Khan Architecture Award for these gardens, the Airport is located 20 kilometers to the west of the center of the Indonesian capital. Terminal 1 (put into service in 1985) and Terminal 2 (1991) were conceived to allow the complex to develop easily to an annual capacity of 50 million voyagers. The arc-like plan of each of the two terminals is matched by a radiating set of three modules with seven satellites each located on the convex side of each arc. It is between these modules that the gardens take on their full significance, visible from almost every angle. Covered walkways permit a real contact with the outdoors, an exceedingly rare phenomenon in the airports of major world cities. It may be interesting to note that Andreu's original color scheme, with a rich red color for the structures of the modules was rejected by Indonesian authorities who considered the shade too "Chinese." They preferred a brown color that the architect has never fully accepted.

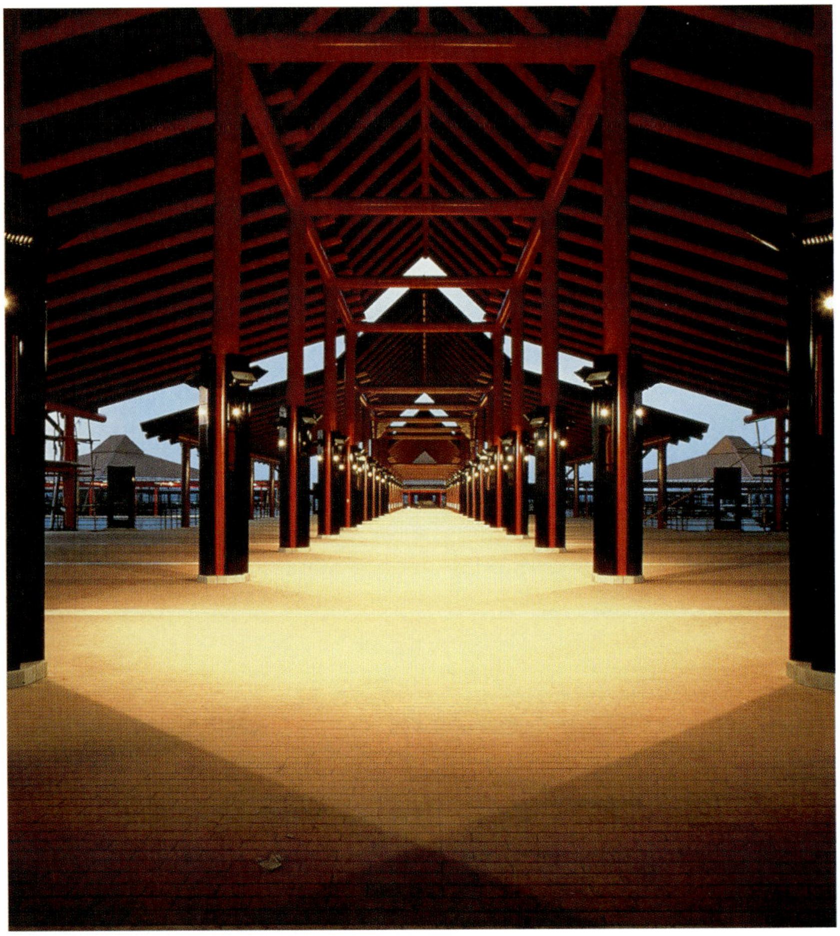

Here as in so many of his other buildings, Paul Andreu has provided for ample space, light and ceiling height. Each of these factors, frequently absent from airport design, serves to make the visitor more comfortable and relaxed before being closed into the metal frame of a jetliner. Despite the size of the Jakarta Airport, its emphasis on gardens and a local flavor blend harmoniously with the conception of space that Andreu impregnates into the design.

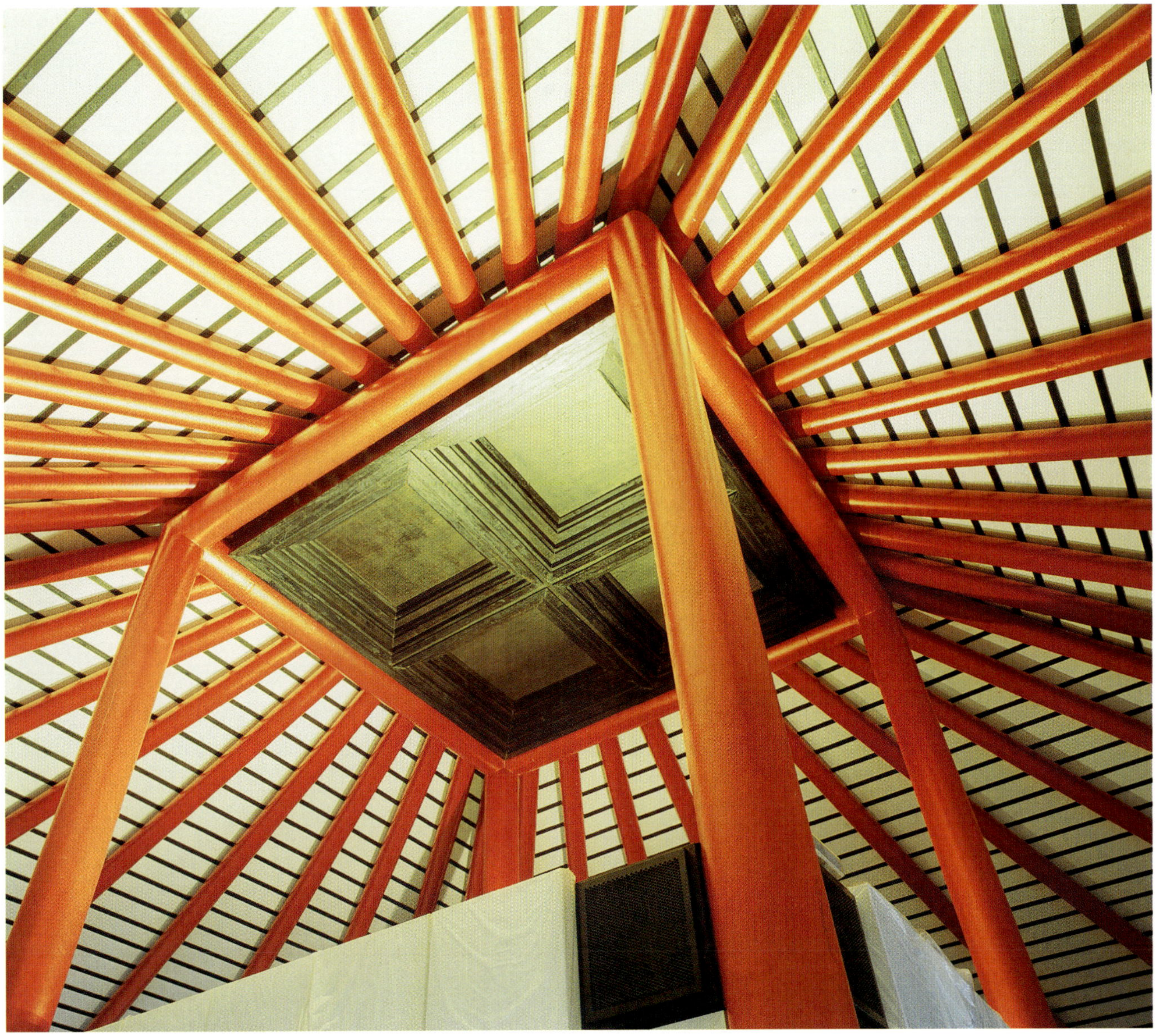

The interior spaces make Andreu's reference to local traditional architecture even more apparent than the exteriors. An appearance of light wooden structure that open out onto the exterior indeed recall the form of houses or palaces seen in the country.

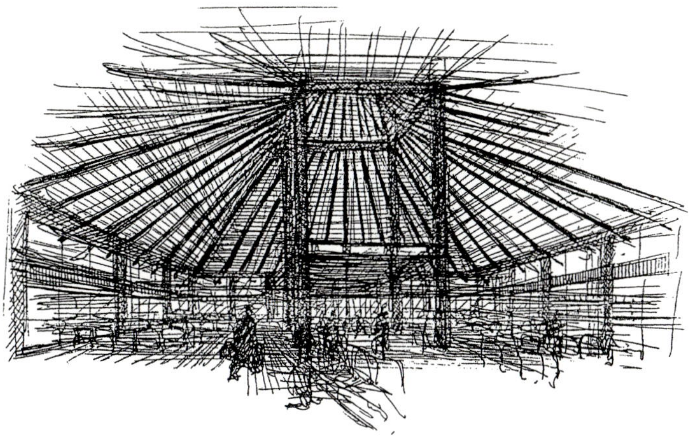

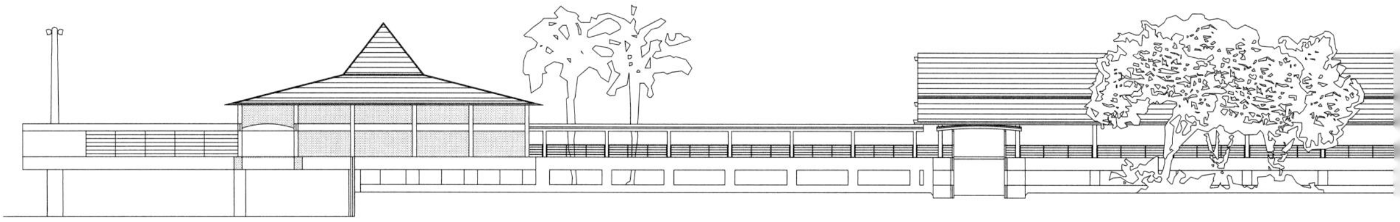

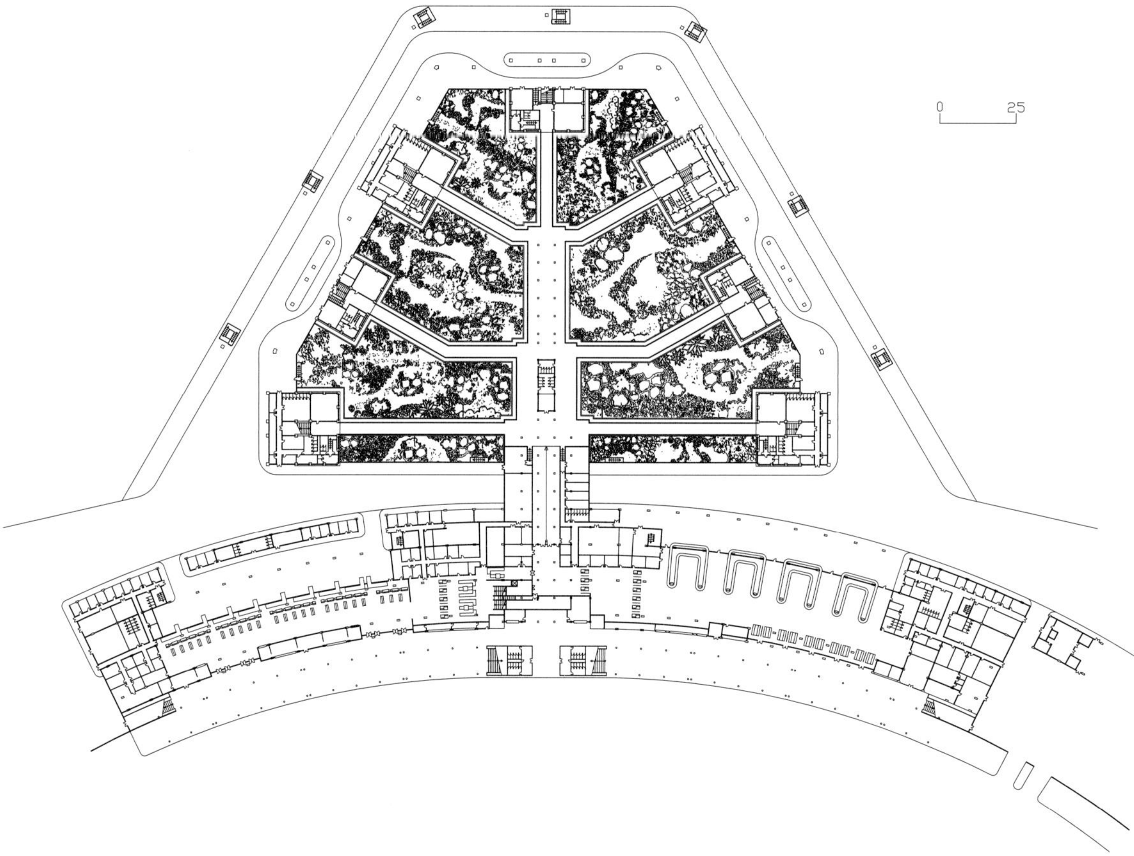

Although the two terminals are of different size (Terminal 2 has a wider circumference), their plans are essentially identical. Nearly semi-circular, the two complexes face each other and give an impression of being related to crystalline or floral shapes. Since each one of these terminals was intended from the outset to handle more passengers than any of the individual Roissy buildings, Andreu has adapted a more complex shape and disposition while retaining the principles of arcs and looping access roads developed in his earlier projects. Despite the passing of the "post-modern" style, the Jakarta Airport does not seem to be fundamentally out of touch with Indonesian reality. Its reference to local architecture in a context that remains fundamentally modern, and as functional as Andreu's other designs is more a source of warmth and identity than it is a sign of an aging esthetic parti pris.

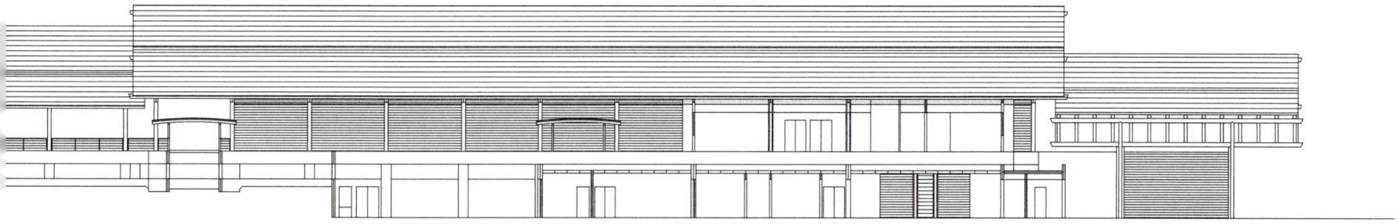

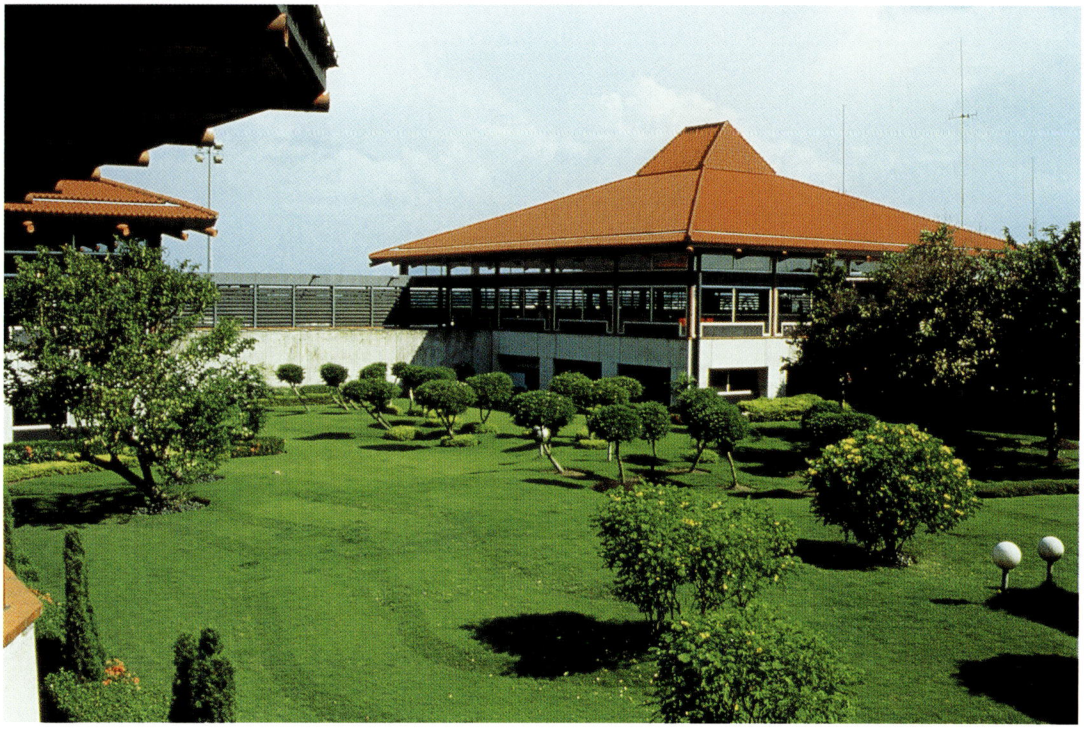

Paul Andreu received the Aga Khan Award for Architecture for his integration of garden spaces with the architecture of the Jakarta Airport. Essentially low-lying, the airport design nonetheless makes space for high ceilings and a feeling of openness that is exceptional in facilities of this size.

Relying on a relatively simple tree-like structure, Andreu gave an open, airy design to Dar-Es-Salaam airport, a mixture of modernity and the kind of organically inspired architecture of engineers like Pier Luigi Nervi.

Dar-Es-Salaam Airport **Dar-Es-Salaam**

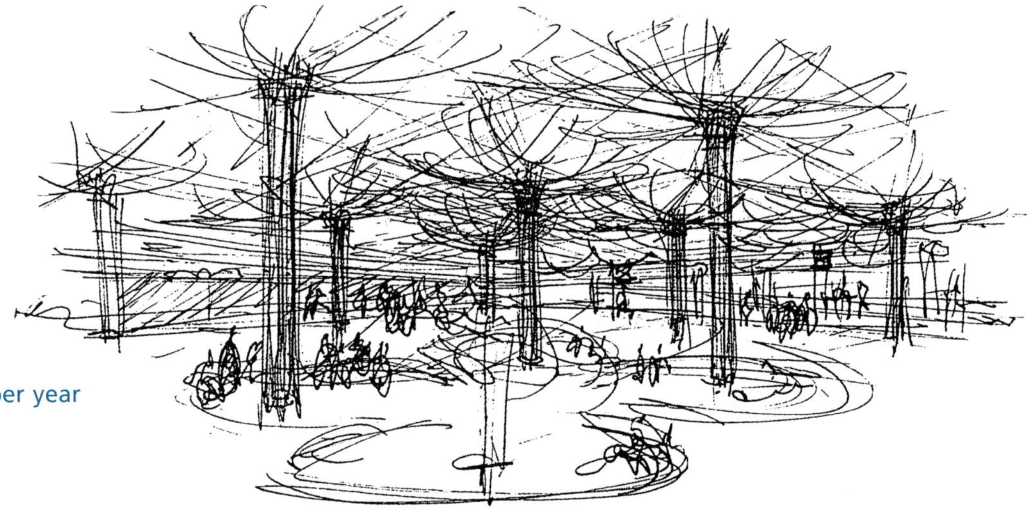

Country: Tanzania
Use: Airport
Start of project: 1977
Completion: 1984
Surface: 15,000 m²
Capacity: 1.5 million passengers per year

The Dar-Es-Salaam Airport put into service in 1984, was intended for 1.5 million passengers per year. There are seven locations for aircraft in direct contact with the 15,000 square meter terminal and 15 more docking points positioned at some distance from the structure. A tree-like reinforced concrete roof covers the lobby and the waiting area situated on a mezzanine. This allows the lobby to have a double-height, confirming Andreu's continual emphasis on space and airiness in his designs. Two cascading, monumental stairs empty obliquely into the lobby space. In fact, the "trees" and their corresponding canopies of concrete, determine the appearance of this structure even more than the facades, which remain more anonymous in their glazed sheathing.

Paul Andreu's sketch and the view to the right of the Dar-Es-Salaam Airport highlight his use of a tree-like form for the successive interconnected roof elements and columns. By accumulating successive geometric elements and skewing them rather than aligning them, Andreu again gives a feeling of movement to the design.

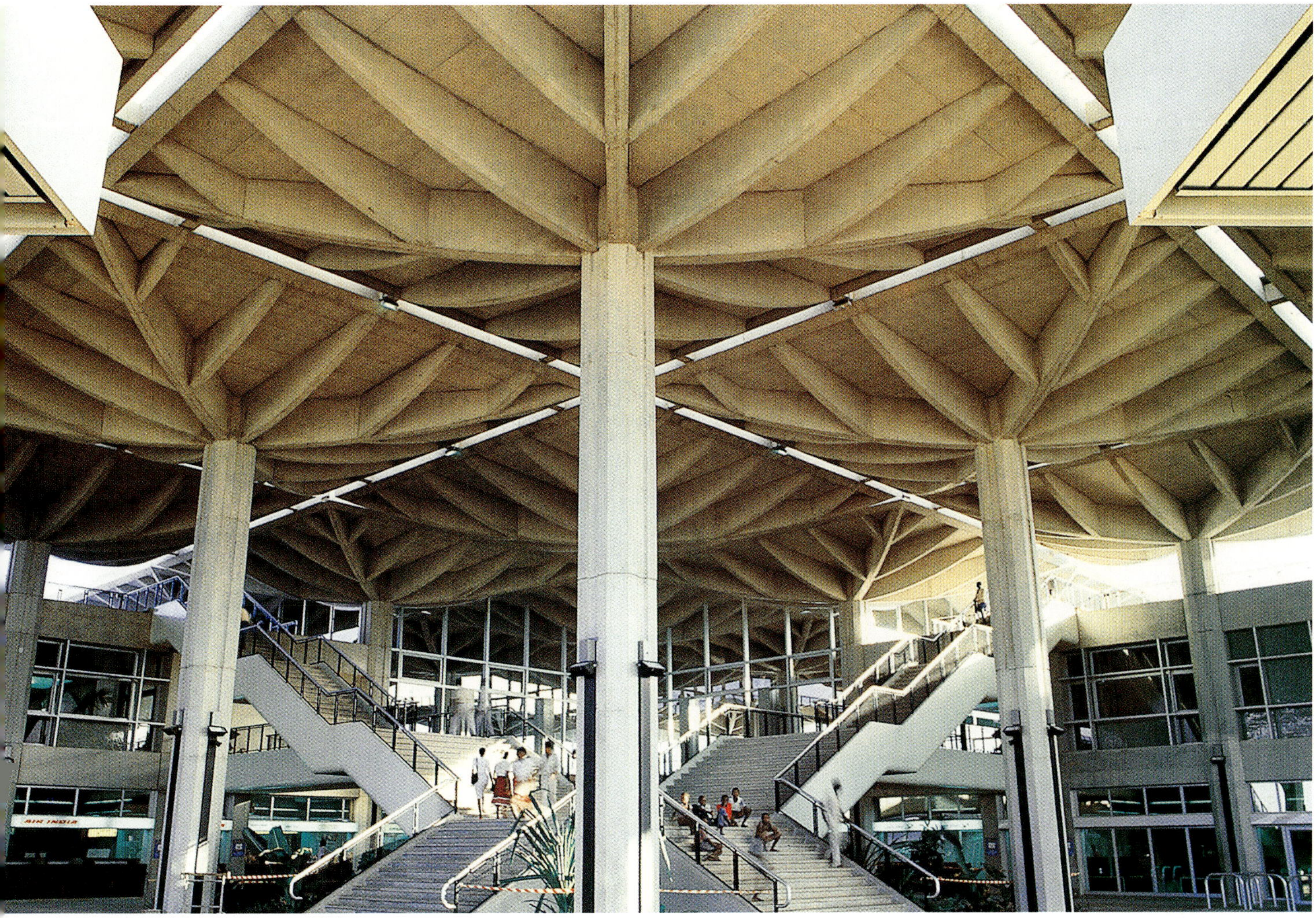

Despite the repetitive use of the tree forms, Andreu does not go so far as to give the impression that this is a kind of exercise in engineering prowess as the Italian designer Pier Luigi Nervi did on occasion. Transparency and opacity are contrasted and natural light comes into the carefully fashioned interior spaces in an agreeable way.

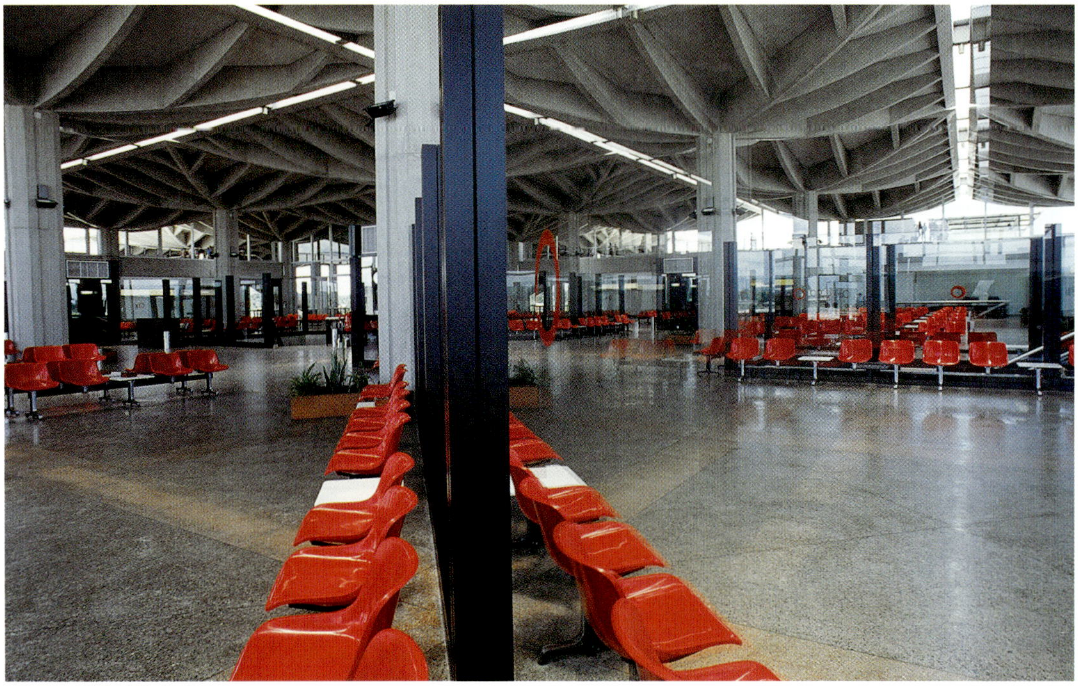

Actually, the glass and concrete combination here gives an overall impression of transparency. A metaphor of the forest is present in the columns and ribbed roof plates, and this despite a fundamentally rigid geometric layout. Unlike his other terminals that have relied to a good extent on curved forms, a square 13-meter grid forms the basis of the plan in Dar-Es-Salaam. It may be that this square grid makes it easier for passengers to orient themselves than the closed, circular design of Charles-de-Gaulle Terminal 1. Here, given the modest dimensions of the airport, issues

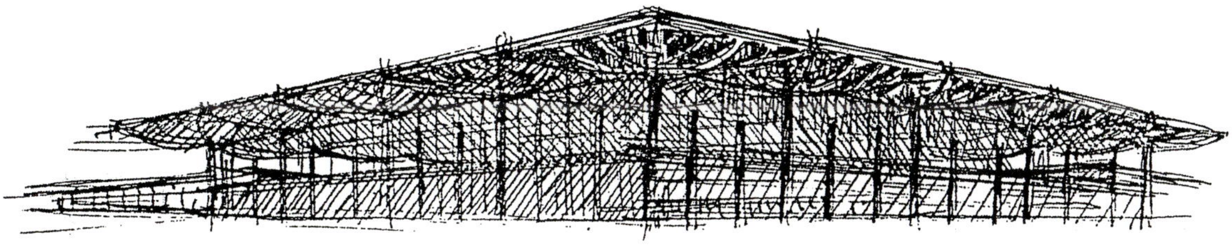

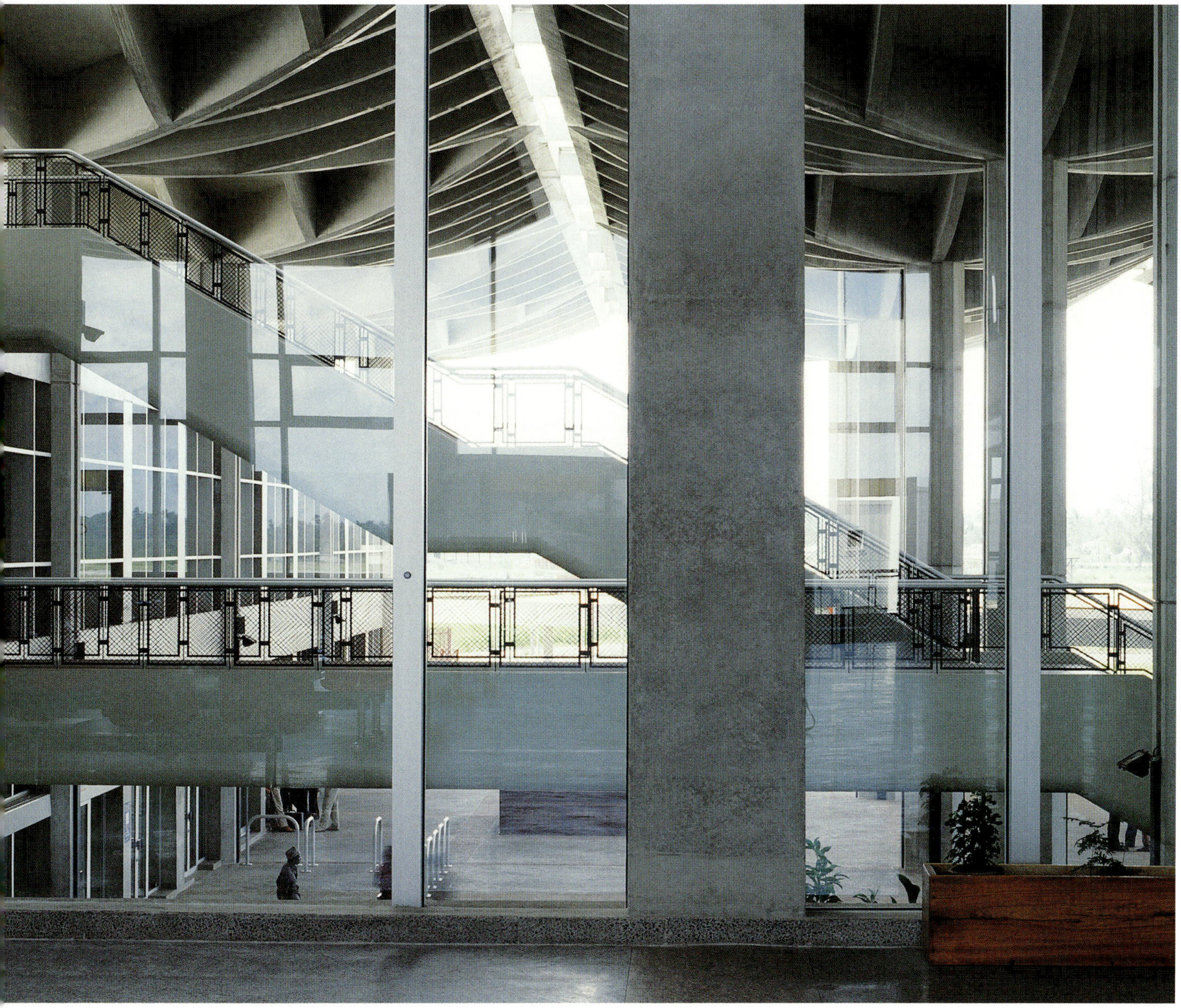

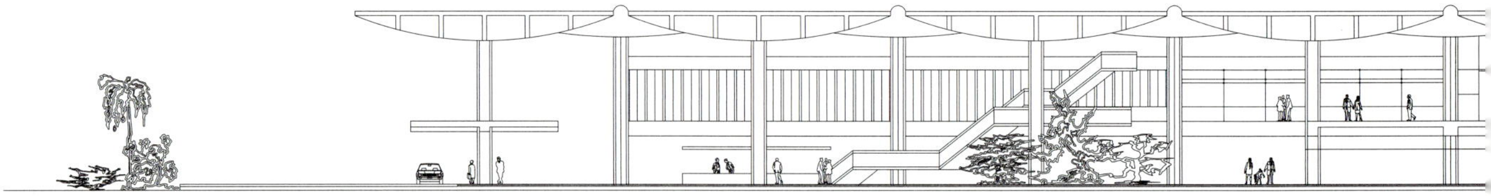

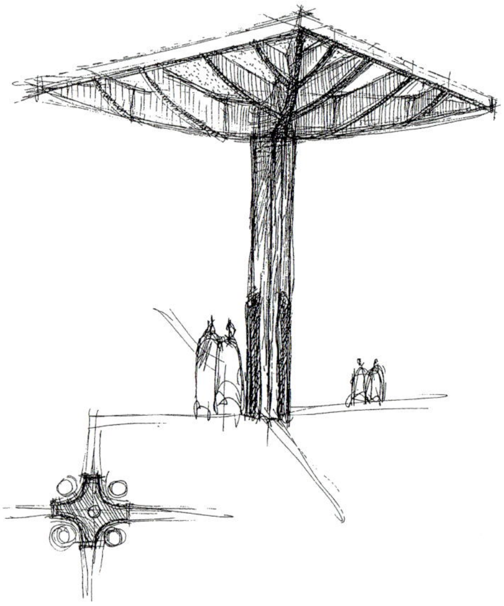

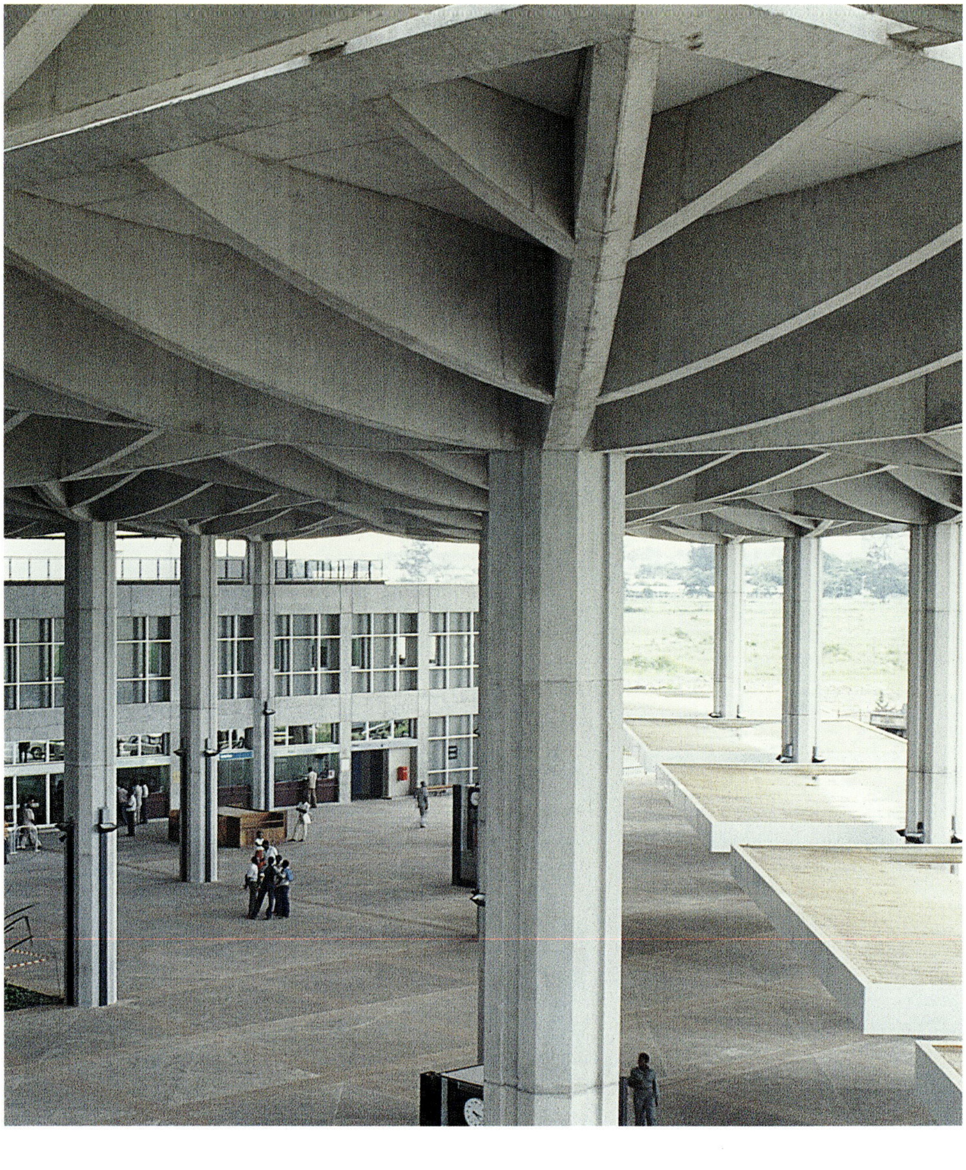

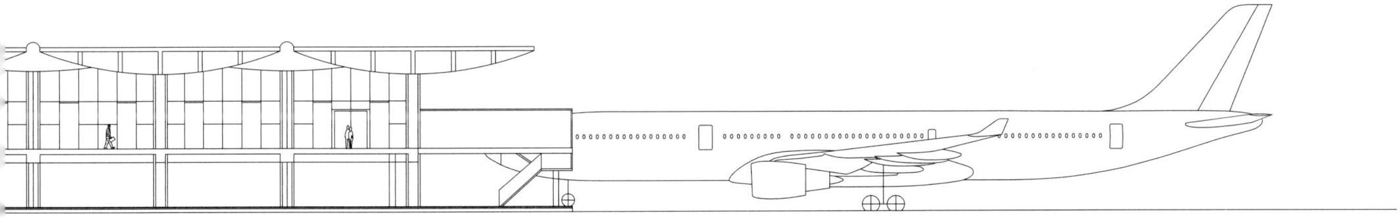

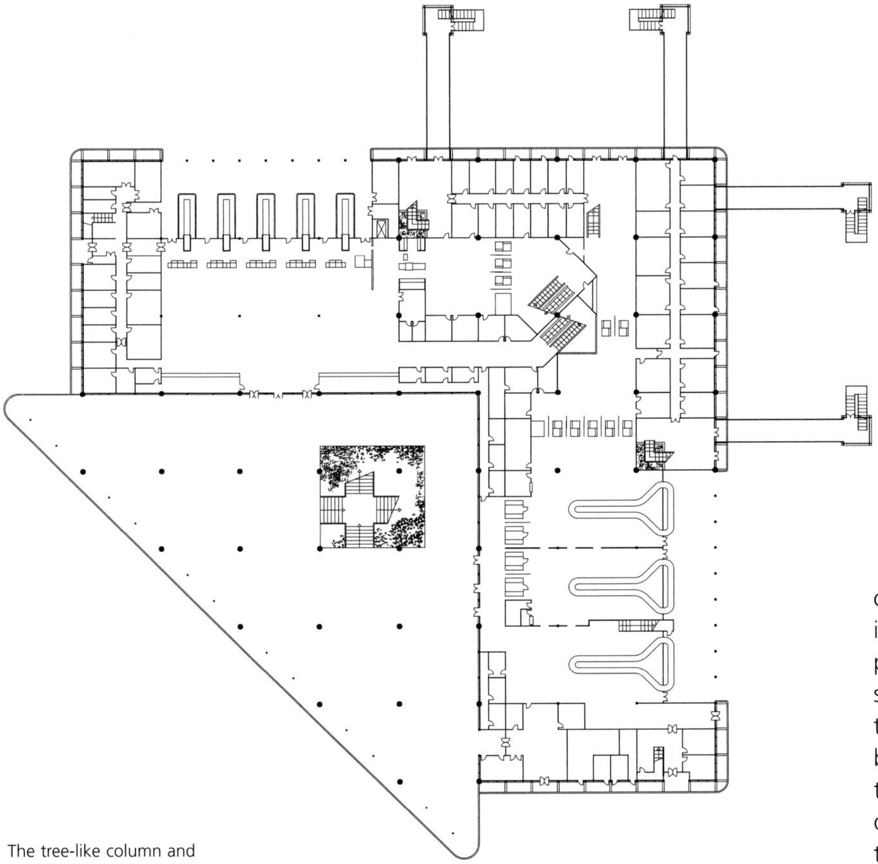

The tree-like column and roof design is extended to exterior spaces underlining the conceptual relation to a forest setting, but as Andreu's plans show, a relentless pursuit of efficiency and simplicity are the real message of this terminal. Beyond any reference to the natural world, moving passengers is what this building is about.

of orientation may not have been as important however. Although the overall plan of the terminal implies a perfect square, it is a notched diamond-shape that emerges from Andreu's use of the basic grid. With its notched side facing the parking lot (500 places) and car or bus arrivals, the square pattern tends toward a complete outer point near the passageways to the aircraft. In other words, despite starting out with the static form of a square, Andreu articulates the plan so that a natural progression toward the points of departure is implied in the architecture itself. Aside from giving a sensation of comfort and open space to travelers, another one of the strong points of Andreu's airport design is precisely this repeated emphasis on orientation and the movement through space.

For the largest Islamic metropolis in the world, Andreu succeeded in using a repetitive geometric pattern that brings to mind the art of the region without confronting the real pitfalls of "pastiche" or superficially historicist architecture.

Cairo Airport - Terminal 2 Cairo

Country: Egypt
Use: Airport
Start of project: 1977
Completion: 1986
Surface: 48,000 m^2
Capacity: 10 million passengers per year

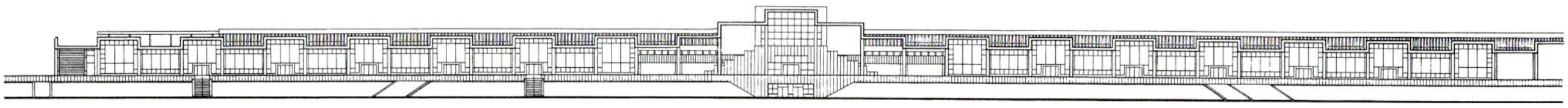

Designed for a capacity of 10 million travelers per year, Terminal 2 of the Cairo Airport encloses 48,000 square meters with a planned total of 96,000 square meters. 3,200 parking spots are provided for and 18 spots for aircraft in contact with the Terminal. The master planning for this airport began in 1977 and called for two terminals with a total capacity of 30 million travelers per year. Andreu's built design is divided into two identical modules, one for domestic traffic and the other for international flights.
The plan of the complex relies on an arc on the automobile arrivals side and two more or less circular boarding satellites. The terminal has two floors on the runway side and a single level on the city side, which emphasizes its long, low appearance.

The succession of square arches laid out again in a broad curve may in a sense recall the design of Charles-de-Gaulle Terminal 2 A and B. And yet with this succession of geometric forms, Andreu again manages to evoke local architecture without in any way imitating existing designs.

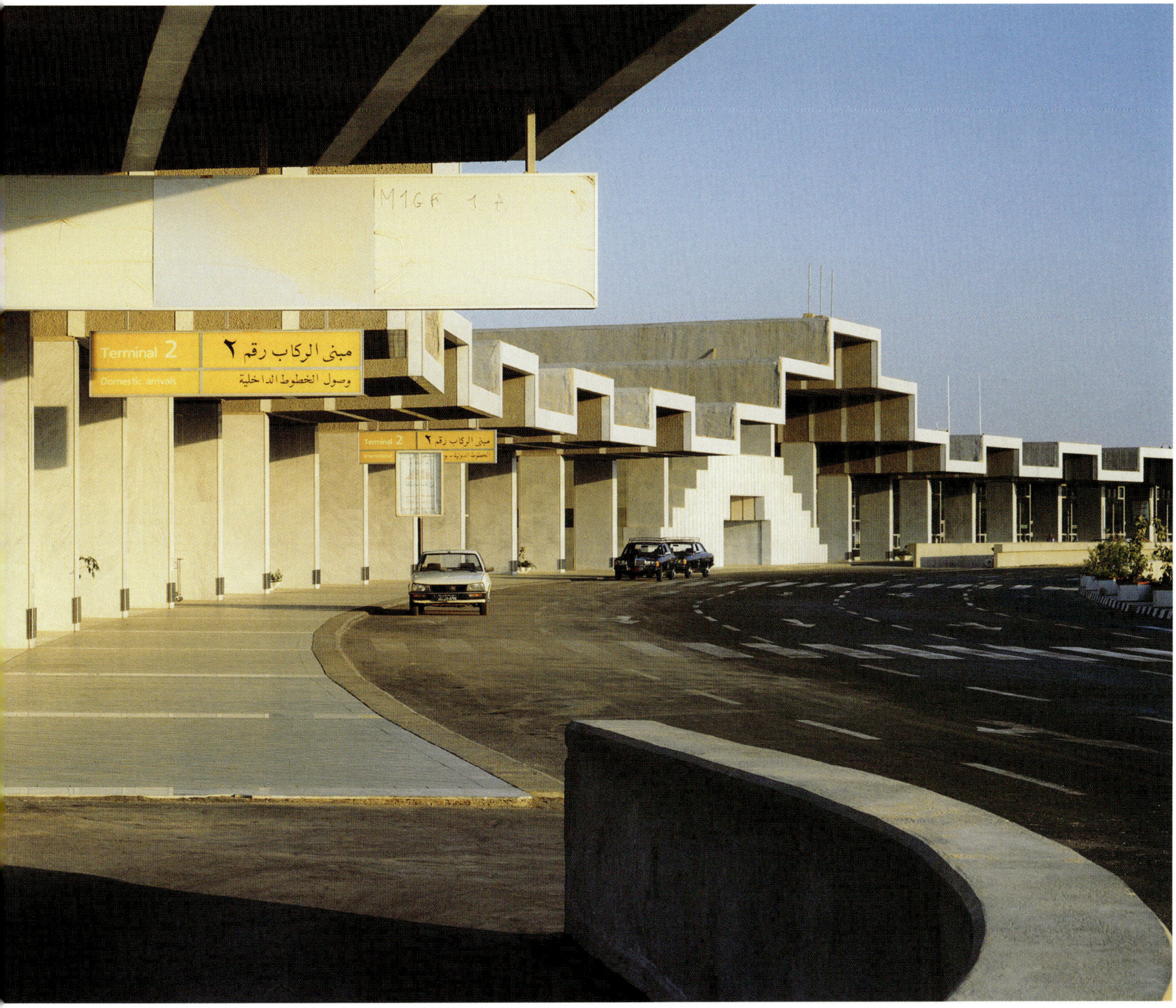

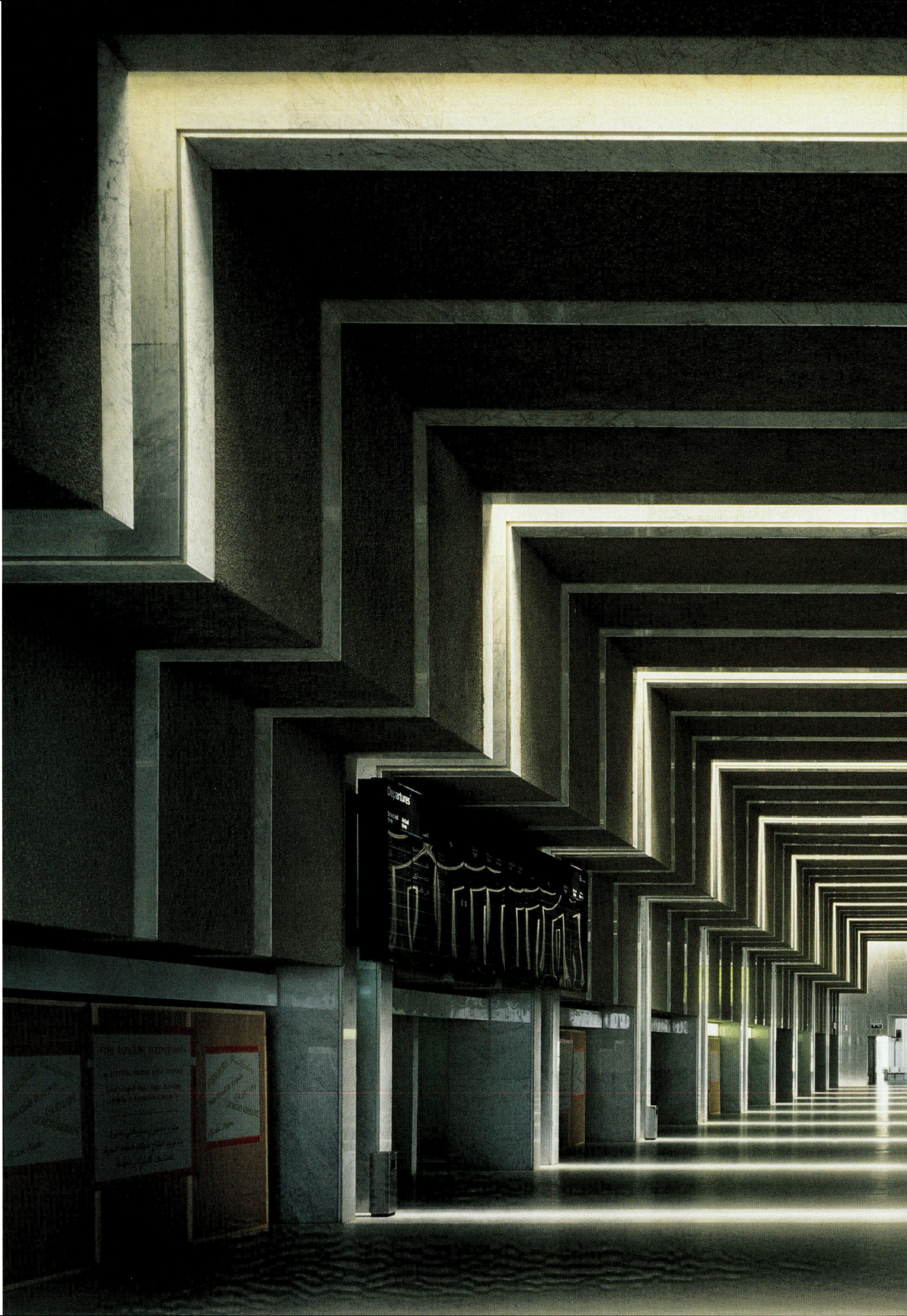
Departures

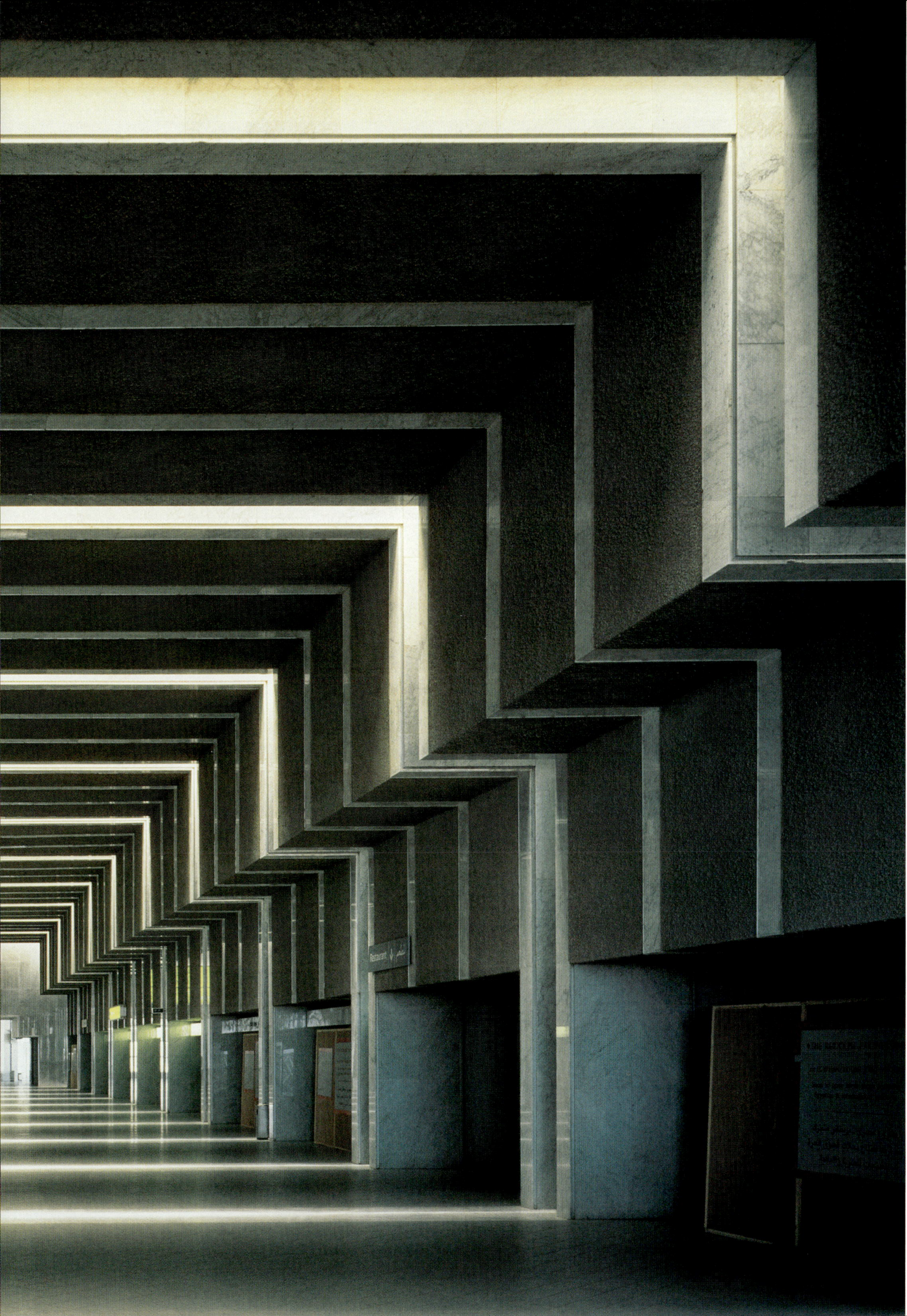

77

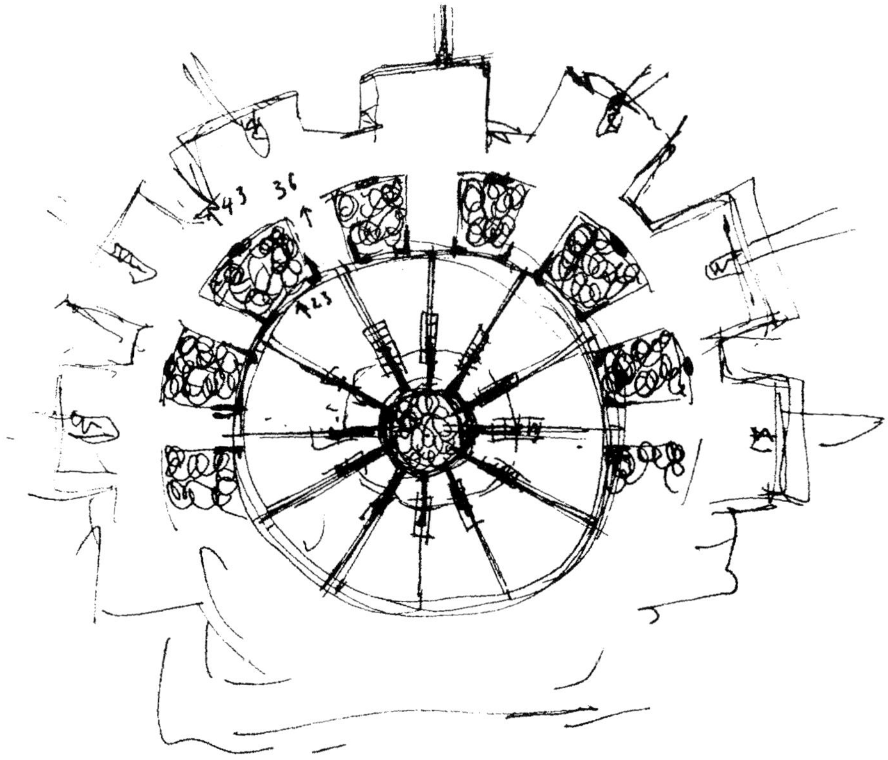

Paul Andreu has placed a great deal of emphasis in this project on the use of light. He goes so far as to say that without the projected light patterns, the structure would not exist as such. Successive door-like squared arches that might be likened to the Moslem architecture bring light into the passageways, but curiously, it is not the architecture of Islam that Andreu cites in explaining his sources of inspiration. Rather, he singles out a drawing of a cut angle formed by a columnless corner in a house designed by the Japanese architect Kiyonori Kikutake. The architect also explains that the basic concept for Cairo evolved from that of Jakarta, but that in the course of design it changed so that only the functional aspects remained similar. Rather than the succession of pavilions he erected in Jakarta, the architect here retains the angled cuts that bring in light and finally fuse the entire terminal arc into a unified whole.

Essentially symmetrical and geometric in its patterns, the Cairo Airport Terminal breaks new ground for Andreu with its complex and changing use of light.

The animation and movement already present through the large number of voyagers finds a more serene counterpart in the slow, inevitable progression of the sun. It is indeed the Cairene climate that permits this kind of architectural device since sunny days are more the rule than the exception. Using light in this way would have been impossible in cloudy Paris for example. Soaring space is not the rule here as much as it was in some earlier works of Andreu, but despite his reference to Kikutake, he does touch on recurring themes of the architecture of Islam in using light and geometry to express himself.

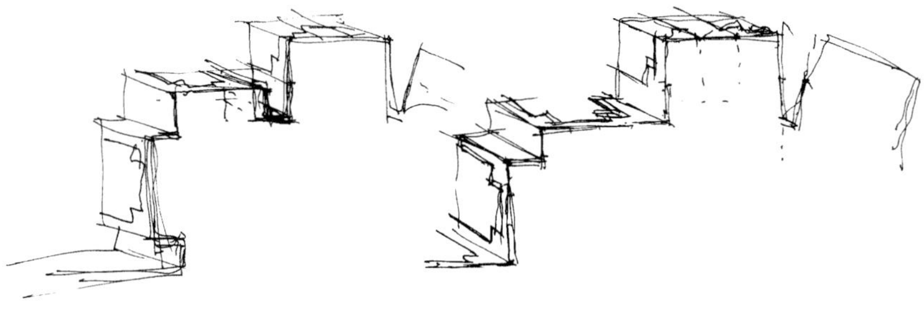

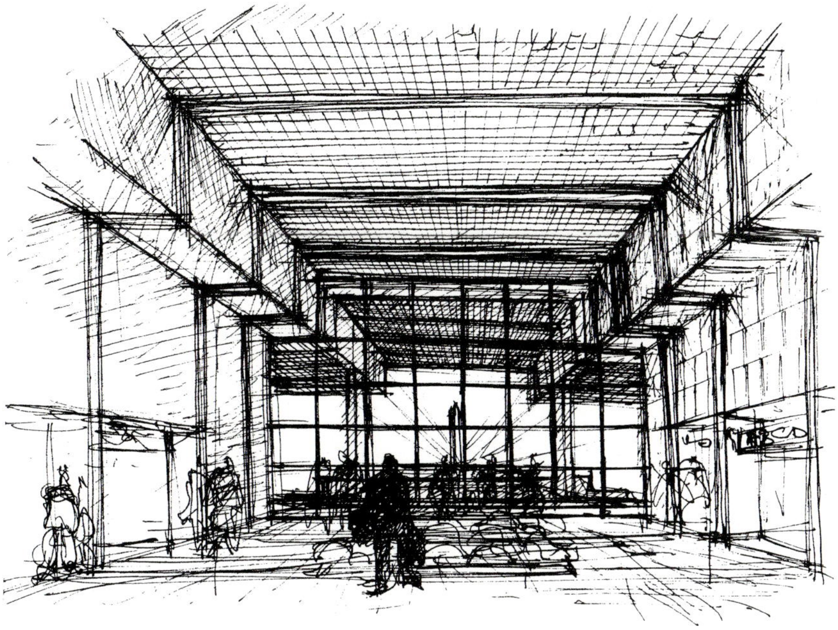

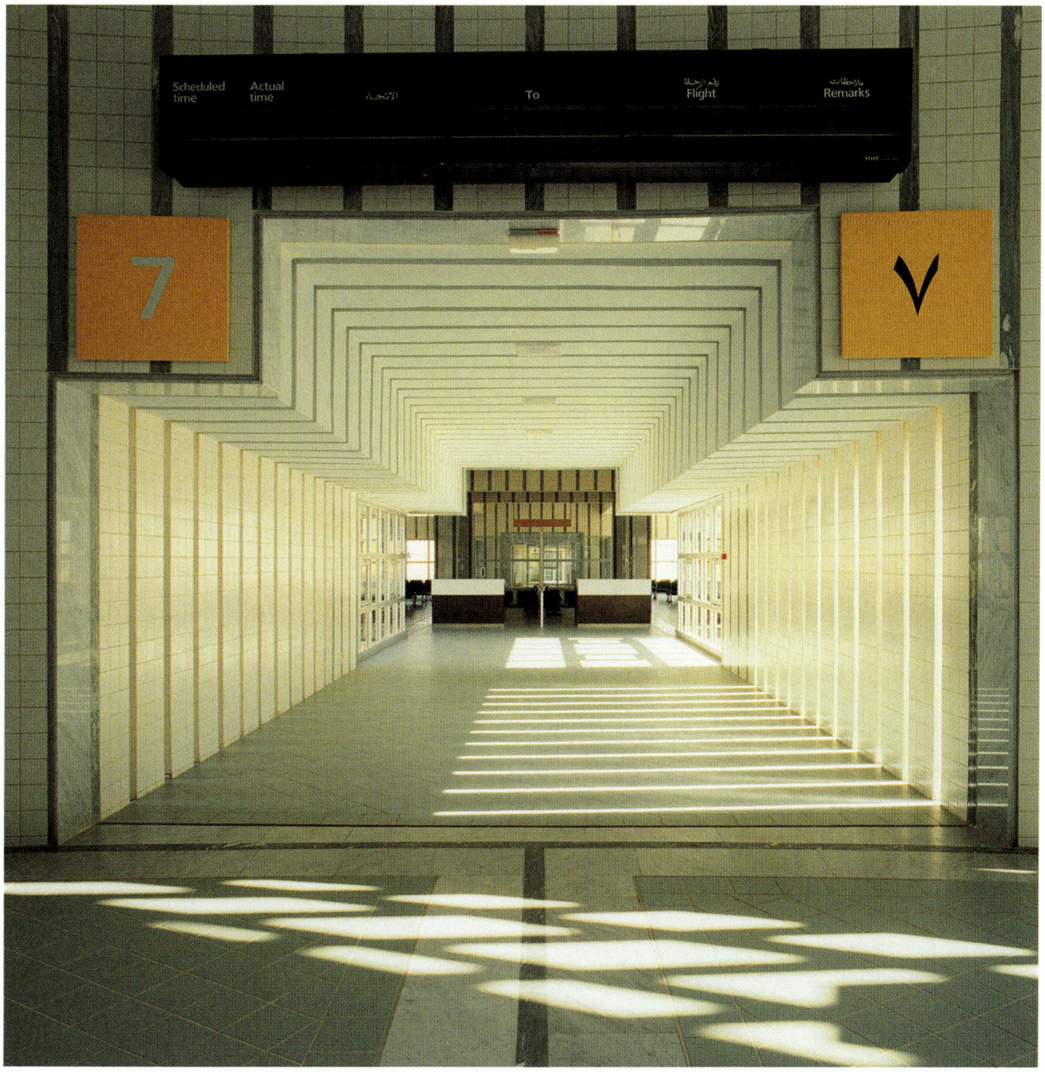

The square, notched arch is also an element of the airport interiors, bringing bands of light that change with the hour of the day. Andreu also makes use of the efficient round form for the boarding zones. Rather than a personal predilection this is undoubtedly a question of how many aircraft can get near the building at any one time.

A light, breezy concept appropriate both to this Mediterranean city and to the seaside location of the airport, the Nice-Côte d'Azur terminal brings Andreu closer to the abundant use of transparency and daylight that characterizes his later work.

Nice-Côte d'Azur Airport **Nice**

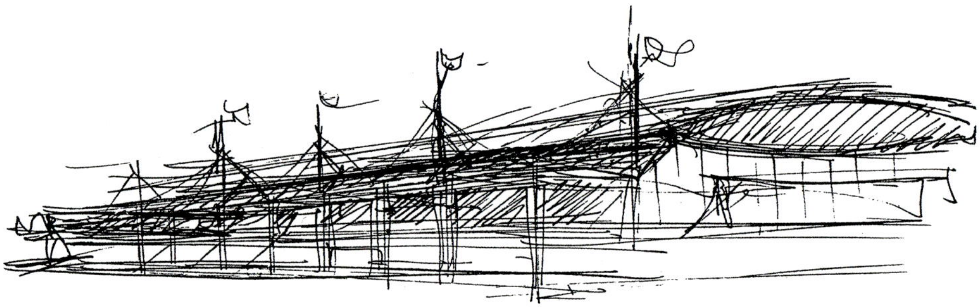

Country: France
Use: Airport
Start of project: 1980
Completion: 1987
Surface: 21,000 m²
Capacity: 2.5 million passengers per year

Designed for 2.5 million passengers per year, Terminal 2 of the Nice Airport relies on some ideas derived from Roissy 2 A and B. This is because the architect decided to place the service elements in a thick roof, accessible from above. A single steel vault running transversally through the space defines the open nature of this design. What is perceived from the interior as only a sweeping curve of the roof, in fact creates the thickness necessary for the mechanicals above. At the leading edges of the roof, both on the city and runway sides, an extremely thin appearance, belies not only its fundamental thickness but also its solidity rendered necessary by the possibility of local seismic activity. The architect likens the sensation given by his roof design to that of the underside of a boat held up with hardly visible stays – it floats above the travelers. Aside from allowing free passage from ground to air, the cleverly designed roof allows the visible floor areas to be completely free of mechanical obstructions. This too goes to giving the whole an impression of freedom and lightness. Indeed, Nice is one of the more spectacular airports to fly in and out of because of the beauty of the surroundings. Approaching aircraft usually fly low off the shore of Cannes and the famous beaches of the Côte d'Azur, and taking off, breathtaking views of the snow-covered Alps are usually visible. With a floor area of 21,000 square meters and just five points of contact for arriving aircraft, this is not

With its mast and rigging image, the Nice Airport evokes the neighboring Mediterranean as much as it does the image of flight. Typically for Andreu, an elevated roadway brings passengers to the upper departures level while allowing access and light to the lower level. The roadway is separated from the building precisely to allow light to reach the bottom area.

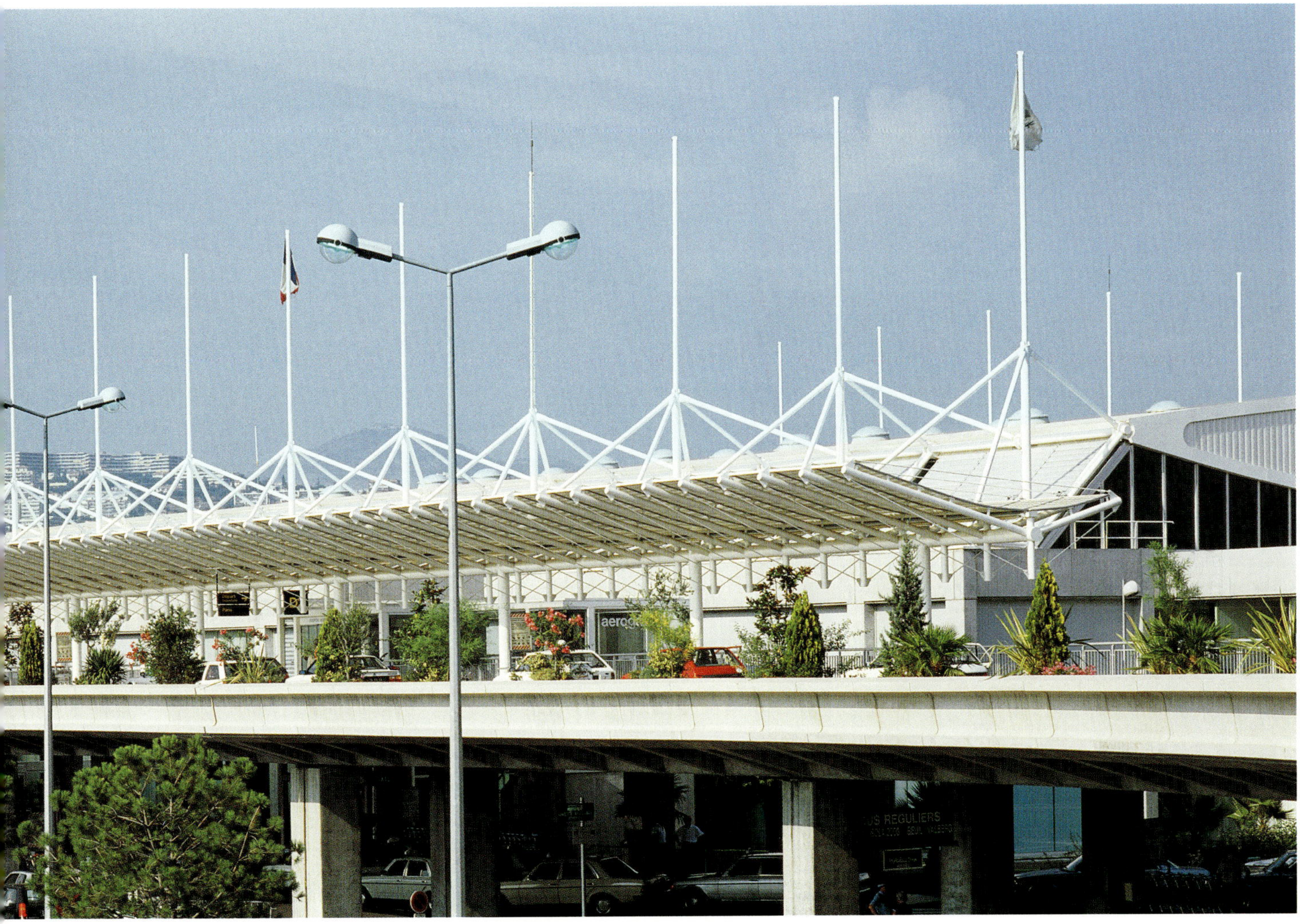

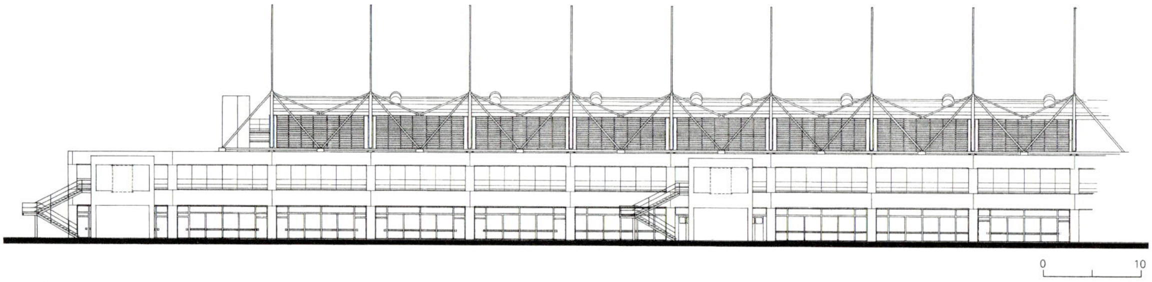

a large facility, but it is an example of complete clarity of movement from the automobile arrivals side (land or city) and the runways sitting in Nice's Baie des Anges. Surprisingly the large vaulted ceiling is black inside, but this serves to draw attention to the two light-filled directions offered to voyages – the city or the skies. Andreu compares the satiny black finish of the roof to paintings by his countryman Pierre Soulages. Inclined windows with grid screens bring changing patterns of light into the main terminal area, and again, in a sunny climate, the architect points out that the shifting lines of light form part of the architecture itself. In a device also seen in some of his later work, the approach overpass is slightly separated from the terminal, allowing the lower level to receive more light. Open, with clear sense of space imposed by its very forms, Nice Terminal 2 fits in well with the warm climate of this region of France. With the shore of the Mediterranean just meters beyond the outer runway, this is in any case a place filled with light, but the architect has built on that fact to allow the light to enter the building, creating an uplifting sensation for arriving and departing passengers.

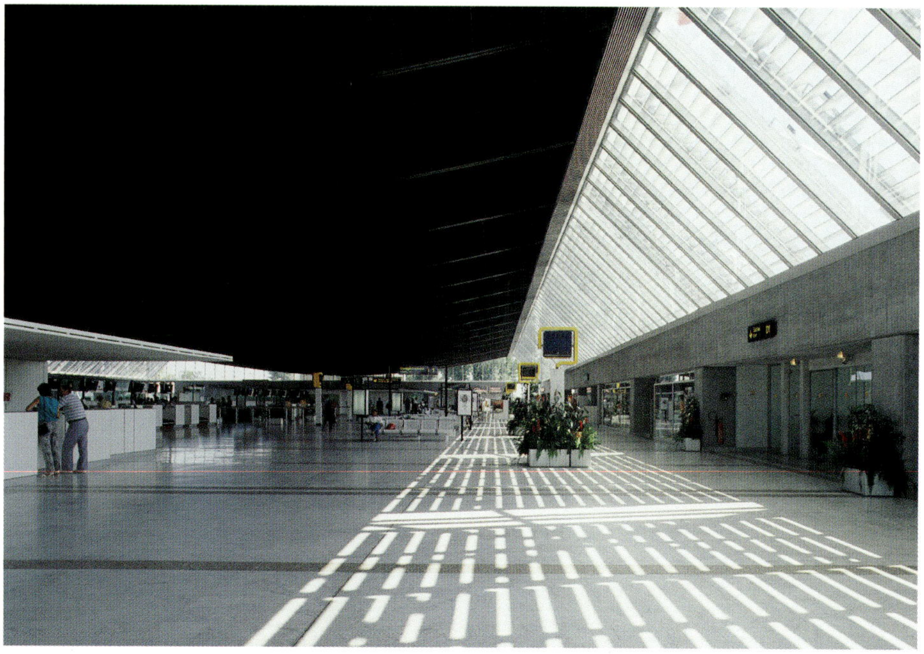

Dealing again with the bright sunlight of the south, Andreu indulges in strong contrasts between light and dark. He shelters passengers from the sun but allows in significant quantities of light that give life to the space as the sun turns above.

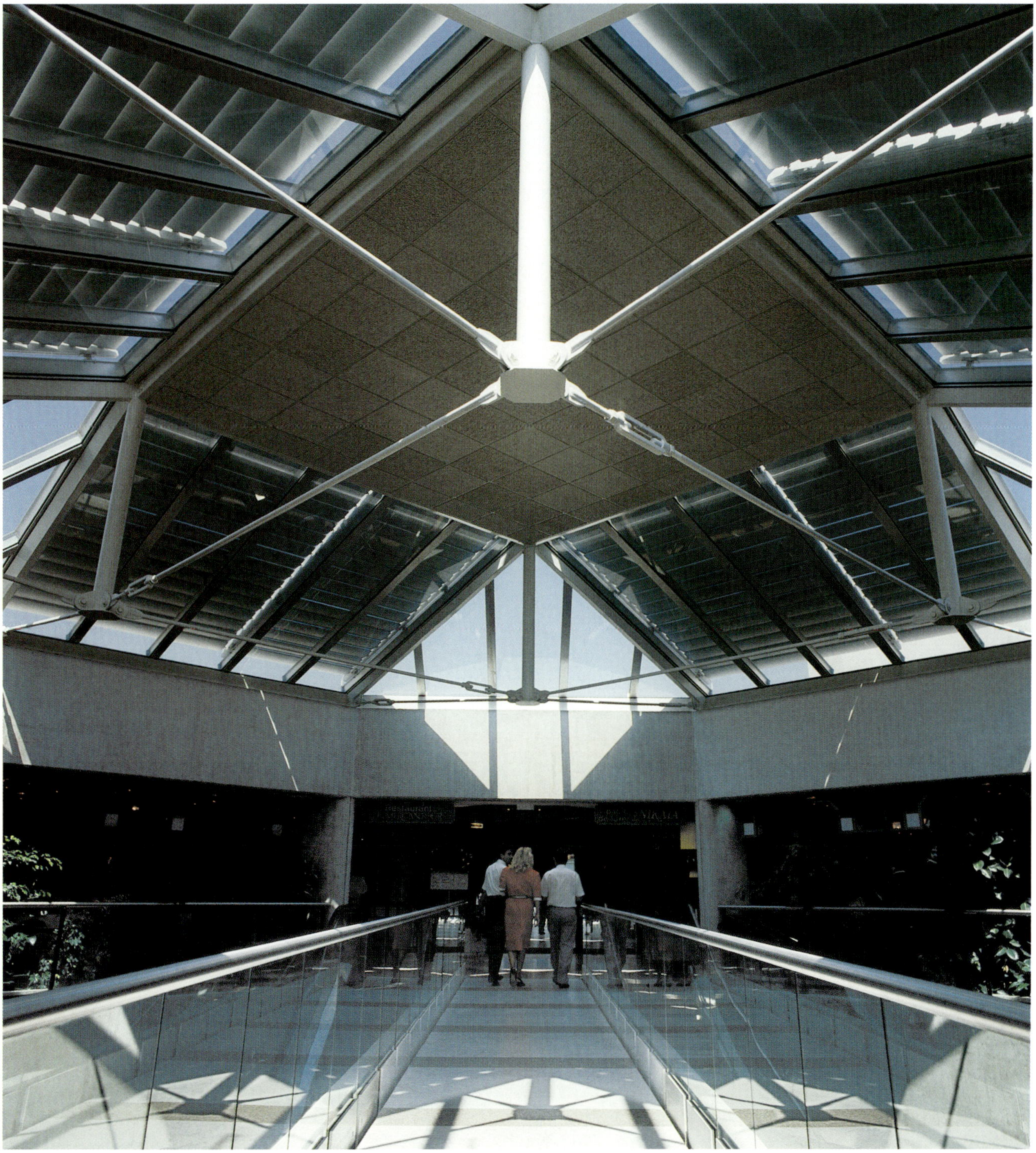

Extension 1997-2002

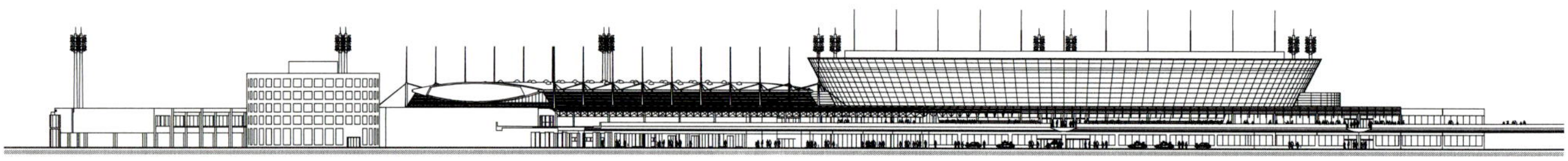

Returning to Nice after his first successful efforts in this Mediterranean resort city, Paul Andreu added a new 27,000 square meter terminal with a theoretical passenger capacity of 4,5 million travelers per year. Doubling the overall capacity of the airport, the architect imagined an unexpected 100-meter diameter circle as the basic form, but built it in an even more unusual inverted cone configuration. Full height glass walls immediately confirm the impression of transparency and lightness he established with his first design in Nice. The glass walls and overall design again permit passengers to clearly see the positioning of the various facilities, and in this instance to have an almost 360° view of the surroundings as well. The 37,000 square meter facility provides for six new aircraft docks and also succeeds in mediating between the existing buildings and possible future extensions. Departure and check-in facilities are located on one level set 5 meters above ground. The actual waiting rooms and departure areas divided into domestic and international areas are set at 6.67 meters above ground. Arrivals and correspondence are below at 2.40 and 3.30 meters above ground, while the baggage carrousels are at ground level. A restaurant with a panoramic 180° view is located atop the new building at 14.2 meters above ground level. Still exploring the ideas of lightness and flight after so many airport projects, Andreu returns to the circular form that he adapted in the case of Roissy Terminal 1. Rather than a concrete ring open in the center, here he changes both materials and direction by reaching upwards toward the sky as opposed to anchoring solidly in the earth. He also points out that the circular form was not derived for the same reasons in Roissy 1 and Nice. In Nice, it is the articulation of

Although making use of a familiar round form, the architect here designs a section of an inverted, glass-clad cone that is rather surprising. In this, he shows an ability to shift styles or layouts within the same airport, as time requires successive development plans. Indeed, Andreu's ability to allow his own architecture to grow is one of his most pertinent qualities.

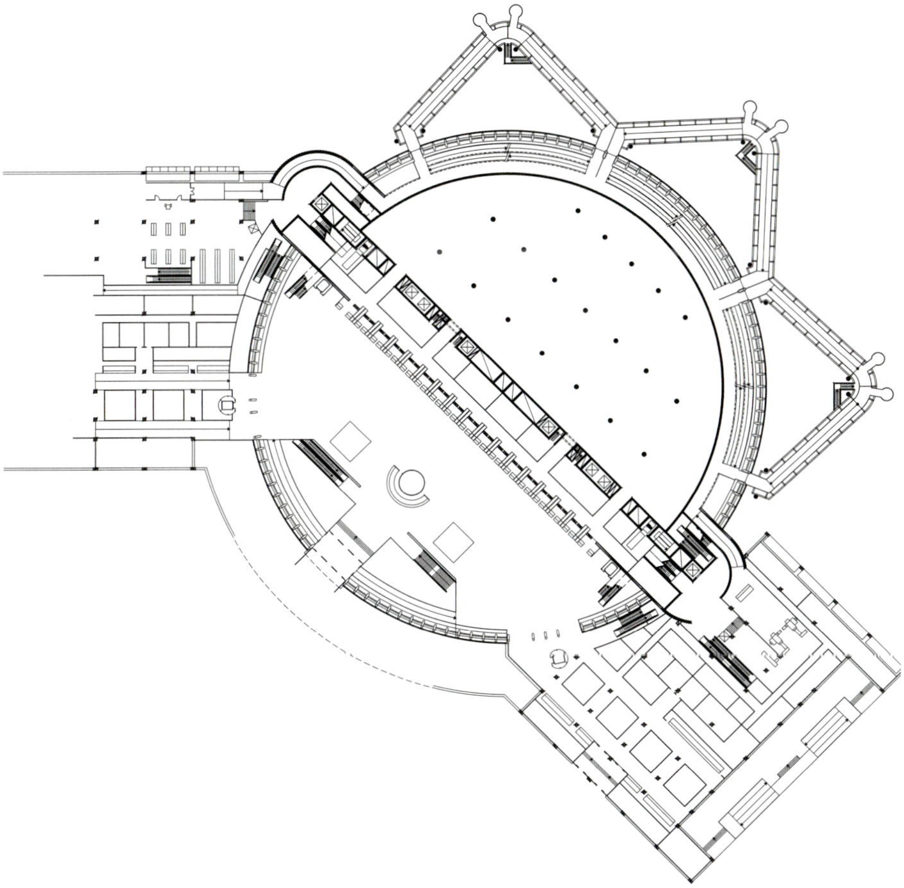

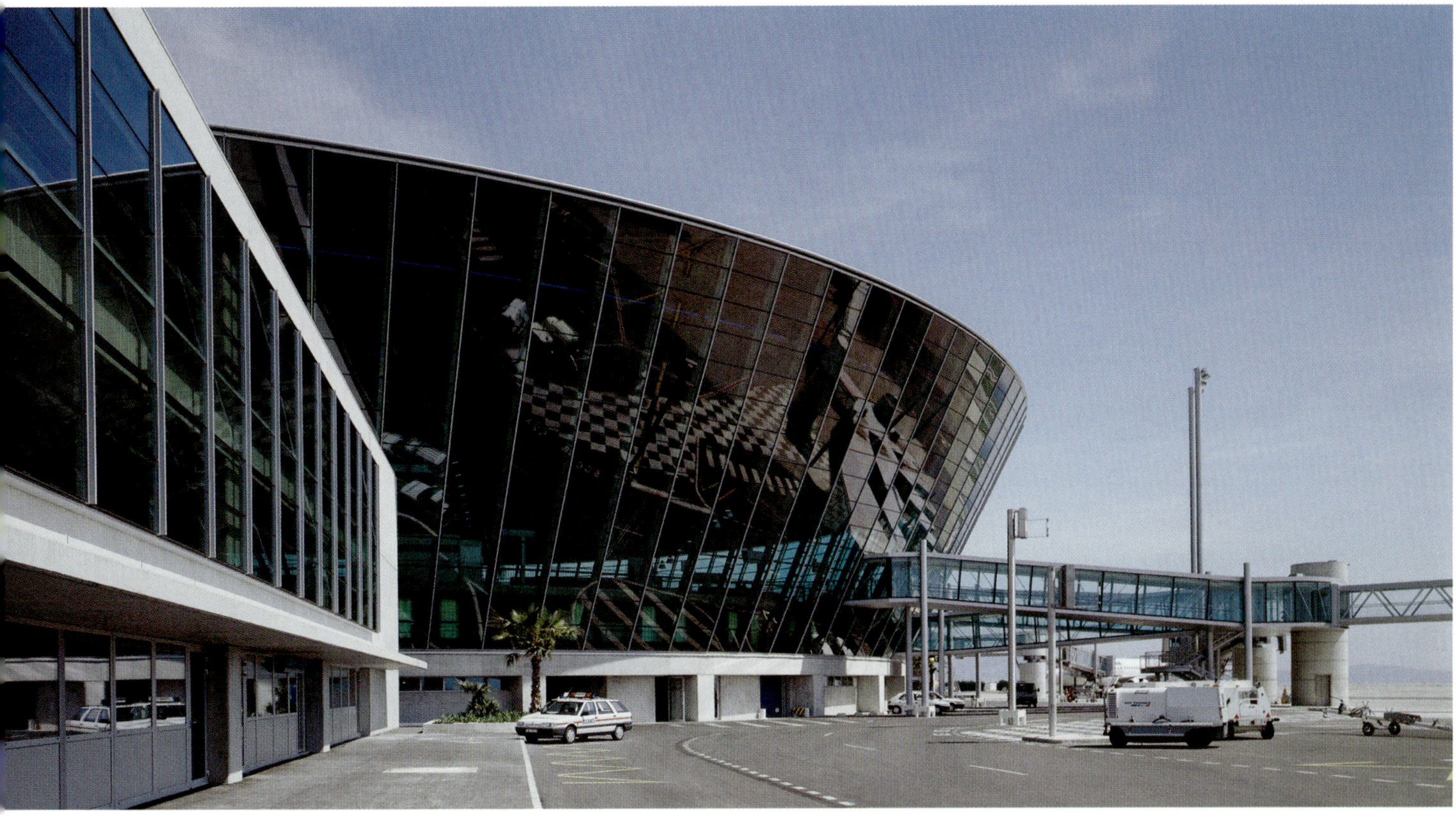

The inverted cone of the extension allows the architect to create unusual interior spaces where the walls lean out rather than in as might more commonly be expected. By creating openings between the different levels of the structure, the architect allows visitors to have an idea of the overall activity of the building while facilitating the penetration of daylight to all areas.

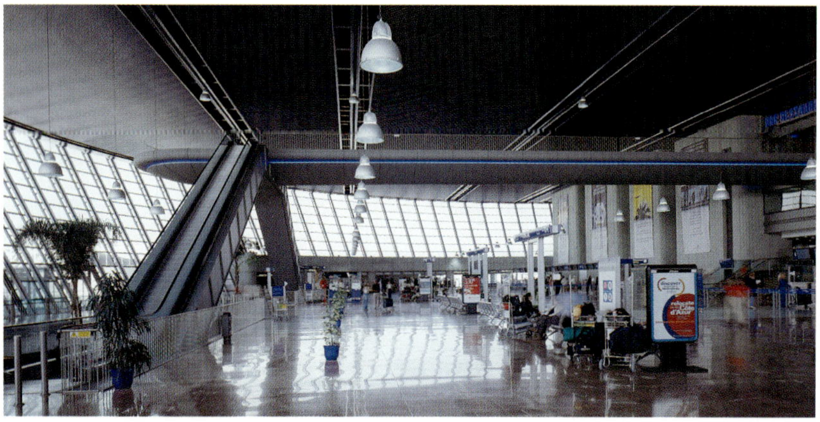

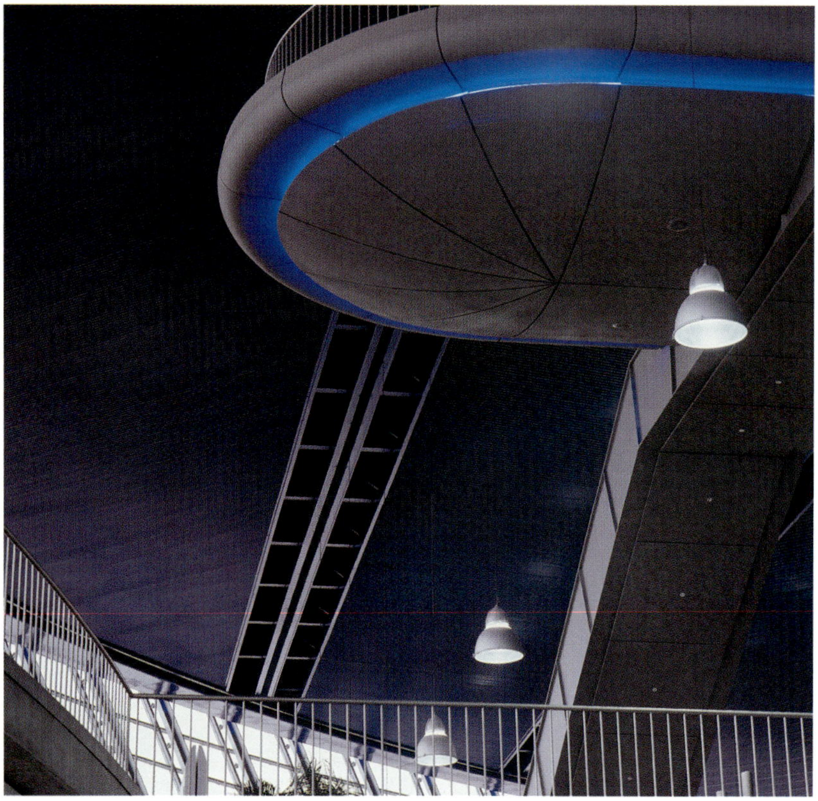

the facility as opposed to an overriding plan that dictated the necessity of this shape. It might be said that whereas Roissy Terminal 1 was imagined in plan more than in section, Nice Terminal 2, Module 2 masters the movement of passengers without sacrificing to a purely technical bird's eye viewpoint. In other words, where Paul Andreu was fascinated with an almost Piranesian vision of complexity at the outset, he has refined his designs, with function becoming almost second nature to him, even as the symbolism of flight, movement and light comes to the center of his thought. This is less of a vortex distributing the movement of cars, people and aircraft in horizontal planes than it is a rising shaft of light. The distinction is considerable and whatever the differences in scale or volume between two projects, that are separated by almost 30 years, there is now an undeniable coming of age, a full mastery of the art of flight one might be tempted to say.

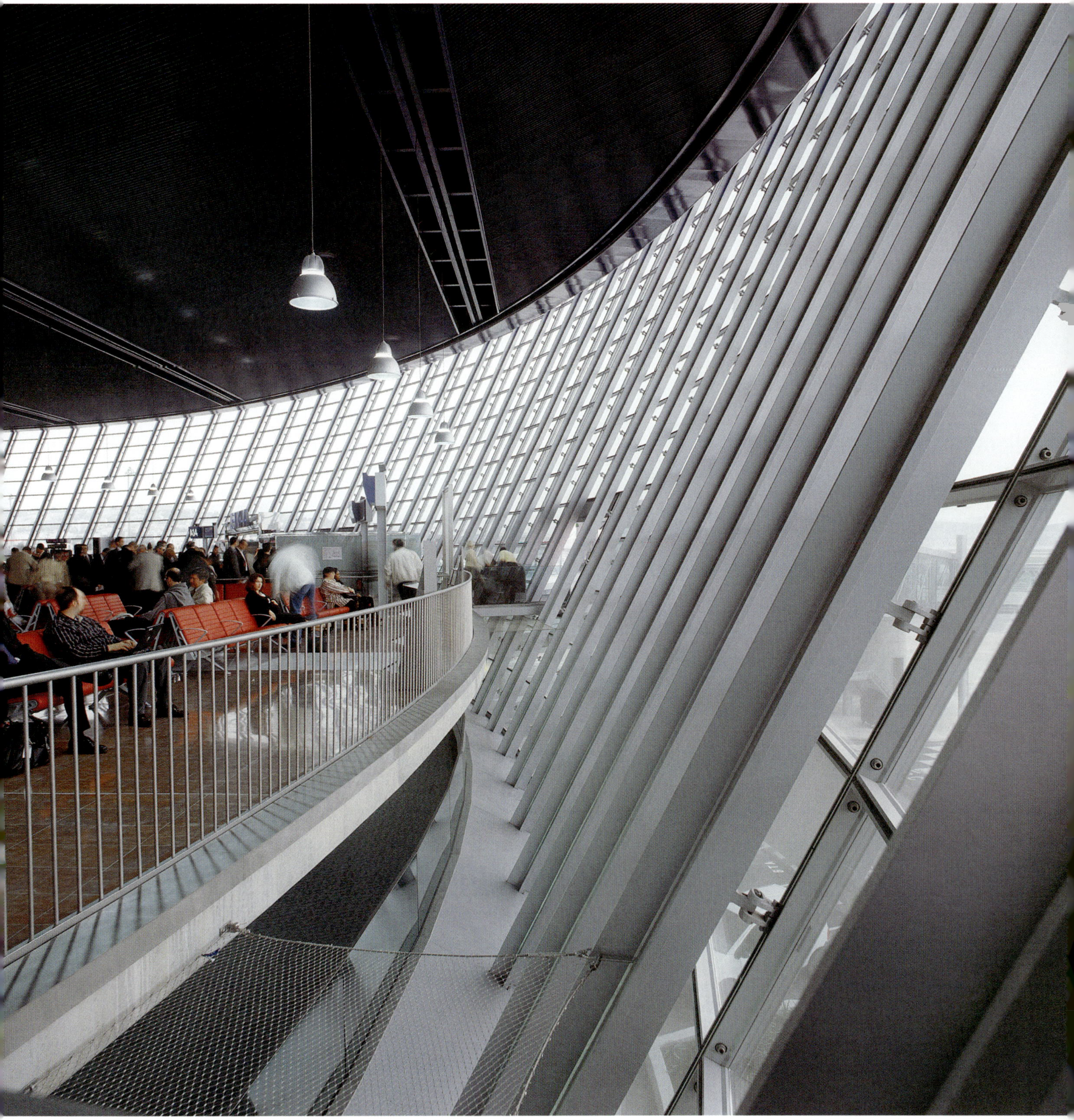

Although Paul Andreu was not the principal architect associated with the Arche, his style and his signature permeates the edifice, especially where the light, so-called "Cloud" that hovers above the inner courtyard of the cube is concerned.

Grande Arche Paris La Défense

in association with J.O. Spreckelsen, competition winner

Country: France
Use: Office Building
Start of project: 1984
Completion: 1989
Surface: 200,000 m^2
Capacity: 80,000 m^2 of office space

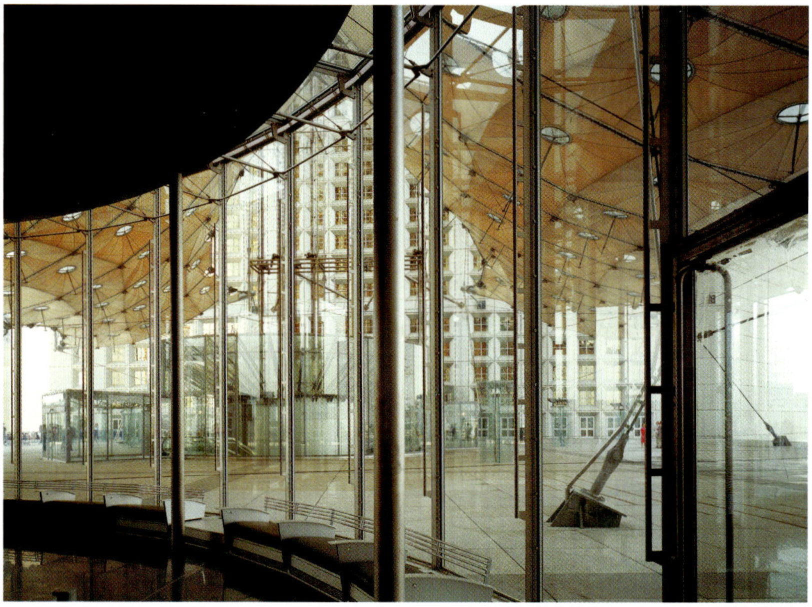

The Défense has an interesting history. In the axis of the Louvre and the Tuileries planted by Lenôtre in 1640, the area took its name from a statue commemorating the defense of Paris by the Commune (1870-71). In 1931, the Seine region organized a competition for the development of the area between the Etoile and the Rond-point de la Défense. In 1958 a quasi-governmental organization was created for the Défense area (EPAD), and as construction began there, various plans were put forward to close the perspective of the Champs-Elysées, or rather open it as I.M. Pei proposed to do with two symmetric towers (1973). An international competition organized at the behest of President François Mitterrand led to the selection of the little-known Danish architect Johann Otto von Spreckelsen amongst the 424 projects submitted in 1983. Spreckelsen formed an association with Paul Andreu for this project in 1984. His open cube structure could not be considered an arch in the traditional sense, but nonetheless the project baptized "Arche de la Défense" began construction in July 1985 with no less than 2,000 workers on the site. In an unexpected turn of circumstances, Spreckelsen resigned from the project one year later and gave responsibility for

Though J.O. Spreckelsen designed the Grande Arche, it does display many characteristics of Andreu's architecture. There is an obvious play on the difference between opacity and transparency, between heaviness and lightness. The suspended "cloud" structure visible inside the opening of the square arch asserts Andreu's presence.

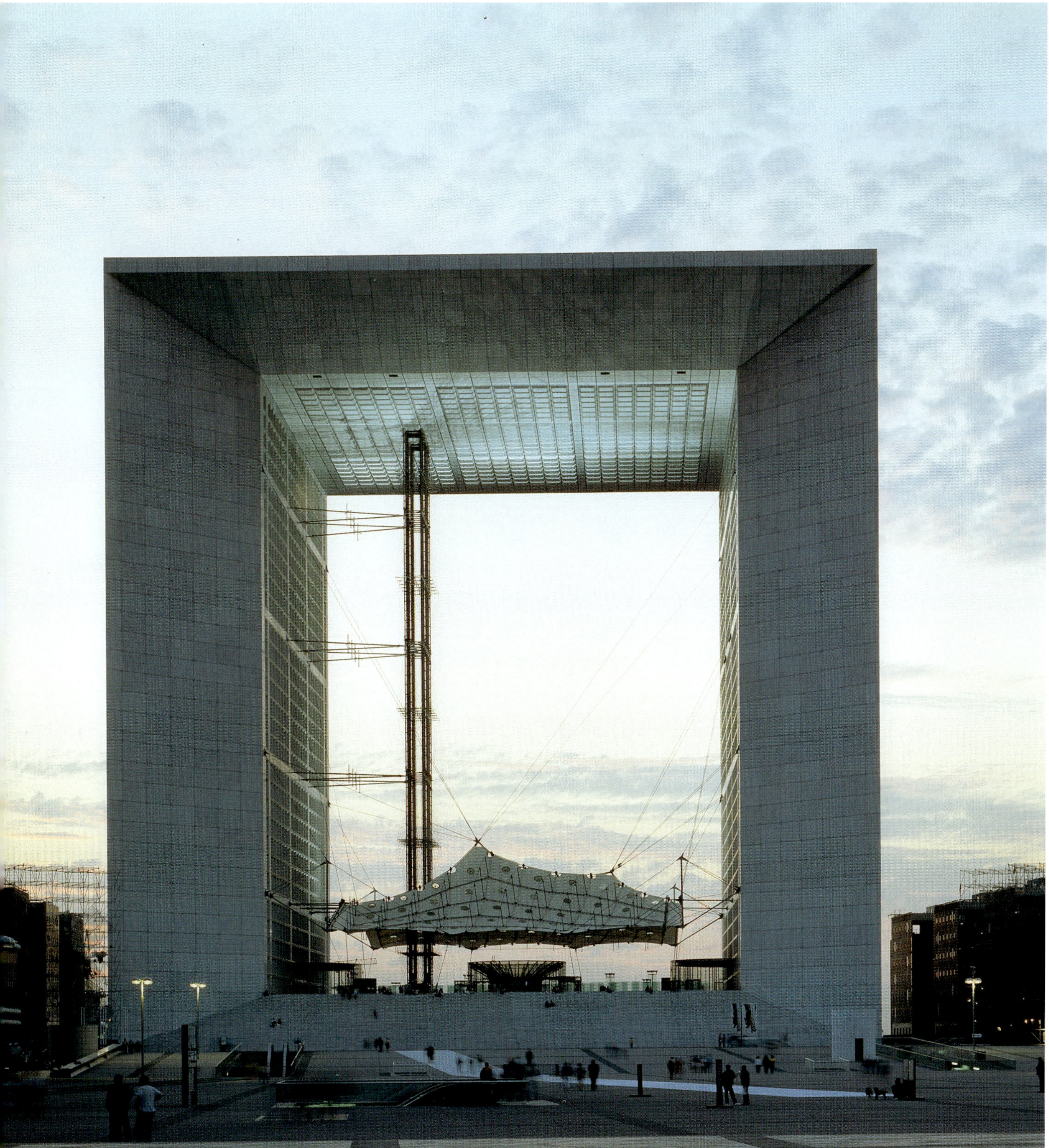

Grande Arche

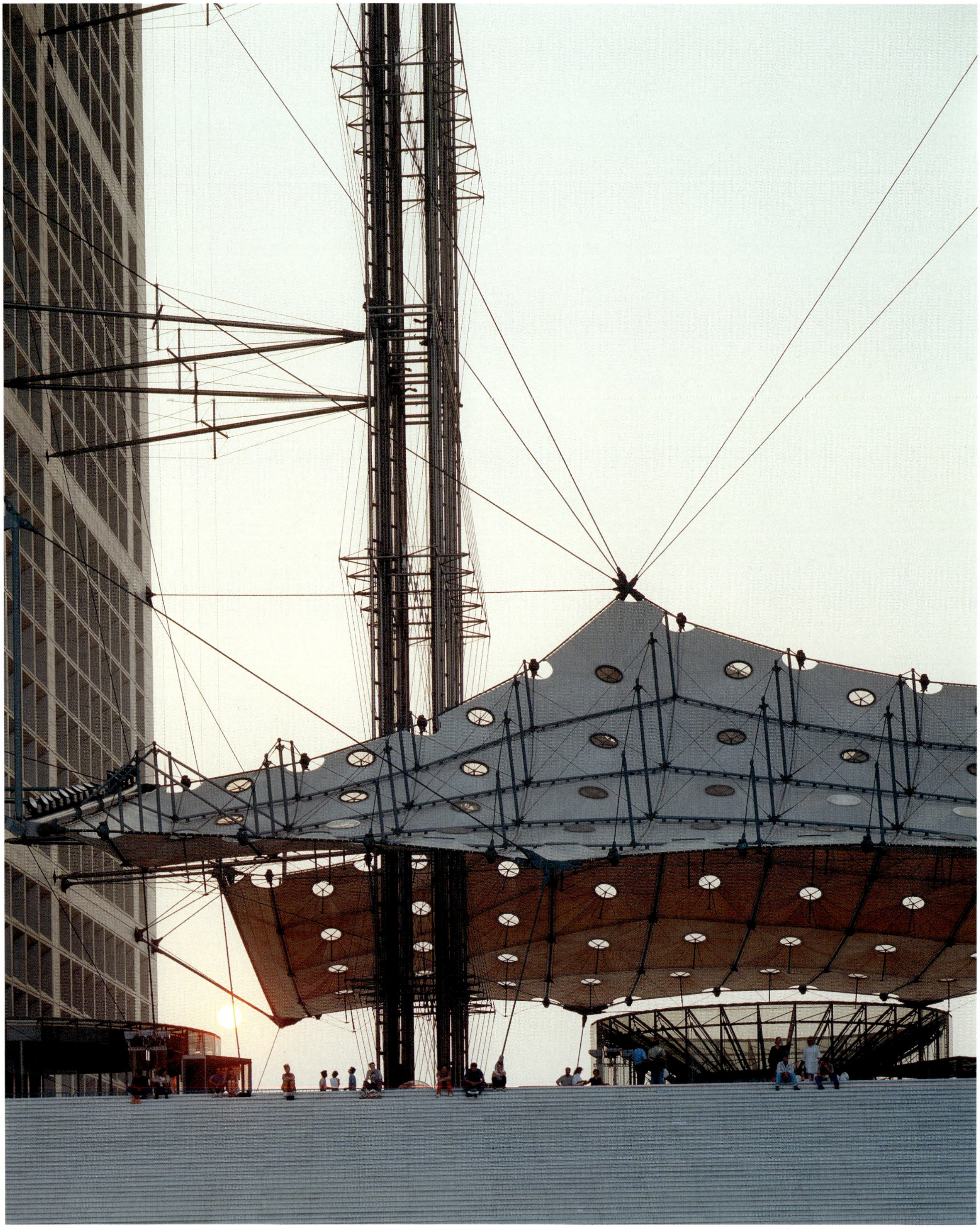

The lightweight and largely irregular design of the cloud is both innovative and efficient. It allows light and air to penetrate while shielding visitors from the sun or the rain. Like a tent that is anchored not in the ground but in the sky, the "Cloud" has some relation to the designs of the German engineer Frei Otto for example.

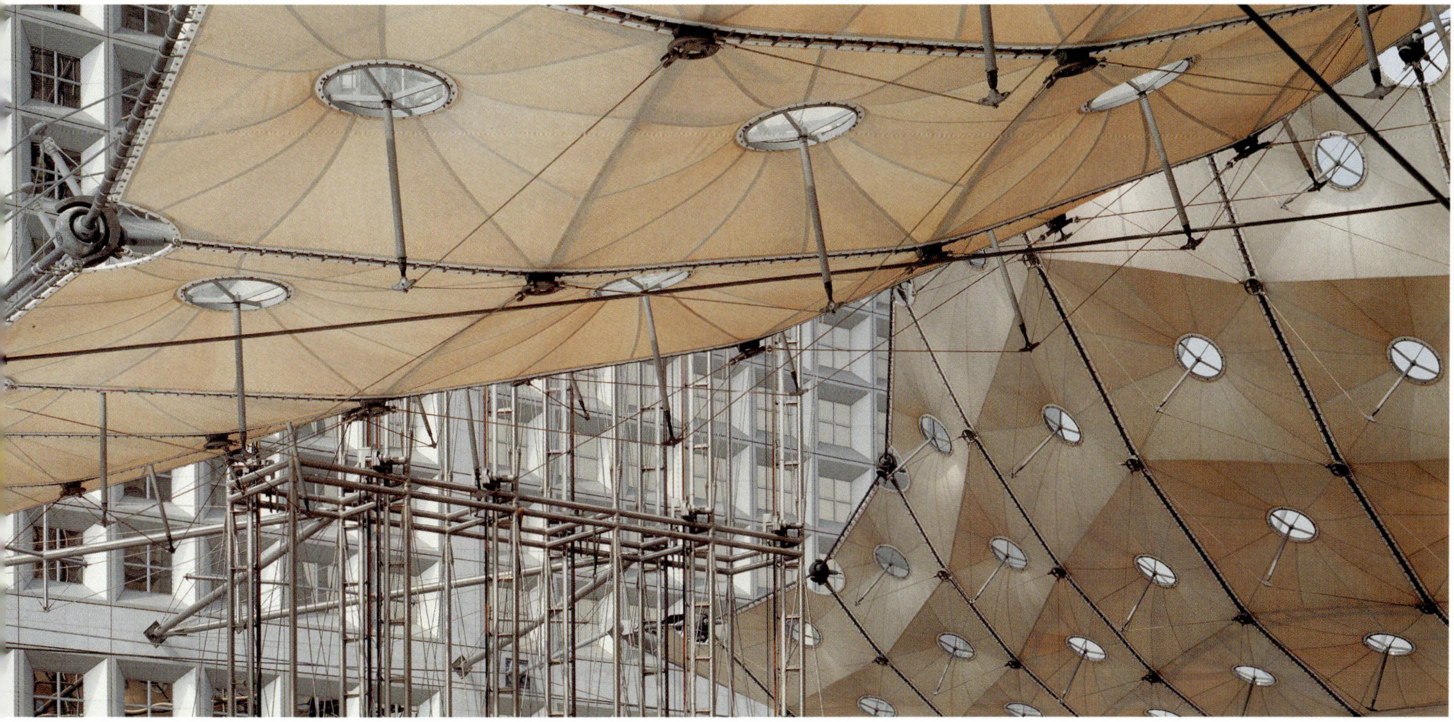

the construction to Paul Andreu. The Danish architect died in 1987. The Arche was nothing short of impressive even by the standards of the very large projects that Paul Andreu has carried forward in other circumstances. Completed in May 1989, the building is basically a 100 meter cube made with 300,000 tons of concrete and 350,000 Carrara marble plaques for the cladding. Andreu had a particular responsibility for the so-called "Cloud" structure he designed with Peter Rice of RFR under the huge opening of the Arch. This stretched Teflon design that resembles a sculpture more than anything else, is supported by a latticework of cables and articulating steel rods. One might say that Andreu is more recognizable in the extreme lightness and elegance of the "Cloud" than he is in the rather heavy Arch itself. Since he was not the design architect of the main structure, this is a rather moot point. Surely, his expertise in engineering was useful to the very last in the erection of this exceptional mega-structure. Whatever its faults, it is one of the enduring symbols of Paris.

Although technically "clones" of the earlier A and B Halls of Terminal 2, Halls C and D nonetheless represent a significant evolution in Andreu's work toward the spare and light-filled efficiency that he is truly well-known for.

Charles-de-Gaulle Airport - Terminal 2 - C and D **Paris**

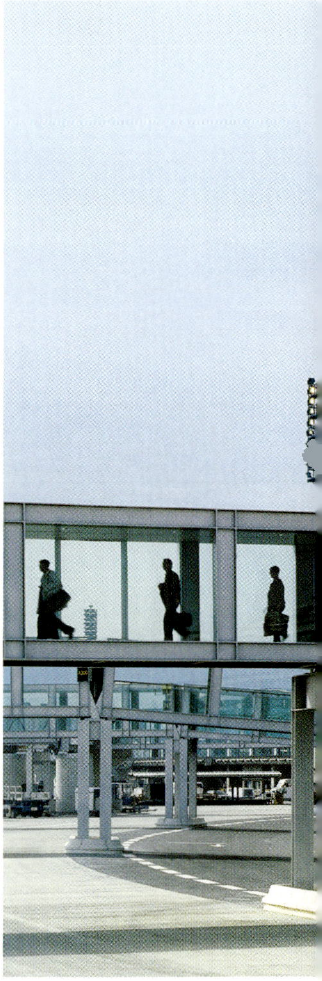

Country: France
Use: Airport
Start of project: 1985
Completion: 1989 (D), 1993 (C)
Surface: 103,500 m^2
Capacity: 10 million passengers per year (2 D: 6M, 2 C: 4M)

Intended for an annual passenger volume of 10 million persons these two structures provide facilities for 15 aircraft in contact with the Terminals, and a further eleven at some distance. Hall D has an area of 46,800 square meters while Hall C is slightly larger at 56,300 square meters. Other facilities include 48 check-in counters in Hall D and 54 in Hall C, as well as 4,000 parking spaces. The external design of these buildings, put into service at an interval of four years (Hall D in 1989 and Hall C in 1993) is identical to that of the A and B terminals. 8.5-meter high double-glazed facades are used in Hall C, whose interior was designed with Jean-Michel Wilmotte. This glazing contributes to the overall transparency of the structures, allowing passengers to at least see the light on the runway side as they arrive from the street side. As was the case in the earlier Roissy buildings, these terminal structures are particularly restrained in their gamut of colors, essentially limited to gray and white. For the architect, color is "added by the passengers." Indeed, with the exception of such buildings as the Abu Dhabi Airport, Andreu himself has often eschewed color. His is an architecture of form and light rather than one of color, and it is true that the typical airport attracts such a variety of travelers and packages that added color may well be superfluous. Intended for longer distance international flights, this building is somewhat higher than its cousins A, B and D. The roof of Hall C was cast in place, while the pre-cast elements of Hall D were simply lowered into space in the kind of rather spectacular construction gesture that has characterized many of Paul Andreu's projects. D was designed for European internal medium-range flights and is a bit wider than the earlier structures. This width (75 meters) is intended to facilitate the movement of travelers and visitors, but also to make

While recalling the eye-like design of its predecessors at Charles-de-Gaulle Airport, Halls C and D are already moving toward the lighter, more largely glazed designs of Andreu's more recent work. Here a glass bridge leads travelers from the terminal to the aircraft, while utility vehicles can drive below.

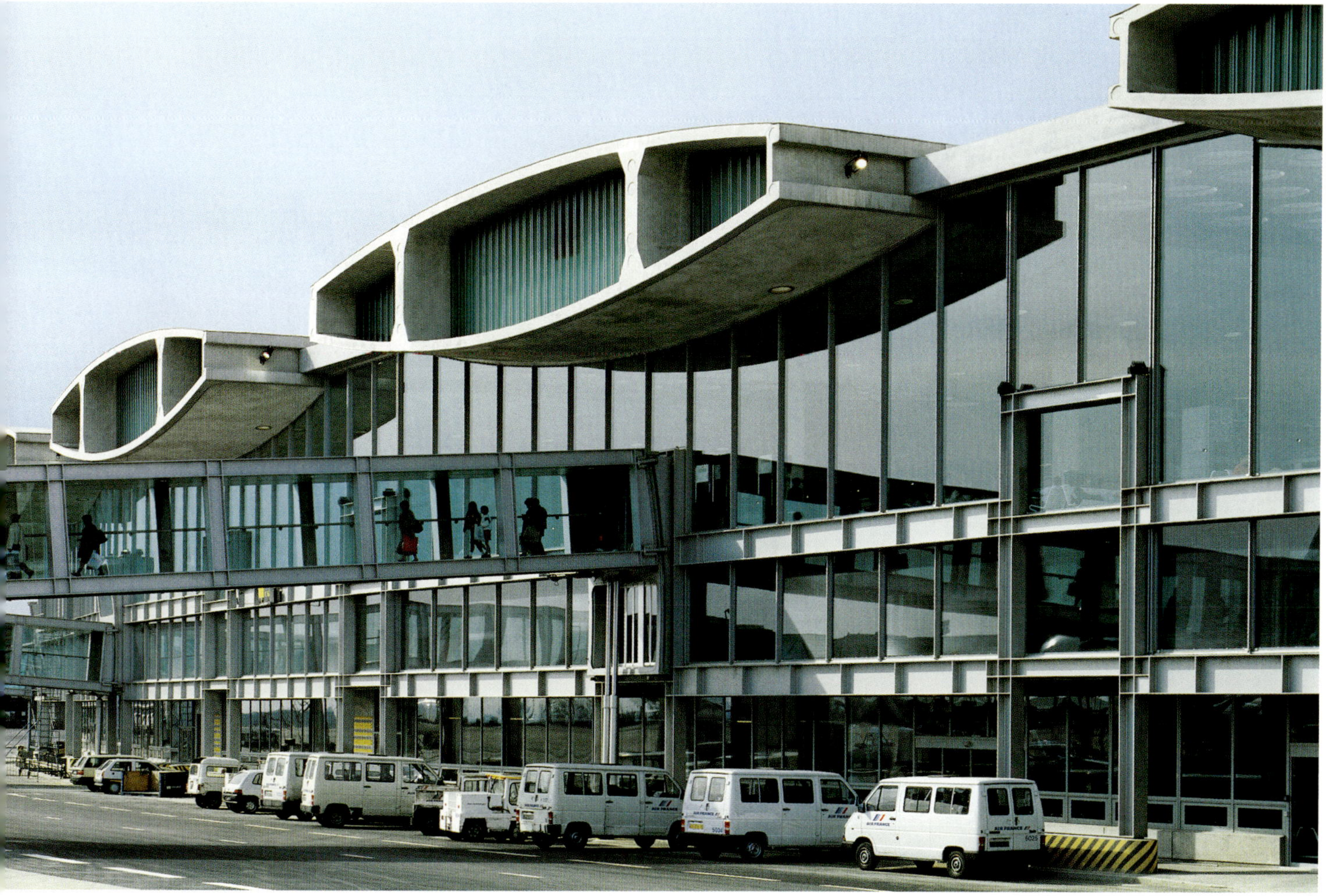

Seating areas that allow travelers to view the activity of the airport as they await their own departure are a hallmark of Terminal 2, much more than in Terminal 1. Andreu's sketches show a particularly developed sense of space that corresponds well to the final, built design.

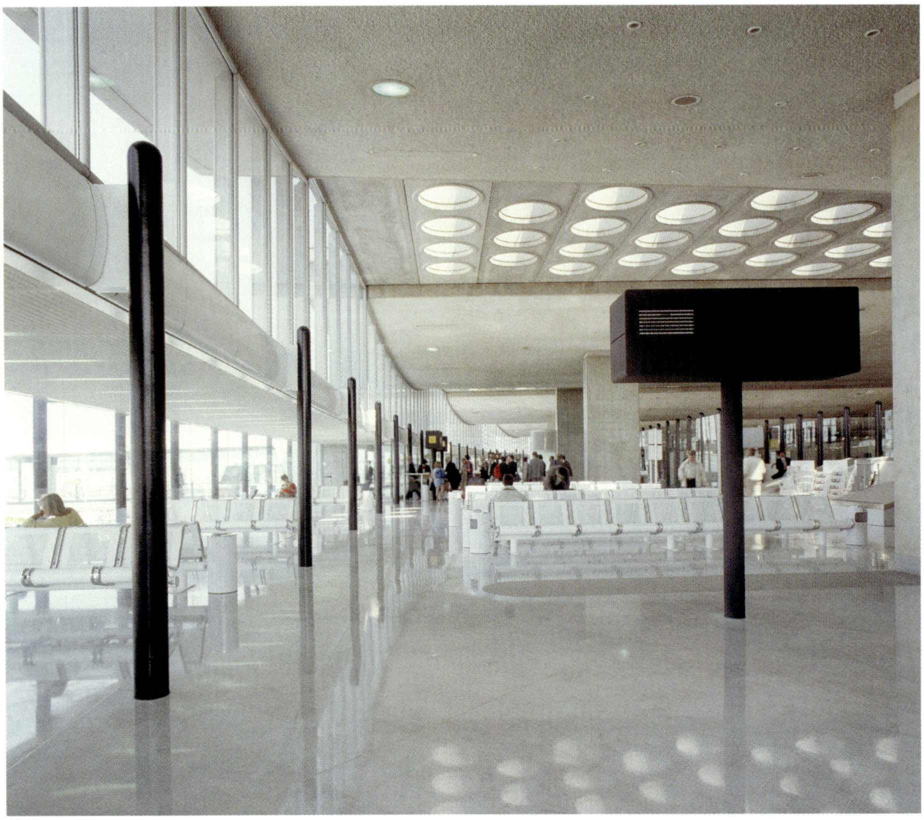

room for boutique space. Mobile loading bridges with glass walls allow a movement from aircraft to the Halls with a more civilized and open feeling than most airport transition spaces. The overall shape and site integration of Halls C and D is identical to that of A and B and the same remarks could be made about the possibly anthropomorphic concept. Yet in repetition, it becomes obvious that the overriding factor in the design of these terminal buildings and their infrastructure is almost totally derived from the practical considerations imposed by the function of the airport. Andreu has clearly mastered the questions of passenger movement and aircraft accessibility that have long dictated airport design. Some of the spaces of these terminals have been filled in or become more occupied with increasing passenger loads and the rising specter of terrorism, but Andreu's

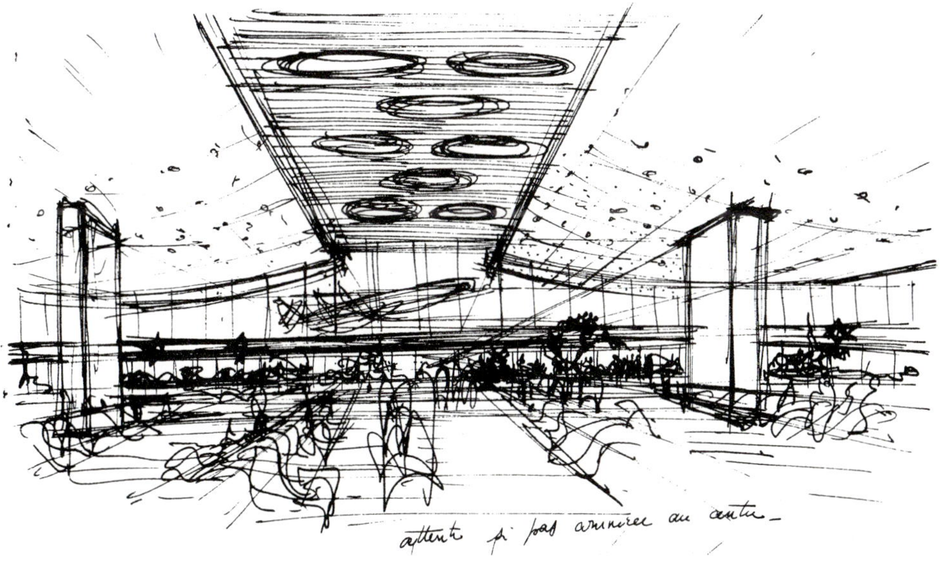

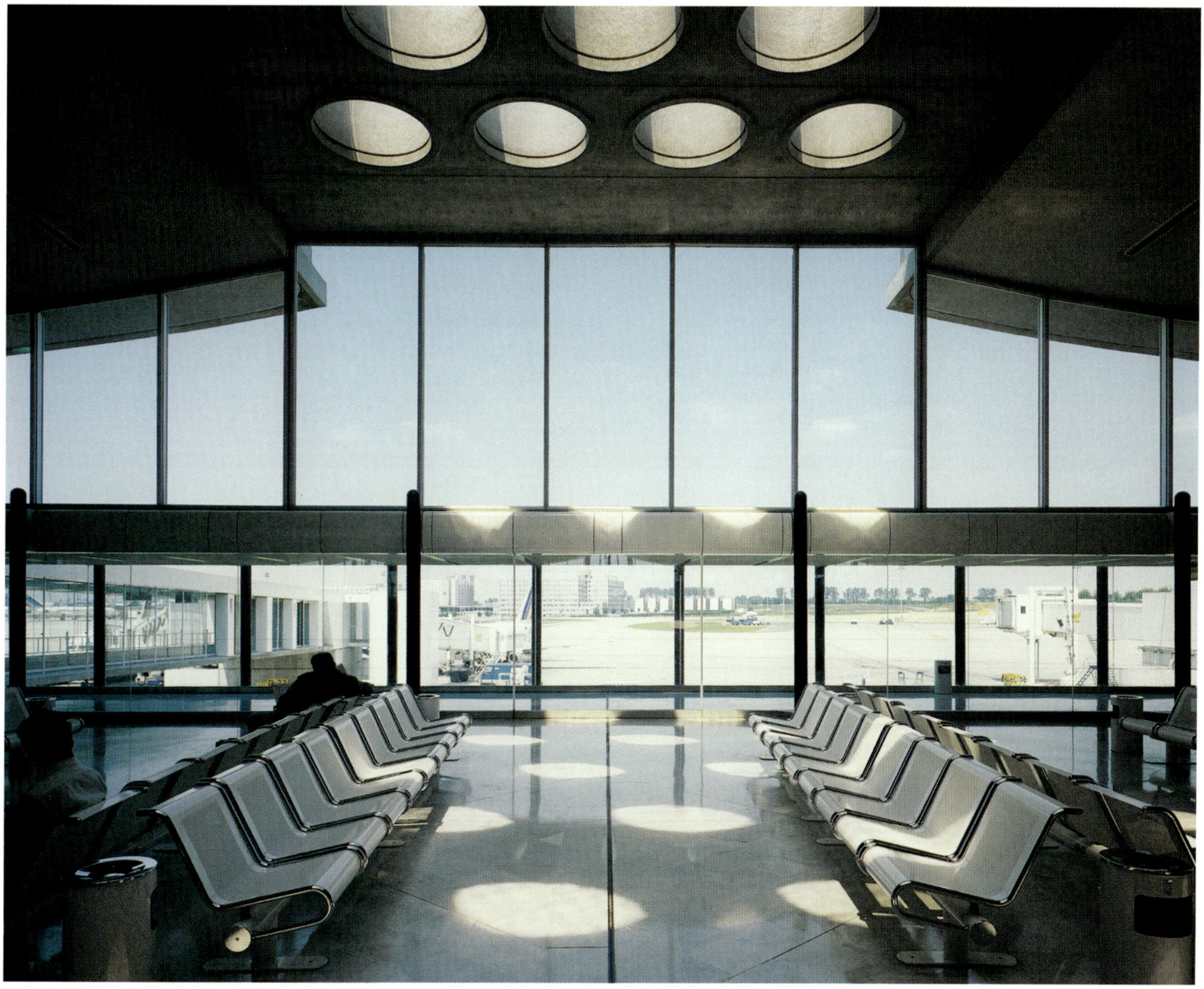

Using openings that allow daylight to move through the space, or an undulating ceiling, as is the case in the image to the right, Andreu continually seeks to animate spaces that retain a fundamentally geometric plan. From the beginning, the architect has shown this tendency to develop designs based on Modernism and yet somehow going beyond the usual rigidities of that school.

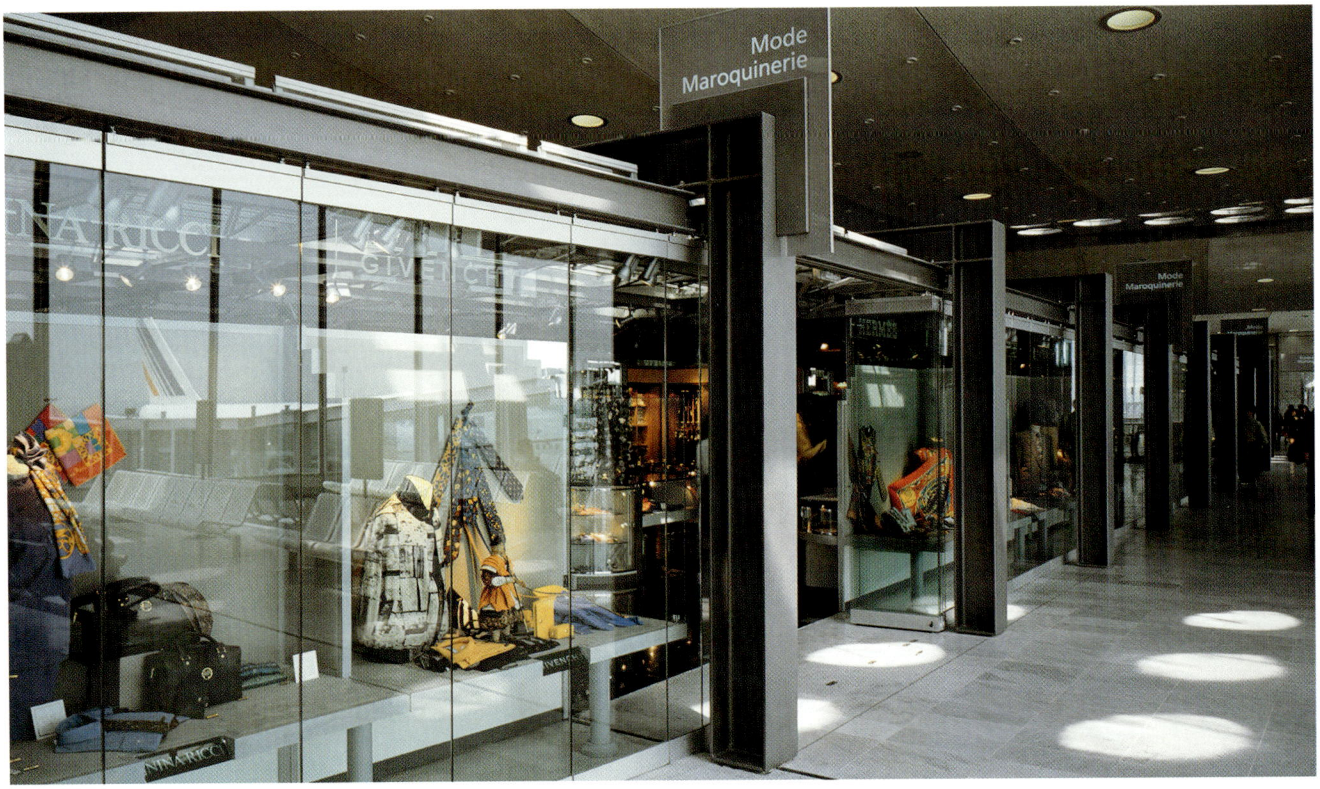

mastery of the basic design retains its practicality. Airport design is indeed complicated and the fact that Andreu and his teams have worked on more than forty facilities worldwide speaks clearly to their success and expertise.

The disposition of the various elements of Roissy Airport and the relative ease with which each terminal can be found are also proof of the intelligence of the overall development plan that has presided over the airport. Some elements, such as the hotels are more difficult to find and to reach in a car. Rather than a purely orthogonal layout which might in other circumstances or countries have been preferred, the looping access roads of Roissy give an impression of complexity which is fortunately not carried over into the actual terminal designs. Andreu's role in road design or green spaces has naturally been less significant than in the buildings themselves.

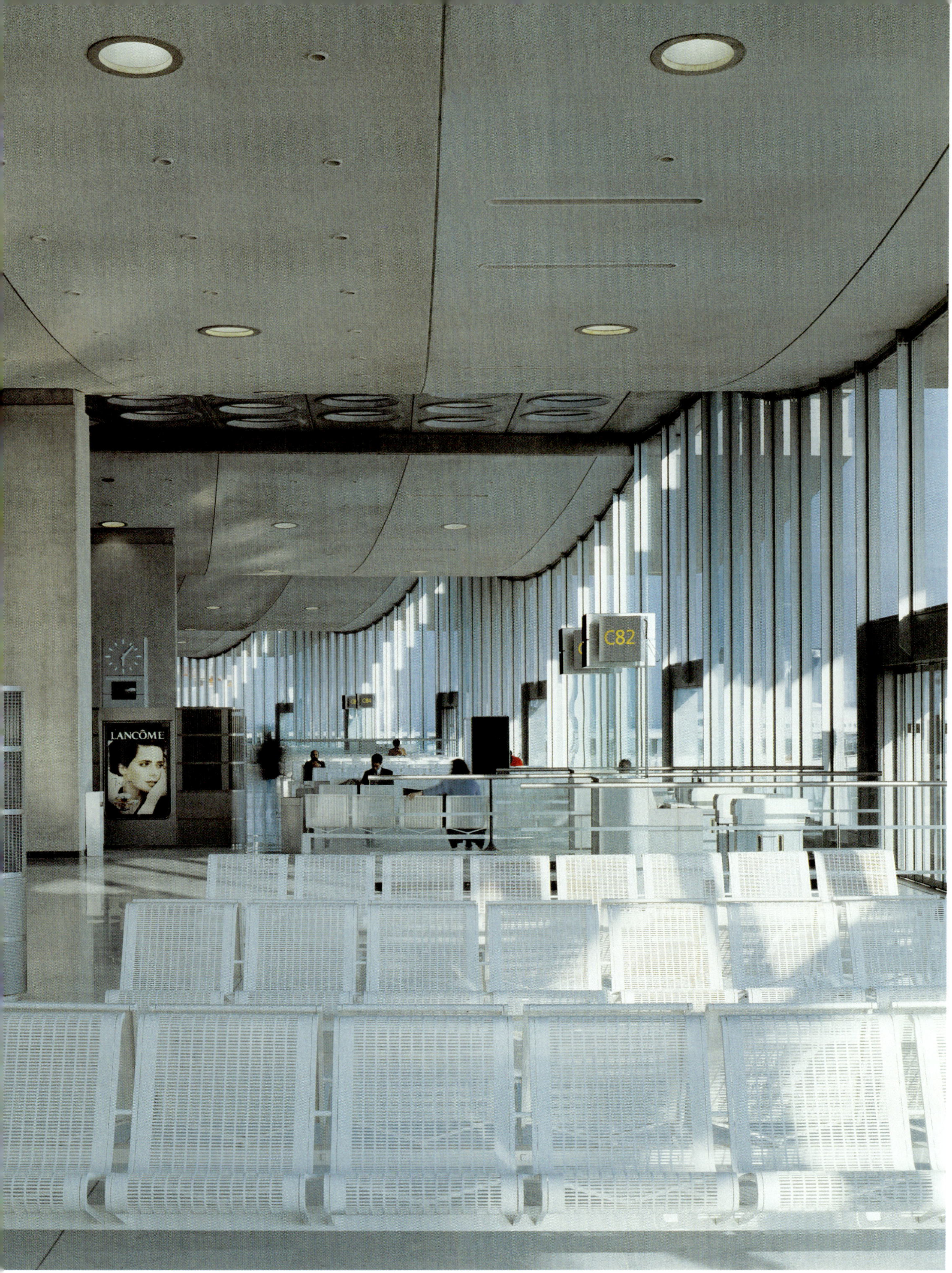
LANCÔME
C82

Breaking out of the airport mold, Andreu is here still dealing with a facility based on the transport of large numbers of people. Devices such as the curved, elevated roadways he often uses in airports are present here, as is an overall impression of technical mastery and "légèreté."

Channel Tunnel - French Terminal and Cité Europe Calais

Country: France
Use: Cross Channel Terminal, Cité Europe, Shopping Center
Start of Project: 1986
Completion: 1993 Cross Channel, 1995 Cité Europe
Surface Cité Europe: 73,000 m^2
Capacity: Cross Channel Terminal: 15 million passengers per year, 7.5 million tons freight

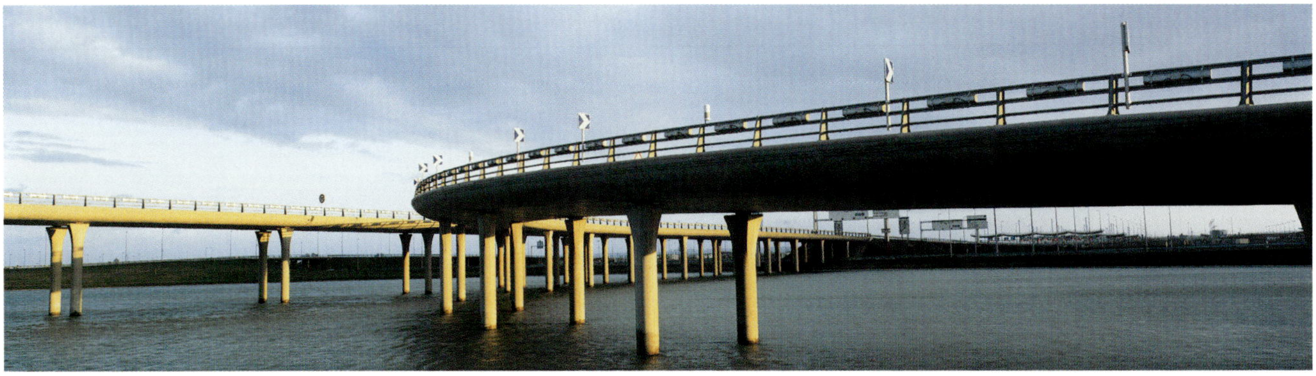

Located at Coquelles near Calais, the French Terminal is just off the A16 highway near the entrance to the Channel Tunnel. Extending his wide experience in the area of traveler movement, Paul Andreu was called on to design the Cross Channel Terminal in Calais. Perhaps more than any other, this project demonstrates the architect's affinity for very large-scale designs. It is difficult to take in the full scope of this

Elevated curving roads, so common in Andreu's airports here take on an almost symbolic dimension, arching over the very large basin that is part of this terminal. Despite creating very large structures, Andreu, at least since the time when he began work on Charles-de-Gaulle Terminal 2, has succeeded in giving a feeling of lightness and clarity to his designs.

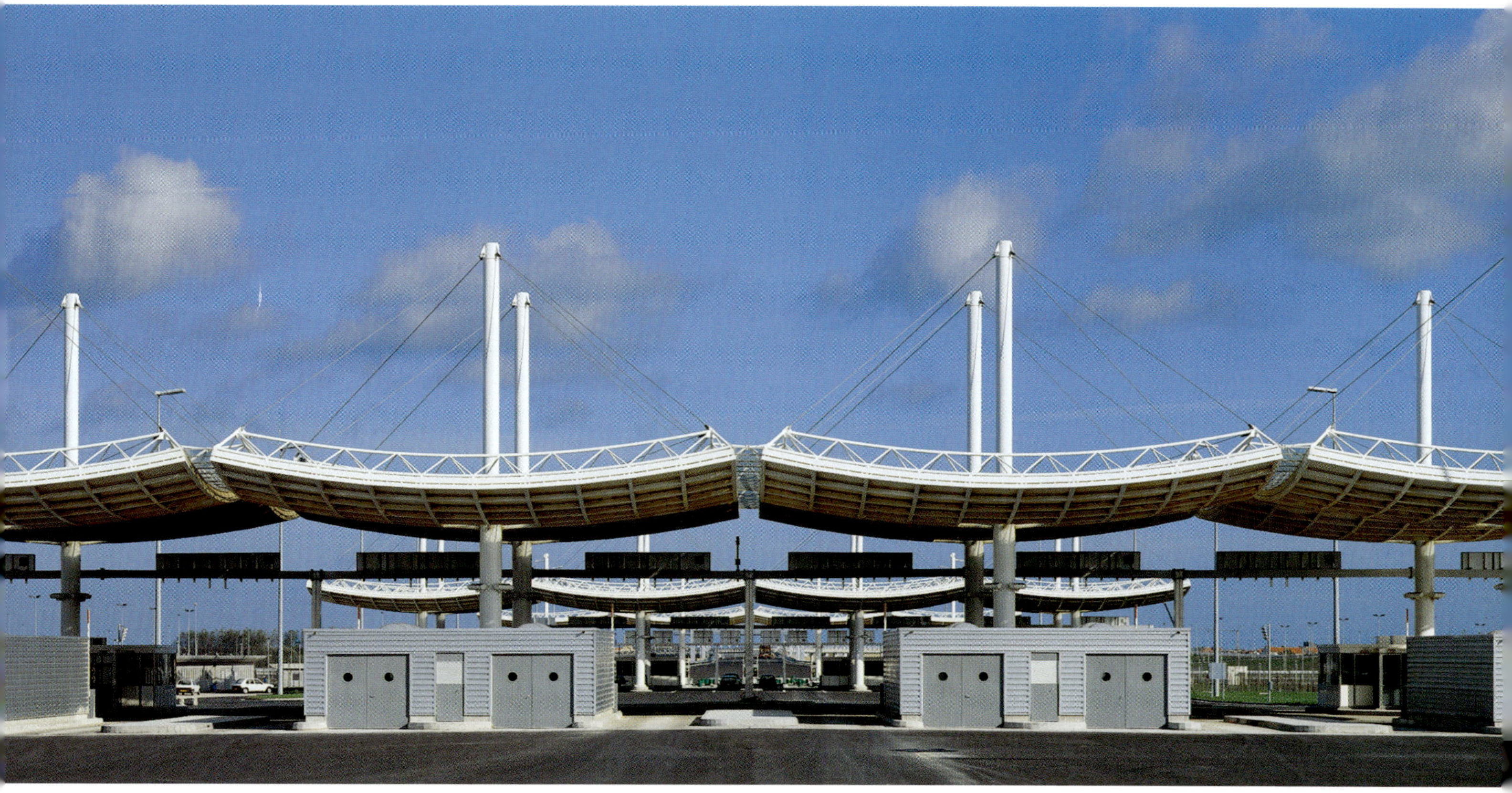

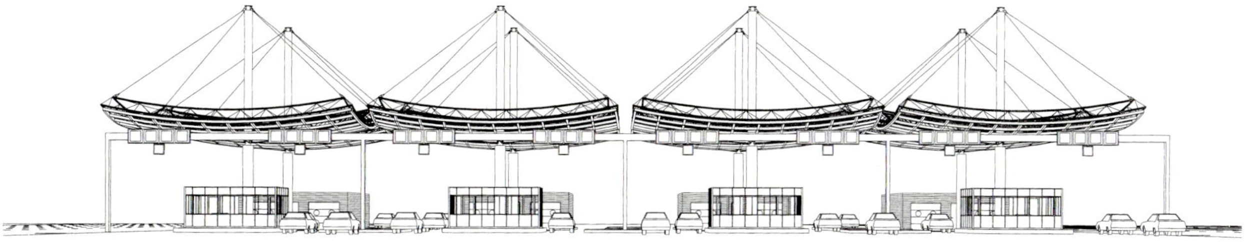

Lofty masts emphasize the impression of lightness that characterizes this design. Metallic screens (right) allow light and partial visibility, giving the impression that the façade is permeable. Below right, spiral staircases and columns contrast metal and concrete in an unexpected way.

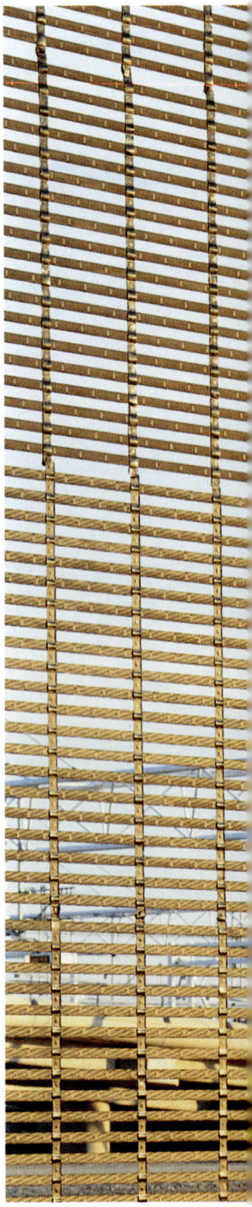

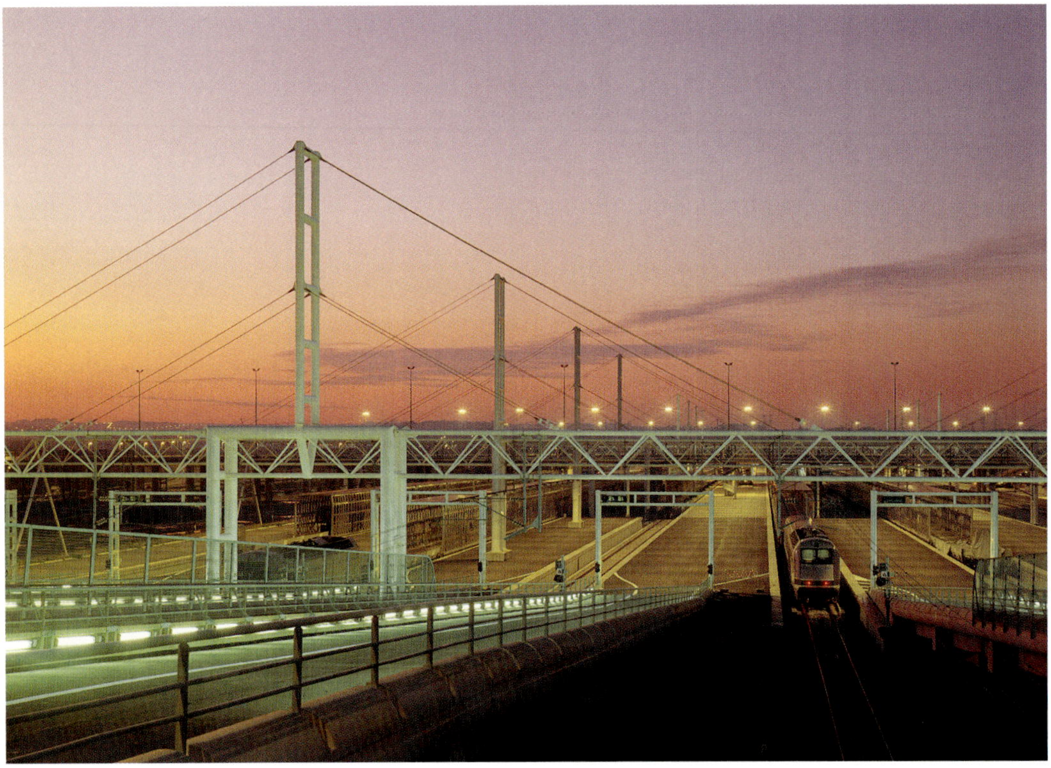

project from any angle but the air. A 400-meter wide reservoir is crossed over by elevated viaducts carrying the main access roads. Within the complex, the Cité Europe shopping center includes a spectacular 24-meter barrel-vaulted space with freestanding monumental facades. The metallic vaults of this space are internally supported and the building also features pyramidal 40-meter high masts, recalling the kind of space that Andreu has created in particular for the recent additions to Roissy. A longitudinal shopping axis brings ample daylight into the boutique areas. Paul Andreu emphasizes the rapport of the complex with the landscape and this use of light within its public spaces as particularly successful aspects of his work. Opened in March 1995, the 100,000 square meters of commercial space in this complex includes 150 stores, one "hyper-market," eleven supermarkets, 30 restaurants and a twelve-theatre cinema facility. In 1998, the Cité Europe generated two billion

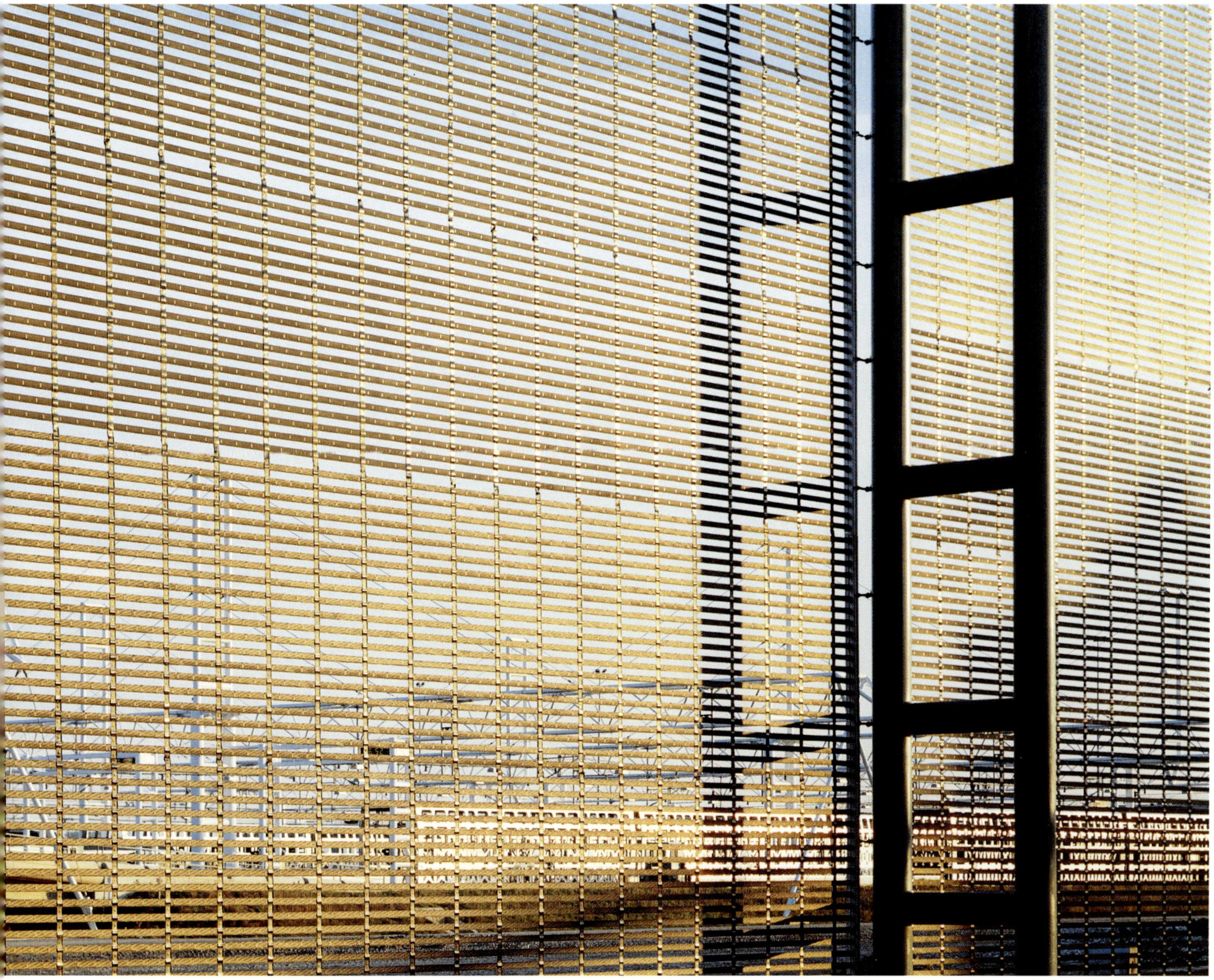

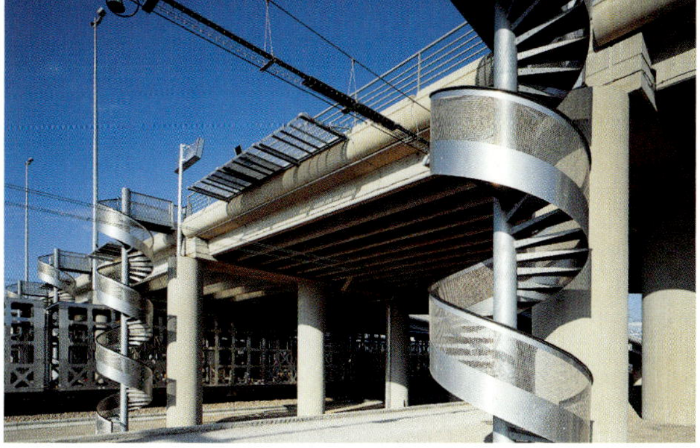

francs in business and received an incredible 19 million visitors of whom 35 percent were English. Called a commercial "cathedral" by the local press the Cité Europe was a design of Paul Andreu working with François Tamisier who subsequently has been involved in the Beijing National Grand Theater. Although this complex is not as vast as Roissy, there is obviously a similarity in the both function and spatial disposition between the two projects. Both are related to transport and both are rather

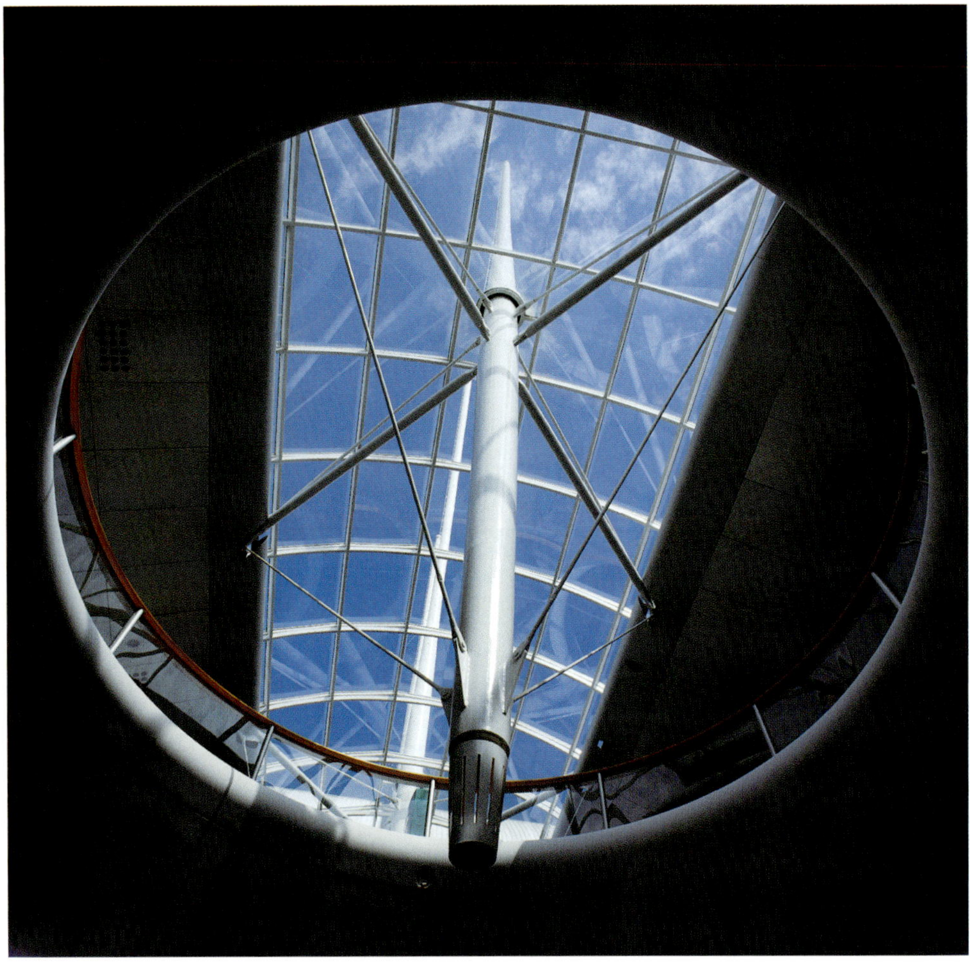

In the shopping center, the architect succeeds in creating spectacular perspectives and indulging in his favorite dark-light contrasts; this is no mean feat in a type of architecture usually devoid of esthetic interest.

pure creations of engineering and the practical needs involved with moving large numbers of people. It might be said, too that Roissy and the Calais project share an urban scale that brings Paul Andreu into the realm of the creation of rather specific types of ideal cities. Of course neither Roissy nor Calais need all of the facilities required by a full city, but the numbers of passengers they handle dictates a logic akin to that of a city. The airport and the tunnel support complex share practicality, a sense of light and space, and an overall efficiency, particularly modern French characteristics. These are in fact qualities shared by some French engineers and designers, Paul Andreu foremost amongst them.

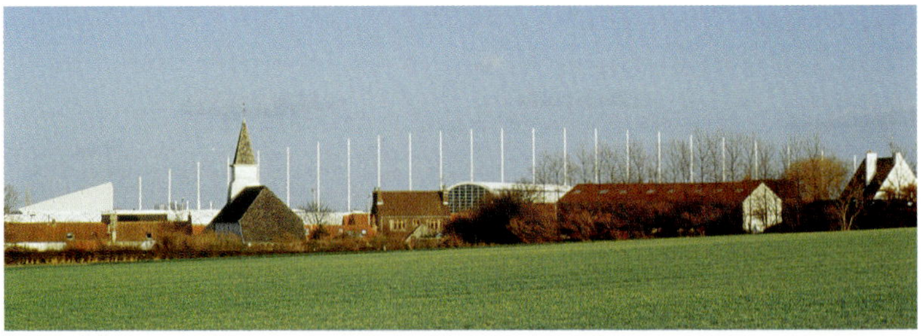

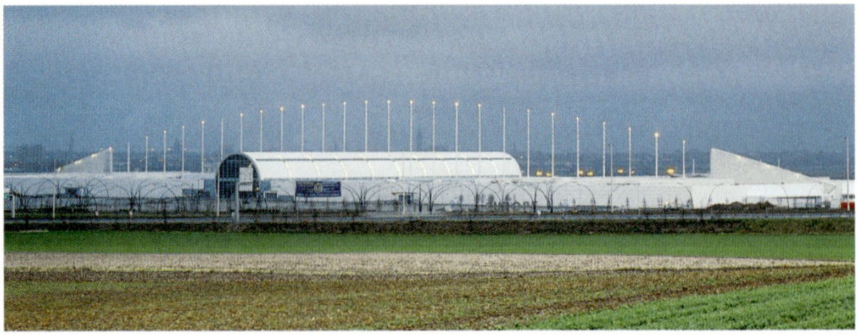

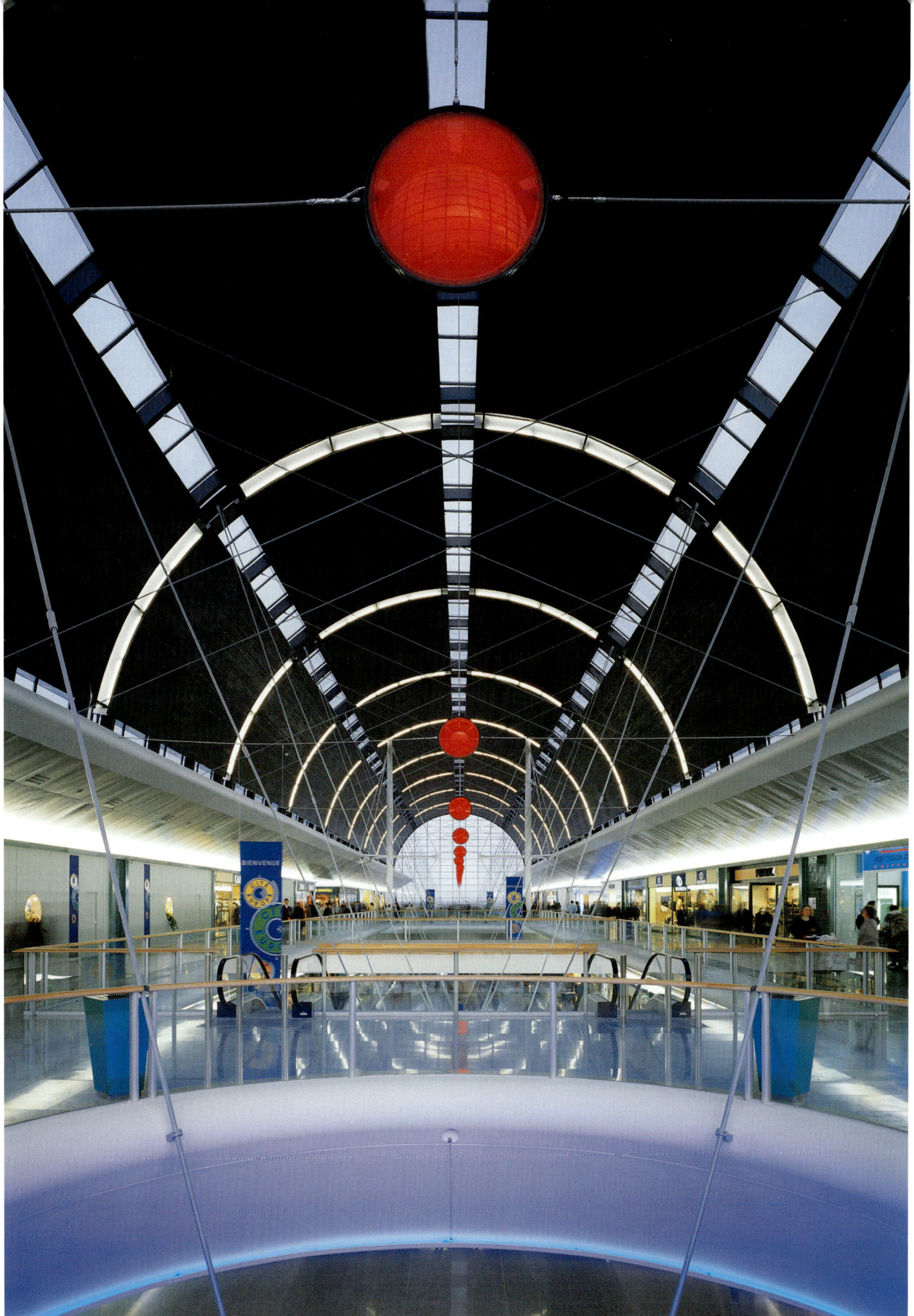

Channel Tunnel - French Terminal

Although the architecture of Kansai Airport was essentially the work of Renzo Piano and his Building Workshop, Paul Andreu laid the groundwork for the initial concept - linear terminals with their levels for the passenger traffic - the "Sandwich concept" and participated in its elaboration. Many of his favorite devices such as elevated roadways separated from the terminal buildings are seen here.

Kansai International Airport Osaka

architect Renzo Piano

Country: Japan
Use: Airport
Start of Project: 1987
Completion: 1994
Surface: 320,000 m²
Capacity: 25 million passengers per year

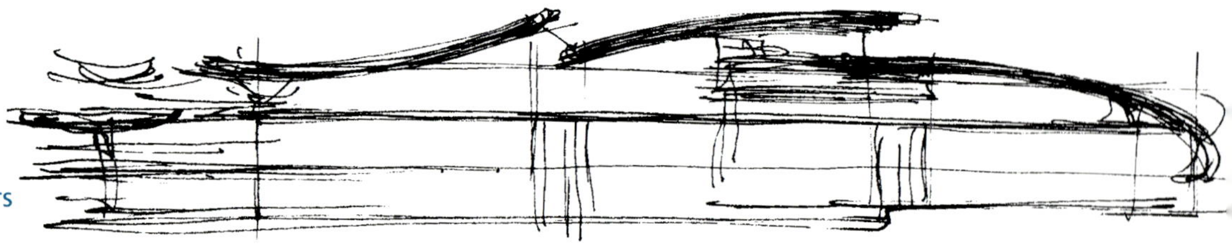

One of the largest architectural and engineering undertakings of the late twentieth century, Kansai International Airport was built on a 511-hectare artificial island located in the Bay of Osaka. Paul Andreu and Aéroports de Paris began working on the project in 1987. Although Andreu was not responsible for the actual architecture of the complex, he did lay the groundwork for the basic designs. An international team that included Nikken Sekkei, Japan Airport Consultants and Aéroports de Paris in fact jointly developed the project. As Andreu points, out, he was the first foreign architect called on by the Japanese authorities to develop a civil project on this scale. Certain concepts seen in at Roissy, in particular in the various halls of Terminal 2, have been used at Kansai. The very long shape of the main terminal building with its 42 contact points for aircraft looks very much like an elongated version of some of Andreu's designs. There is also a direct relation between the dissociation of entry roads and the "canyon" between the approach ramps and the terminal later seen in Andreu's Roissy 2 E and F buildings as well as his Bordeaux terminal. Andeu links this concept to his own observations of the St. Louis (Missouri) train station. The difference between this project and Roissy however is that it was built in a single phase. Given the high volume of traffic and the distances involved, devices such as an automated train to carry passengers to their gates were necessary. Nonetheless, simplicity and clarity, hallmarks of Paul Andreu's work on airports around the world are clearly present here. Renzo Piano as the architect was selected from a prestigious field in an international competition in 1988. The unusual curved shape of the 1.7-kilometer long main terminal building, is related to air traffic

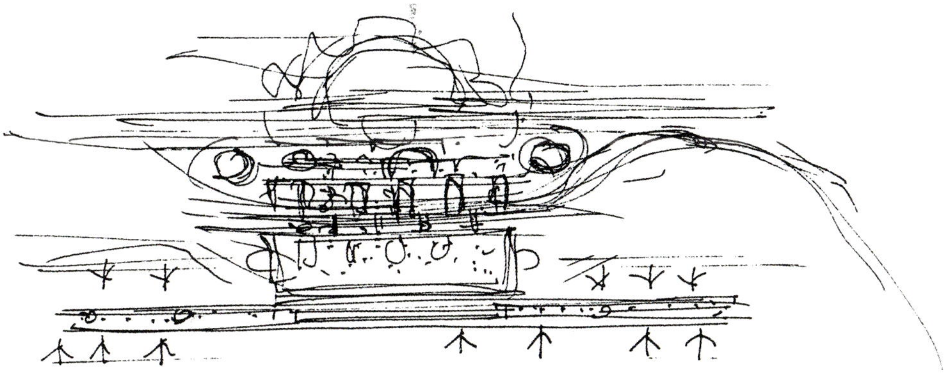

On the left a sketch by Paul Andreu shows a proposed curving roof pattern for the airport. On this page, an aerial view of the spectacular completed facility, which is entirely built on an artificial island. Paul Andreu's drawings, reproduced here were made before the competition, won by Renzo Piano and after the choice of the overall concept by the Japanese authorities.

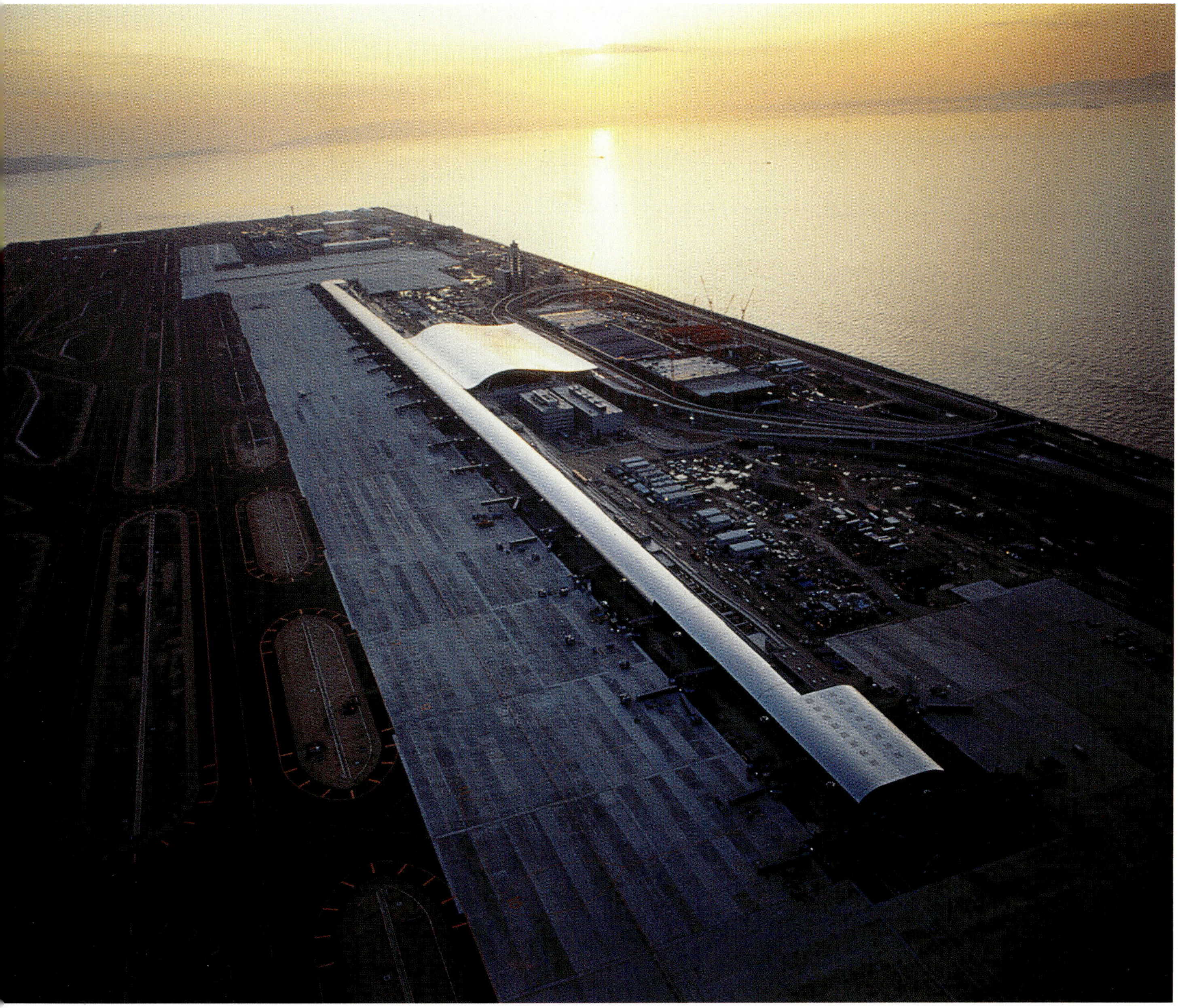

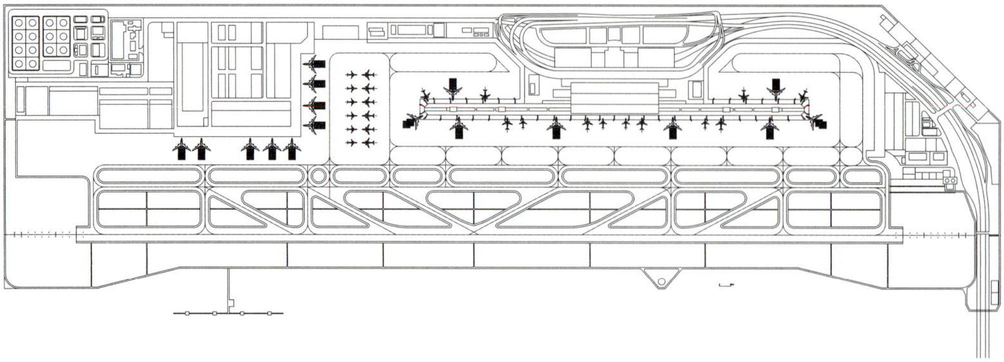

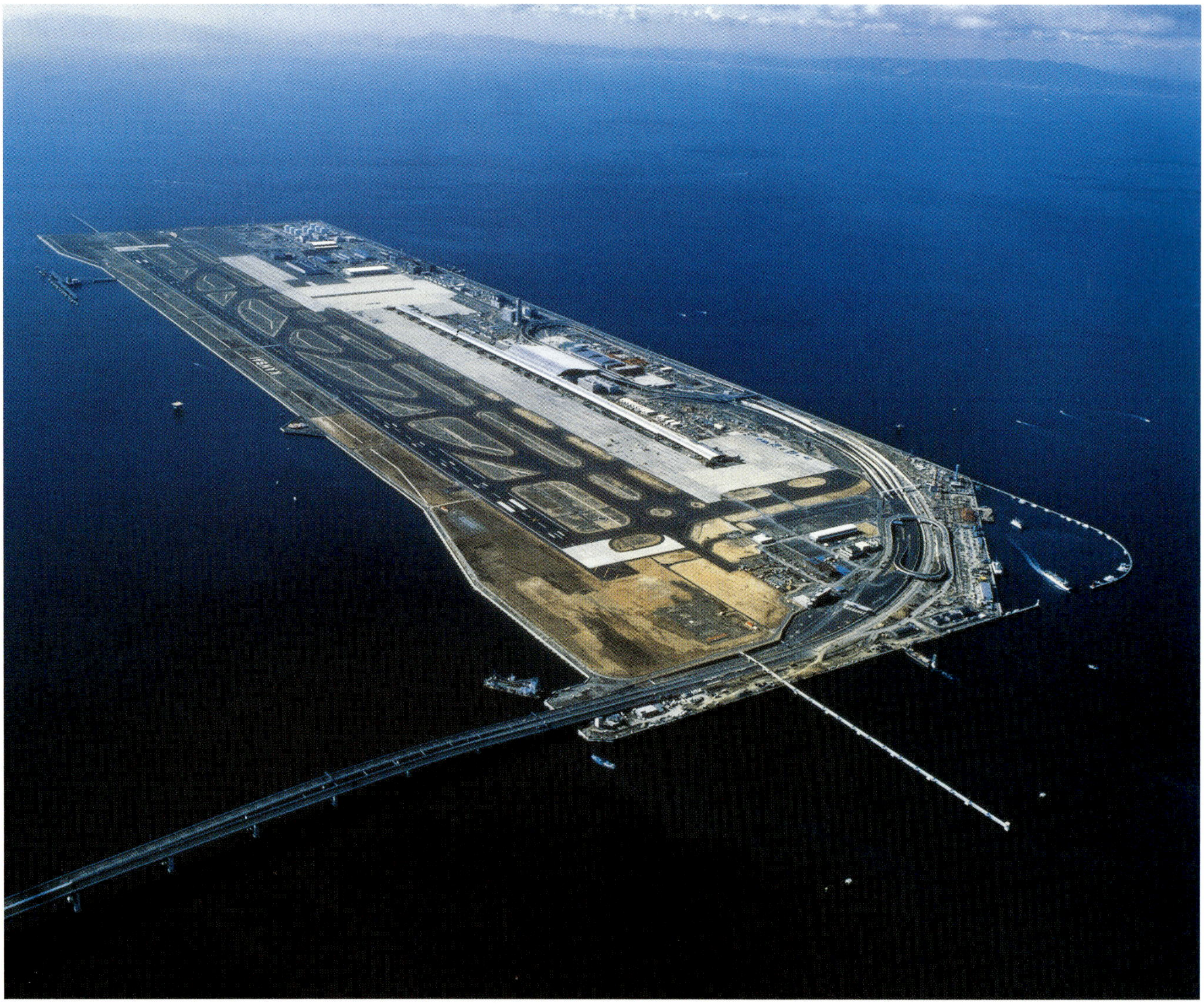

Andreu's drawings for the airport confirm the fundamental outline of the completed facility as seen in another aerial photo. It can be said that the functional aspects of Kansai Airport are directly related to Paul Andreu's studies of the subject.

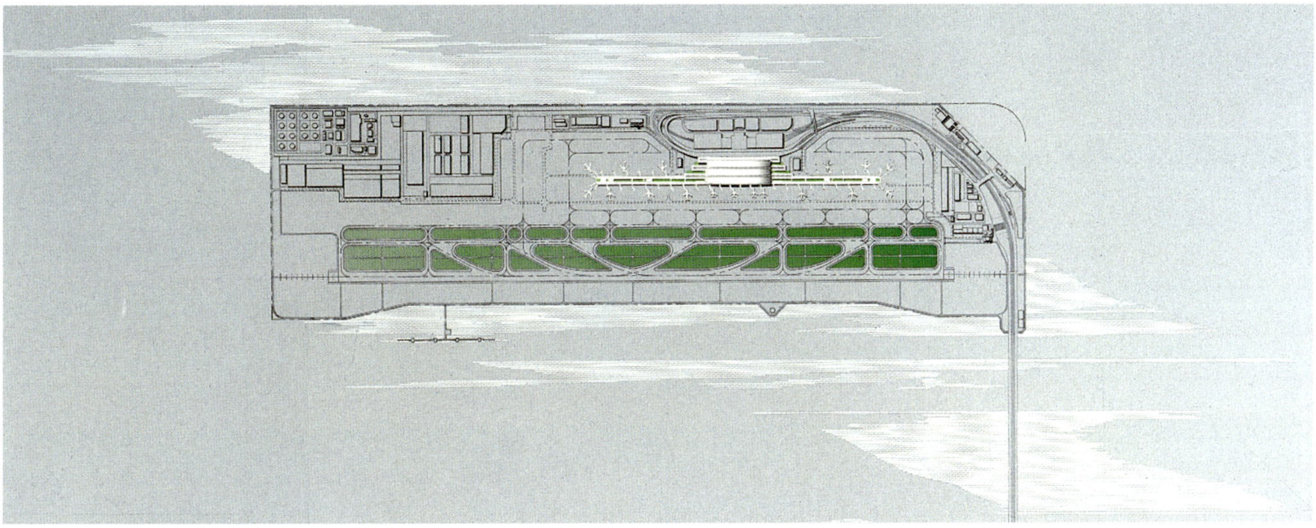

control need to maintain visual contact with taxiing aircraft at all times. The curve of the terminal was in fact conceived as a small section of an imaginary 32.8-kilometer diameter torus, whose main volume would be underground. With its 83-meter long arches on the upper floor, the terminal offers a real feeling of freedom to travelers. It should be noted that the construction of such a large building on an artificial island posed many technical problems, solved in good part with the assistance of Ove Arup & Partners using a system of hydraulic joints designed to compensate for the predicted settling of the landfill. Simply put, the traveler finds his way easily in this airport and even more important feels comfortable at all times. Seen from the air, the 82,000 stainless steel panels covering the 90,000 square meter roof often shine in the sun offering a more congenial image than almost any other modern airport in the world.
The 320,000 square meter facility completed in 1994 was designed for annual traffic of 25 million passengers. The scale of Kansai International Airport is such that it coincidentally gave rise to a series of other projects, such as Tadao Ando's Awaji Yumebutai complex built on the nearby island of Awaji on the site deeply scarred by the extraction of landfill for the airport. Paul Andreu and his collaborators put a great deal of time and effort into developing the second phase of Kansai Airport in the late 1990's, but this expansion, which will eventually be necessary, was put on hold because of the prevailing economic situation.

Working on a smaller scale than in most cases, Paul Andreu here succeeds in putting forward not his own ego as an architect, but rather the function and beauty of a sport. This acceptance of the modesty befitting of the designer who serves his client and his project is a tribute to Andreu's personality.

Ski Jump - Winter Olympics **Courchevel**

Country: France
Use: Ski jump
Start of project: 1988
Completion: 1991
Lenghts of jumps: 70 m / 90 m
Capacity: 24,000 spectators

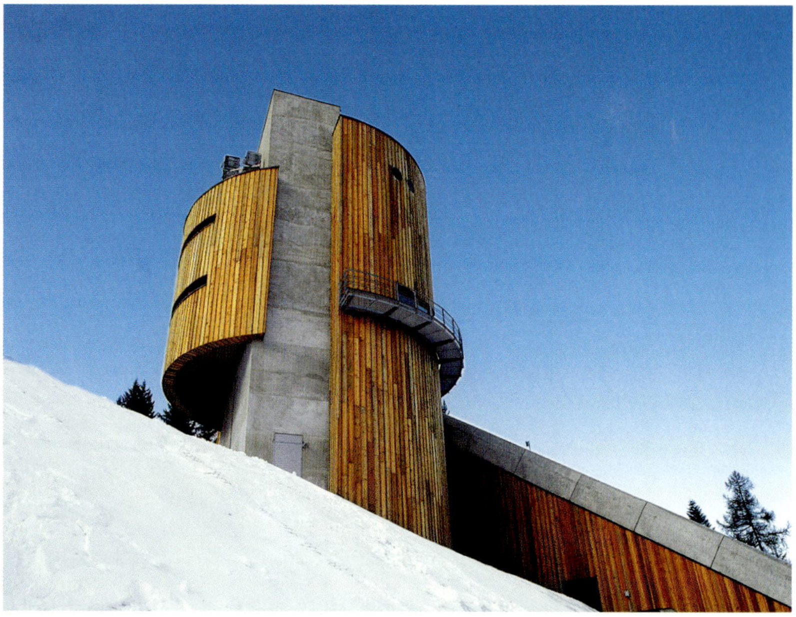

The simple powerful lines of the ski jump give an indication of Paul Andreu's ability to adapt his talents to the very specific requirements of this sport. Far from attempting to give an "airport" feeling to the facility, he has given the leading role to the ski jump, and thus to the athletes themselves.

The Three Valley ski area of France is the world largest with 188 ski lifts and 600 kilometers of trails. It includes five resorts: Courchevel, Meribel, Val Thorens, Les Menuires and La Tania. Paul Andreu was called on to design the ski jump facilities in Courchevel in time for the 1992 Winter Olympics. Though the Winter Games were based in nearby Albertville, the Ski Jumping event took place here. Taking on a task that was obviously quite different than airport design, Andreu went about his work in a carefully studied way. "I spent a lot of time trying to understand the mechanics of ski jumping," he says, "from beginning to end. I mean from the time the skier leaves his or her hotel, takes the life, warms up, concentrates, and finally faces the terrifying slope to do the best and longest jump possible." The architect underlines the basic

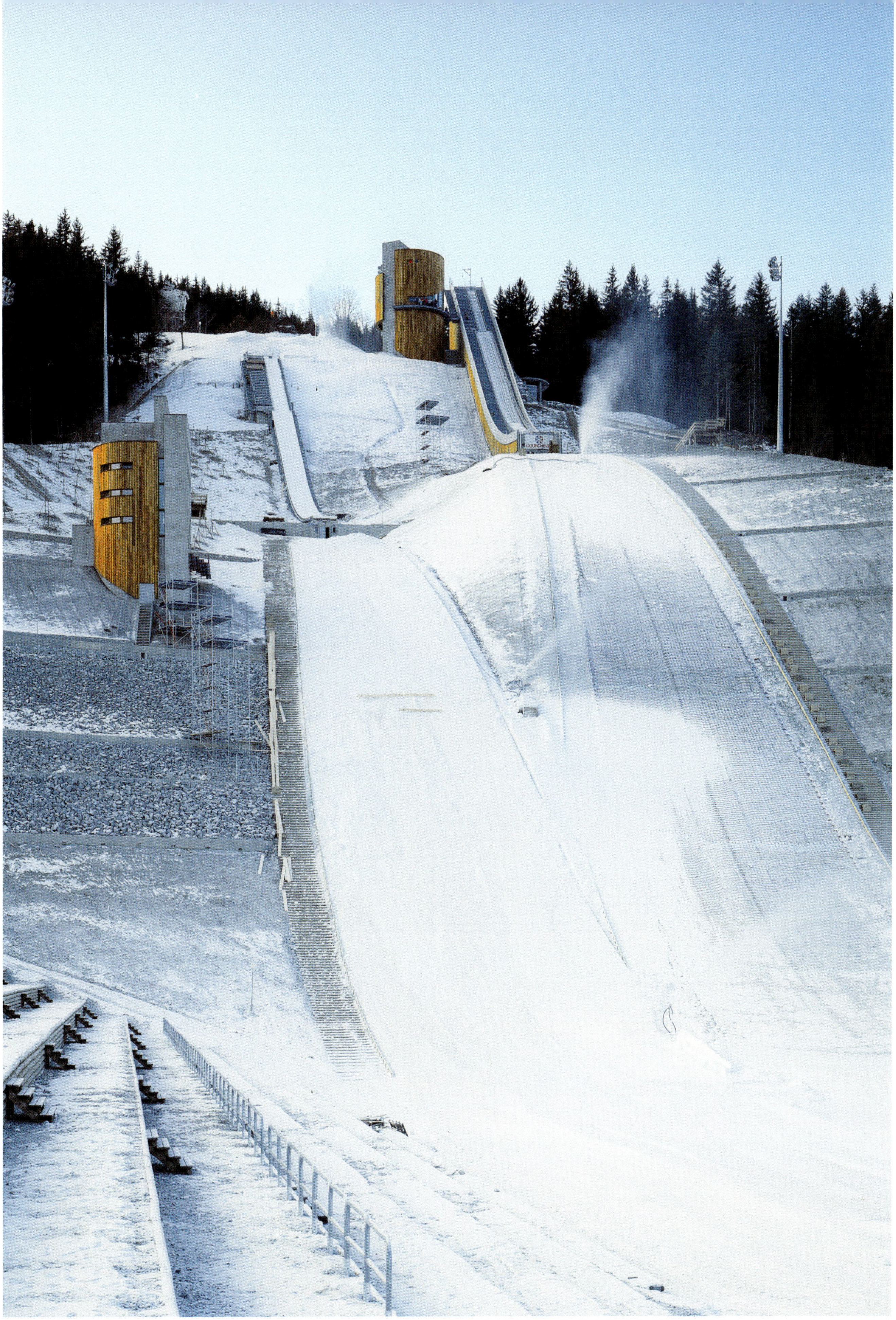

The curved forms and the use of concrete and wood corresponds well both to the natural environment, the site and the architectural style of ski resorts. With its angled windows, the tower to the right emphasizes the slope and indeed gives some of the sense of movement that Andreu often gives to his work.

functional geometries that dictate form in this instance, much as he would analyze transportation facilities. It should be obvious that the case of the ski jump is somewhat particular and does also involve flight, albeit in a less industrial mode than airports imply. "There are at least seven or eight geometrical constraints determining the settling and the form of the building: vertical and horizontal viewing angles, relative heights, etc.," says Andreu, "I grouped the judges tower for both jumps in the same construction. Afterwards, I decided not to try to do anything more than transcribe the functional exigencies, so that the close relationship between the judges' tower, the ski jumps and the surrounding landscape could be understood or felt." Working with the Committee for the Organization of the Olympic Games (COJO) and Aéroports de Paris, Andreu created a facility with two jumps – 70 and 90 meter runs, and a capacity of 24,000 spectators.
Paul Andreu also puts great emphasis on such basic matters of the line of sight of visitors, judges and skiers. His design is obviously subordinated to functional constraints, but in a way this is a signature element of his style. First he solves the technical problems involved with a project, he seeks out the most efficient engineering and architectural solutions for the basic shape keeping in mind not only the basics, but also the overall effect of the design. In this instance, he has truly concentrated on the needs of the facility, creating

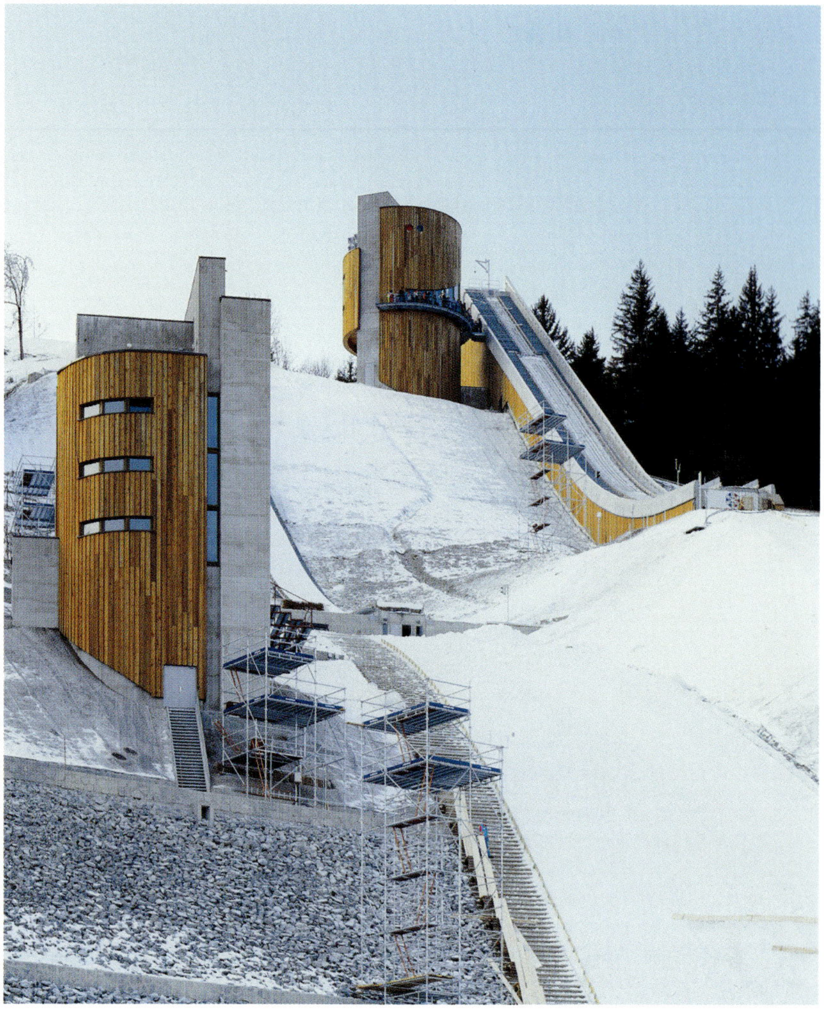

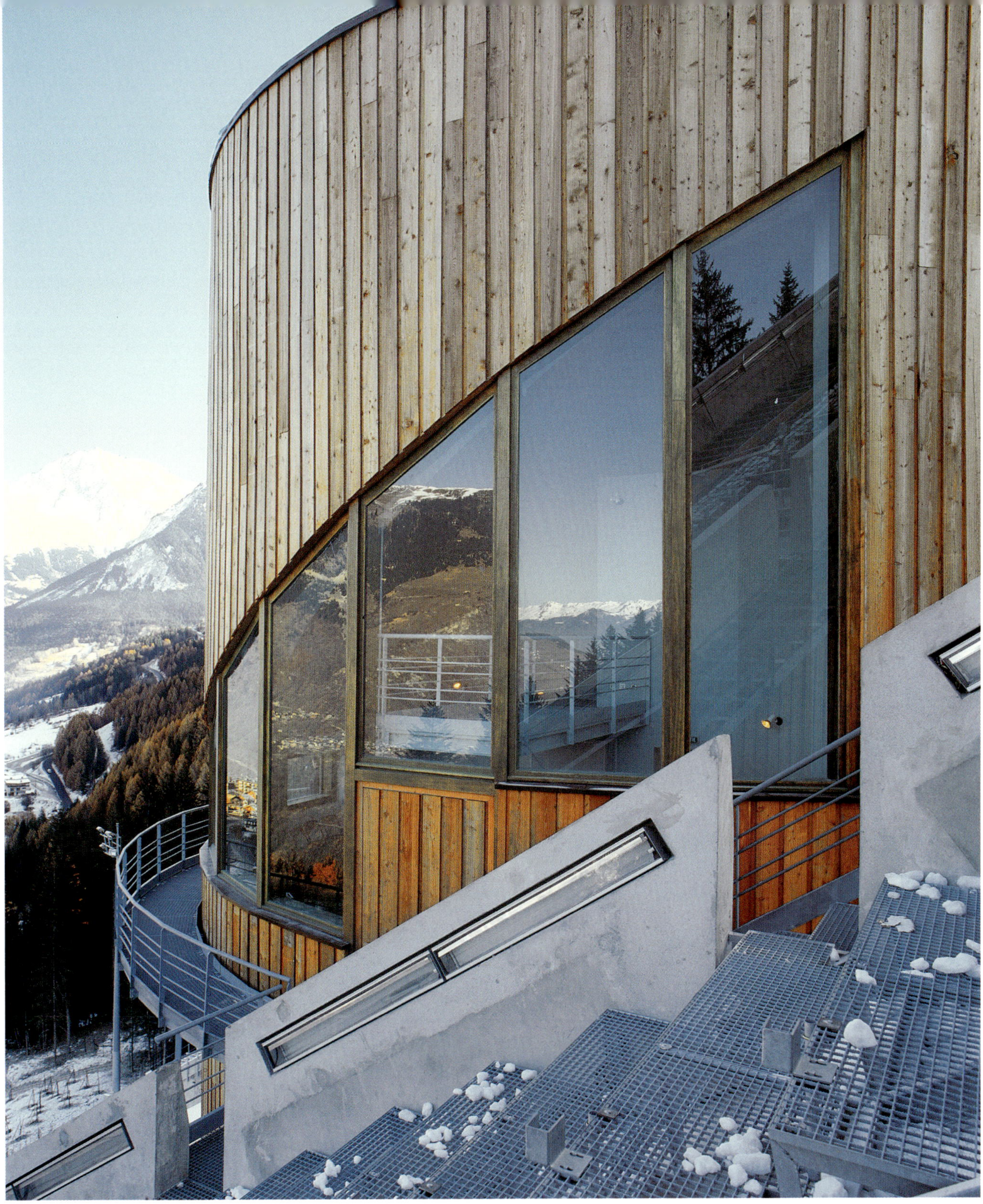

an elongated six-level semi-circular tower at the top of the jump for the various facilities. Andreu compares the focus of this structure on ski run, sky and earth to the single-minded organization of the observatories at Jaipur with their oblique ramps. "For the rest," he says, "everything is simple and associated to the landscape: the buildings are faced with wood in their rounded parts, whereas the flat parts expose the concrete. The same materials are used for the ski run, faced with wood over its entire height and ending in banks of concrete, a line in space, what is left of the idea that everything 'floats' in the air."

With its airy, undulating roof the Bordeaux airport achieves new standards of combined efficiency and transparency. Having mastered all the basics of airport design, Andreu is here free to let his imagination soar, despite, or perhaps because of the small size of the project.

Bordeaux Mérignac Airport **Bordeaux**

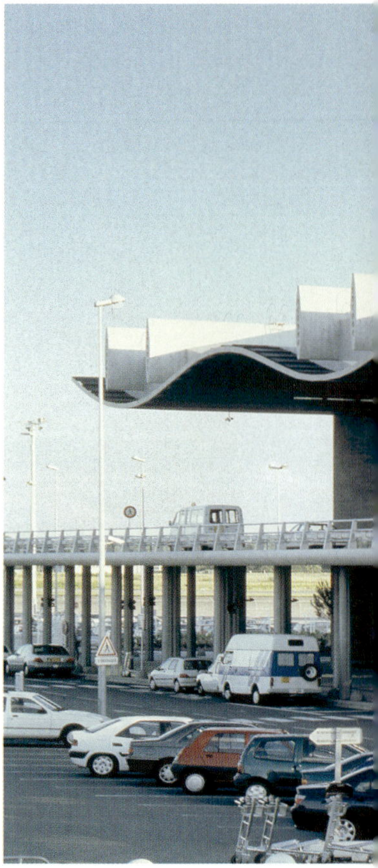

Country: France
Use: Airport
Start of project: 1989
Completion: 1996
Surface: 15,000 m^2
Capacity: 2.5 million passengers per year

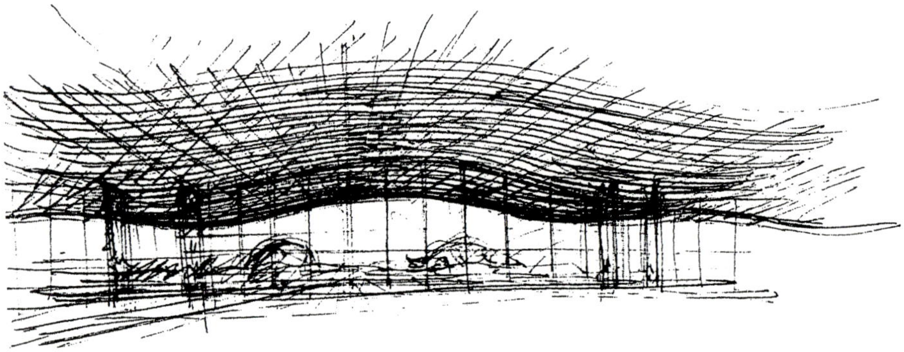

Put into service in 1996, this small facility is intended to handle 2.5 million passengers per year. With a terminal building area of 15,000 square meters, it has four locations for docked aircraft and includes 4,000 parking spots. As Andreu points out, the concentration of airport facilities in a relatively restricted volume does not simplify the task of the architect; rather it becomes more difficult to achieve the high degree

With its undulating form, the Bordeaux Mérignac airport provides a recognizable architectural form evoking waves or flight while retaining the transparency that has come to be a hallmark of Andreu's architecture. An elevated access roadway allows, as is frequently the case in his airports, light to enter all levels.

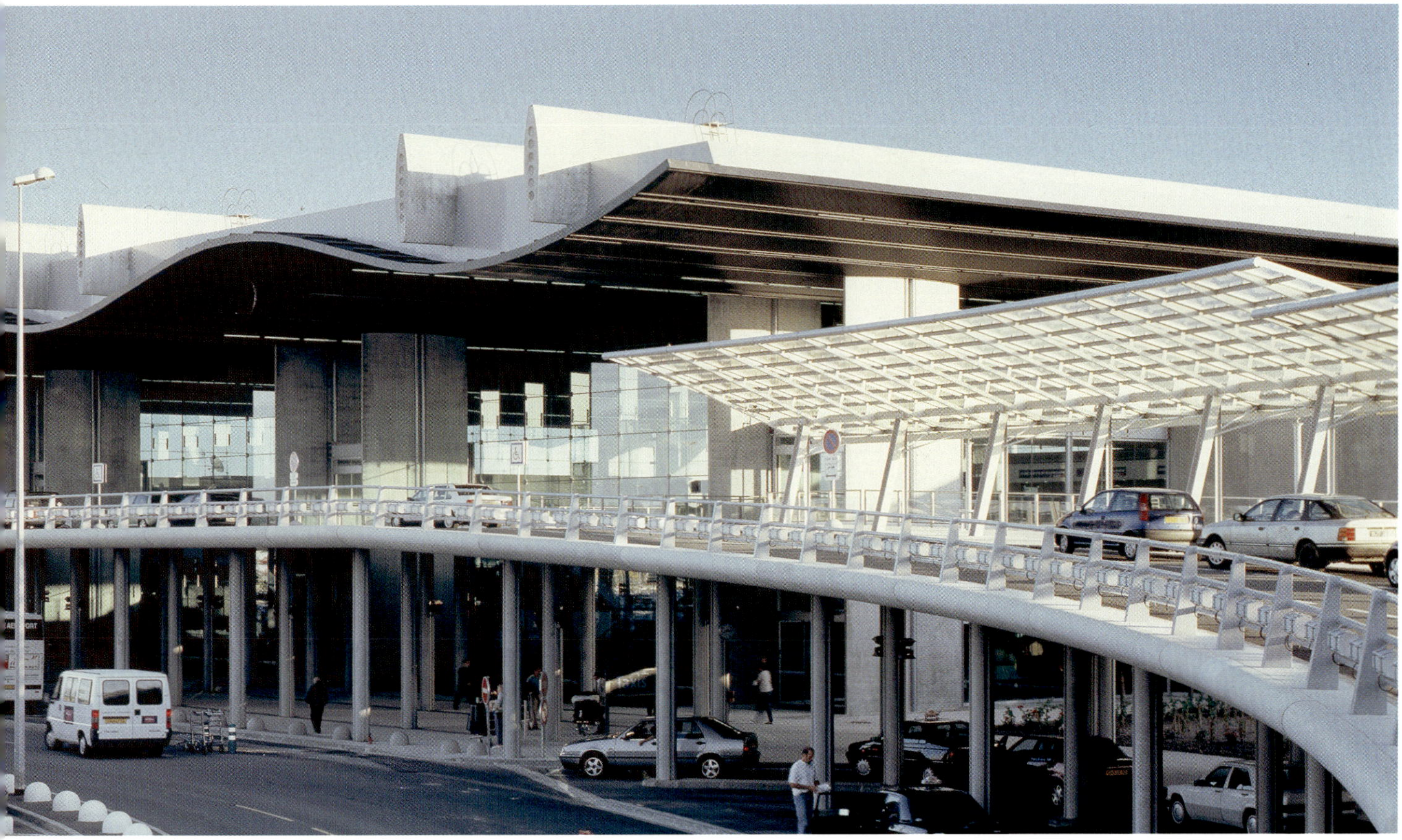

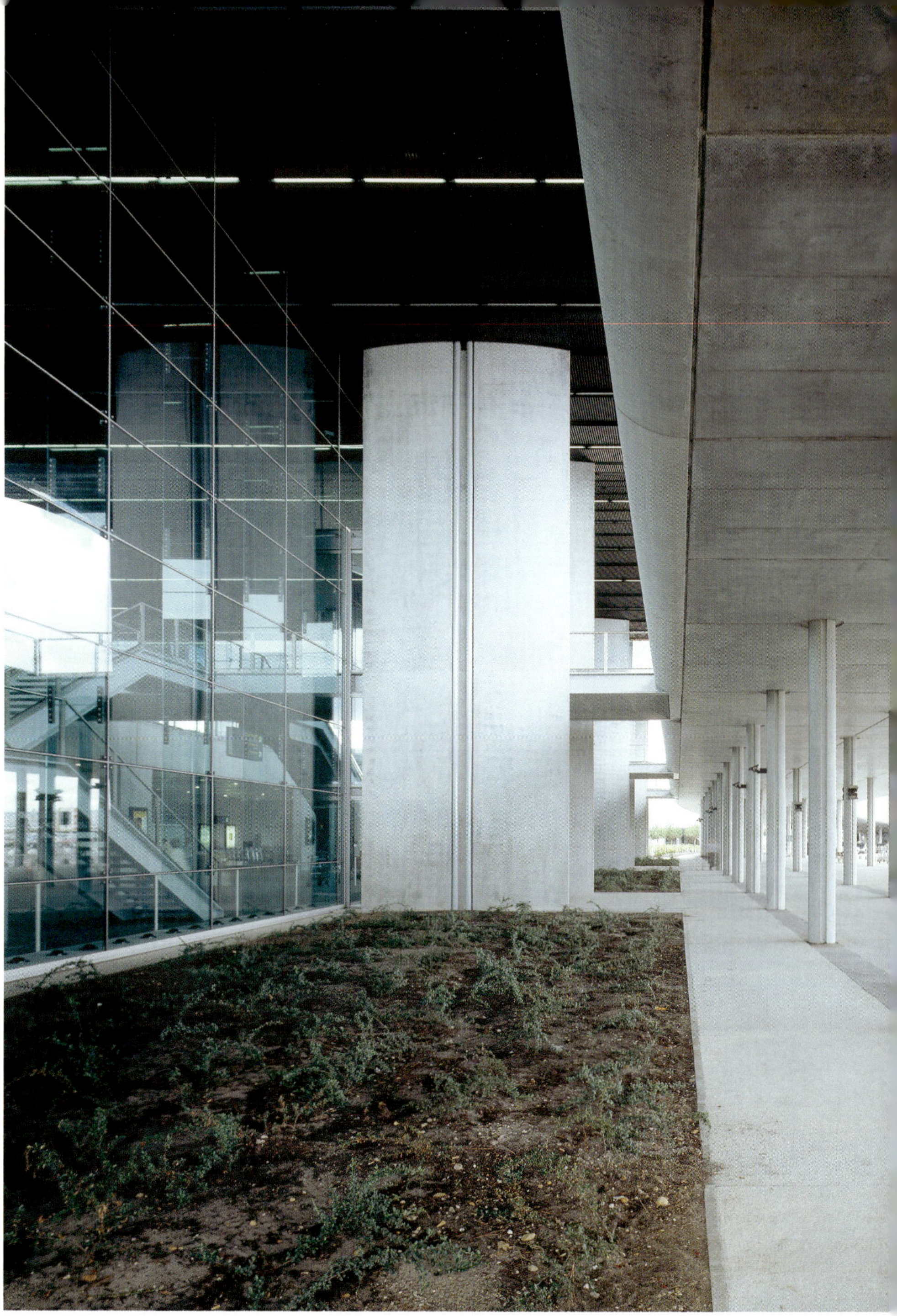

114 The elevated roadway seen from below, with its gap or "canyon" between the actual deck and terminal building is a clever device for making both the upper and lower levels equally attractive and light-filled. Andreu also carefully finishes the underside of the roadway to make it appealing and not give an impression of overhanging weight.

of transparency and simplicity that he seeks in larger airports. Here, Paul Andreu faced the complex task of integrating a new terminal into existing facilities, and simultaneously providing for future expansions. His solution, a strong, undulating, open-ended roof appears to solve all of these problems at once. With its inherently repetitive pattern, this roof seems to invite extension, and indeed does facilitate it in technical terms. Eight pairs of columns support four 80-meter long double beams that permit wide-open interior spaces. The idea of a "canyon" also seen in Renzo Piano's Kansai Airport is given form here albeit on a smaller scale. A 16-meter high glass wall divides the interior and exterior elements of this high public space that offers views of each level. Ticketing counters,

Inside the terminal, the contrast between the undulating roof and the transparency of the glazed walls is very much in the spirit of Andreu's architecture. His use of dark surfaces and spaces only gives more value to the presence of light.

boarding areas, baggage claim spaces below and escalators are all visible to travelers practically from the moment they step out of their car or bus. Partially inspired by Terminal 2 at the Nice Airport, this structure is in Andreu's mind even simpler, more direct in its approach. The ceiling inside is made up of black tubular panels running in the same direction as passenger flow. Paul Andreu, who also used a black ceiling in his first Nice terminal, says, "black more than any other color, reflects the subtle nuances of sunlight." The architect also took into account the appearance of the terminal from the approach road, and as he says, the undulating roof draws a simple line in the sky with the setting sun behind

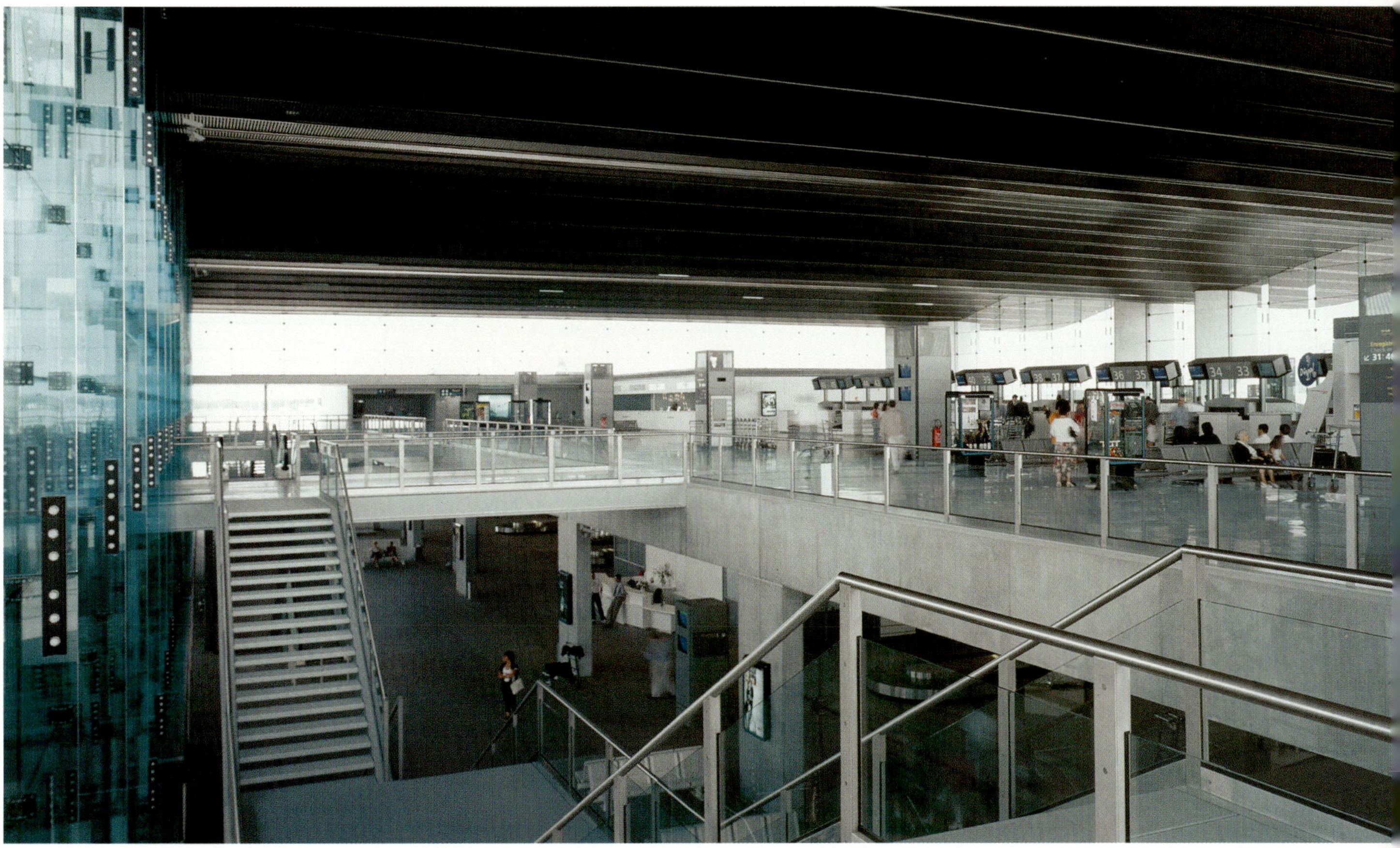

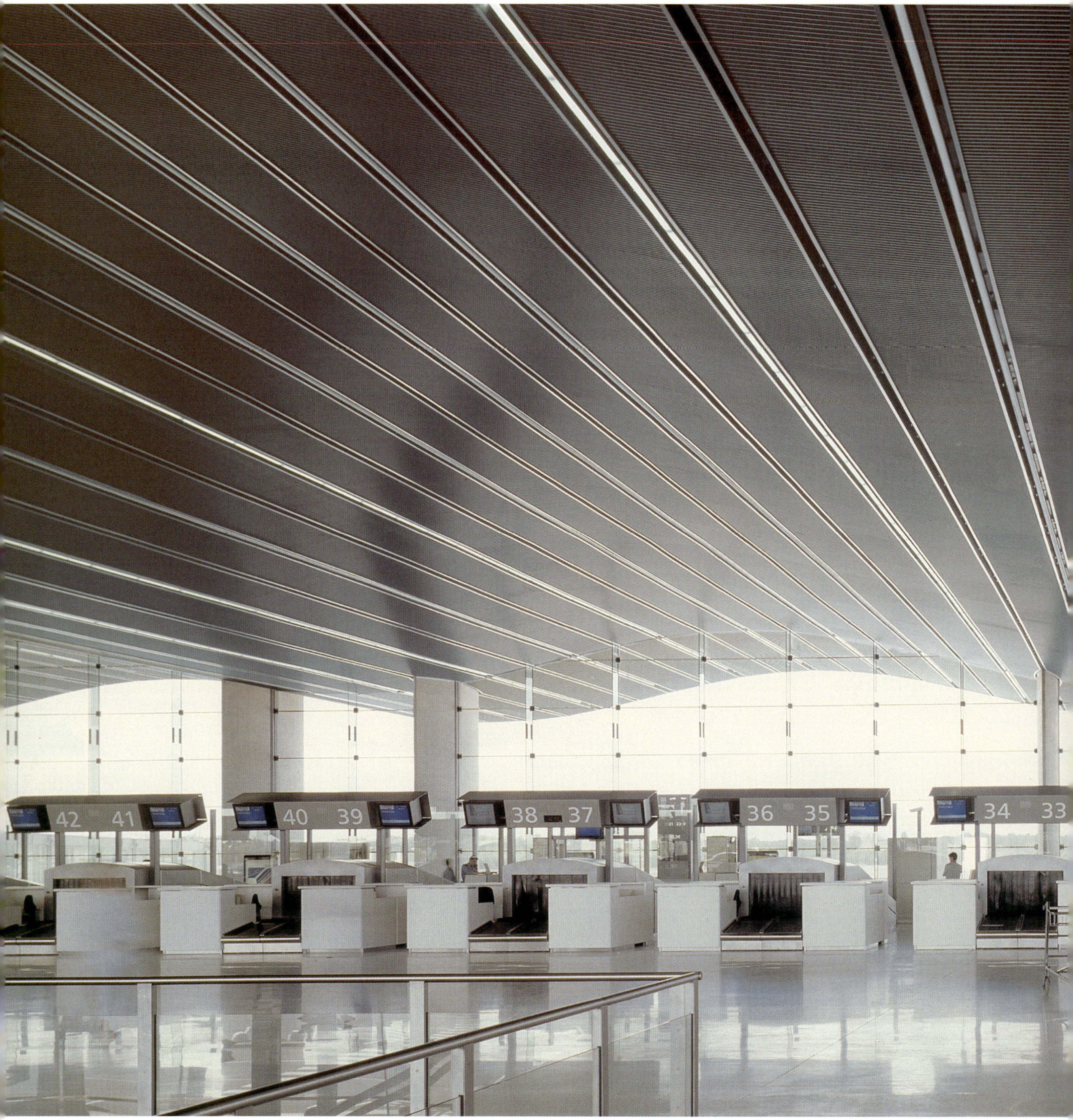
42
41
40
39
38
37
36
35
34
33

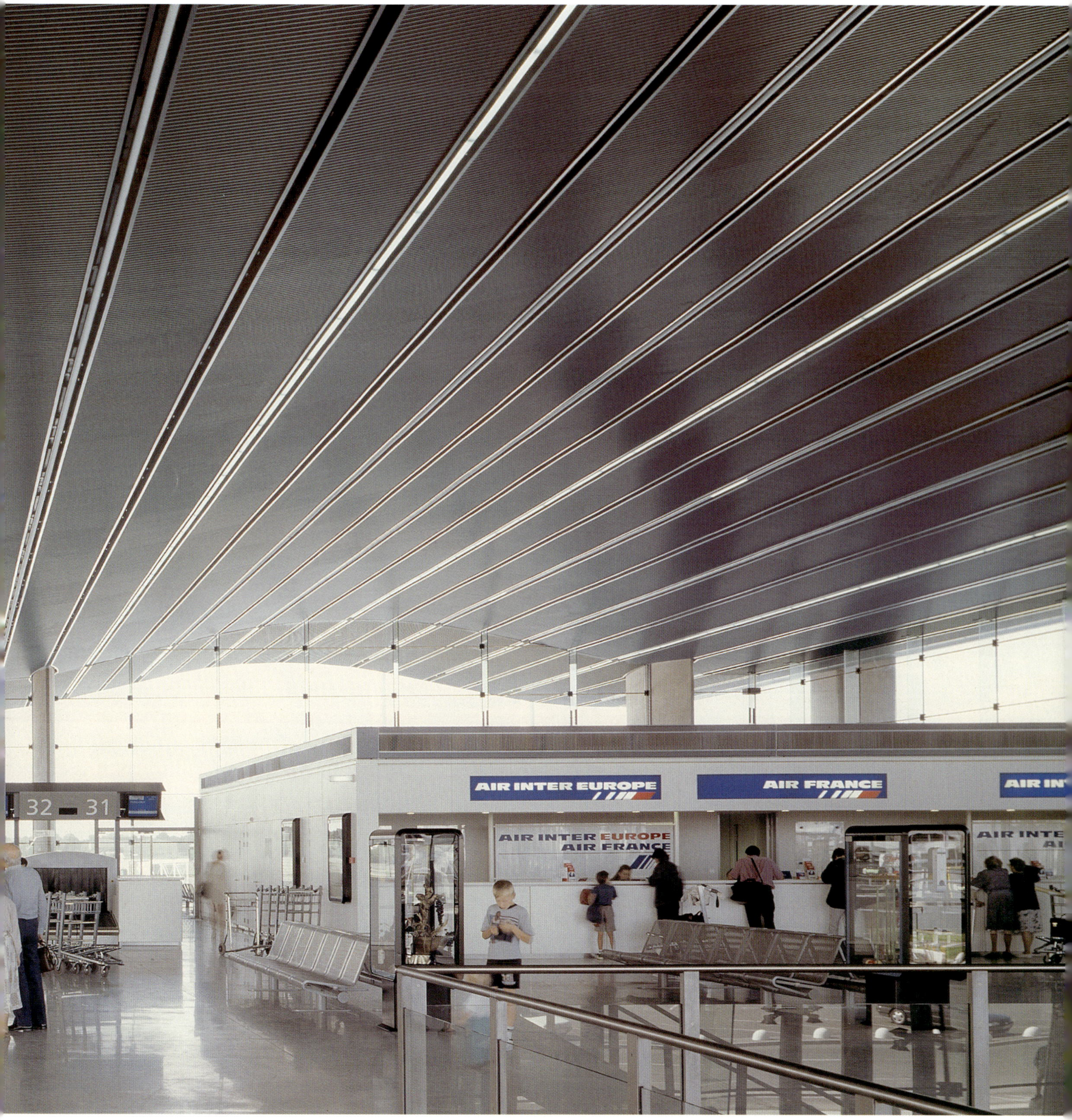

Bordeaux Mérignac Airport

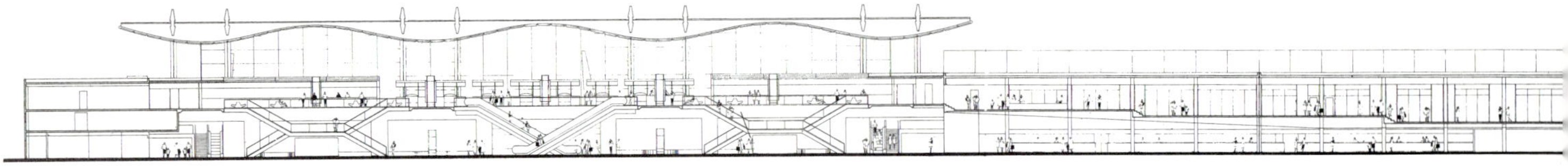

it. In both plan and section, Bordeaux Mérignac Terminal 2 is one of the most straightforward of Andreu's projects, adopting an almost orthogonal (rectangular in this case) layout. Even the car park, which sometimes tends toward amoebic shapes in his designs is essentially rectangular here, while approach roads avoid some of the complex loops seen for example at Roissy. In a way, Mérignac may be one of the first clear signs of a growing maturity and simplicity in Andreu's airport design and architecture in general. Whereas his earlier work did make use of simple forms, the swirling complexity of buildings such as Roissy Terminal 1 is replaced in an admittedly smaller building in Bordeaux by an almost rectilinear purity. Light, always important in Andreu's designs seems now to make its way more readily into his buildings, though contrast between light and dark (black ceilings in Nice or Bordeaux) remains a steady element. An absence of strong color is also a steady factor together with an engineer's reliance on rather spectacular techniques to achieve the apparent simplicity of completed spaces. Flexibility in the face of existing installations or future expansion is another factor that Andreu's airport work almost imposed on him – and yet many architects never learn to master this kind of complexity. How to be repetitive out of necessity without ever lapsing into boredom and lack of inspiration – this is a question that lies at the heart of Paul Andreu's success as an architect.

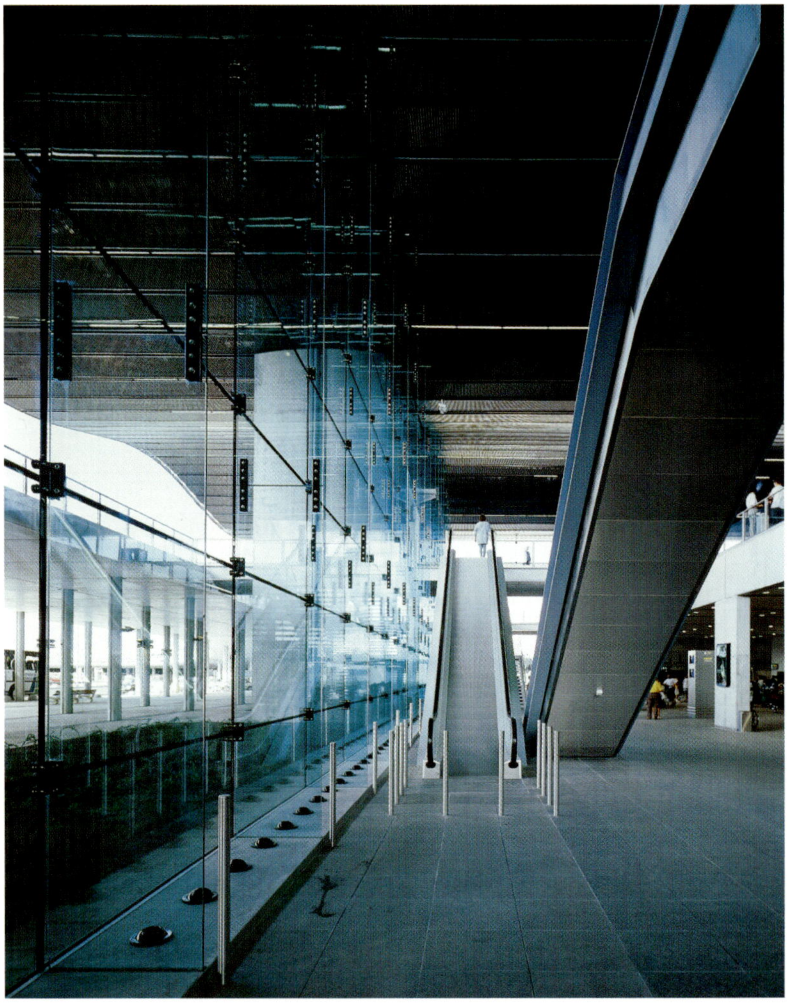

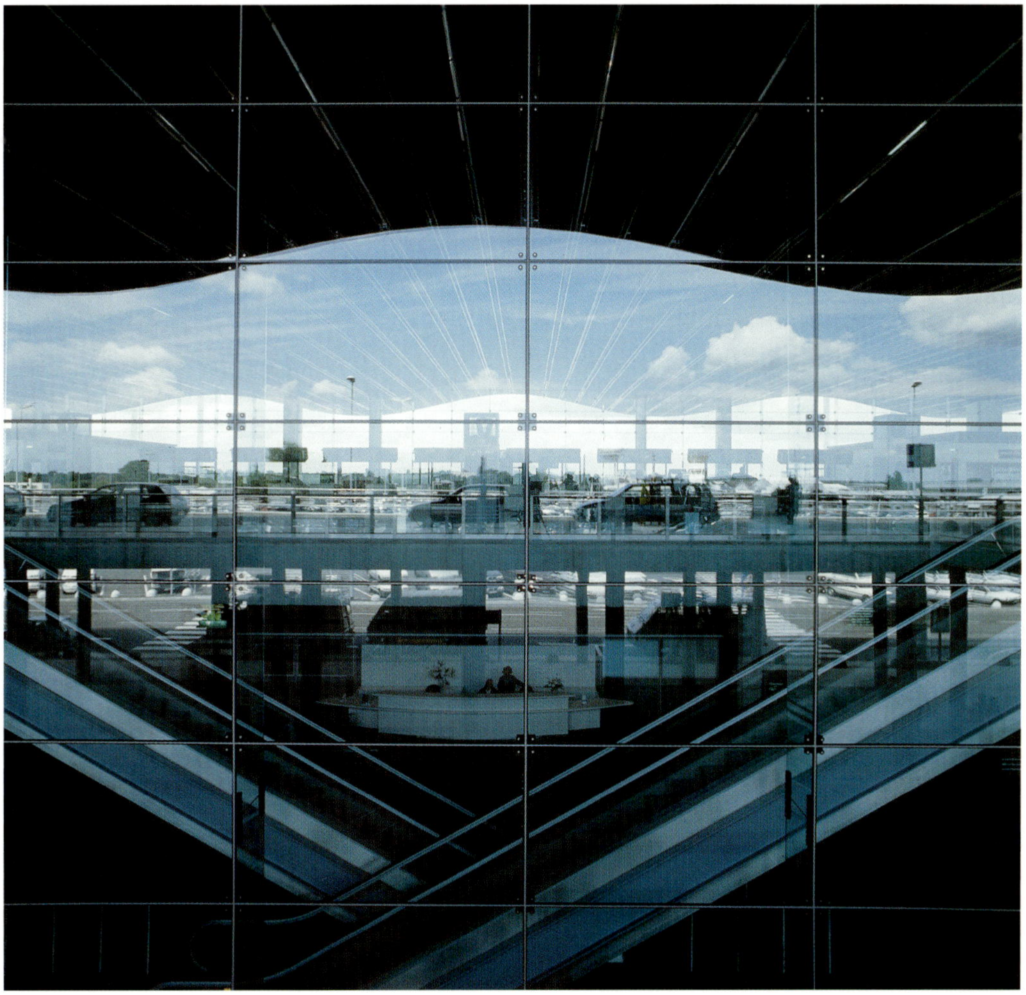

With the large openings and suspended moving walkways, the interior of the terminal continues the impression of lightness and flight already given by the undulating roof. Relatively small by the standards of Andreu's usual airport work, Bordeaux Mérignac achieves standards of openness and coherence that surpass those of some naturally more complex large facilities.

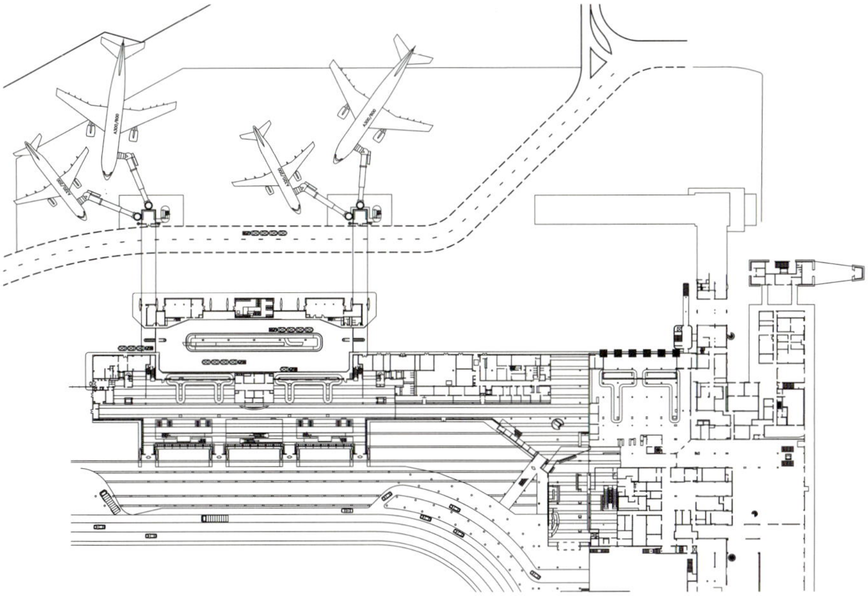

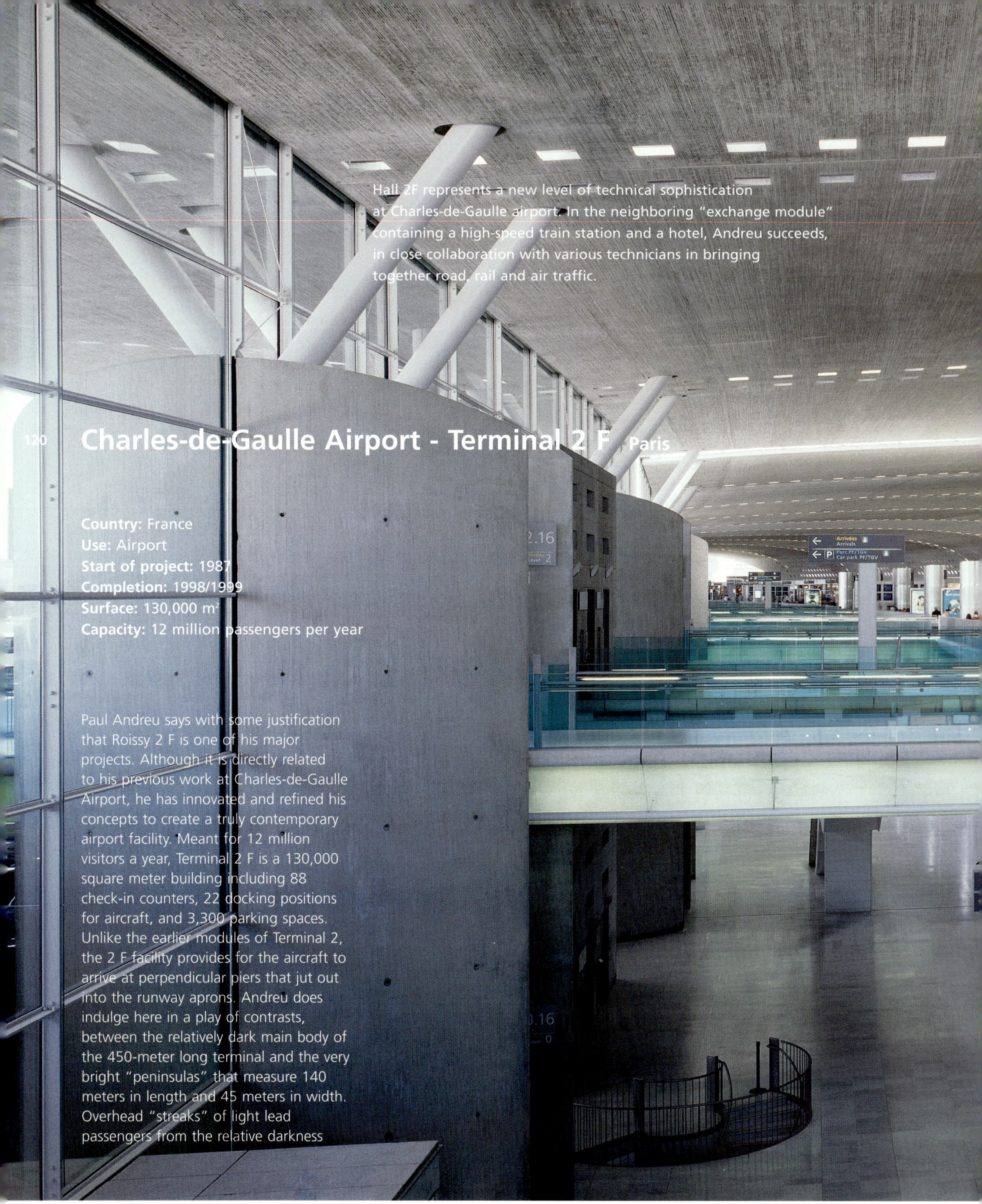

Hall 2F represents a new level of technical sophistication at Charles-de-Gaulle airport. In the neighboring "exchange module" containing a high-speed train station and a hotel, Andreu succeeds, in close collaboration with various technicians in bringing together road, rail and air traffic.

Charles-de-Gaulle Airport - Terminal 2 F Paris

Country: France
Use: Airport
Start of project: 1987
Completion: 1998/1999
Surface: 130,000 m^2
Capacity: 12 million passengers per year

Paul Andreu says with some justification that Roissy 2 F is one of his major projects. Although it is directly related to his previous work at Charles-de-Gaulle Airport, he has innovated and refined his concepts to create a truly contemporary airport facility. Meant for 12 million visitors a year, Terminal 2 F is a 130,000 square meter building including 88 check-in counters, 22 docking positions for aircraft, and 3,300 parking spaces. Unlike the earlier modules of Terminal 2, the 2 F facility provides for the aircraft to arrive at perpendicular piers that jut out into the runway aprons. Andreu does indulge here in a play of contrasts, between the relatively dark main body of the 450-meter long terminal and the very bright "peninsulas" that measure 140 meters in length and 45 meters in width. Overhead "streaks" of light lead passengers from the relative darkness

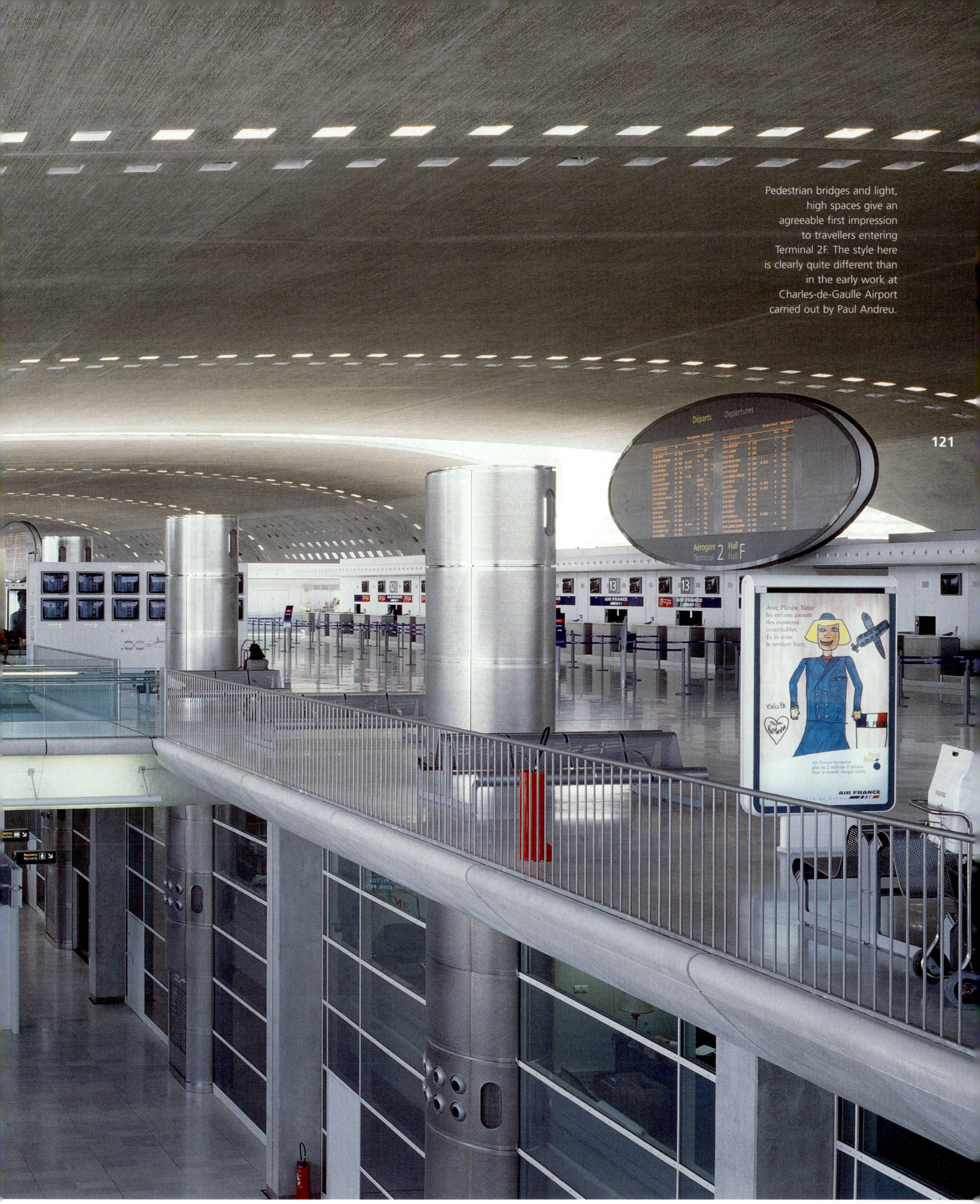

Pedestrian bridges and light, high spaces give an agreeable first impression to travellers entering Terminal 2F. The style here is clearly quite different than in the early work at Charles-de-Gaulle Airport carried out by Paul Andreu.

In the actual boarding areas, the 2 F Terminal takes on an entirely different appearance than its predecessors. With its large glazed openings and soaring forms it evokes flight in a much more "airborne" mode than the other Roissy facilities. Though views to the aircraft are available, the traveller is also drawn upwards by the skylights.

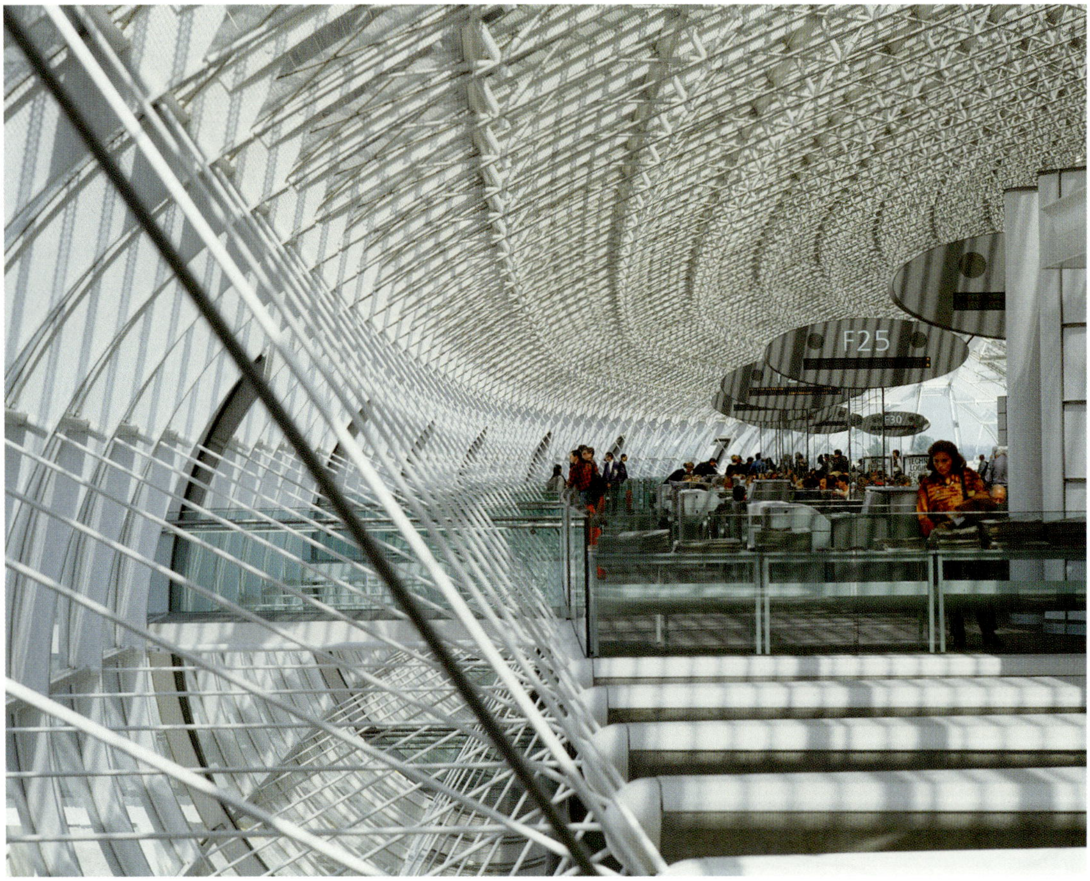

toward the bright space reserved to their departure, but even in the main body of the terminal, there is an undeniable feeling of generous space, due to the 70-meter span of the shell. Once in these spaces, travelers need only walk a few steps to get on the aircraft. Lounge areas located in the leading volumes of the peninsulas are particularly luminous and

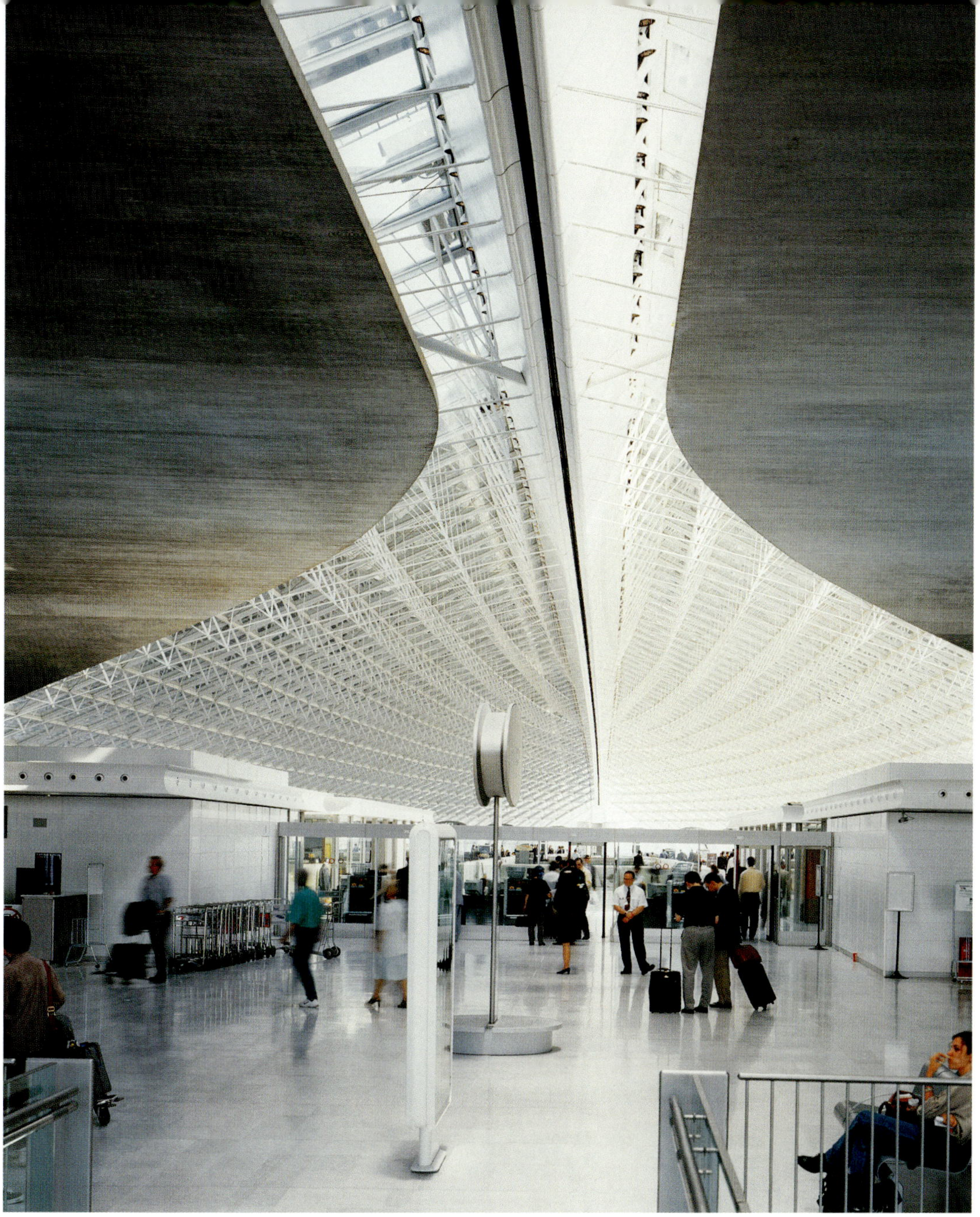

123

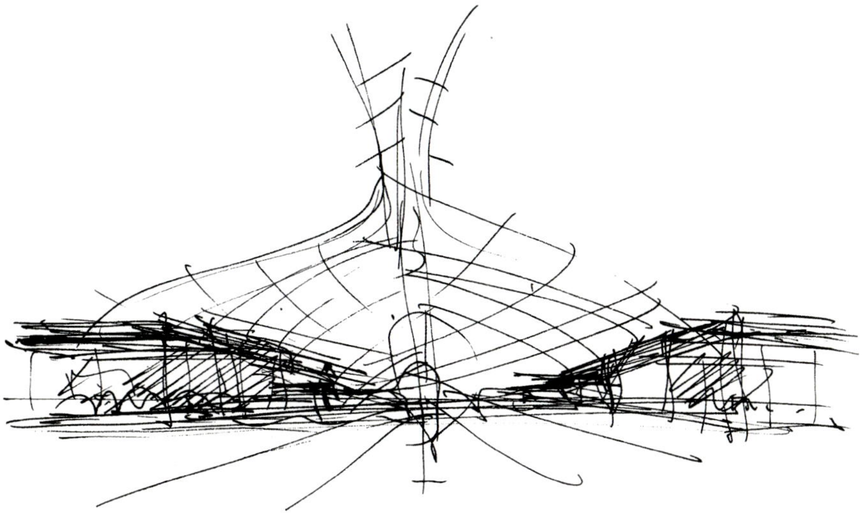

Charles-de-Gaulle Airport - Terminal 2 F

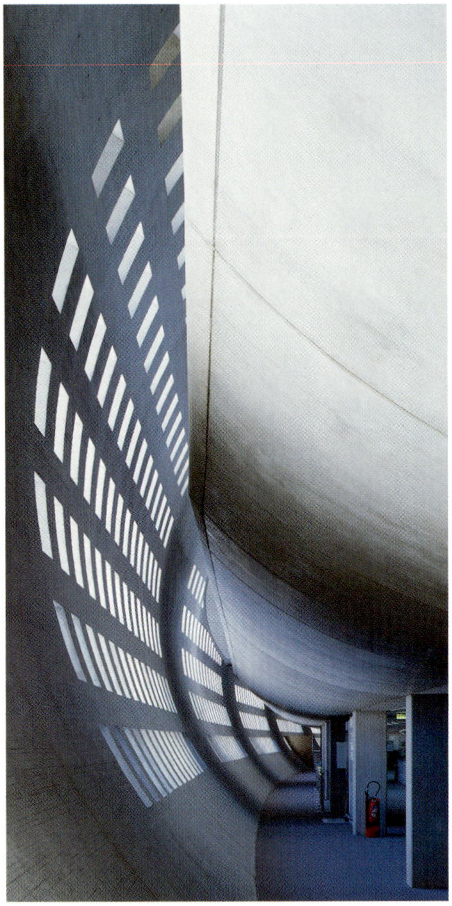

Wrap-around, curving forms define the exterior presence of Terminal 2 F as seen from the runway side (right). Within, these curves correspond to largely glazed walls that bring ample natural light into the building during the day. The effect of transparency is reversed at night when the Terminal glows from within.

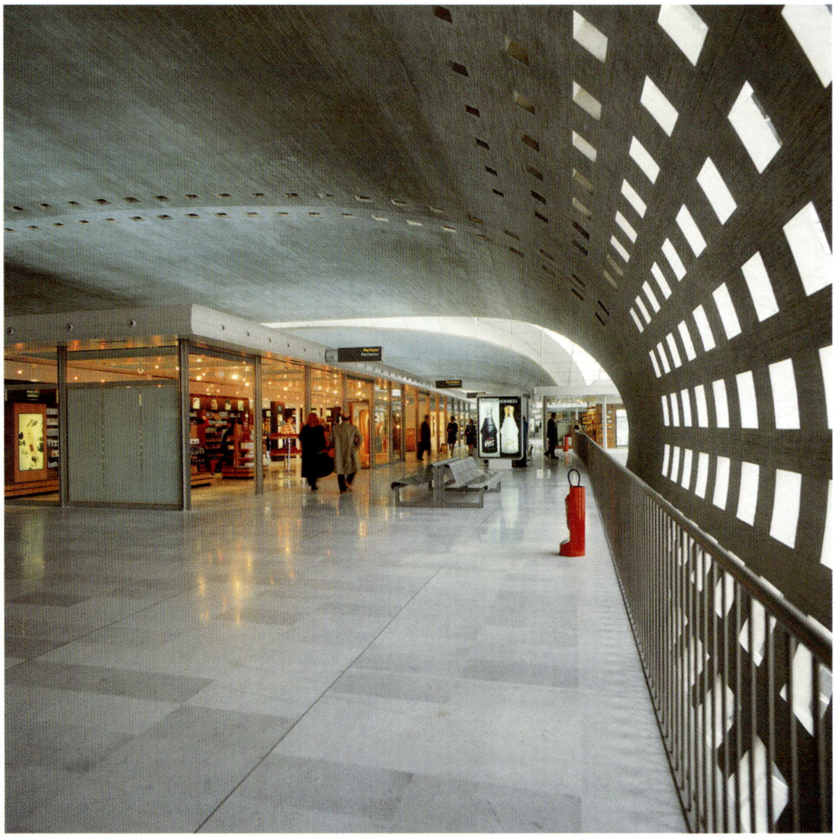

comfortable. A perforated stainless steel screen is used on the ceilings of the peninsula areas, giving a certain lack of definition as to the precise height of the natural light source. As he has in other terminals, Andreu provided for a gap, in this case of 18 meters, between the approach road and the actual body of the terminal. This element, that he calls a "canyon" serves to allow light to reach the lower level and to give visitors a precise idea of the volumes and layers of the structure.

Terminal 2 F does in many senses represent a high point in Paul Andreu's design of airport facilities. Whereas large passenger volumes and tight budgets have often been the justification for mediocre, boring architecture, Andreu has turned the very scale and means

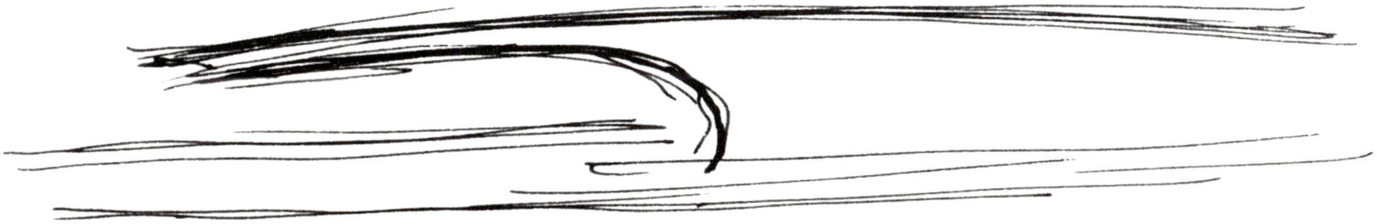

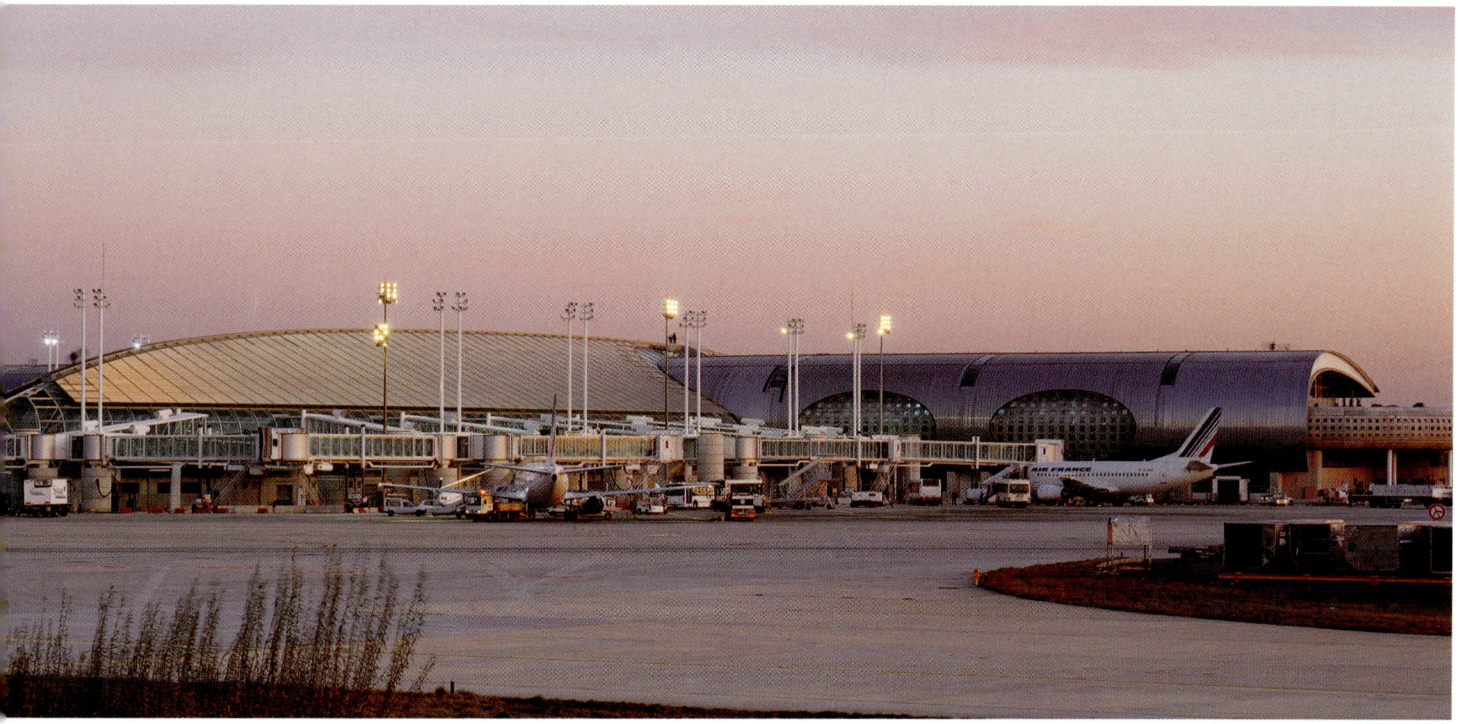

of airport construction to his advantage, and to that of the traveler. Using techniques that are surely sophisticated, Andreu and associates like Duthilleul and Rice who worked with him on the neighboring TGV Station, have brought a new standard to public transportation facilities without having recourse to inflated budgets. In a sense, Paul Andreu has democratized quality architecture more than almost any other designer active in the world today.

TGV Station 1989-1995

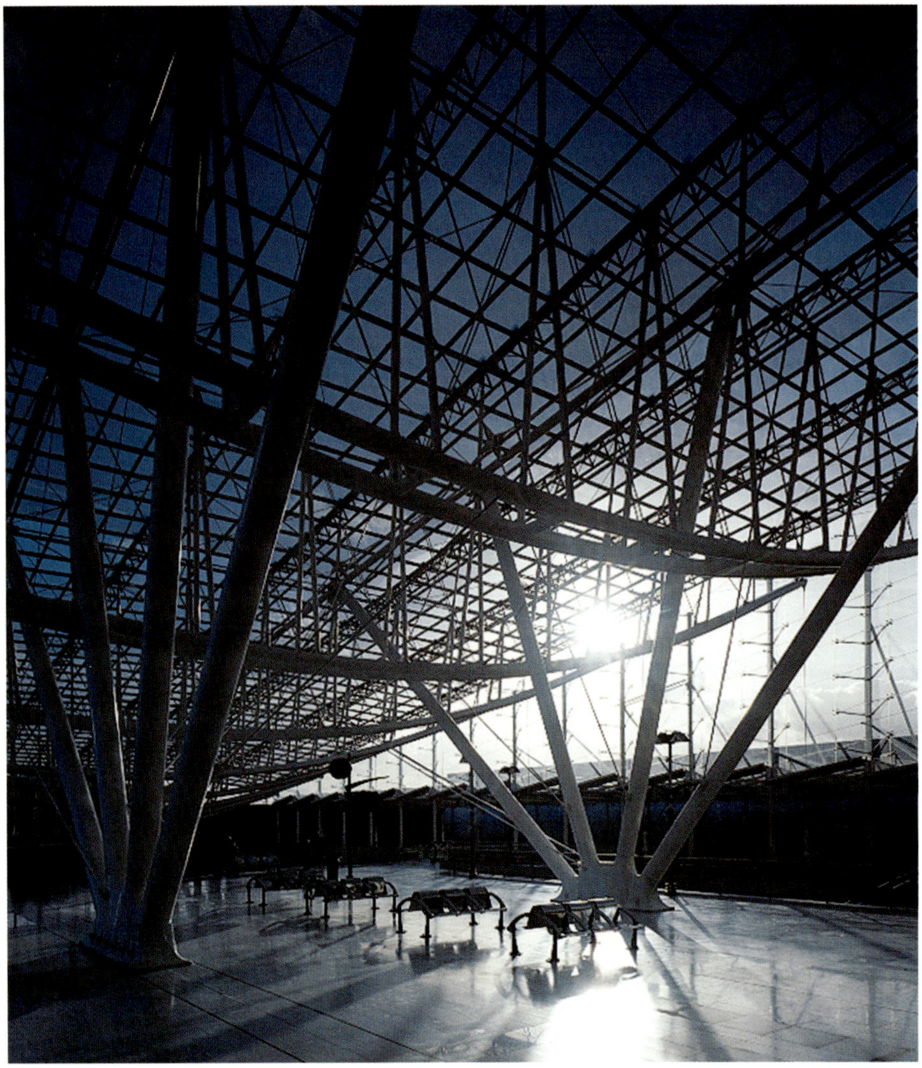

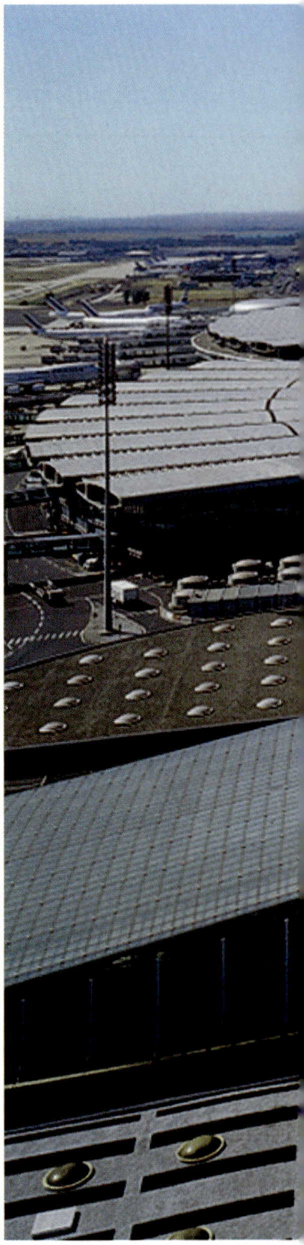

Baptized the "Exchange Module," Roissy Terminal 2 includes not only a hotel, but also, significantly, a station for the high-speed TGV trains, designed in collaboration with Jean-Marie Duthilleul of the Agence des Gares, architect for the French railways (SNCF). Intended for a theoretical annual passenger traffic of 13 million persons, the TGV station includes a floor area of 100,000 square meters. Both TGV and local RER lines are brought together here to allow passengers to arrive or travel on by car or rail. Although the SNCF actively developed the idea of such exchange modules even before the creation of the Roissy TGV station (for example with the Lyon Satolas station designed by Santiago Calatrava), the reality of extensive transfers from rail to air has yet to fully materialize. Be that as it may, Andreu has taken on and mastered the extreme technical complexities of this conjugation of travel facilities and produced one of

A view down on the spectacular glass roof of the TGV station, located to either side of the oblong Sheraton Hotel confirms Andreu's desire to make not only 2 F but its entire environment bright and open. To the left, the station seen from within.

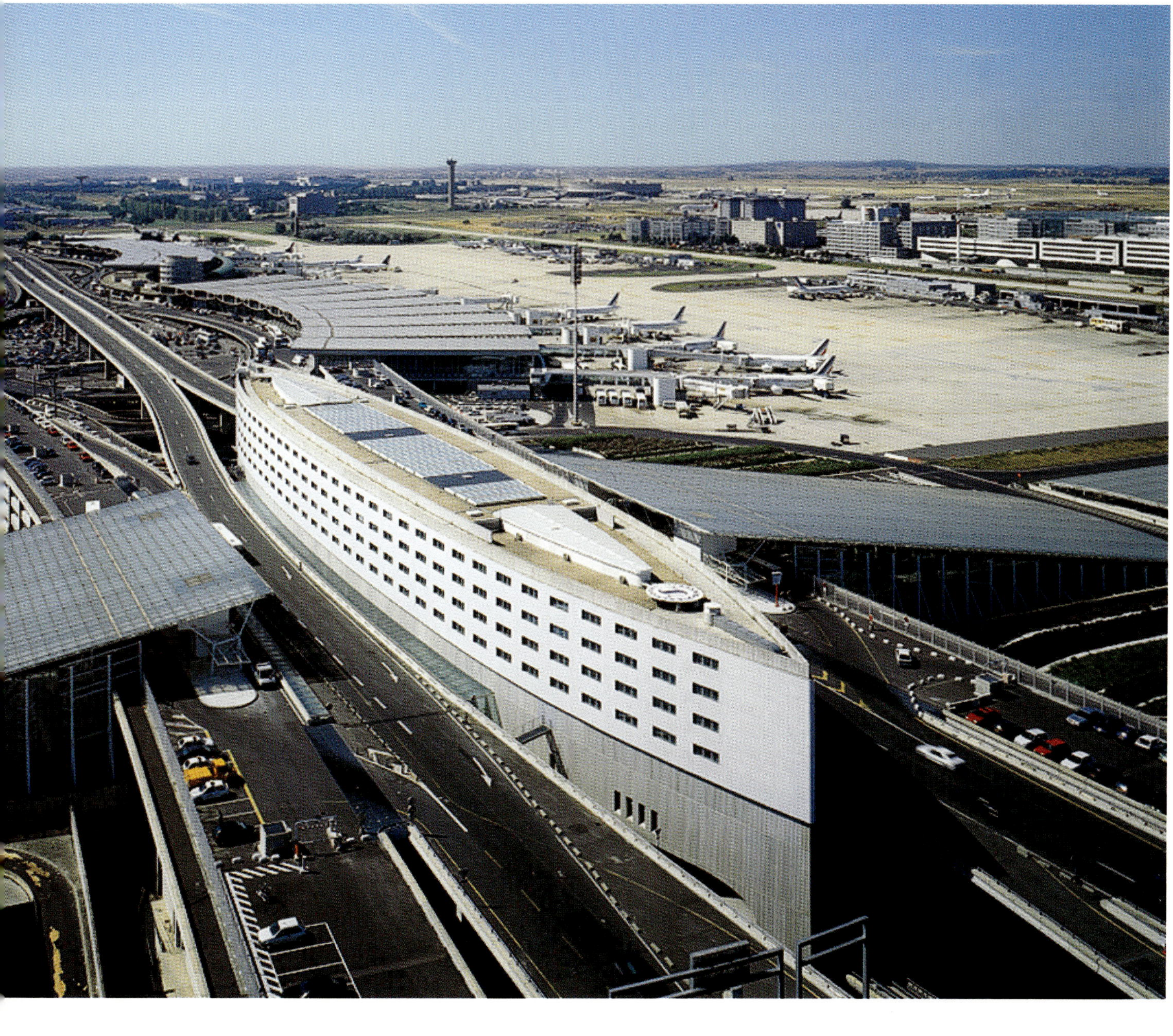

Movement through the passageways connecting the terminals, TGV Station and Hotel is coordinated in an architectural style that gives unity to the whole.

the most attractive and efficient terminals in the world. This success is also an indication that the planning that went into the previous phases of Terminal 2 providing for future extensions worked much as they had been planned – no small feat in itself. The basic lines of communication are built around an east-west access road and the north-south rail lines. Although much of the TGV station design was the work of Andreu, he met with a kindred spirit in Duthilleul, who has been responsible for making recent SNCF stations, such as those of the new TGV Mediterranean line open and generous in their proportions. Looking back to the great glass-covered train terminals of the 19th century, the two architects, together with the brilliant engineer Peter Rice (RFR) imagined a 2,800 square meter glass roof supported by no less than 2,000 tons of steel, over the 500-meter long station. It is almost as though Paul Andreu's growing interest in light has reached an apotheosis in this fully glazed, spectacular space. The unfortunate breakage of some glass panels above this space has long required the use of unsightly nets over the passenger areas, however it would appear that faulty glass panes rather than any architectural or engineering difficulty are at the origin of these problems. It may even be that vandalism was involved. The hotel, whose axis follows that of the access roads, is described as a "tear" in the fabric of these arteries. In fact, it sits in a perpendicular alignment atop the railway station.

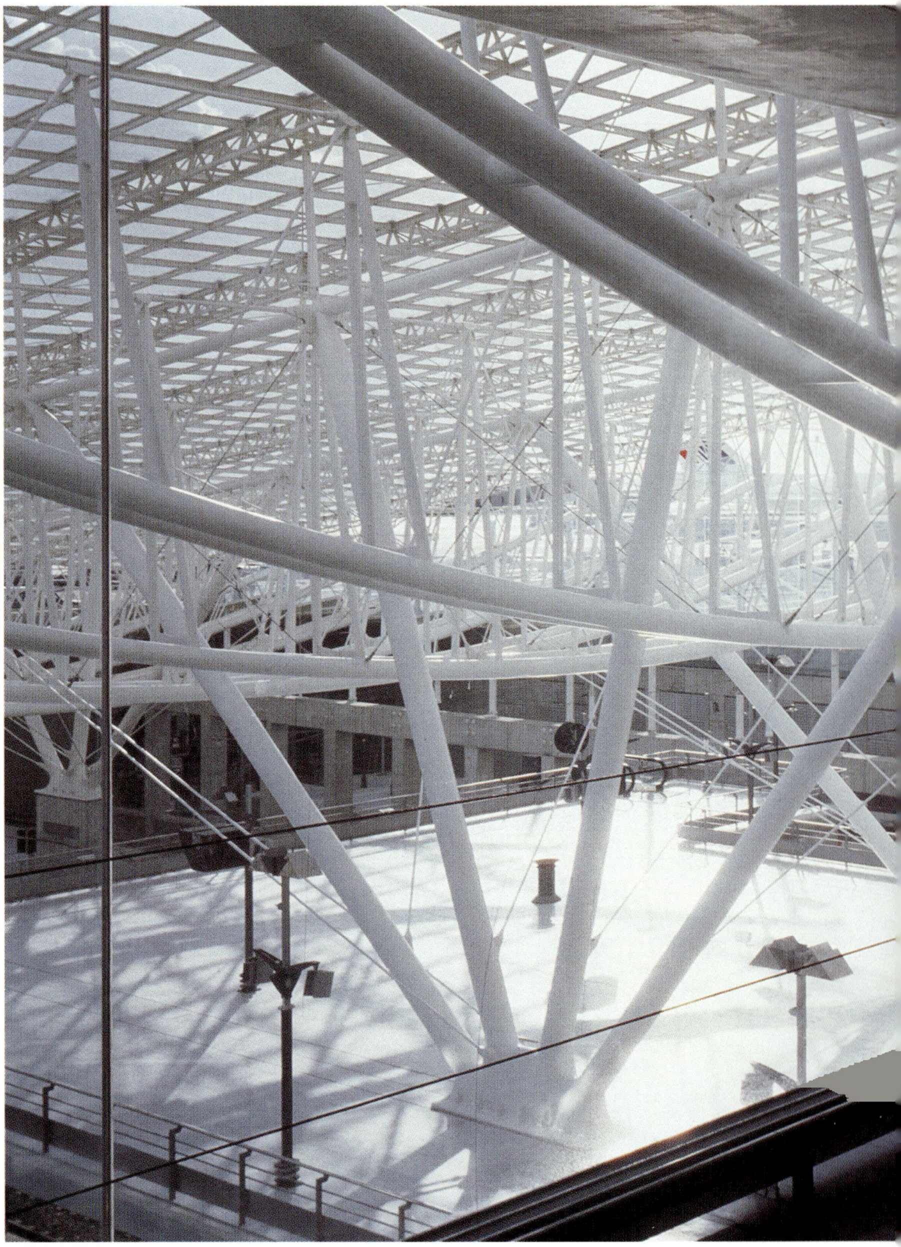

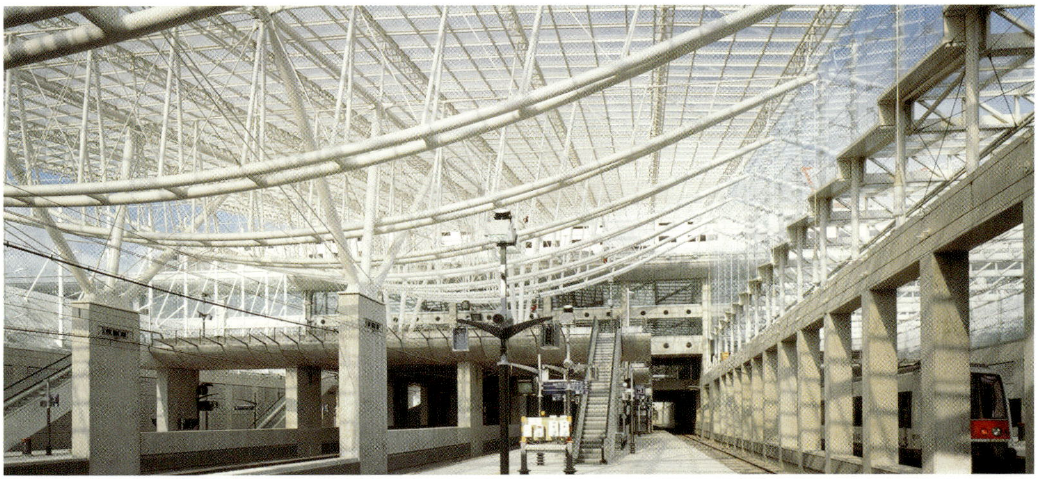

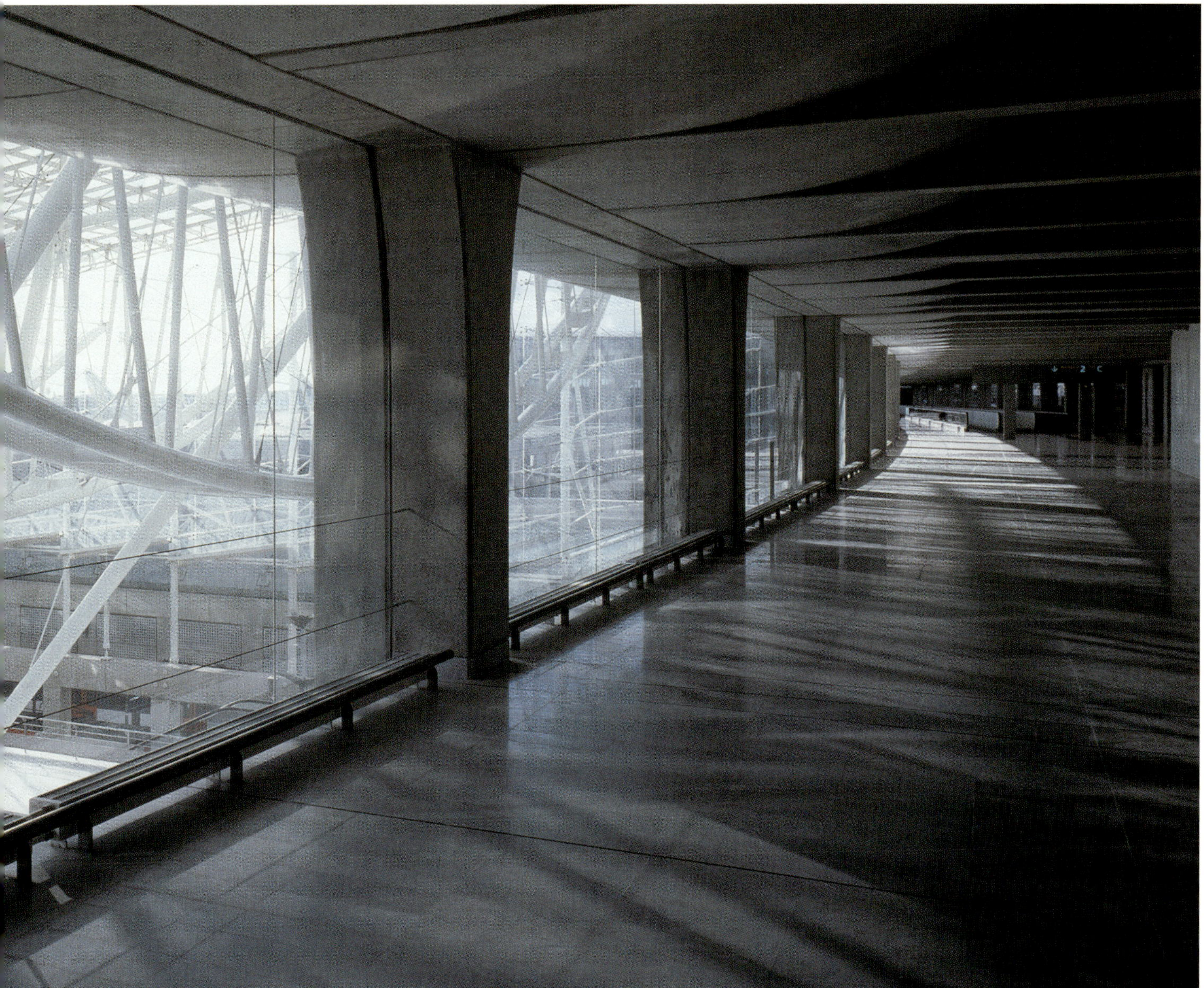

Sheraton Hotel **1994-1996**

With its elevated approach roads and very open central volume, the Sheraton Hotel almost appears to float in its central location – a logical consequence of the placement of the perpendicular axes representing air and rail travel.

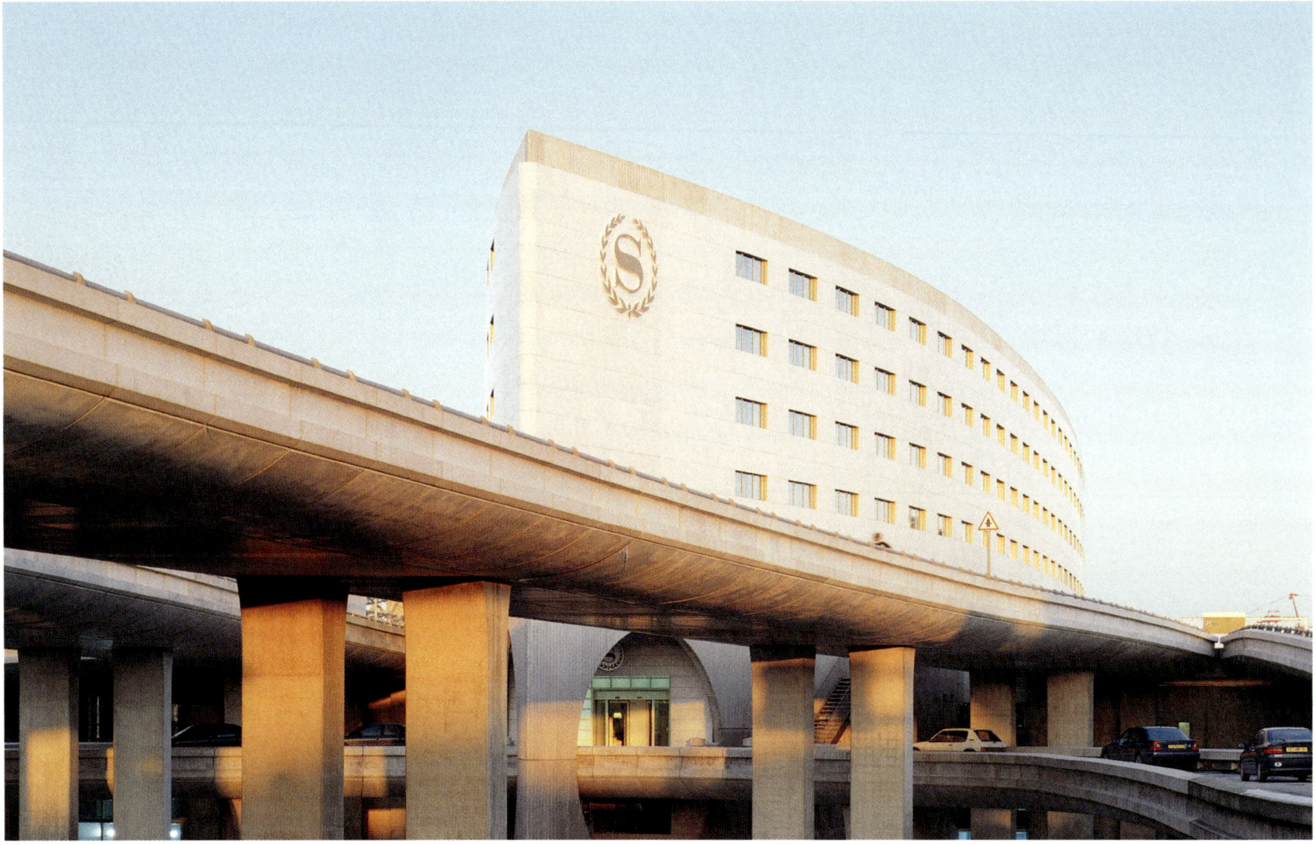

Inaugurated on January 16, 1996, the Sheraton Hotel has 256 rooms and is located in an oblong site just above the TGV Station and close to Terminal 2 F. It is set in an east-west orientation, as opposed to the north-south axis of the intersecting train station. TGV and RER access is provided on the lowest level, transit to the airport terminals one level up and the actual hotel facilities on the upper four floors. Paul Andreu has carefully created openings toward the station and the airport that highlight the central location of the hotel and permit travelers to orient themselves easily. With the roads that bend around it, the Sheraton is in a sense the heart of the idea of the Exchange Module – air, rail and road traffic all converge here.

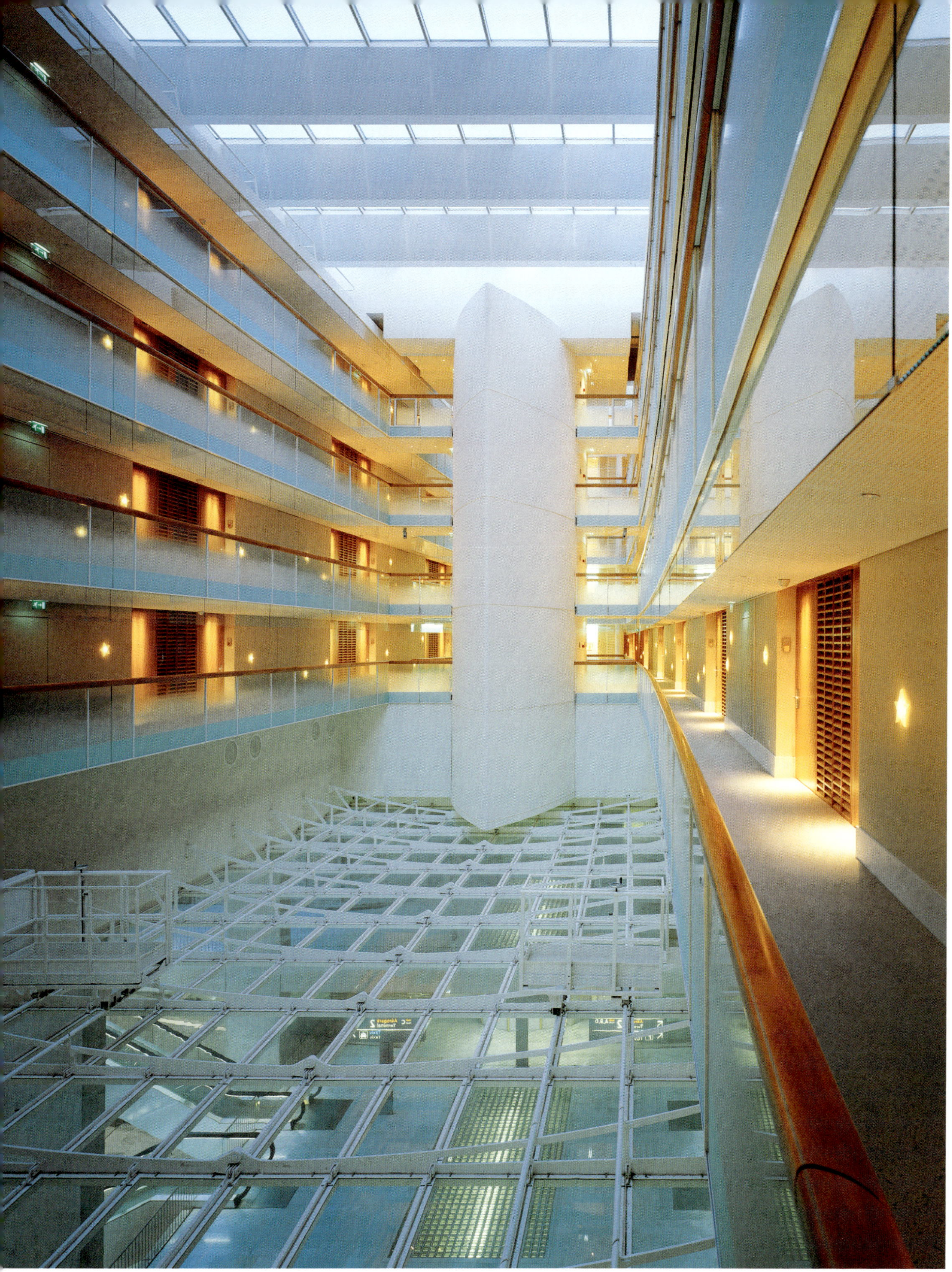

Charles-de-Gaulle Airport - Terminal 2 F

Building on the concept of the geodesic dome pioneered by Buckminster Fuller, Paul Andreu creates a luminous globe sitting in the water of the Bay of Osaka and dedicated to the city's rich maritime history.

Osaka Maritime Museum **Osaka**

Country: Japan
Use: Museum
Start of project: 1993
Completion: 2000
Surface: 20,000 m^2
Capacity: 150,000 visitors per year

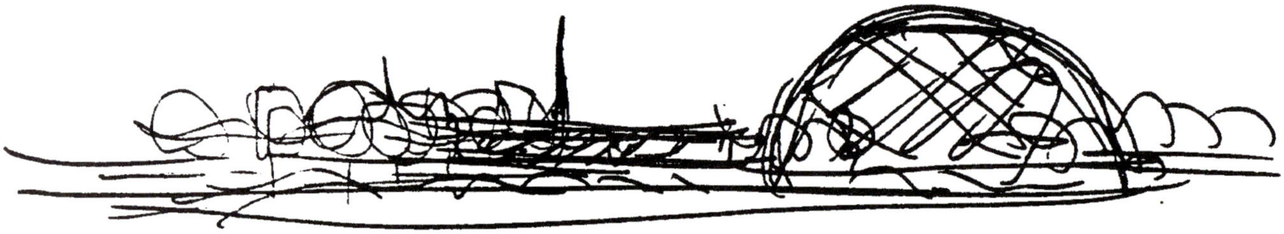

With the international reputation garnered as he developed airports all over the world, Paul Andreu has begun to move actively beyond the areas that made his reputation. One of the first major projects outside of France of this nature to reach completion was the Osaka Maritime Museum. Located in a newly developed office city area not far by subway and elevated train line from the heart of Osaka, the new facility is unusual in that it lies in a 300,000-square meter basin, dug out of reclaimed land to again become part of Bay of Osaka, and indeed of the Pacific Ocean. A bit like the upcoming Beijing Opera,

A geodesic dome sitting
in an artificial extension
of the Bay of Osaka, the new
museum is spectacularly
simple in its appearance.
Andreu's sketch gives
an accurate impression
of the appearance
of the finished structure.

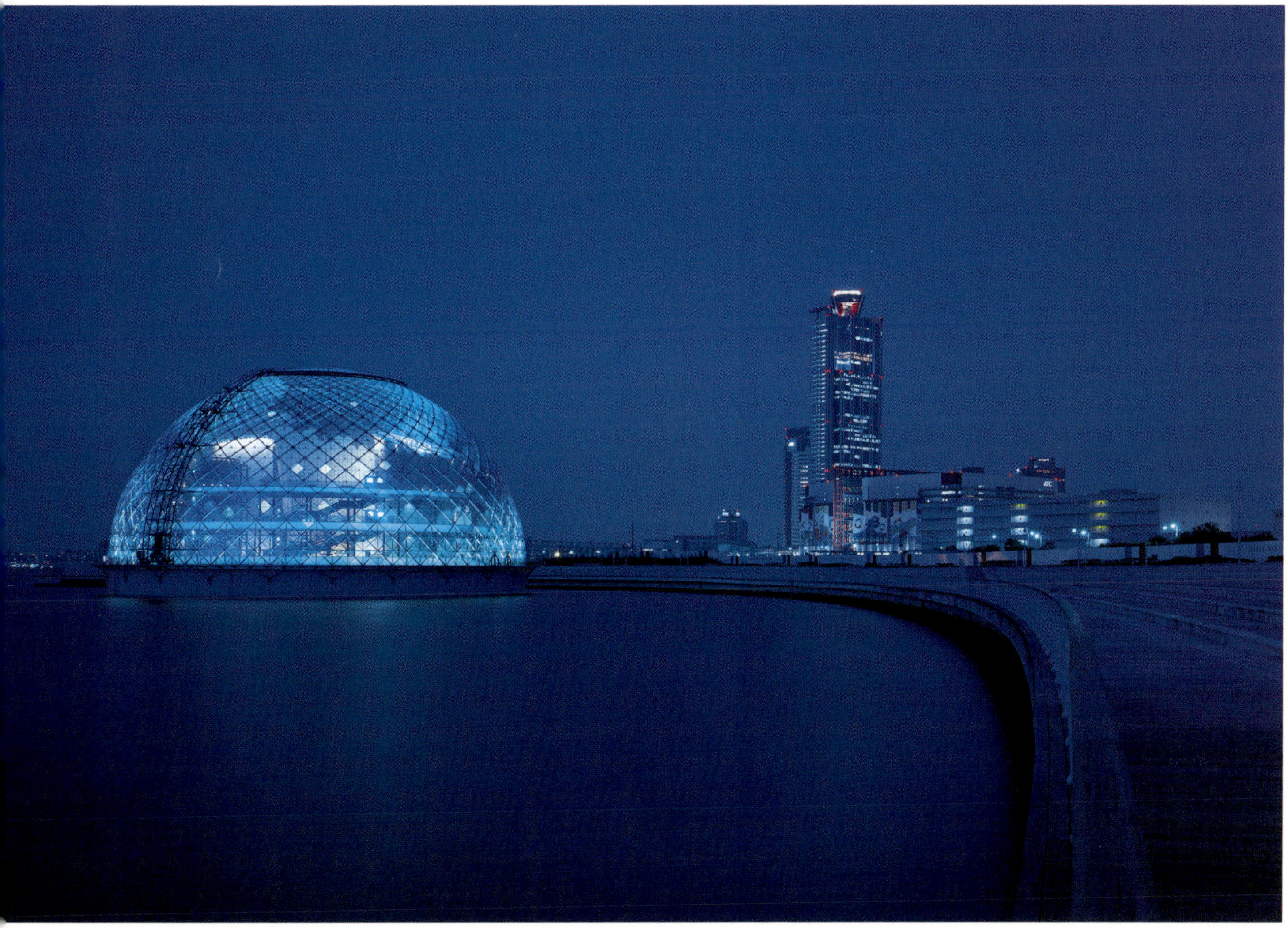

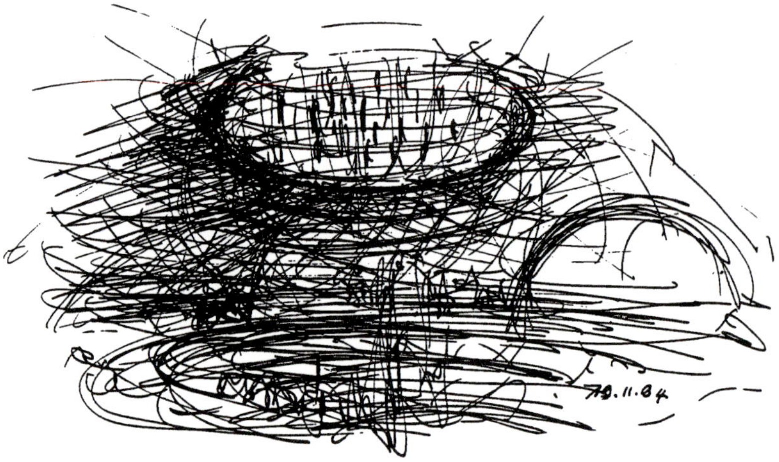

this structure is approached through an underwater tunnel. The architects, who included François Tamisier and Masakazu Bokura for this project, had the daunting task of designing a structure for a collection that was not really formed when the work got under way. What was known was that a large restored wooden ship would be the centerpiece of the museum, and that it would be devoted

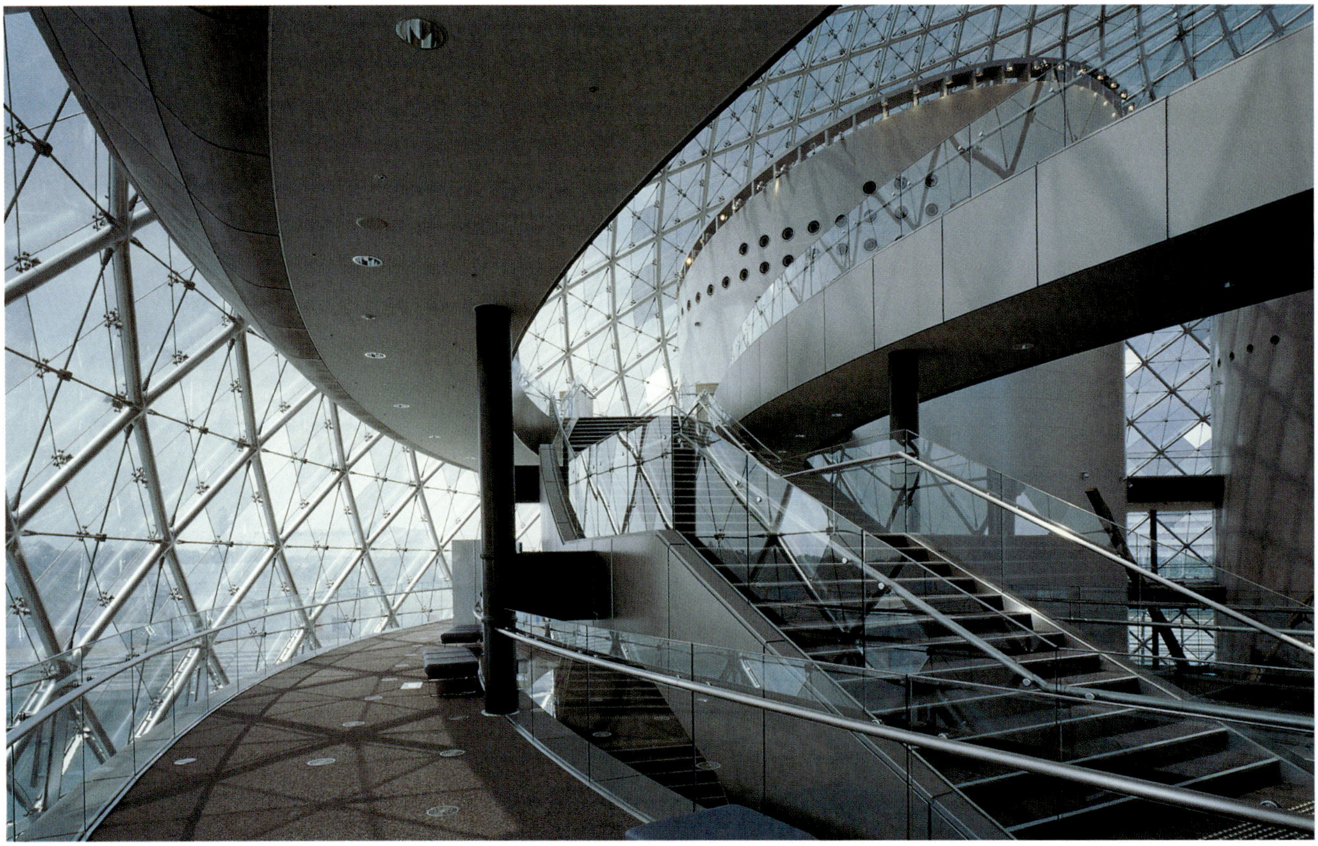

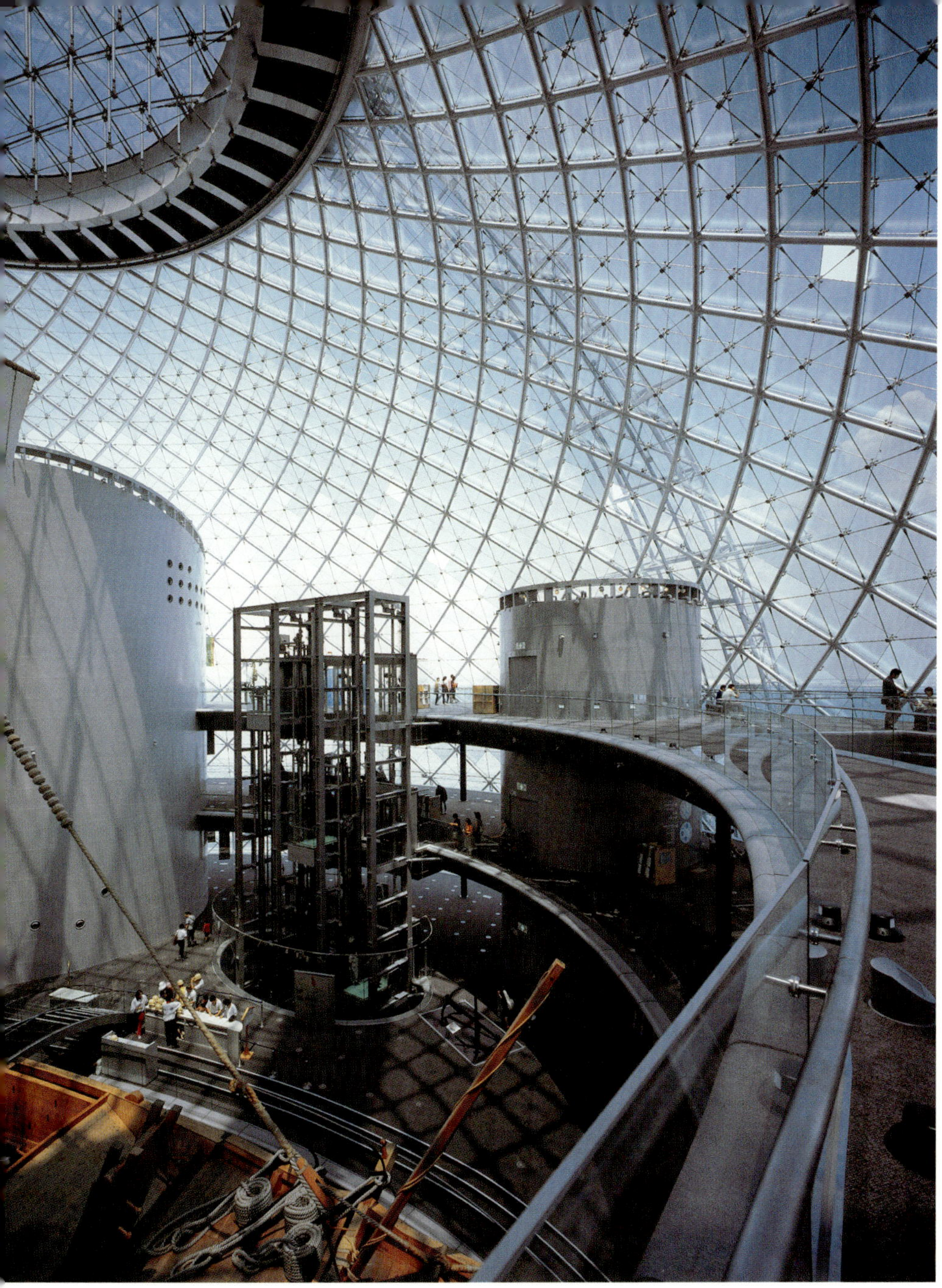

Despite its ultimate transparency, the interior of the museum is somewhat more complex than its outward volume would suggest. Andreu's sketch again suggests this finished appearance that brings to mind his occasional penchant for almost Piranesian complexity.

to the maritime history of this great port city. Developing this singular form on the basis of Buckminster Fuller's geodesic domes, Andreu went substantially further in refining the structural aspects so that stringent Japanese seismic rules could be met. Using a so-called "lamella grid" to make up the spherical shape out of flat lozenges whose size diminishes with rising height, the Andreu team managed to hold the glass together with a "ten point" system using only silicone joints without a metallic frame. Two sheets of 15 mm glass with a layer of perforated galvanized steel were employed – the perforations varying according

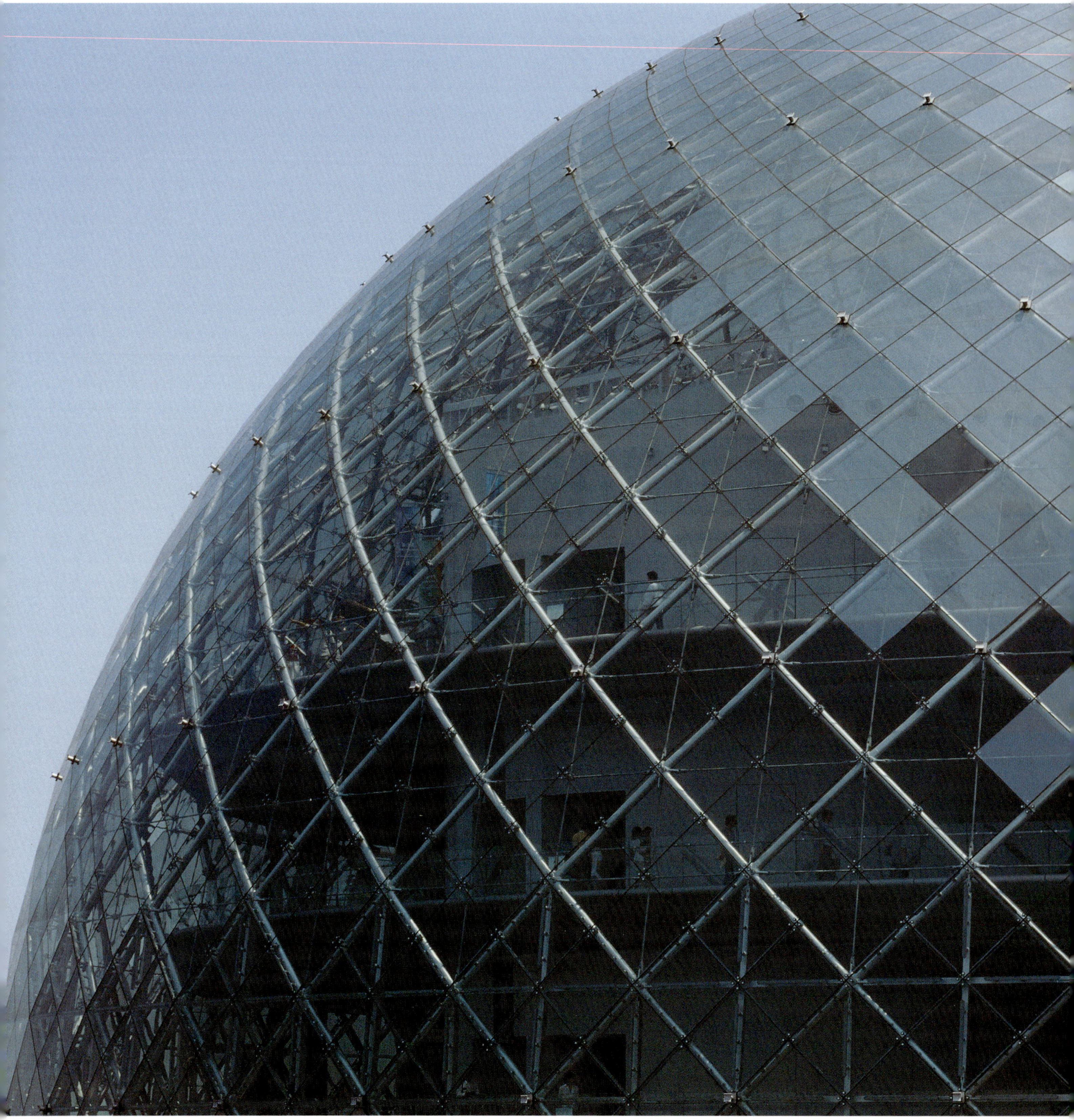

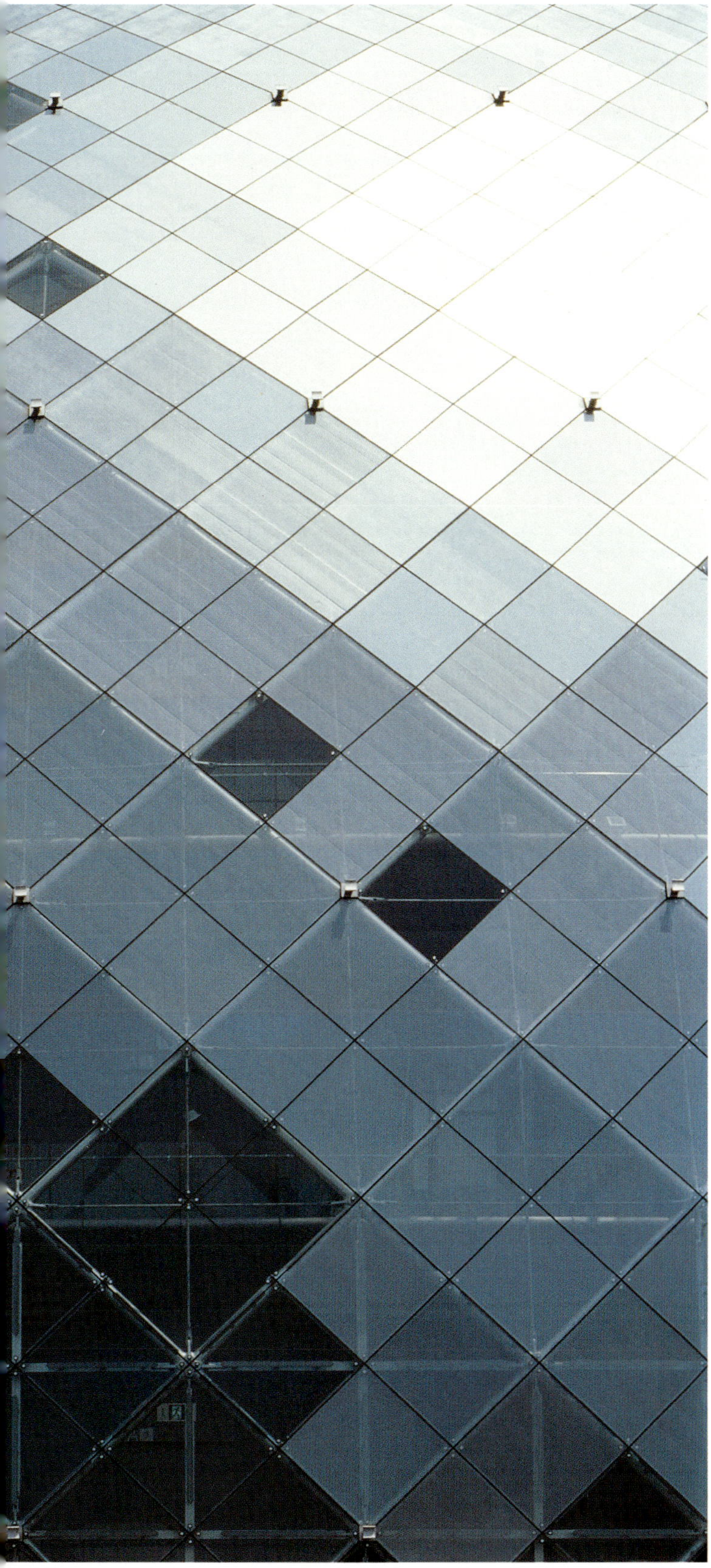

Building a glass dome of these dimensions in an area prone to earthquakes is naturally an engineering tour-de-force. Here, the transparency of the shell allows visitors within to be seen from the outside.

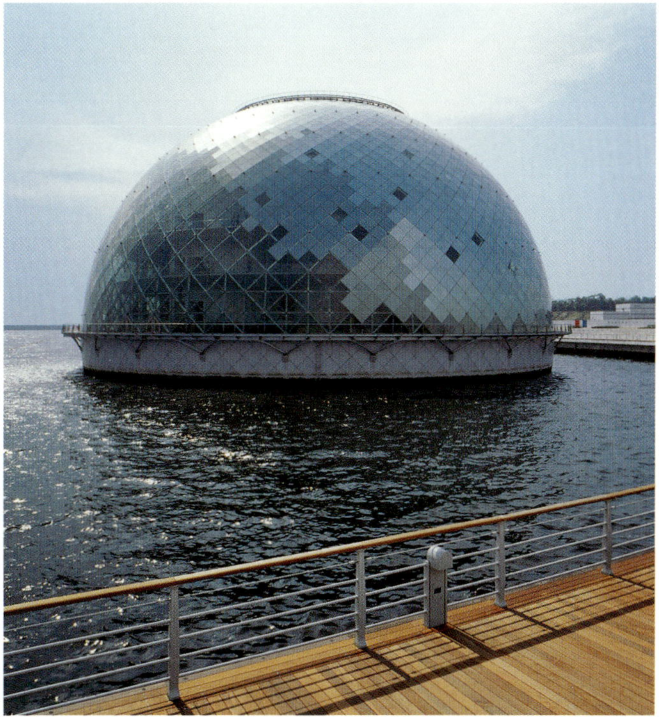

to orientation to diminish heat gain, or an excessive "greenhouse effect." Although it might be imagined that such a remarkable crystalline cupola would be highly fragile, one of the most interesting aspects of the construction was that the entire dome was brought in a single piece on barges and lowered into place on November 8, 1999. This is a stunning example of how Paul Andreu has used his real knowledge of engineering and his taste for rather spectacular gestures together half way around the world from his own country. Assisted by the French-

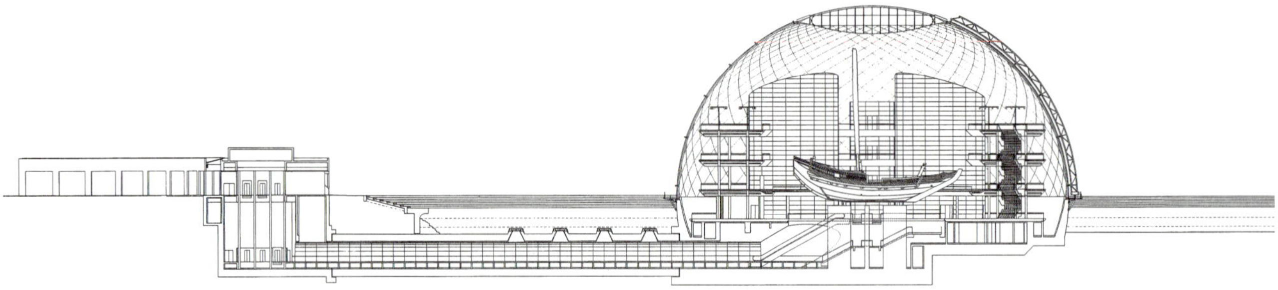

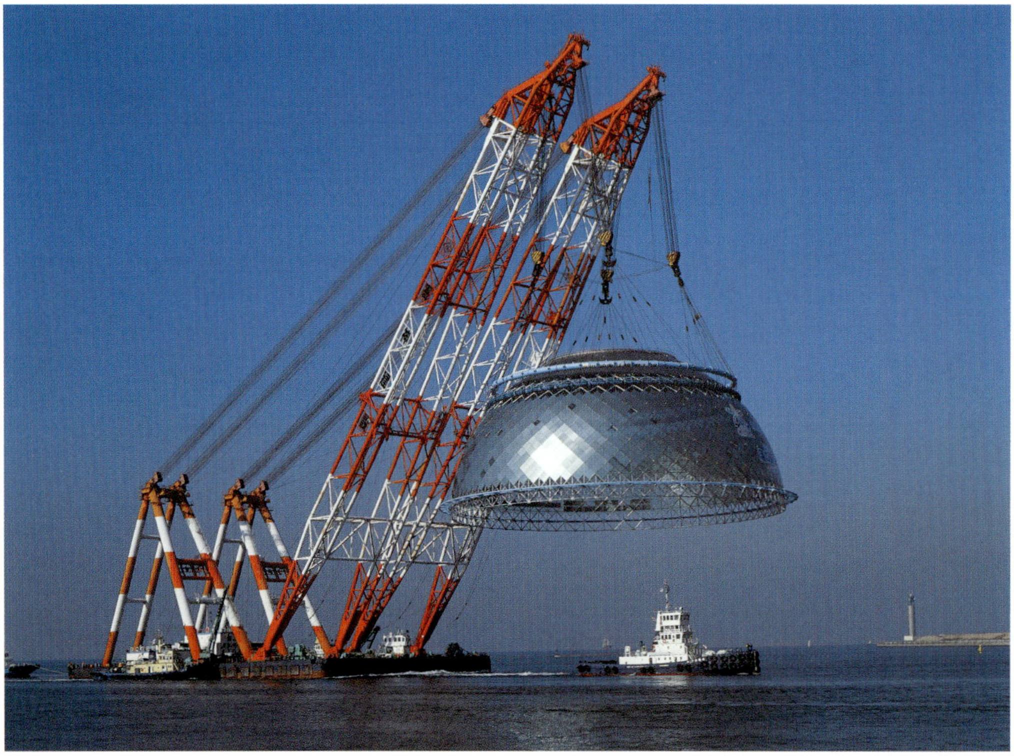

The nearly complete dome being delivered by a sea-going barge. Plan and section show the long underwater approach tunnel visible in the preceding double-page. Andreu also uses the idea of an underwater approach in the Beijing National Grand Theater.

speaking Japanese architect Bokura, Andreu also mastered the complex Japanese construction and public authorization procedures in this instance. He was also quick to seize on the capacity of the Japanese to work to very high quality levels that area almost impossible to obtain on Western projects. A 5,000-square meter entry pavilion is located on the landside of the project, and a 1,000-square meter, 60-meter long tunnel links this portal to the actual 14,000-square meter museum.

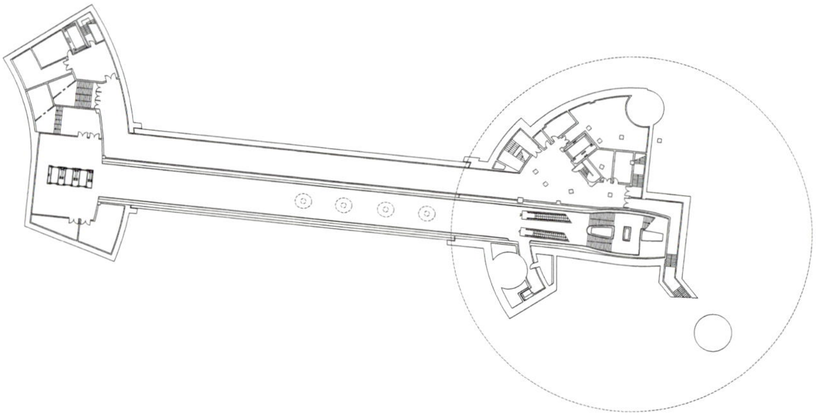

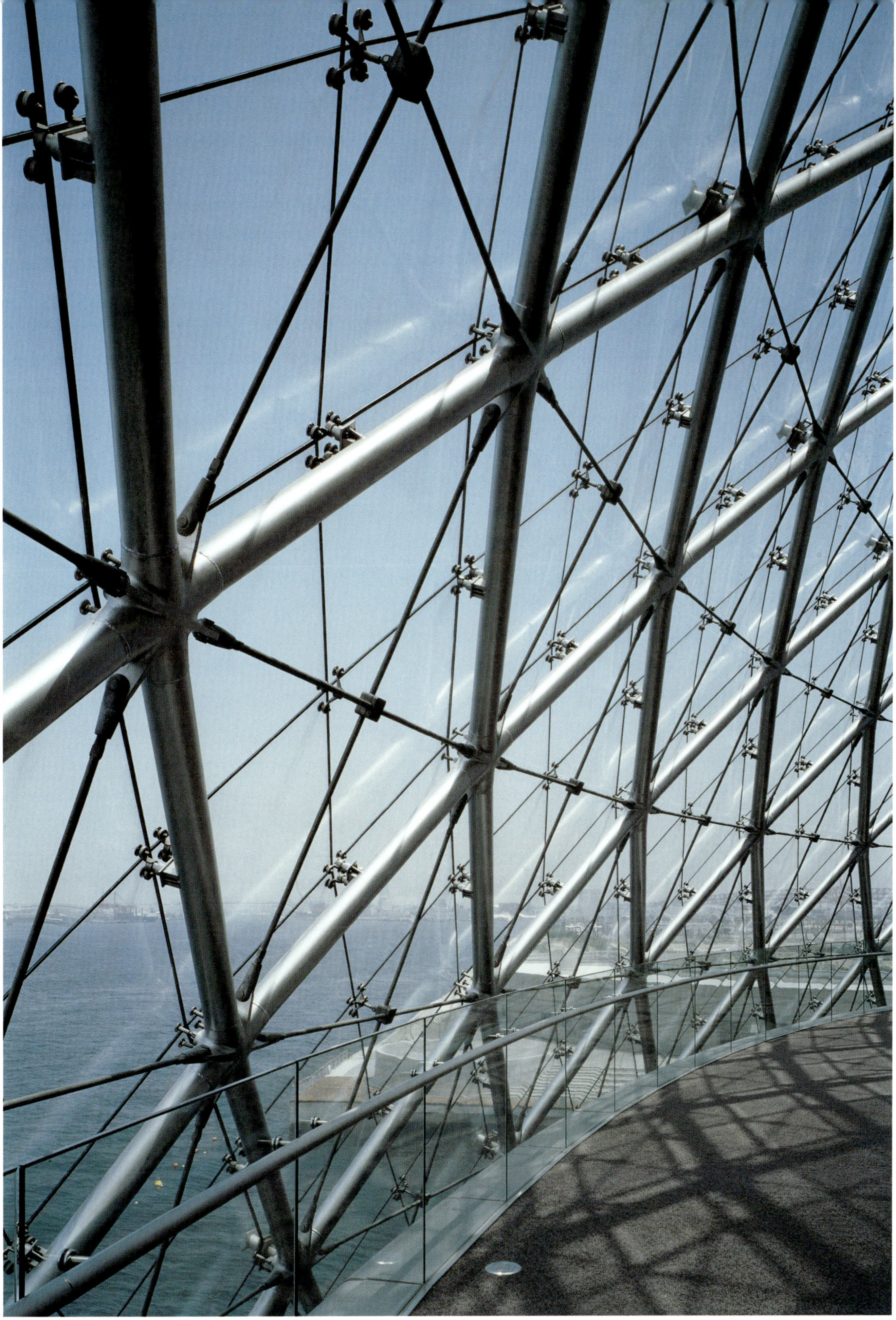

Though it was built on a very fast schedule and without the type of close control that the architect usually exerts on his projects, this new Chinese airport is symbolic of the rising economic power of the "Middle Kingdom."

Shanghai Pudong Airport Shanghai

Country: China
Use: Airport
Start of project: 1996
Completion: 1999
Surface: 220,000 m^2
Capacity: 20 million passengers per year

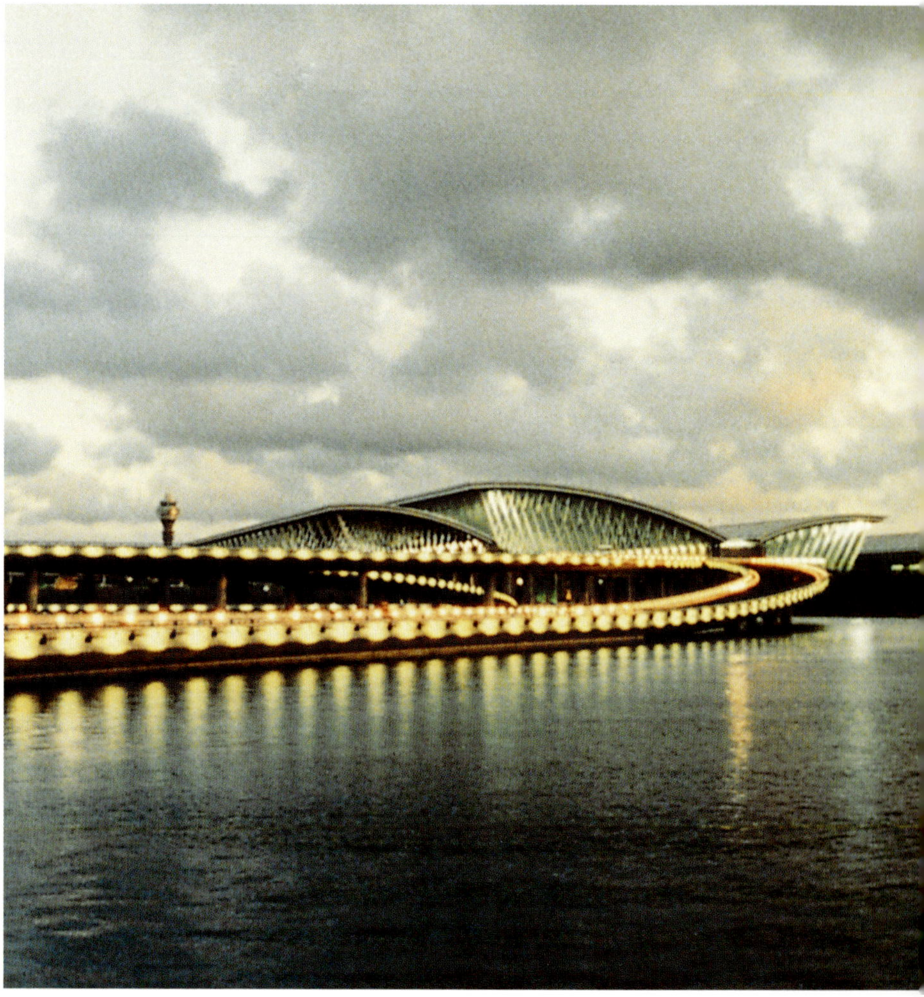

The explosive development of the economy of the Shanghai area has led to a corresponding rise in the demand for air travel. The airport that Andreu designed for the new Pudong area was intended for a theoretical passenger capacity of 20 million persons per year. An original terminal of 220,000 square meters is designed to eventually be increased to no less than 840,000 square meters in the future. Parking is provided for 3,180 vehicles and the airport's organization divides passenger movement into two levels – boarding, deplaning passport controls, and train and car access on level one; departures, check-in, passport and security controls as well as shops on level two. Large stretches of water and planted areas give a more humane touch to this large facility than it might otherwise have.

Elevated roadways arch over the water here and the winged appearance of the terminal buildings is evident to approaching travellers. Clearly Andreu often carefully considers the appearance of his airport buildings as they look to people coming from the outside. More and more over time, he has given an uplifting sensation of flight to these designs.

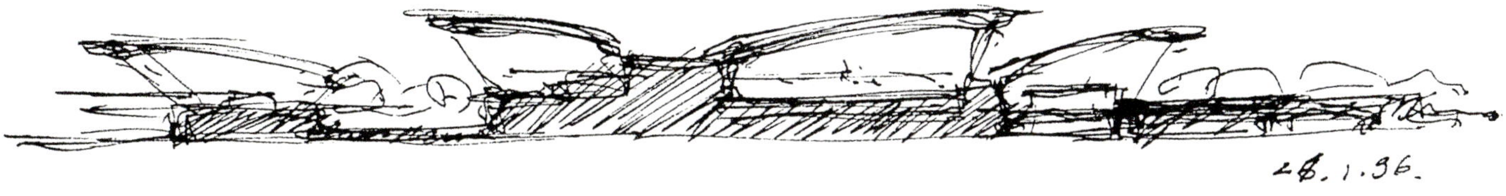

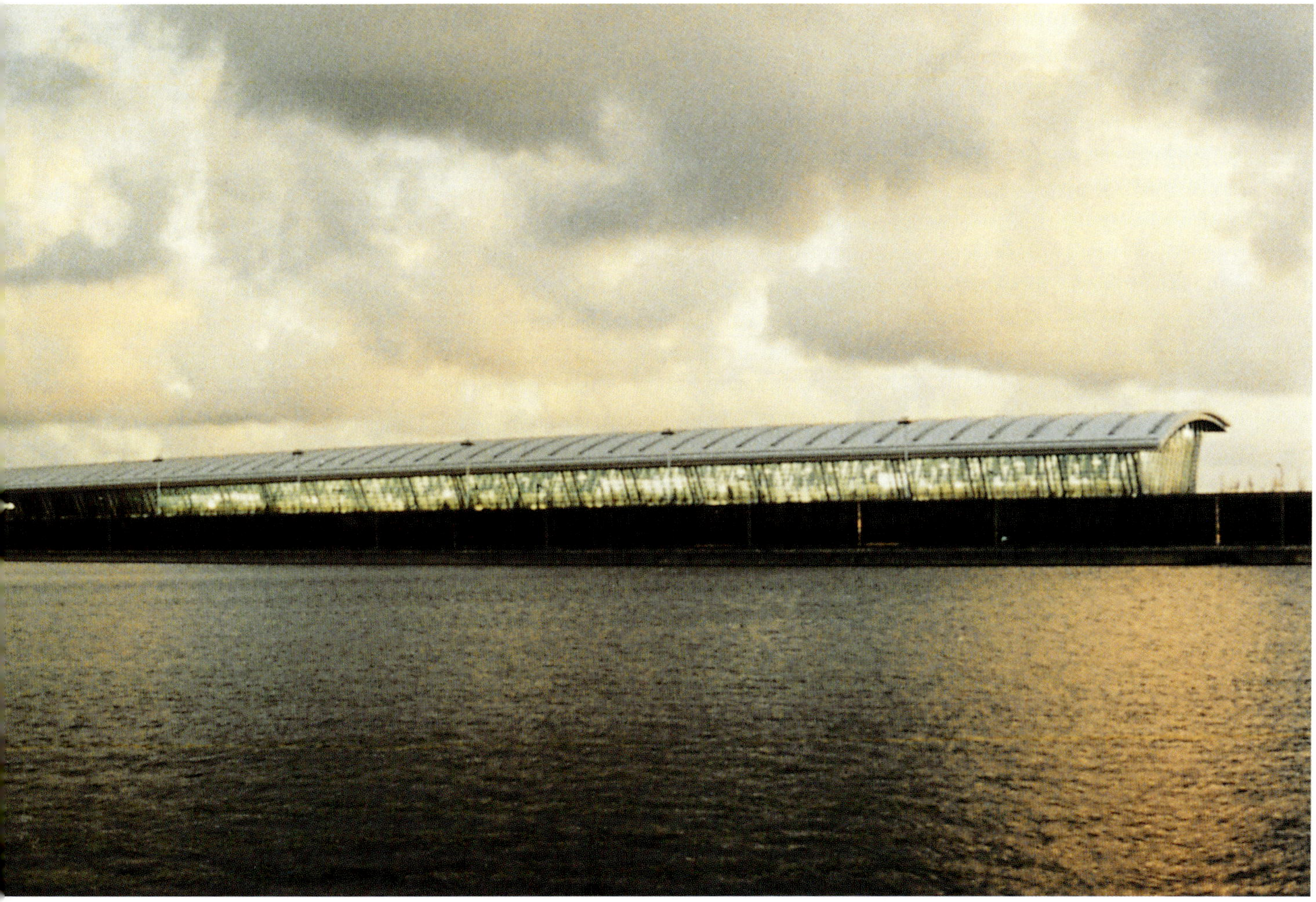

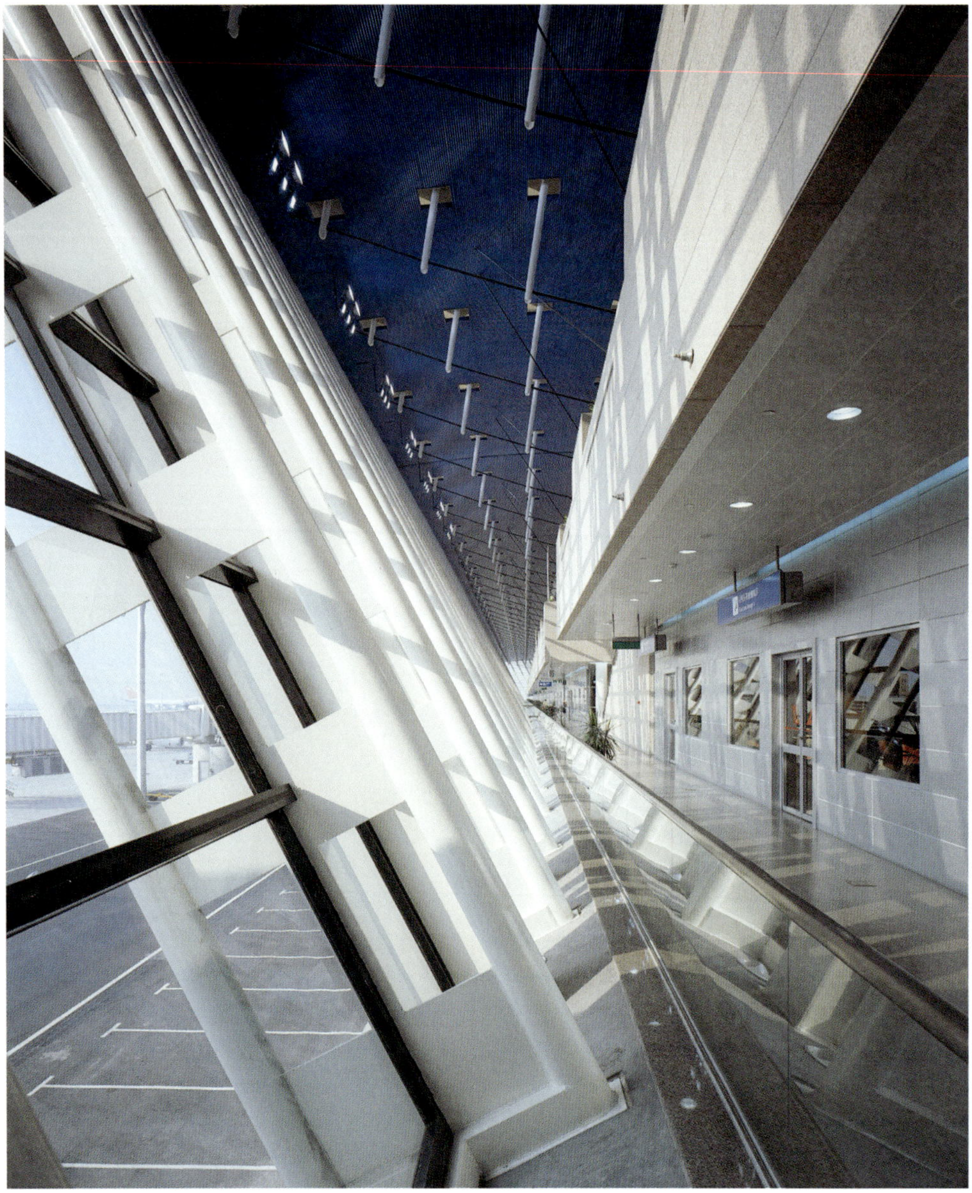

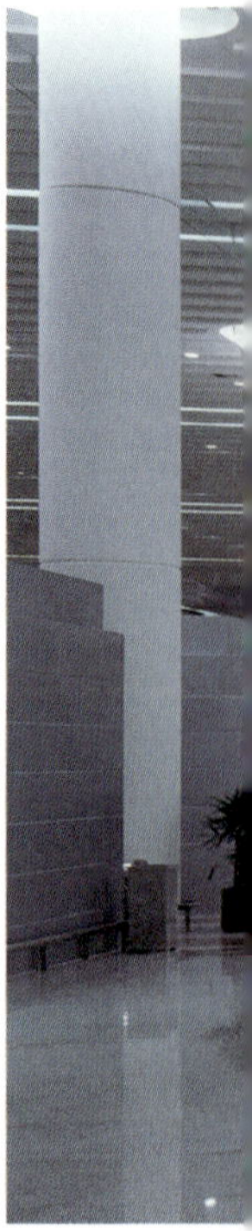

A very large square pond and canal mark the entrance to the centrally located terminal areas. Although Paul Andreu stresses that approach roads enter the complex obliquely rather than in a frontal manner, the overall plan of the airport remains very symmetrical and on the whole rectilinear. Even if there are some loops in approach roads, the tendency of Andreu to simplify and concentrate functional elements is apparent here. Runways are located on either side of the

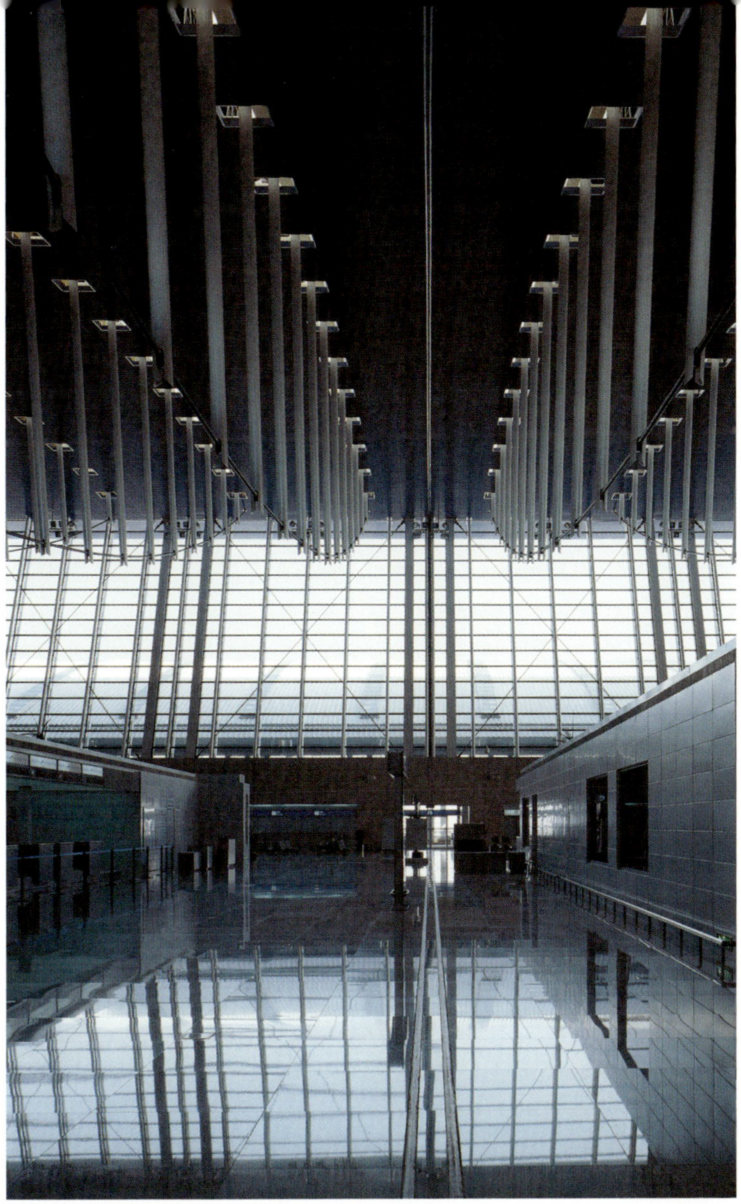

Perhaps somewhat less original than a terminal like Charles-de-Gaulle 2 F, the Shanghai facility nonetheless makes use of Andreu's typical large windows and is the product of his mastery of airport efficiency.

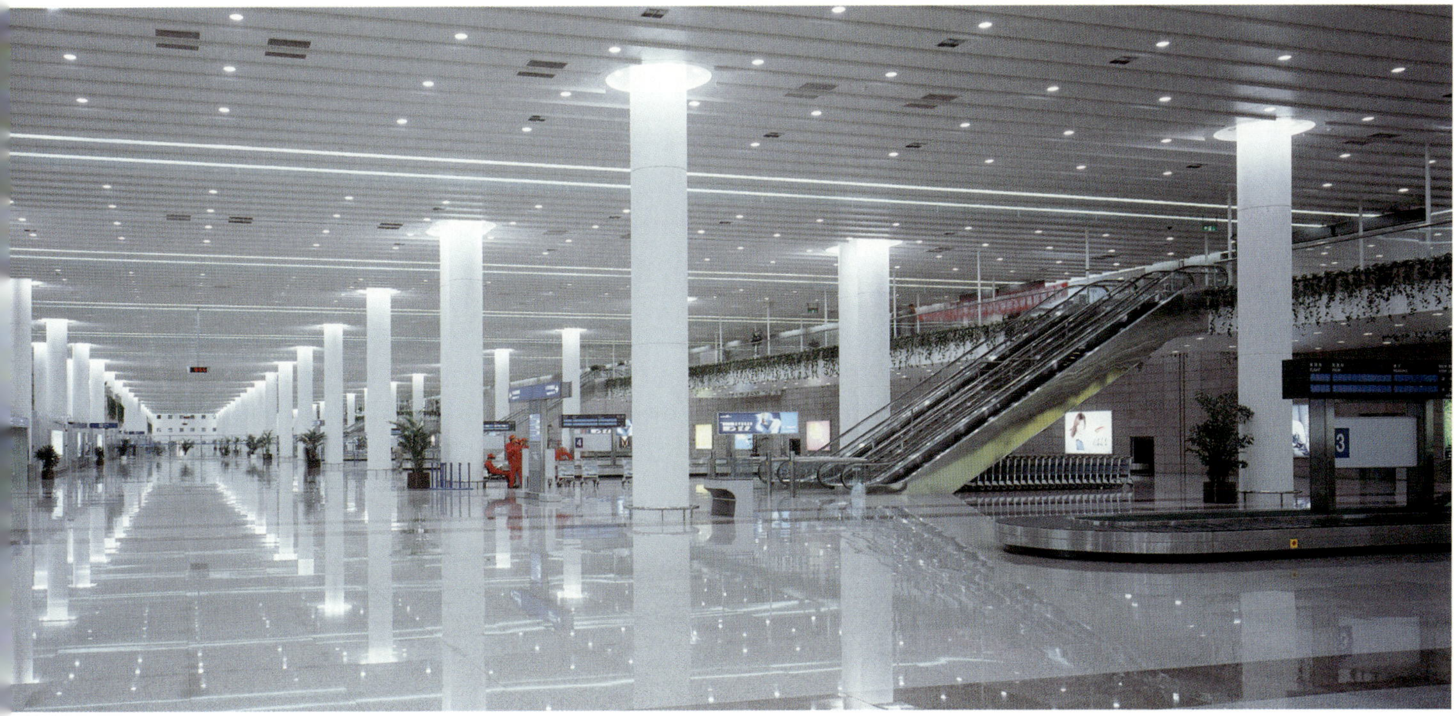

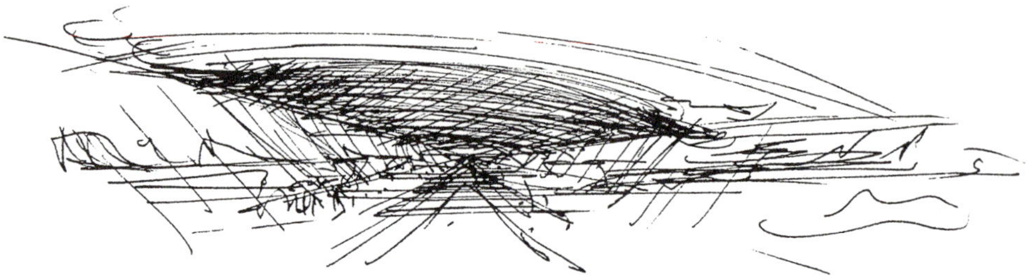

basically rectangular plan terminals but the buildings themselves are set in a great square planted with trees. Andreu stresses that despite its size, the Shanghai Pudong Airport maintains the kind of functional simplicity he has come to master so well in other projects. A succession of gently curving light steel roofs that Andreu likens to "the petals of a flower, the wings of a bird or the widening ripples formed by the breeze in the water" sits on a strong concrete base. The upward sweep of the roofs is oriented in each case in the direction of passenger movement – either toward land for the arrivals or toward the runways and the sky for the departures. The pre-stressed metal roof has no

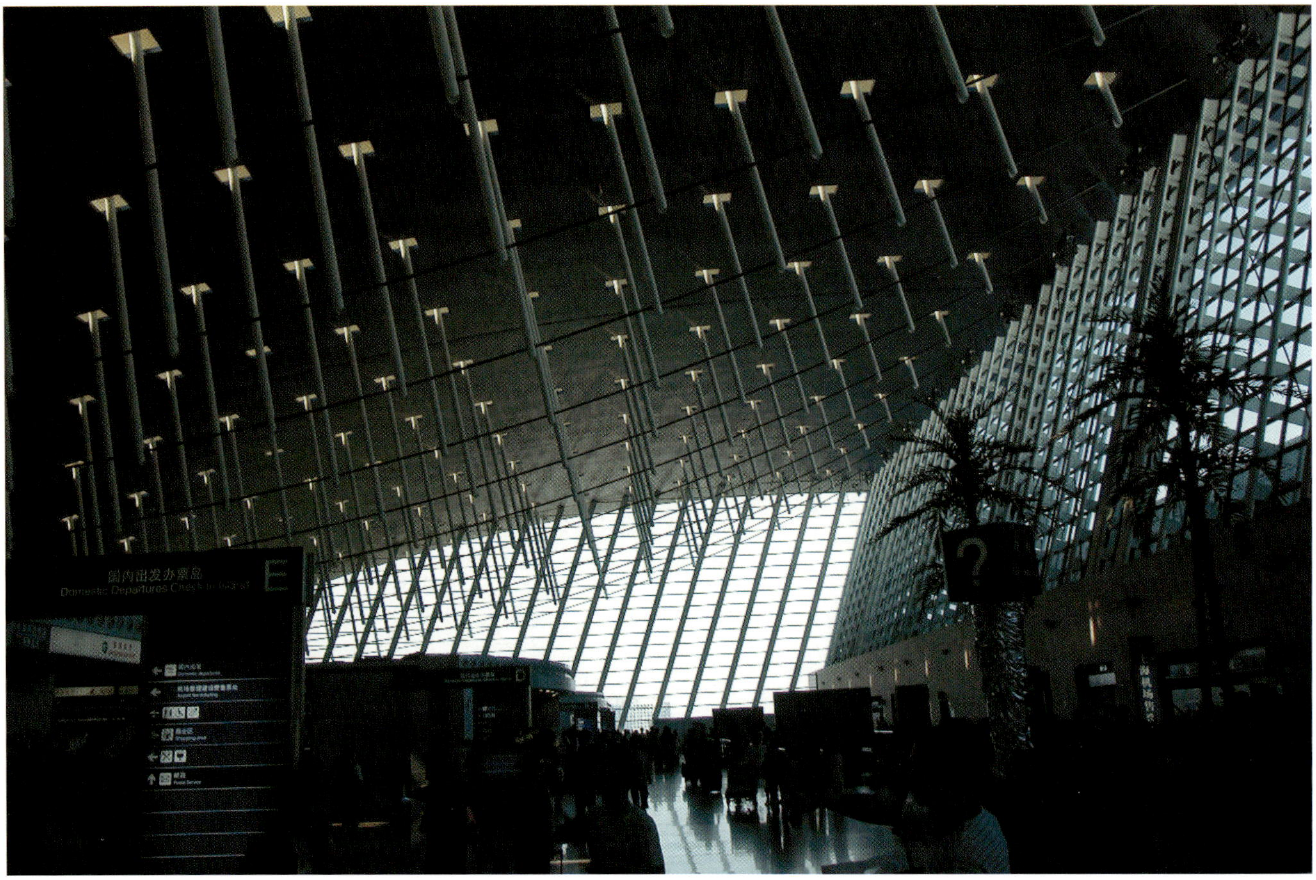

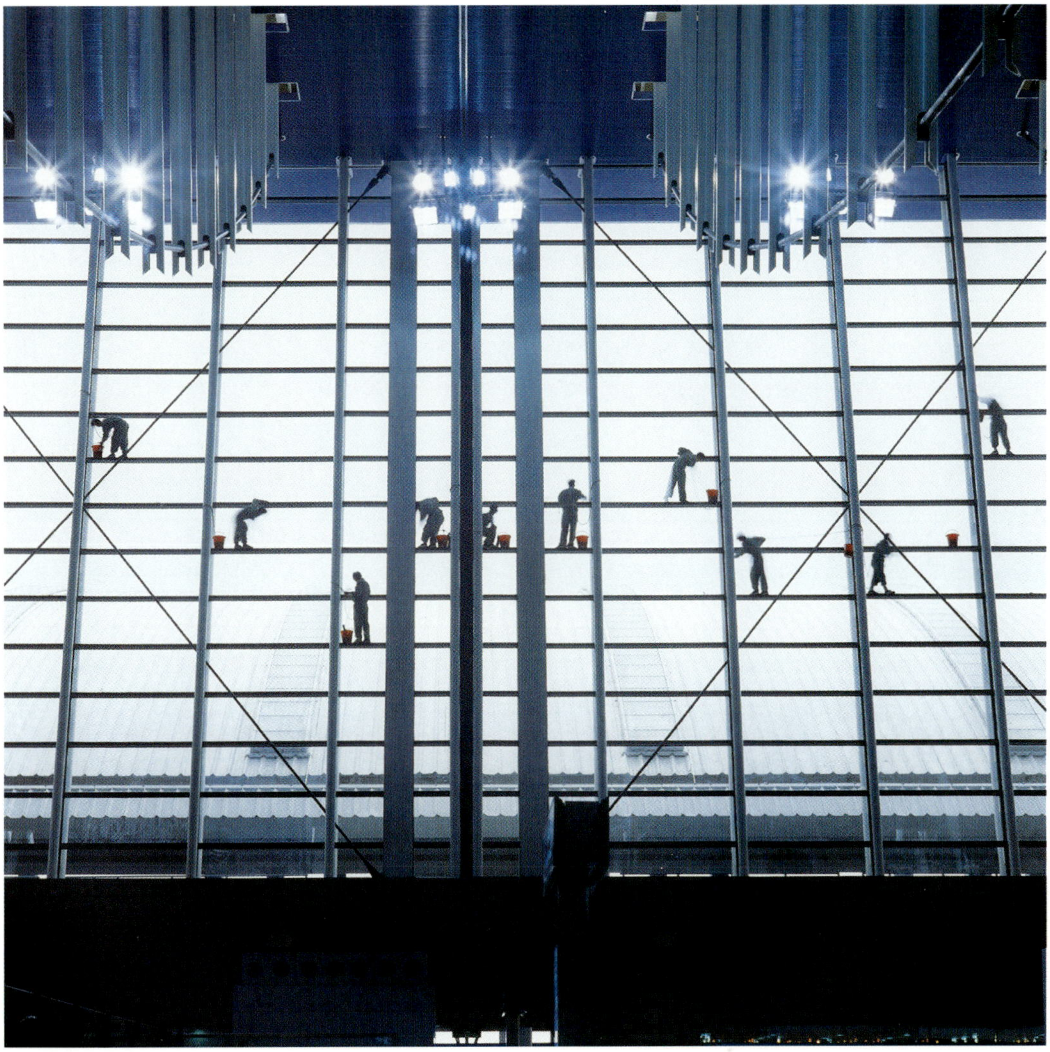

The entrance canopy and slanting glazed walls are even more clearly marked by Andreu's recent style than the somewhat less stunning interiors. Movement and transit are clearly inscribed in the design as seen from any angle or in drawings.

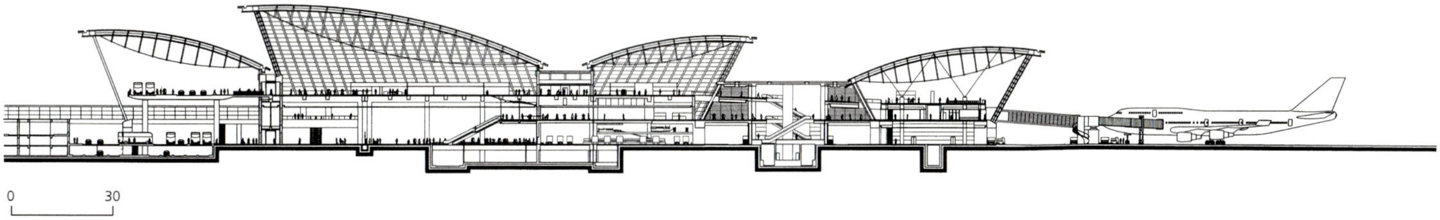

The scale of the airport and its walls and ceilings is emphasized by these views, where workers can be seen against the glass (on the preceding page) or the spiked curving roof defines the long interior spaces (right).

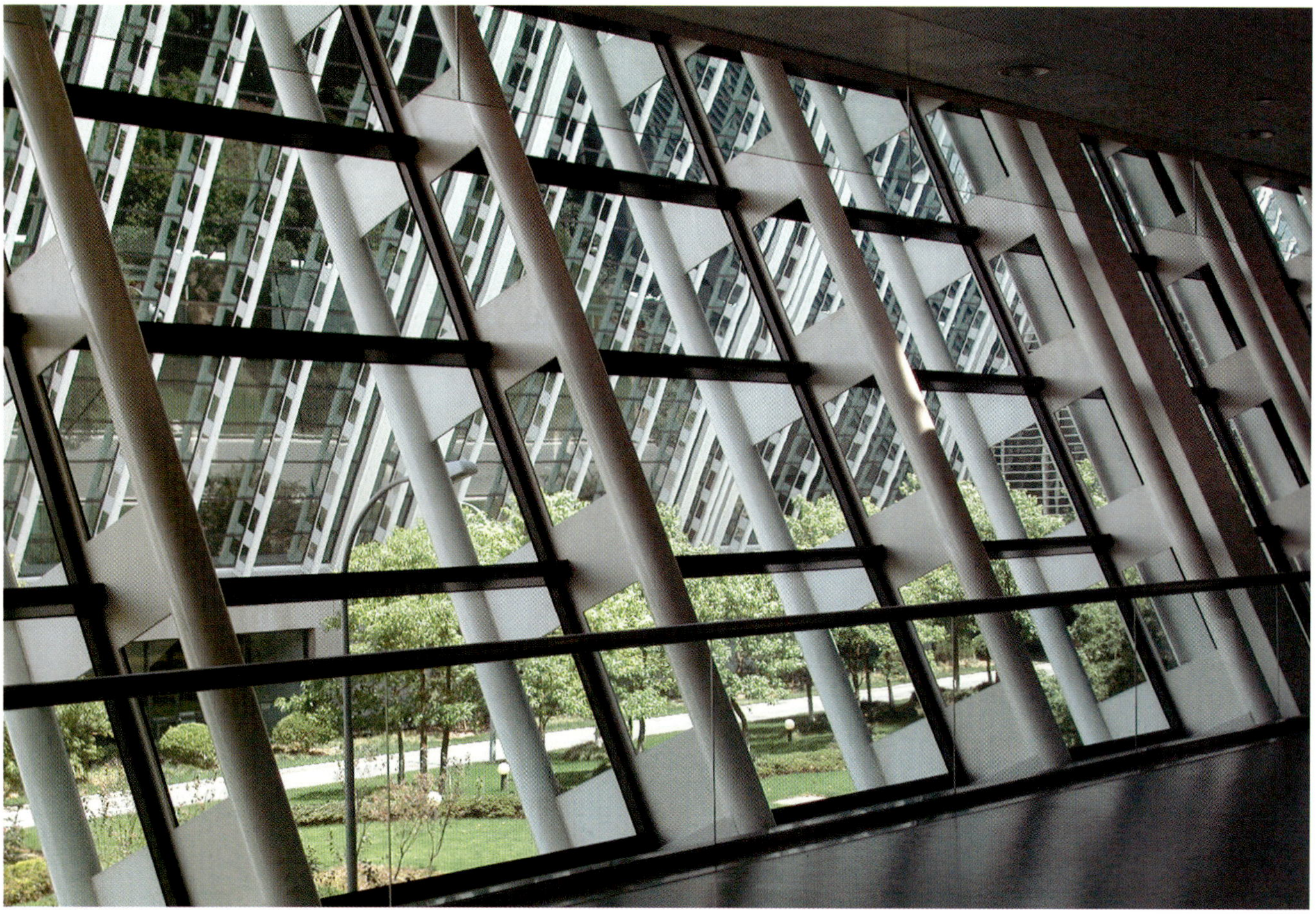

diagonal bars, while the vertical supports enter the dark blue ceiling through openings that also admit light during the day. True to their usual methods, the Chinese construction "institutes" took on the task of building Shanghai Pudong airport with a massive effort involving as many as 10,000 workers simultaneously on-site. Paul Andreu may not have controlled each detail of construction as fully as he has in the case of the Beijing Opera for example where his close collaborator François Tamisier has been permanently stationed.

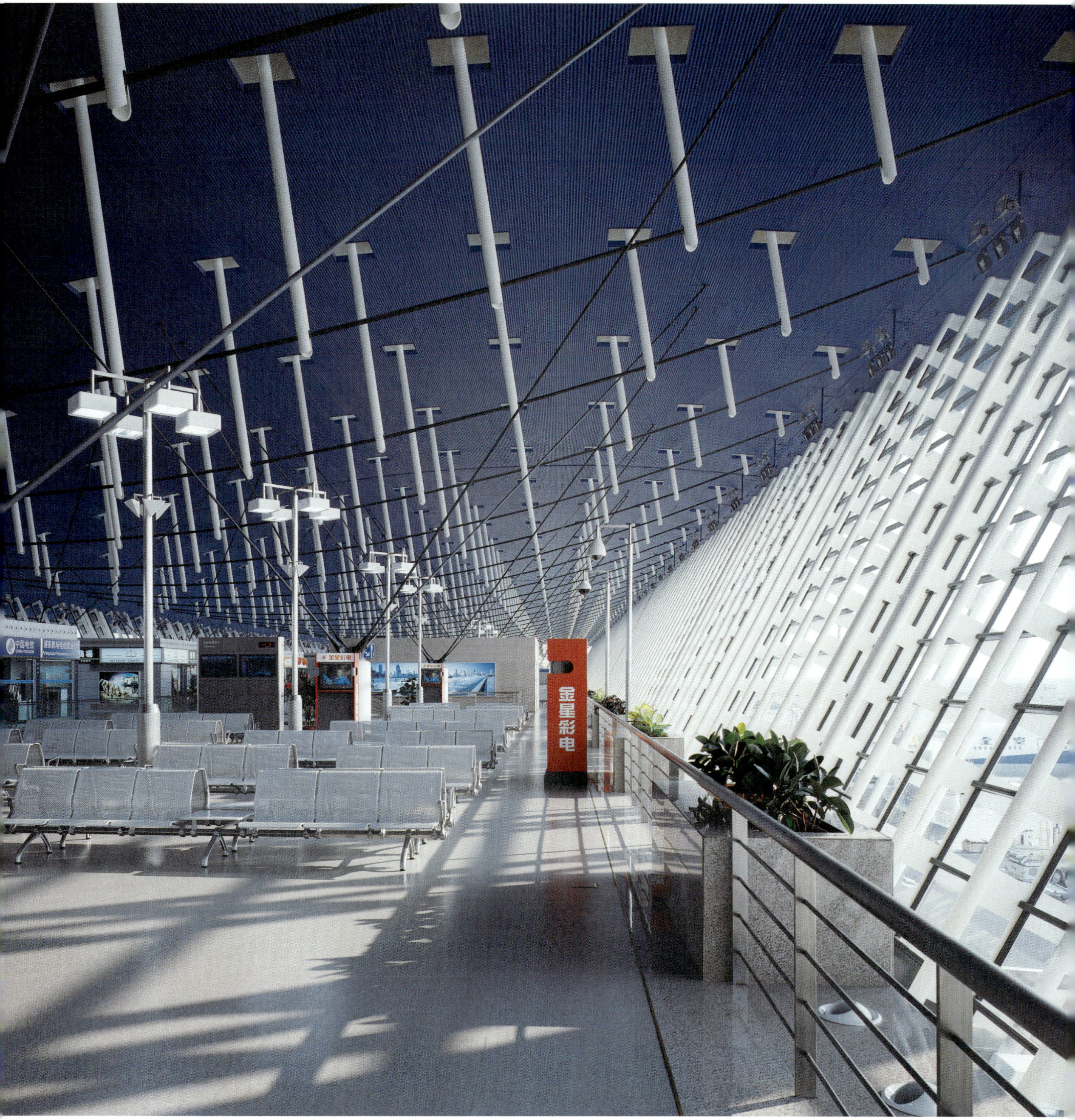

Shanghai Pudong Airport

The last large section of Charles-de-Gaulle airport to be designed by Paul Andreu, Hall E shows just how far he has come in his conception of the modern airport since Terminal 1 was hailed in 1974 as a new type of design.

Charles-de-Gaulle Airport - Terminal 2 E Paris

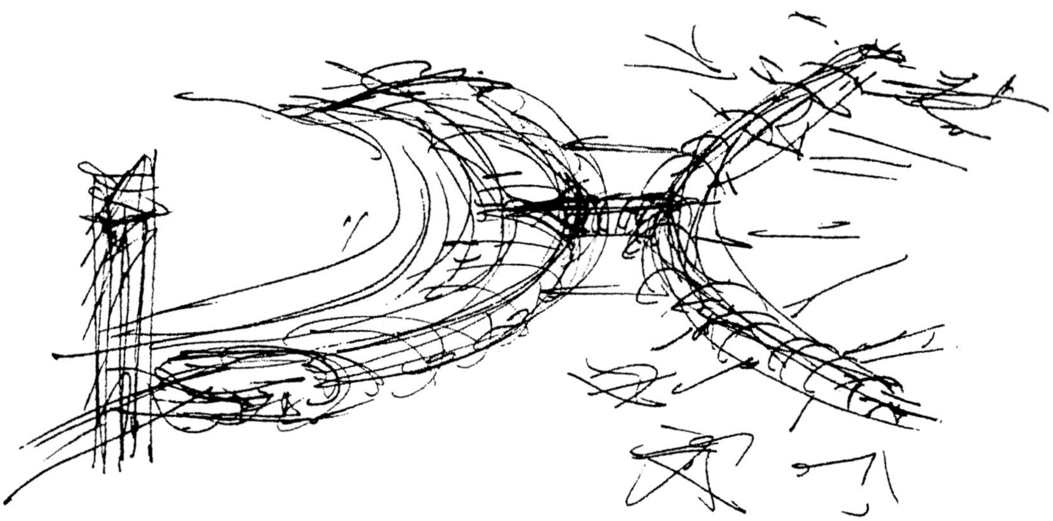

Country: France
Use: Airport
Start of project: 1997
Completion: 2003
Surface: 220,000 m²
Capacity: 11 million passengers per year

The most recent, though surely not the final extension of the Charles-de-Gaulle Airport in Paris is Terminal 2 E, completed in 2003. With a theoretical capacity of 11 million passengers per year and an area of 230,000 square meters, 2 E is larger but less complex than the airline terminal 2 F. Considered the "final link" in the Terminal 2 complex, it has the largest capacity of any of the completed modules (possible maximum capacity 18 million travelers). It also has more shops and more security checkpoints than the rest of Terminal 2. 2 E is an outgrowth of

Although it takes up the long curving volumes seen in Terminal 2 F, the newer building is quite different in both external appearance and internal design.

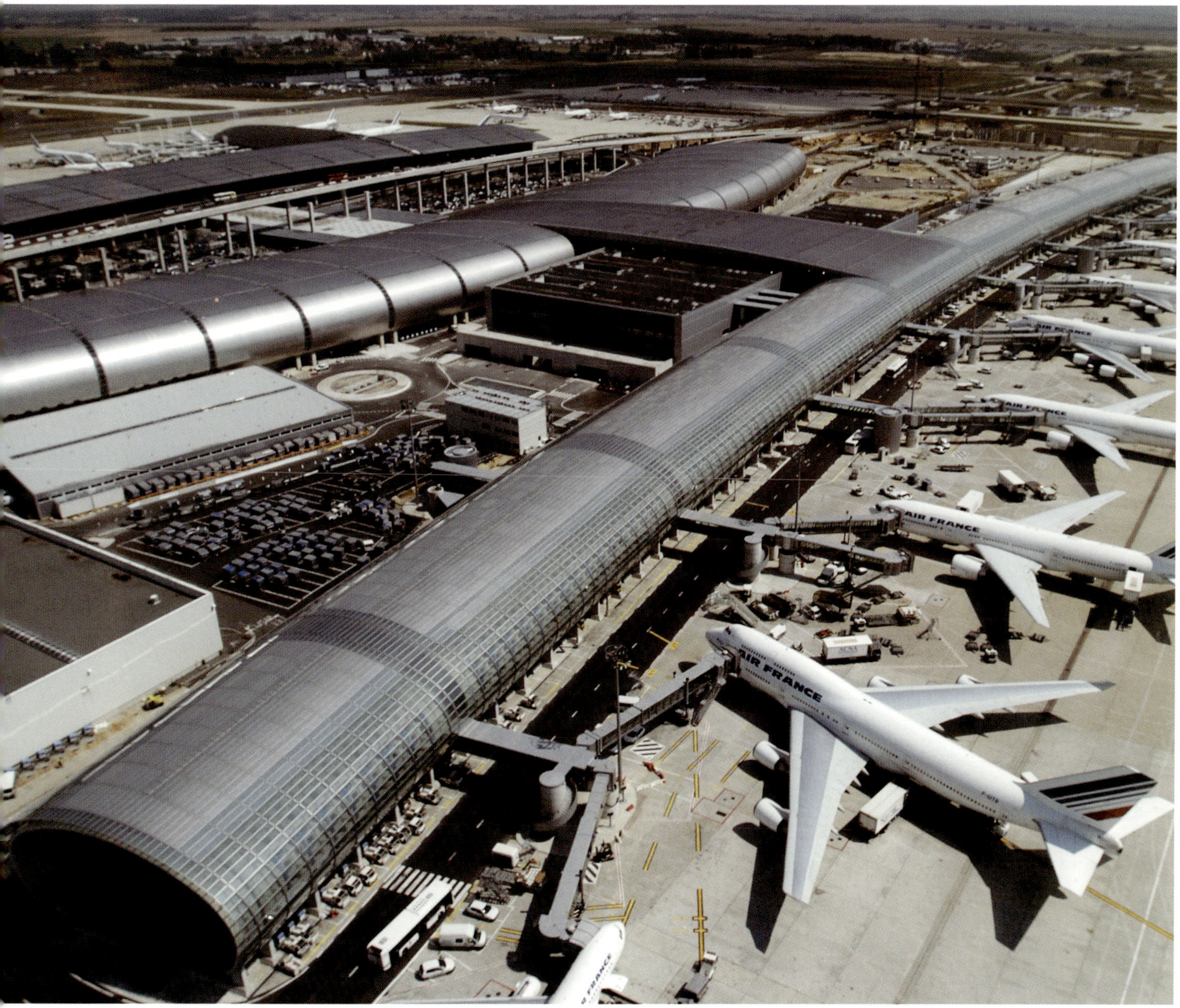

The tubular, concrete glass and metal-enclosed shell of the terminal is visible in these pictures of the interior.

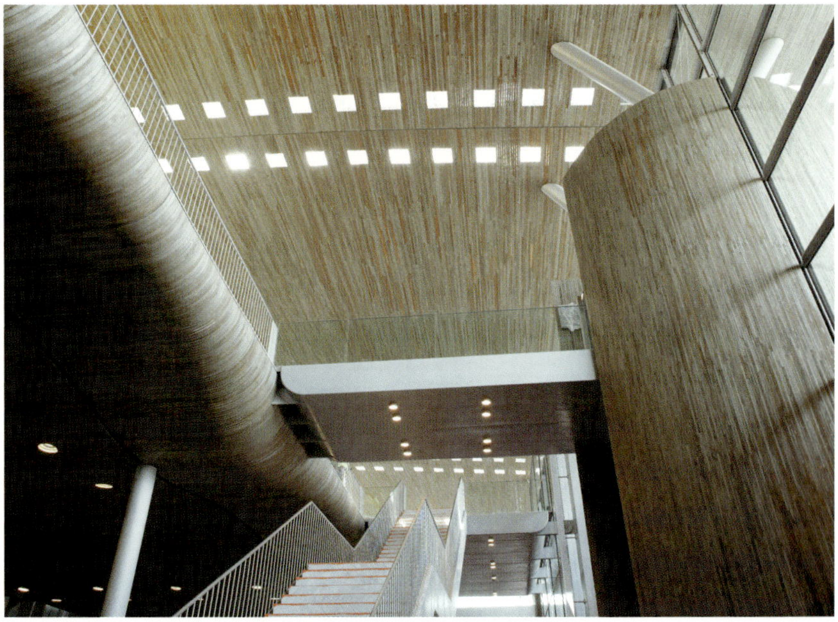

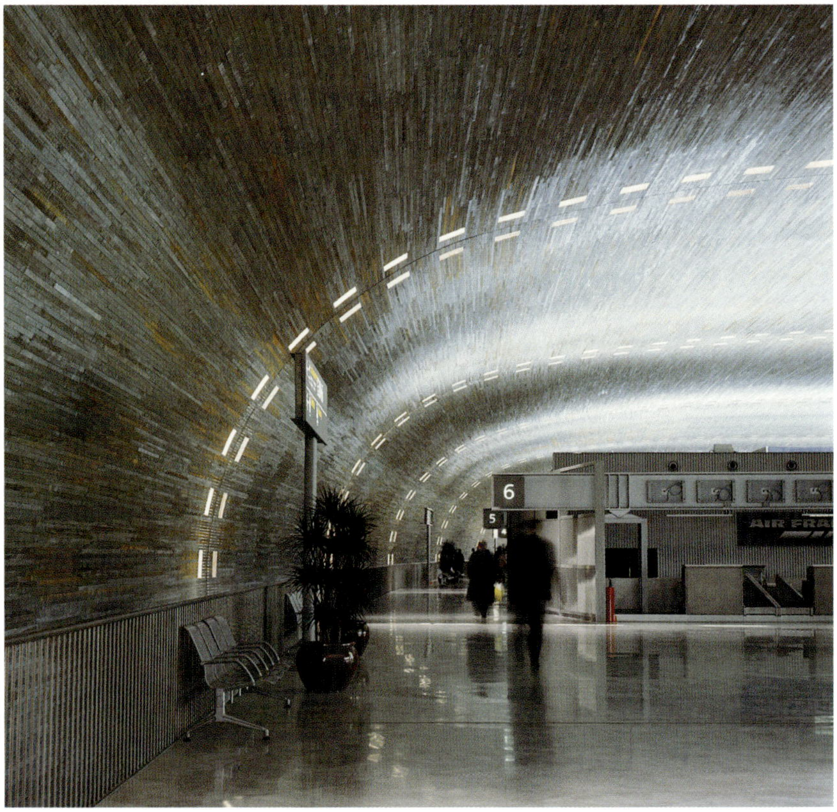

Andreu's work on 2 F, but as was the case in the previous phases of the Charles-de-Gaulle Airport, the architect has insisted on developing and changing the design, rather than permitting a sterile reproduction of earlier designs. Rather than the modular, repetitive system used at Roissy by Andreu for the other structures, 2 E has a continuous, gently curving double-shelled skin. Air ducts for the boarding area are located between the two skins as is artificial lighting. 140 check-in counters are located at a level situated 7.5 meters above ground level in this facility which is in a sense the other "half" of Terminal 2 F which it faces. The boarding "pier" is a structure made up of 4-meter wide assembled elements consisting of a 40-centimeter thick concrete shell, steel arcs and double-glazing. Intended for international traffic, 2 E is to be served by two satellites, situated respectively at 570 and 1200 meters from the center of 2 E and F. They are oriented along a north-south axis. Like its cousin 2 F, 2 E has a "canyon" on the approach side that permits a clear readability of its layers, and it succeeds in clearly dividing ingoing and outgoing passenger flows, a key to coherent design that Andreu clearly mastered with more and more success as he advanced in his work at Roissy. A new access road to the east of the Terminal 2 complex in a sense completes the composition. As Paul Andreu points out, his work on Roissy, with its ongoing ramifications has been a labor of no less than forty years – beginning in 1969 and slated to end in

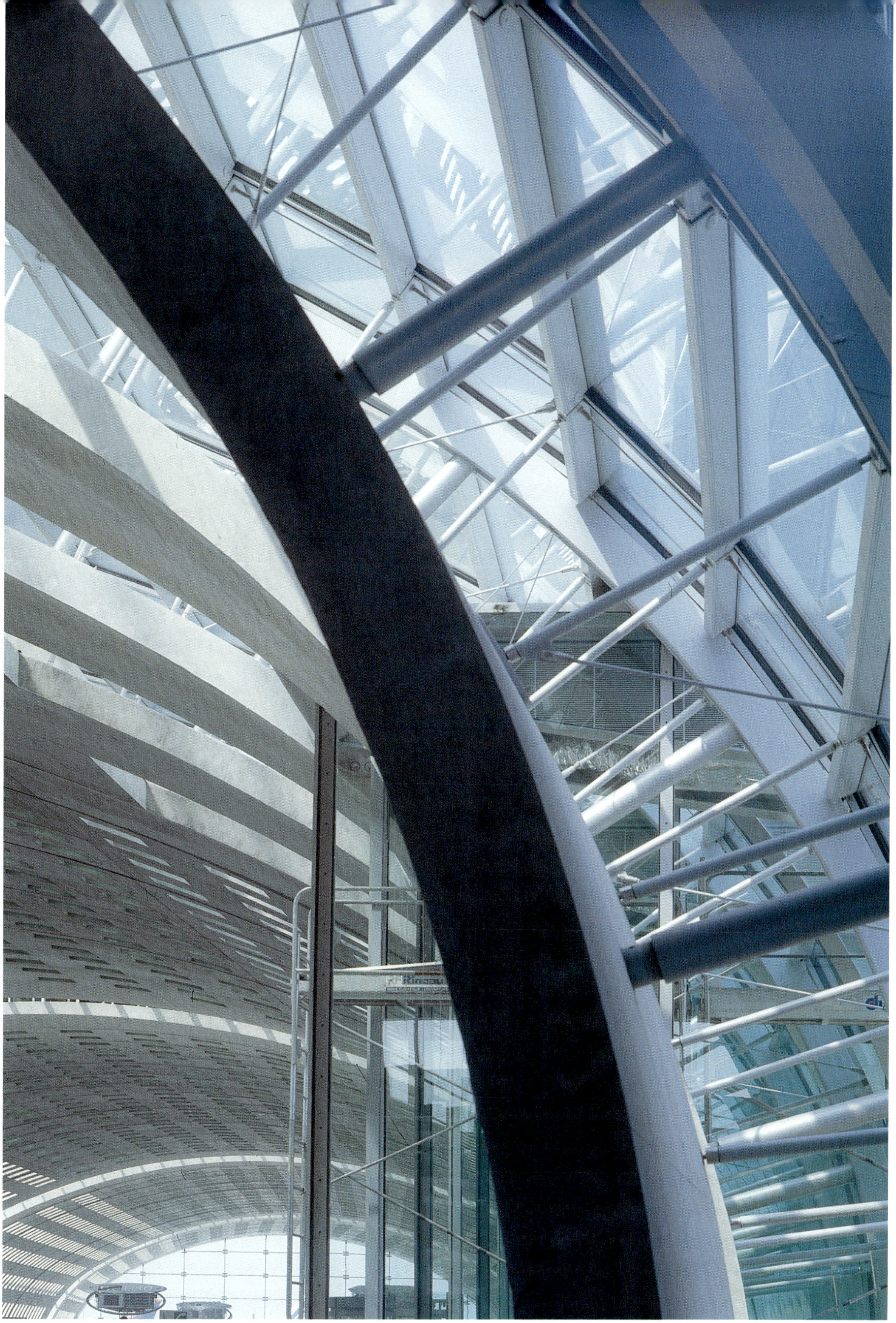

Charles-de-Gaulle Airport - Terminal 2 E

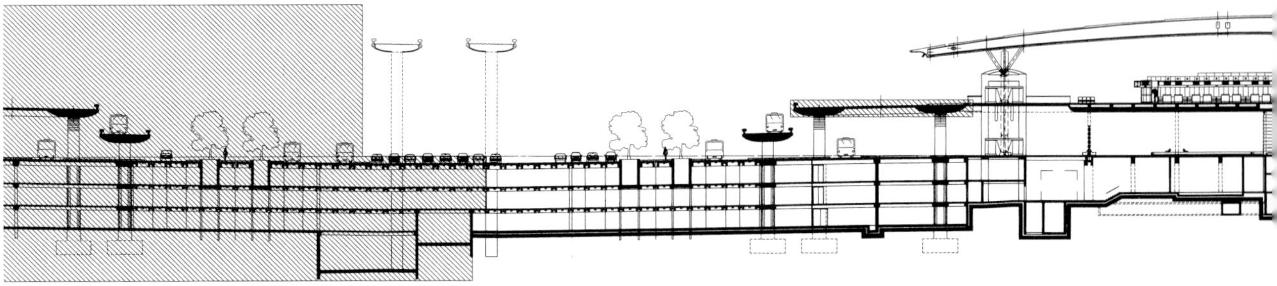

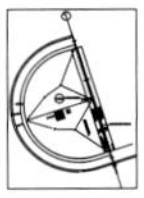

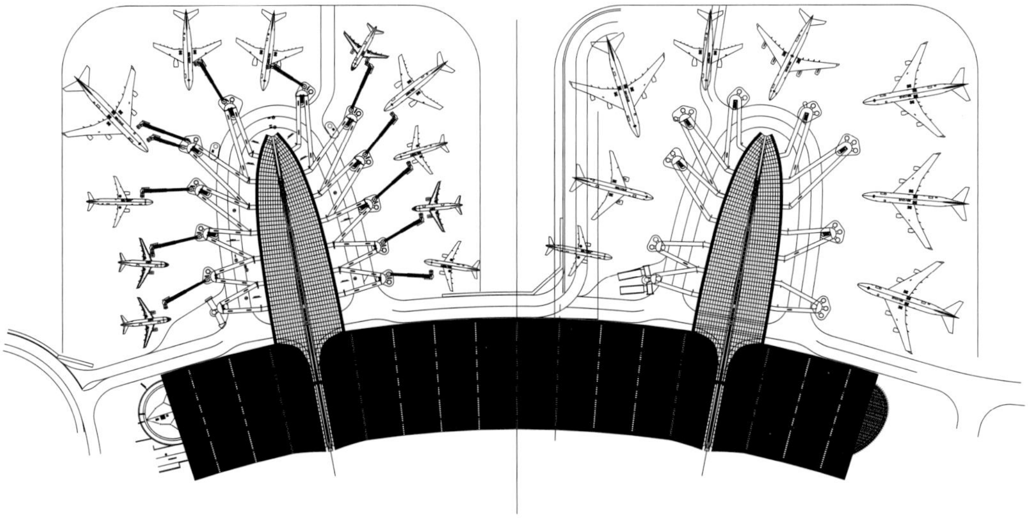

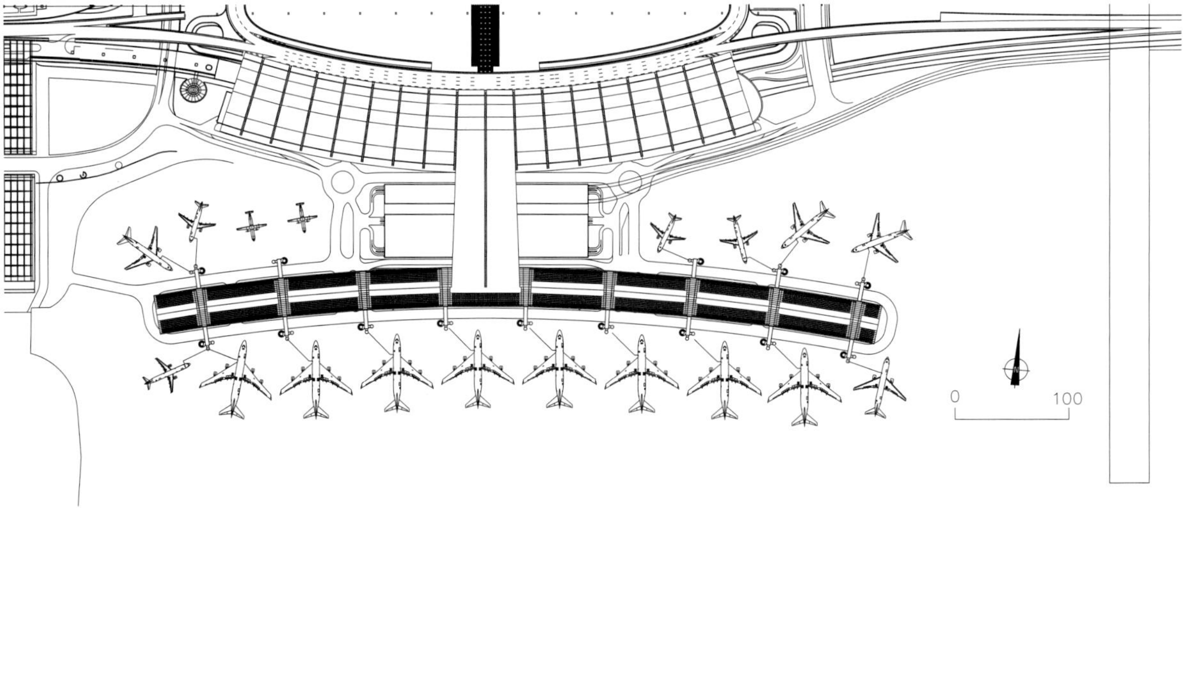
0
100

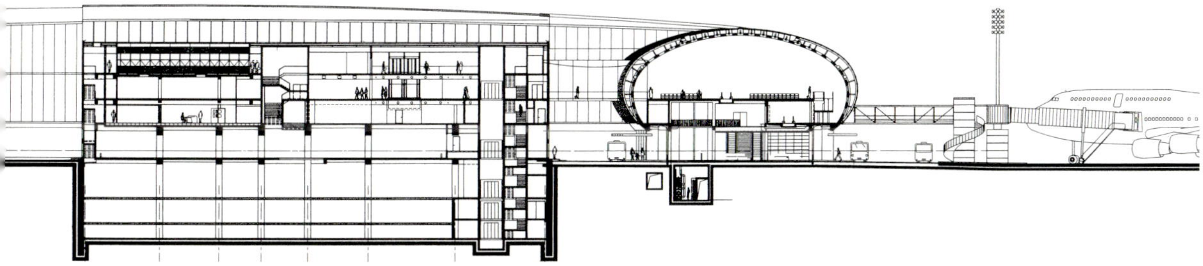

Successive curving bands of pierced concrete or metal and glass characterize the terminal whose function, like that of Terminal 2 F is laid out in two extrusions where airplane boarding is handled.

2008. It is certainly a rare occurrence that a single architect – albeit in this instance one who is ably supported by the teams of Aéroports de Paris – should preside over the destiny of such a visible and significant complex as Roissy Charles-de-Gaulle. Other modern architects, like Japan's Fumihiko Maki with his Hillside Terrace complex in Tokyo have demonstrated a similar devotion to a single zone. But Andreu's designs are

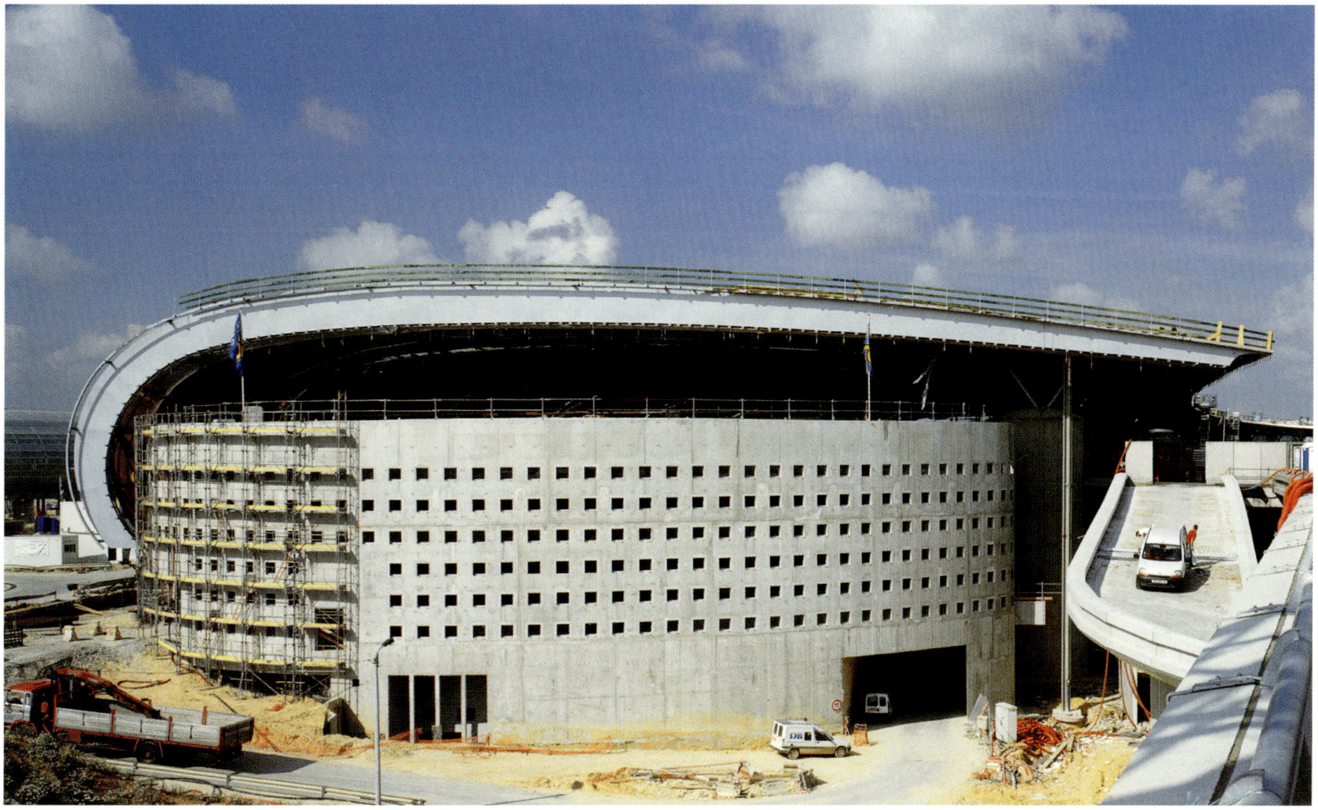

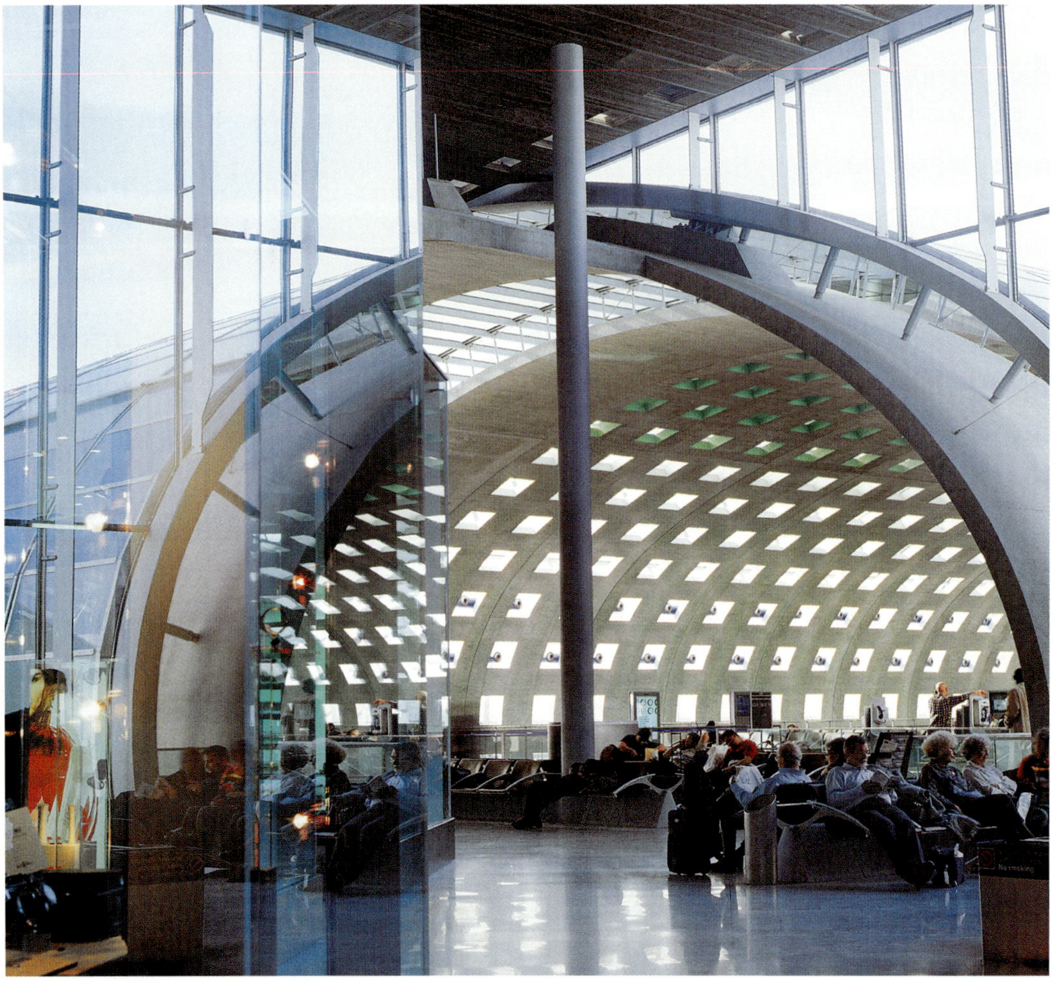

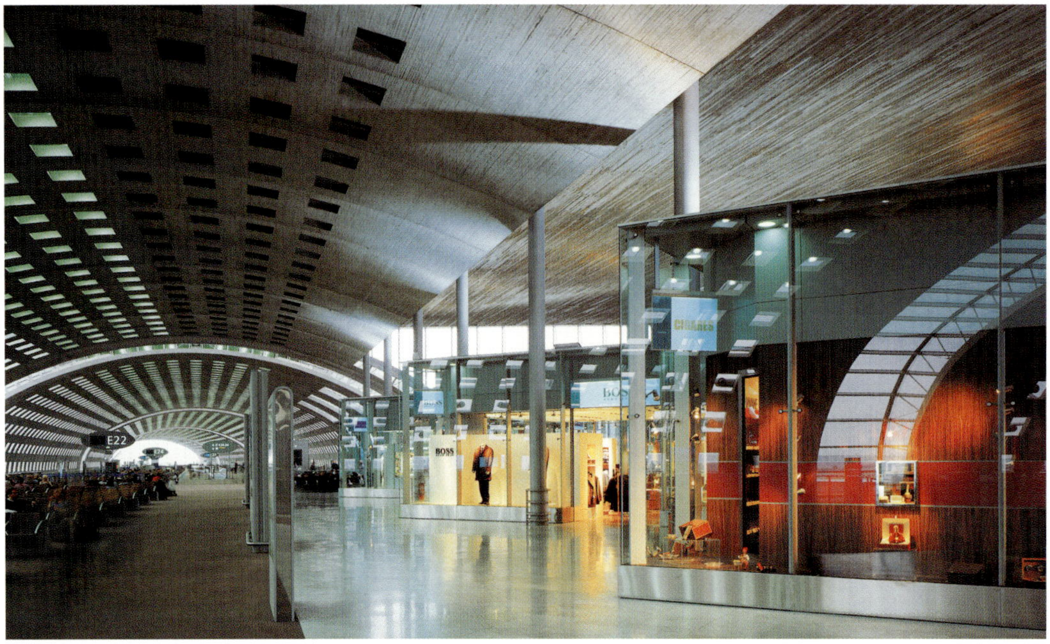

With its pierced concrete shell system, Terminal 2 E reveals more of its structural workings than most of the previous buildings at Charles-de-Gaulle Airport, with the possible exception of Terminal 2 F, conceived in a similar transparent mode.

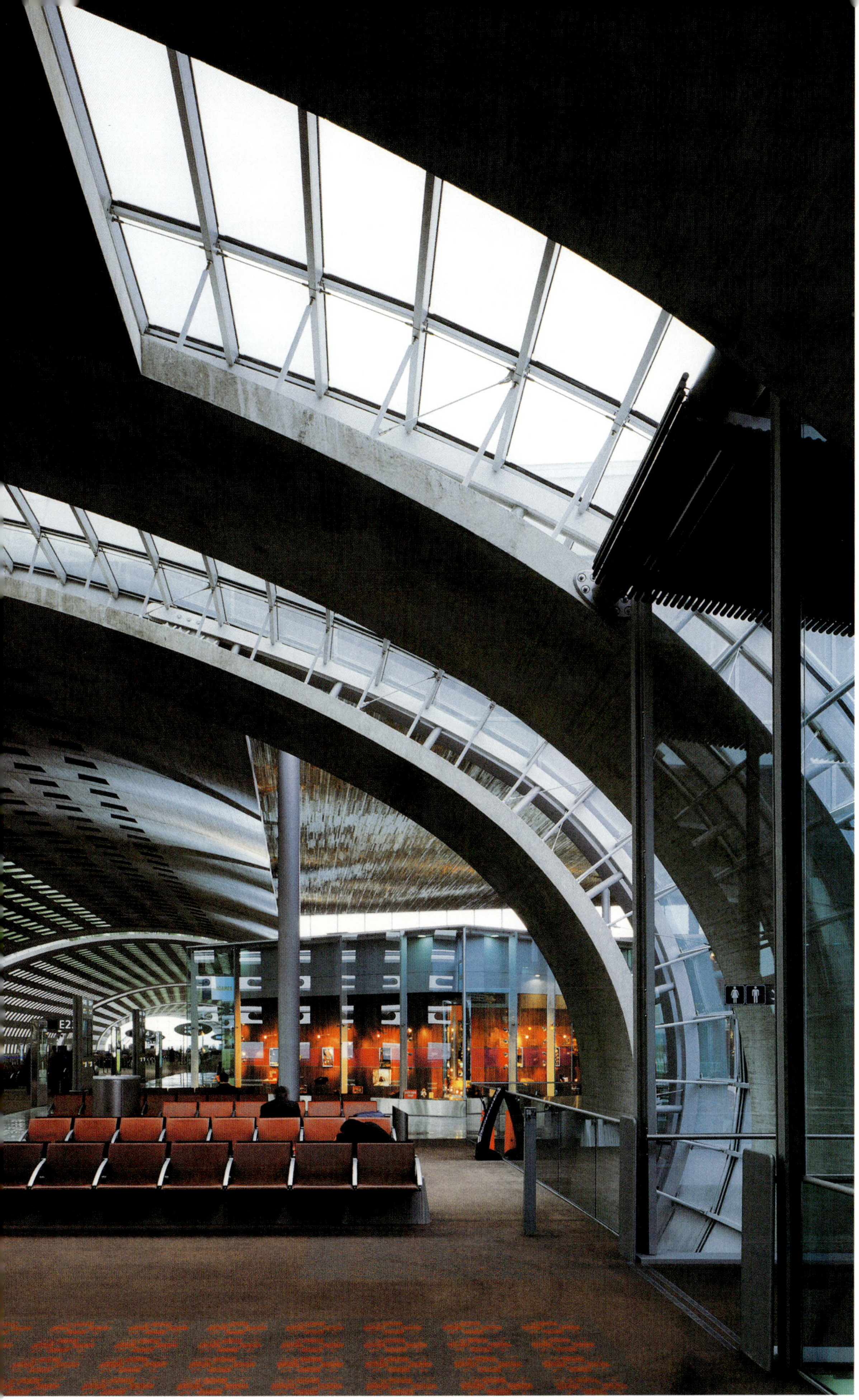

Interior spaces are carefully provided with natural light entering either through large glass walls or through square openings in the outer shell. Though the tubular volumes may recall those inside of actual aircraft, their dimensions are sufficient to avoid any of the impression of claustrophobia that some suffer in planes.

Waiting areas again avoid the feeling of enclosure that might have resulted from the flattened tube design through a clever and consistent use of light. The light comes not only from the end of the volume, but also from the top and sides thanks to the repetitive square openings.

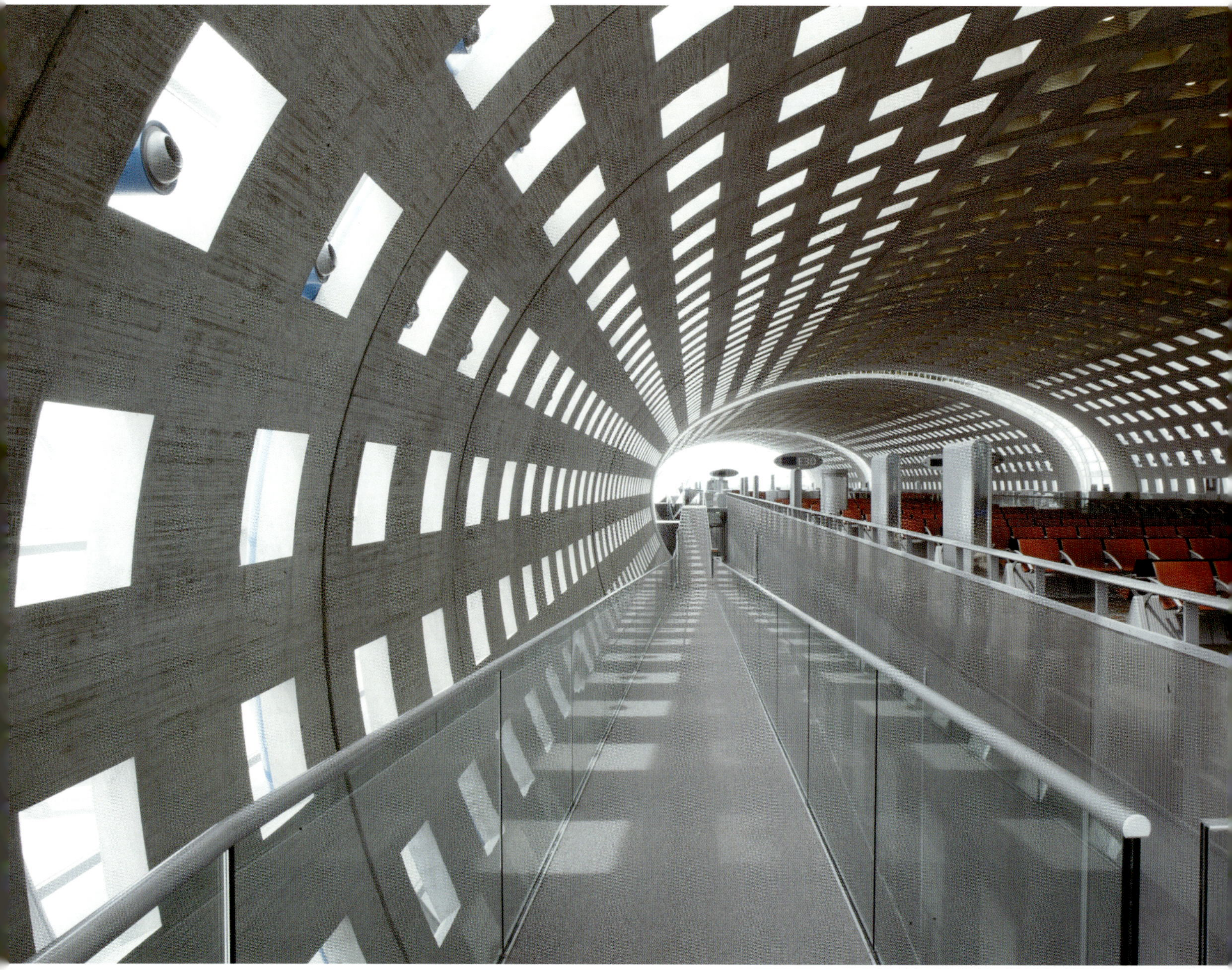

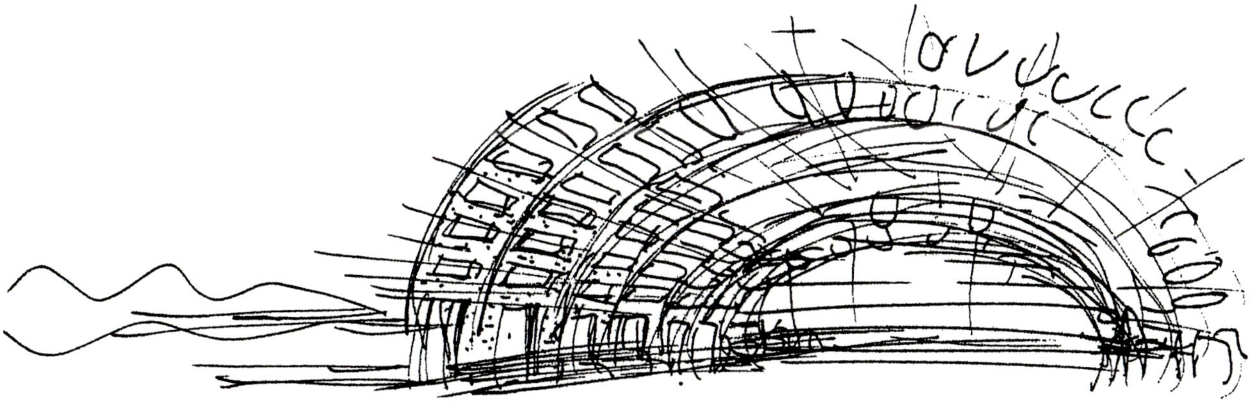

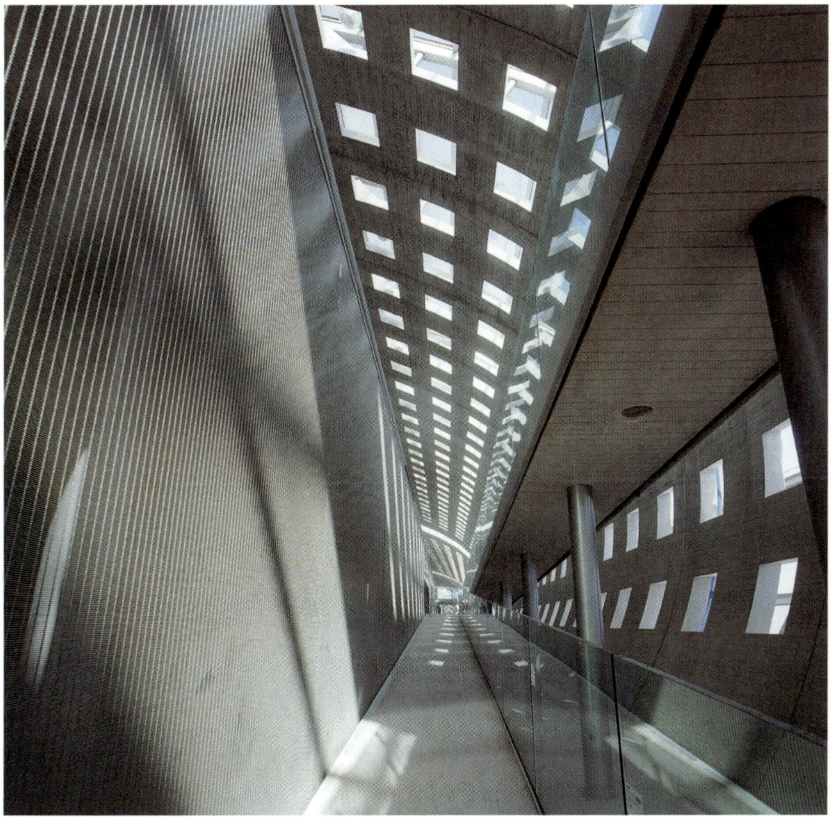

in many cases, the first contact of foreigners with France and as such, they may well serve to establish a lasting impression of the country. The functional elegance and carefully mastered architectural and engineering aspects of Roissy make it one of the most successful major airports in the world. While staying within the confines of a relatively bureaucratic and complicated system, Andreu has found his path – one that first and foremost takes into account the necessary utilitarian elements. But Andreu, unlike so many of his contemporaries who stop there, goes on to make a virtue of necessity, to make beauty out of what could so easily be banal. Light and space have gradually taken centre-stage in his airport terminals, perhaps because the practical considerations became second nature to him at a certain time. Roissy Terminal 1 was striking, especially when it first opened, but it had an underlying complexity that is akin to the realization of many French engineers in other domains. Terminal 2 has been a steady progression toward the light, and it is the travelers who benefit from this transition. Those with an eye for architecture look, and others just feel a sense of ease and comfort that is exceedingly rare in modern air transport.

Moving further from airport design with this new complex, Paul Andreu resolves the complicated programmatic issues with an ease born of his earlier experience. Unexpected curves and angles give a sense of movement to the whole.

Guangzhou Gymnasium **Guangzhou**

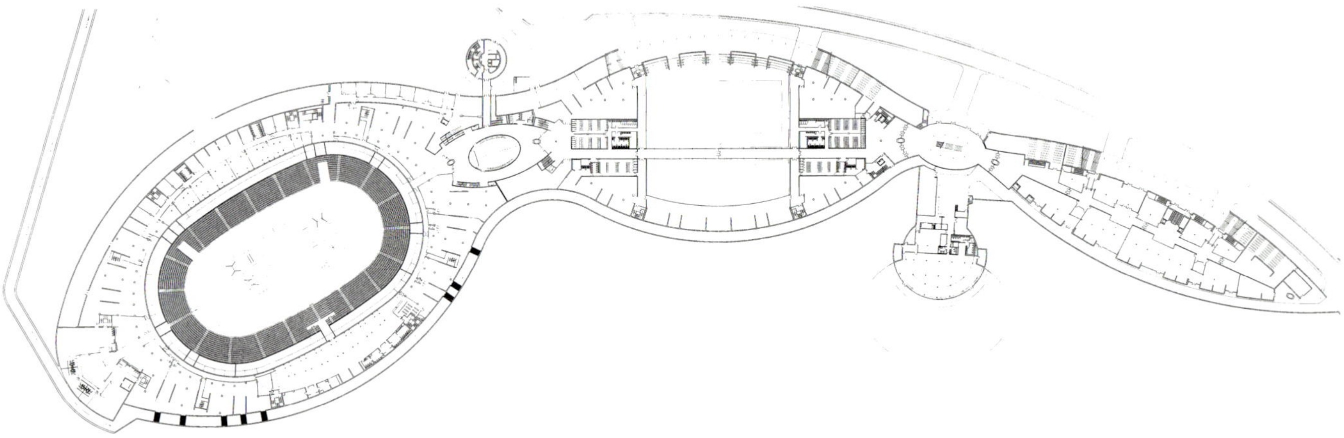

Country: China
Use: Sports facilities
Start of project: 1998
Completion: 2001
Surface: 100,000 m^2

Located to the northeast of the International Airport and Natural Park of Guangzhou, this is one of the major elements built for the 9th National Games of the People's Republic of China (2001). Three shell-shaped buildings with white roofs, and a strong link between each other contain all the facilities. The semi-transparent 30,000-square meter roofs are an essential element of the composition. As Paul Andreu says, "Each of the elements that constitutes the sports complex has a semi-transparent roof designed to ensure during the day quality uniform lighting, perfect for television broadcasting, and to stand out at night like a great light signal, visible from the road and the hills. The supporting frames resemble the ones used in Terminal 2 F of Charles-de-Gaulle Airport in Paris, but here the maximum span of 160 meters is much greater. Once

A night view of the complex gives a glowing, almost organic impression of the successive forms. As he does in airport design, but with somewhat more liberty here due to the less restrictive program, Andreu uses unexpected angles or spatial variations to give an impression of movement to his architecture.

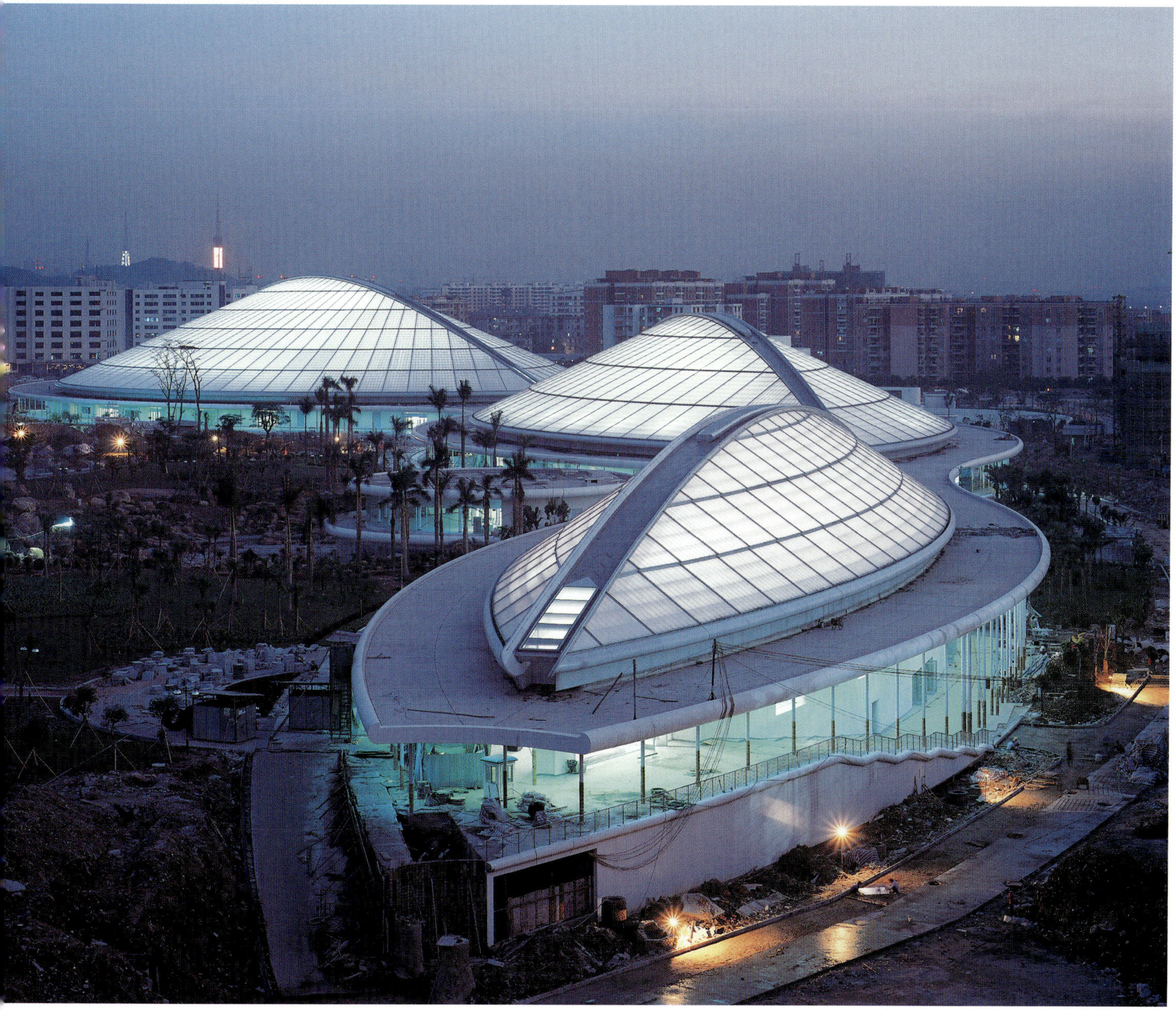

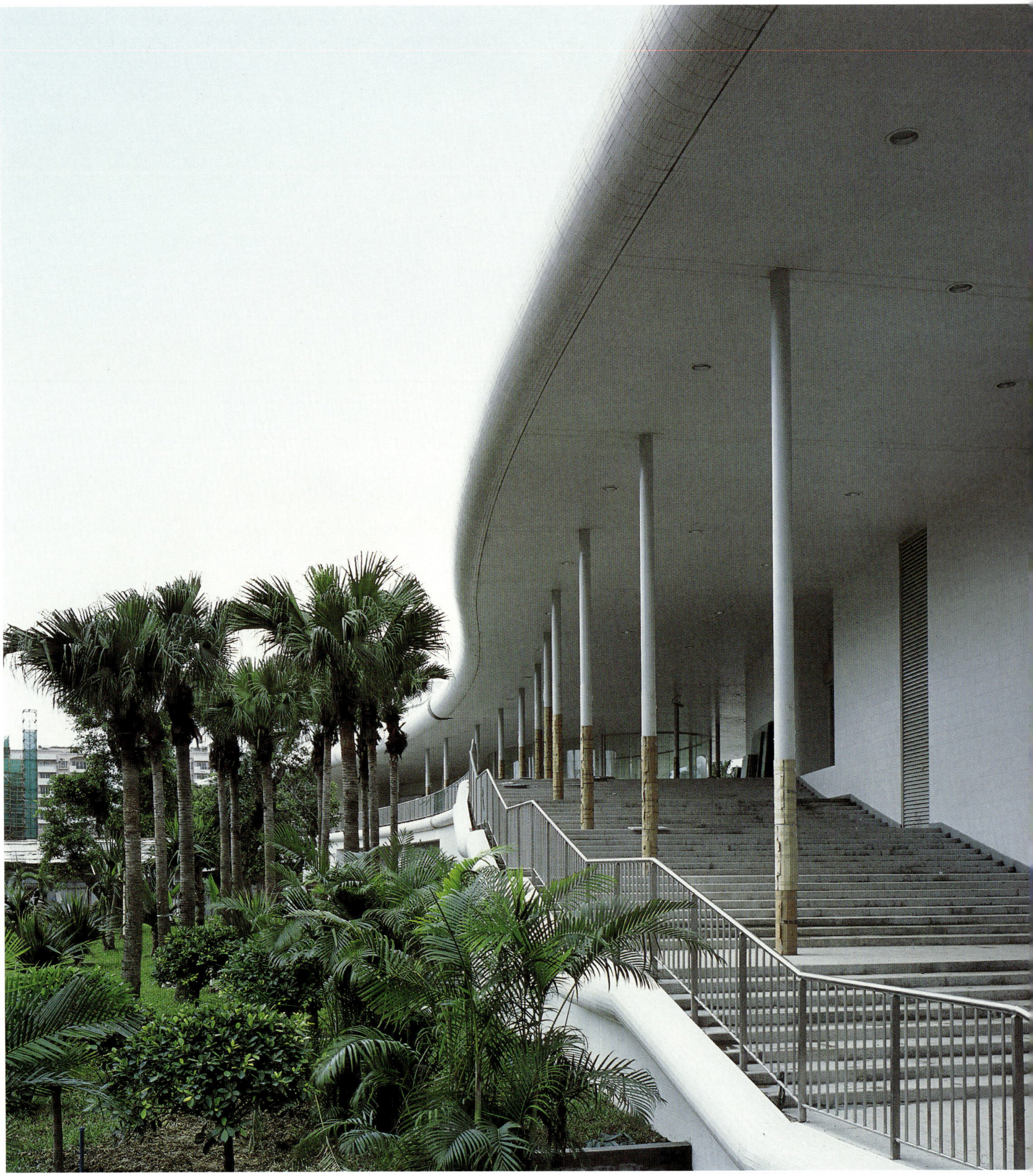

Open canopied areas with very thin columns allow users to be covered and yet to be exposed to the natural surroundings. Gentle curves also animate the structures and avoid the boredom that a rectilinear vocabulary would have produced.

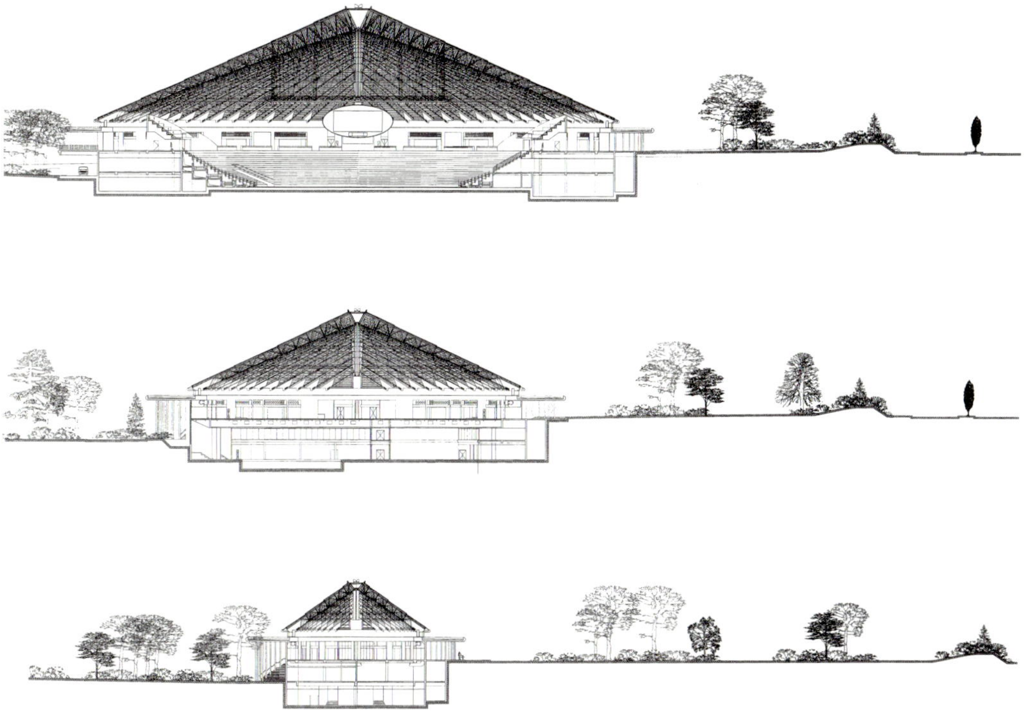

again, the upper ridge serves as a technical space where the cross beams can be joined in such a way that the framework remains a lightweight structure which, together with the semi-transparent roof, forms the luminous material which has been the object of so much of my work." The three buildings have the following functions: a main covered 6,500-seat stadium which can adopt a variety of configurations for athletics, gymnastics, team sports, tennis, ping-pong (10,000 seats) or various forms of entertainment; a training area that includes a large hall, an Olympic-size swimming pool and a series of rooms designed for special sports; and a public sports center. In addition to this 100,000-square meter complex on the eight-hectare site, there are parking lots, an office building, a restaurant and an athlete's village, designed by another group of architects. The entire complex is intended to form a logical transition from the urban landscape to the neighboring Baiyun Hills. As Paul Andreu declares, "In response to the brief for the design competition launched by the municipal

The vast glazed roof of an open sports area is the internal complement to the glowing exterior view seen at the beginning of this chapter. As the section on the previous page shows, the architect inserts the volumes into the slightly different ground levels rather than sitting the building on top of the land in a more traditional way.

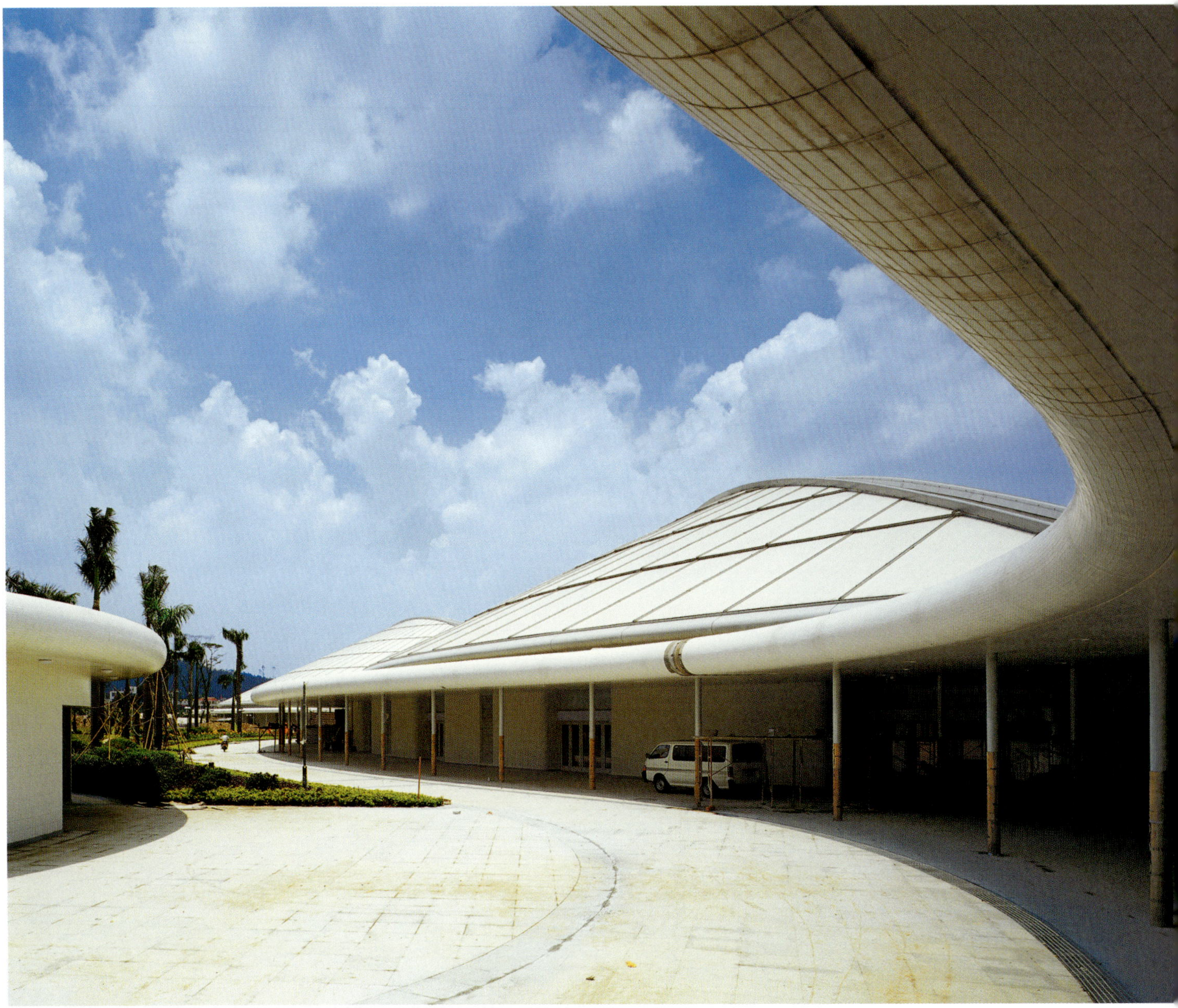

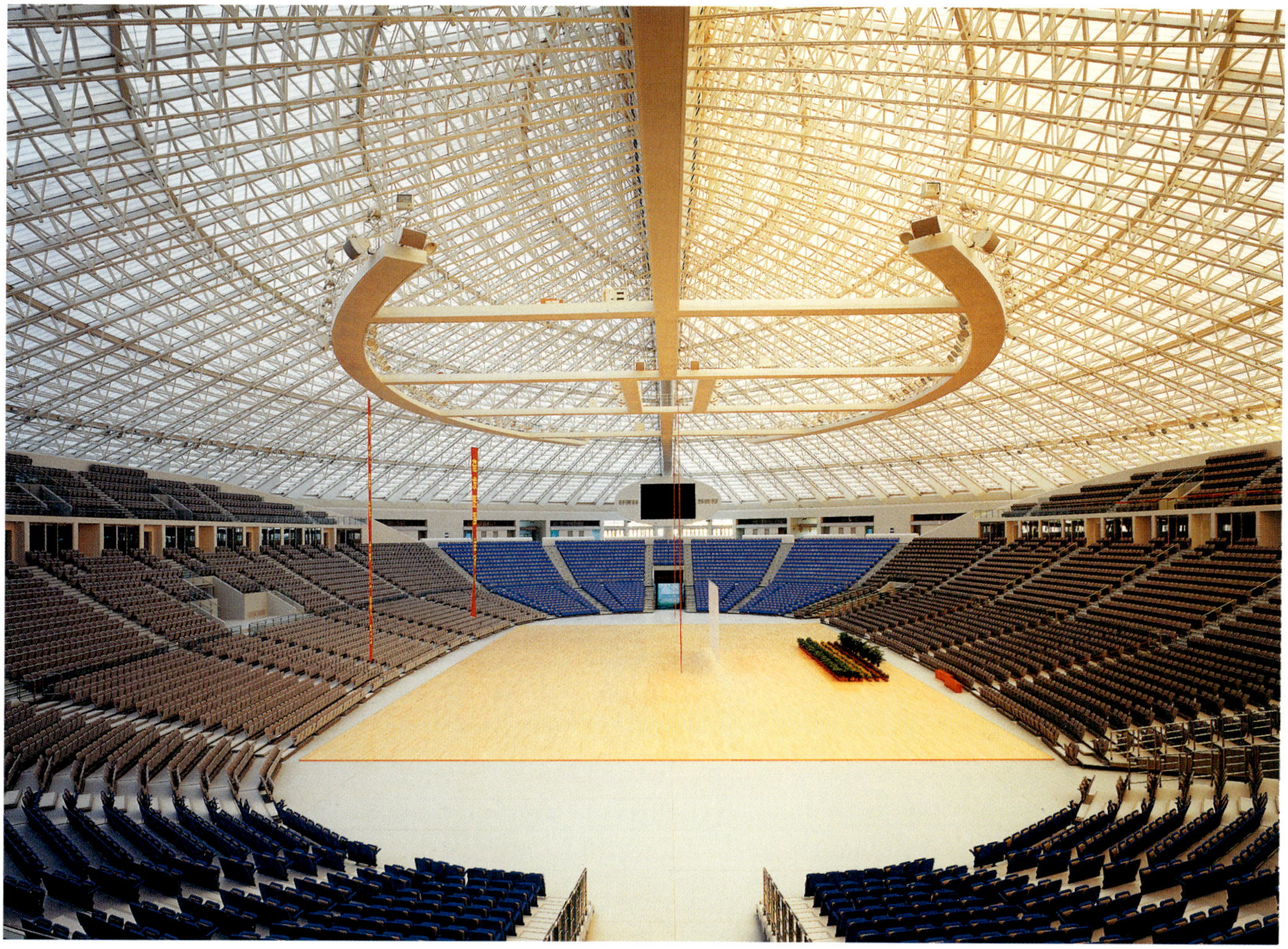

government of Canton (Guangzhou), we decided that preserving the view of the protected landscape of the Baiyun hills was to be the main element of our project. The facilities were designed to create a smooth transition between the cityscape and the countryside. Whence the idea of a low-lying structure on a human scale, partially set under ground level in order to obtain the necessary interior space to accommodate major sports events. From this base, we designed three emerging roof structures, three small fairly round and geometrically pure hills, forming a sort of landscape in the landscape. This movement is what led us to the roof material. We wanted the complex to stand out during the day in pearly white amidst the surrounding greenery, and to shine at night, when it would be illuminated from inside, like some sort of unreal vision against the dark hills in the background." Working with François Tamisier who is also responsible for the Beijing Opera project, Andreu here begins to affirm his gradual move away from the world of airport design. Like any good architect, he learns from his previous work, employing a roofing system similar to that of Charles-de-Gaulle 2 F for example, but both in terms of working conditions and of the interest of the design, this project, along with the Maritime Museum in Osaka, are Andreu's declaration of independence, a fact to be confirmed in a spectacular manner when he completes the Beijing Opera.

By far the most prestigious contract to have been awarded to a foreign architect since China began its recent economic rise, the Beijing National Grand Theater also confirms the country's desire to adapt a resolutely modern vocabulary for its symbolic edifices.

National Grand Theater of China Beijing

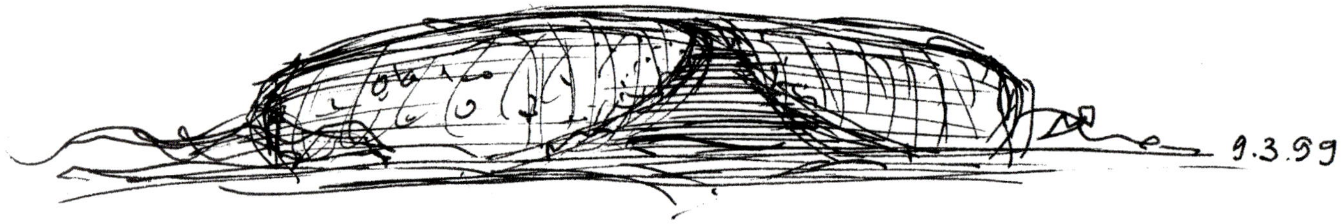

Country: China
Use: Theater
Start of project: 1999
Completion: 2005
Surface: 149,500 m^2
Capacity: 2,416 / 2,017 / 1,040 seats

Awarded to Paul Andreu in August 1999 as a result of an international competition that he won in the last phase against Carlos Ott, author of the Paris Bastille Opera and the English architect Terry Farrell, as well as a Chinese group from Xinghua University, this 149,500-square meter structure is being erected just behind the Great Hall of the People, near Tien An Men Square, and thus very close to the entrance to the Forbidden City. It is a 212-meter long ellipsoidal titanium shell that will house three halls of 2,416 seats (opera), 2,017

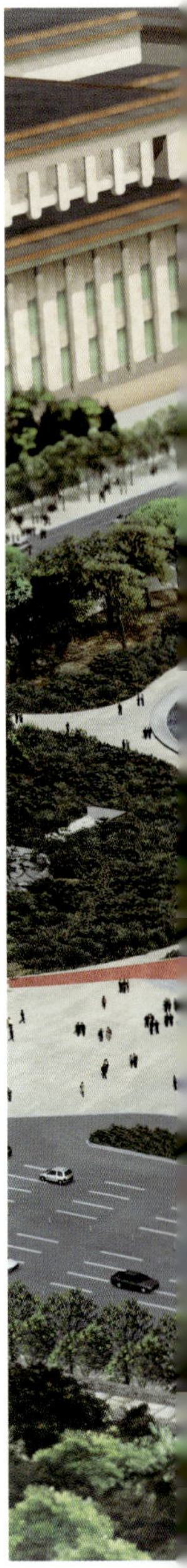

A sketch by Paul Andreu and a virtual aerial view of the Theater give a clear impression of the environment and exterior appearance of the completed structure. Visible to the left on the computer view is the rear façade of the Great Hall of the People, recalling the proximity of Tien An Men Square and the Forbidden City.

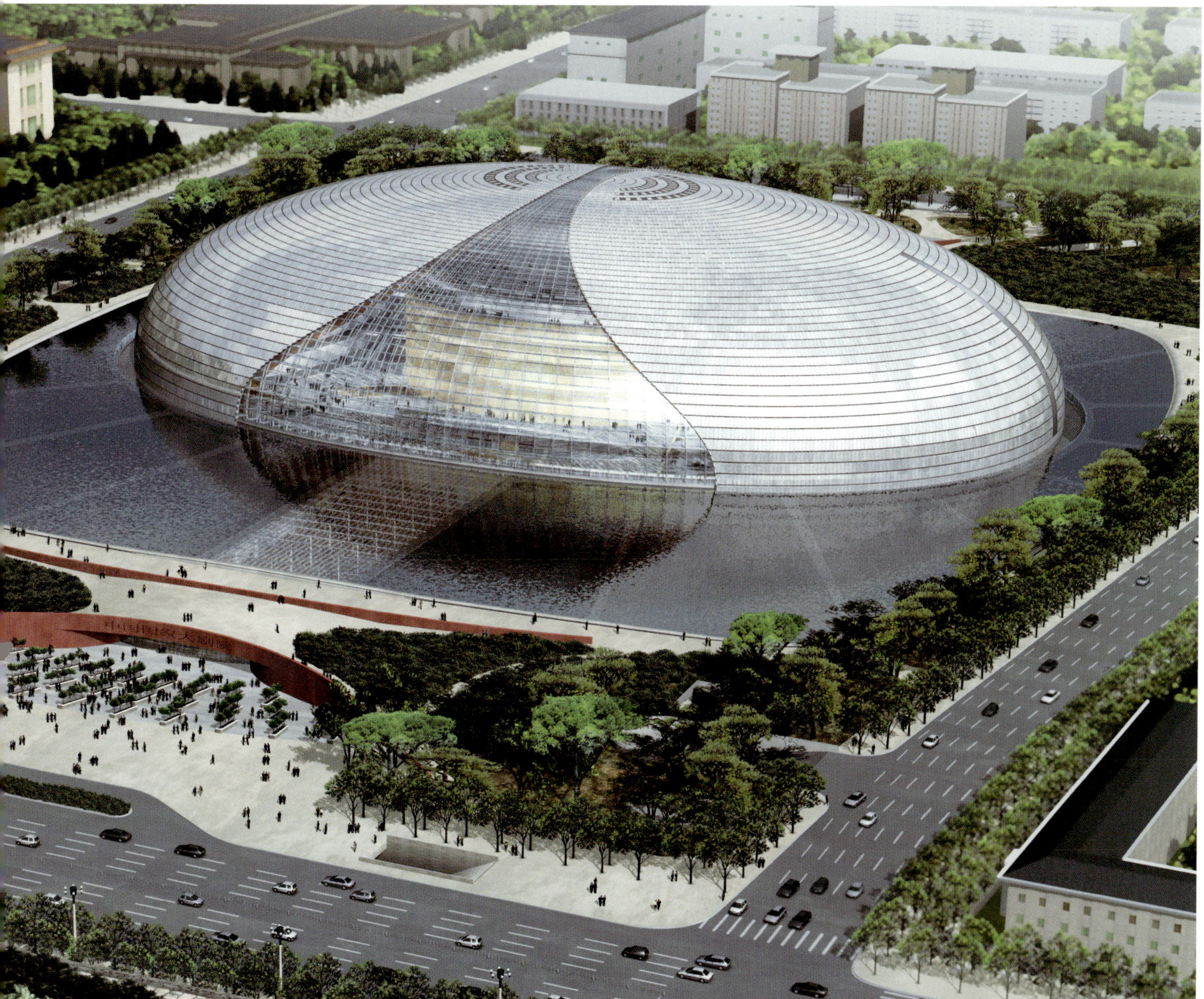

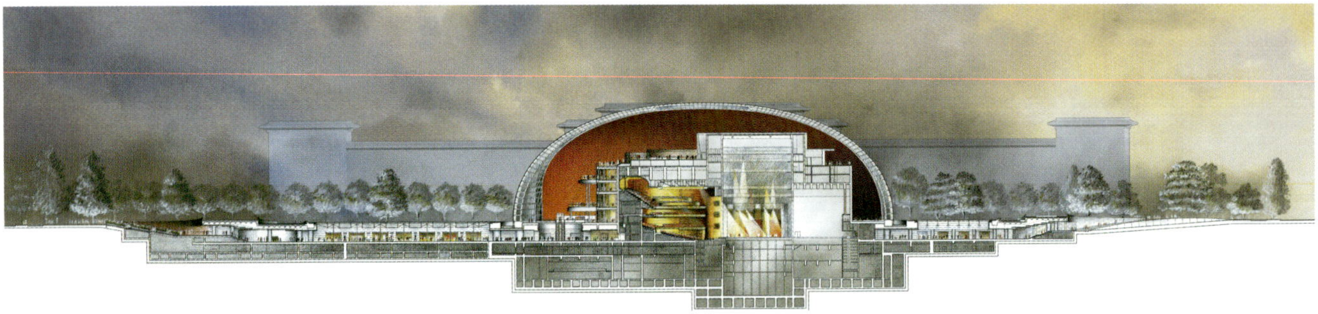

The external shell houses the different performance and technical facilities. Though the insides of the building are complex, the whole is ordered in an almost mathematical perfection that brings to mind certain natural phenomena. It might be recalled that in Chinese mythology, the tortoise is the symbol of longevity and wisdom. It is said that its shell represents the vault of the universe.

seats (concerts) and 1,040 seats (theater). The shorter axis of the structure is 143 meters long and the height of the shell is 46 meters. In order to leave the external shell intact, the architect has chosen to provide public access through a transparent 60-meter long tunnel that will pass beneath the basin that surrounds the building. This is a device similar to the underwater tunnel he used in the Osaka Maritime Museum. Andreu emphasizes that the tunnel is an essential design element since it represents a transition space between the bustling outside world and the world of culture

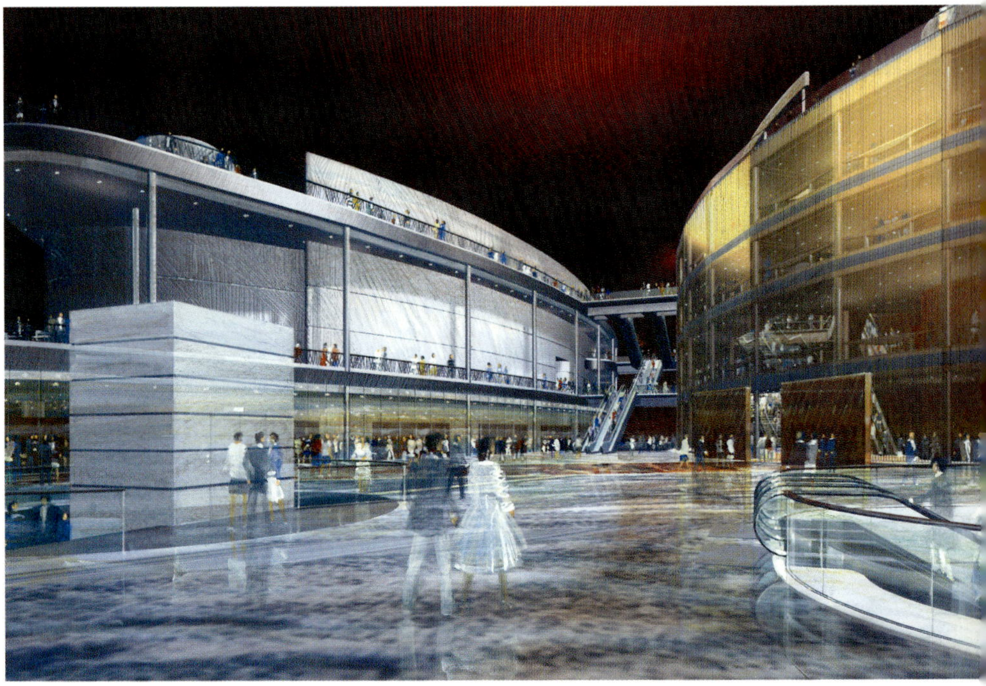

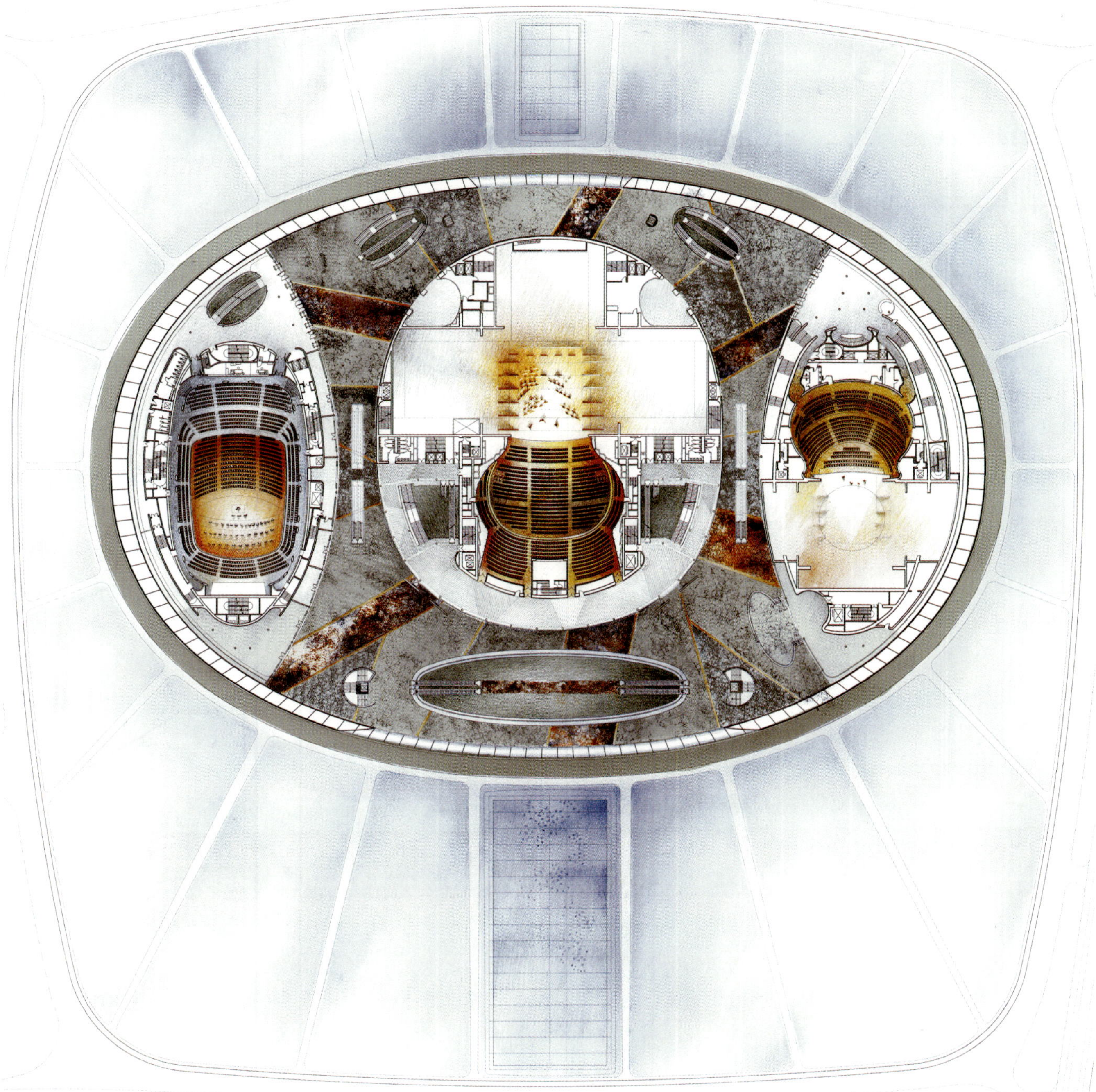

The plan shows the disposition of the three facilities within the main shell of the Opera. The egg-like outline gives an almost biological appearance to what is a purely functional disposition of the theaters.

A construction photo taken early in 2004 (below) and a virtual image of the completed Opera (right) show the close correlation between the original project and the almost completed structure. Below, a sketch of the foyer, and right, an overall plan of the Opera.

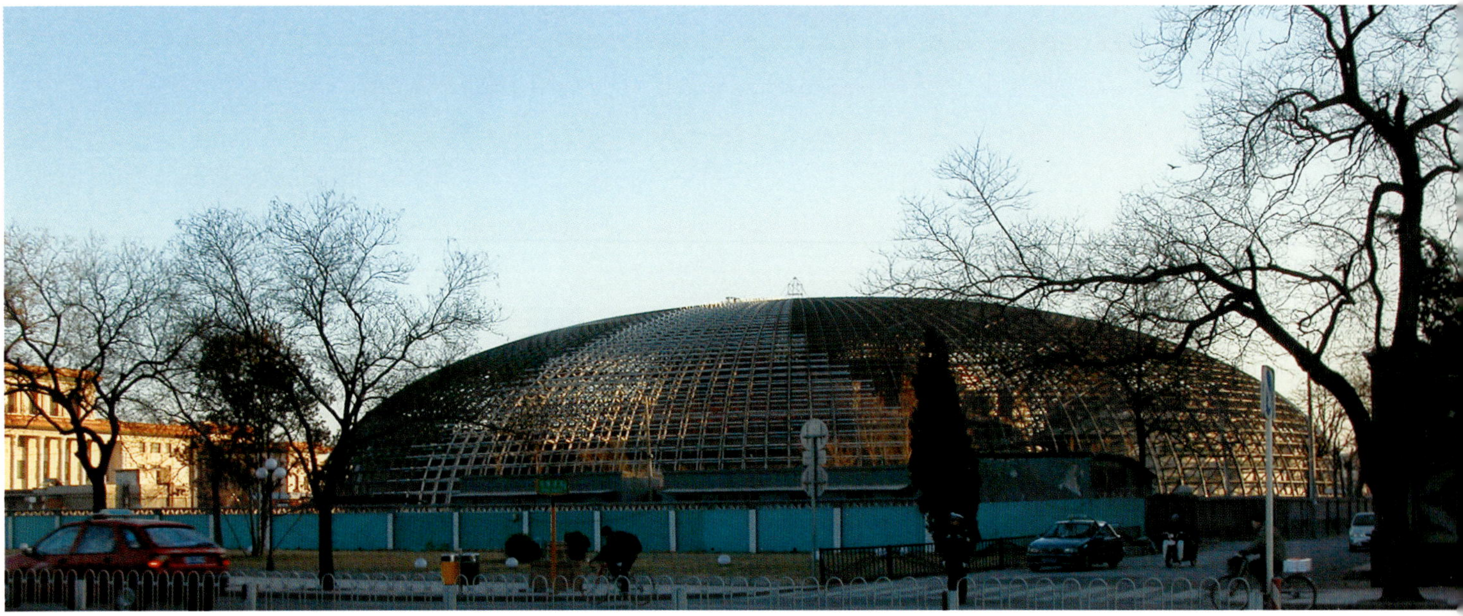

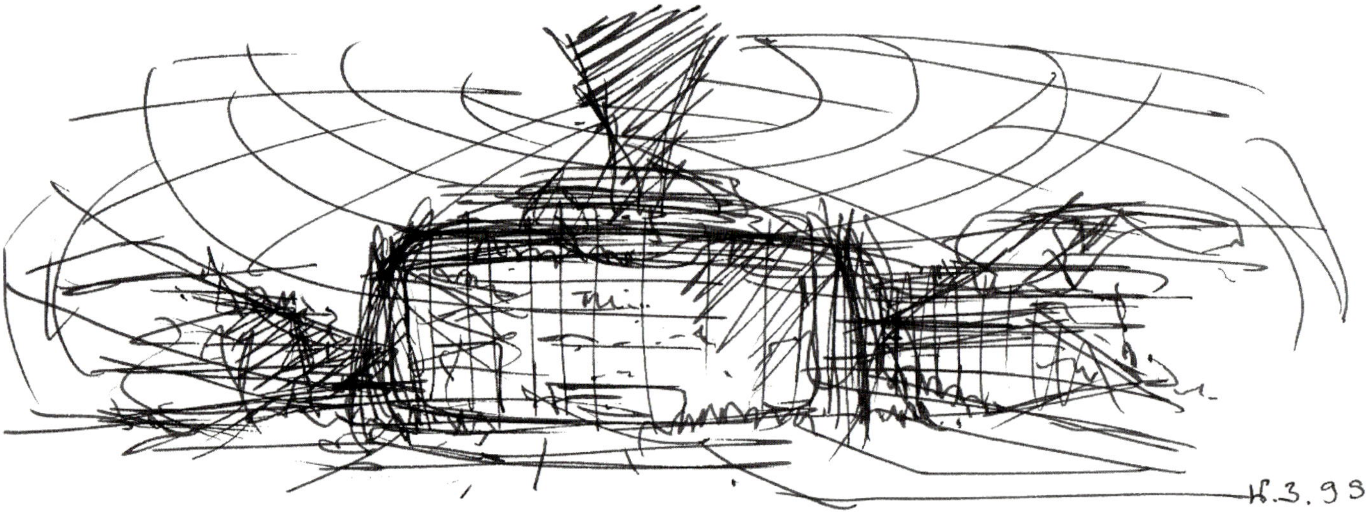

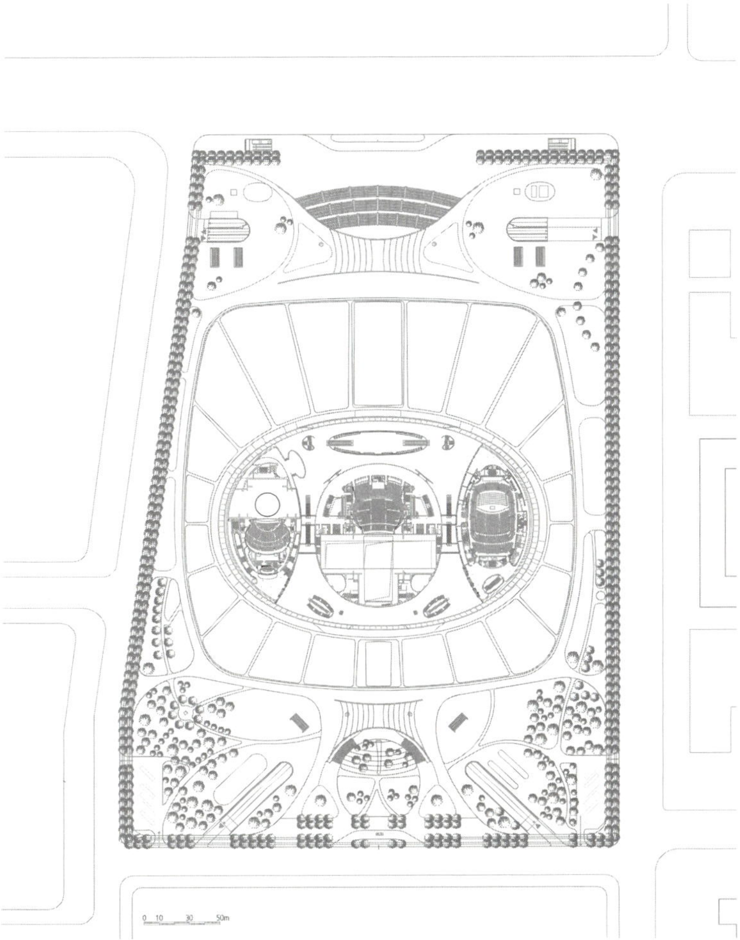

within. Extensive urban renewal efforts have made way for a large park area around the Opera that was erected on a very fast schedule with the opening planned for the end of 2004. Andreu faced extremely stiff resistance to his project, both within China and curiously in his native France, where the daily *Le Monde* published an almost vitriolic attack against the design. As Andreu says, "I am not used to projects that receive intense media scrutiny. I must admit that for the Beijing project, I have

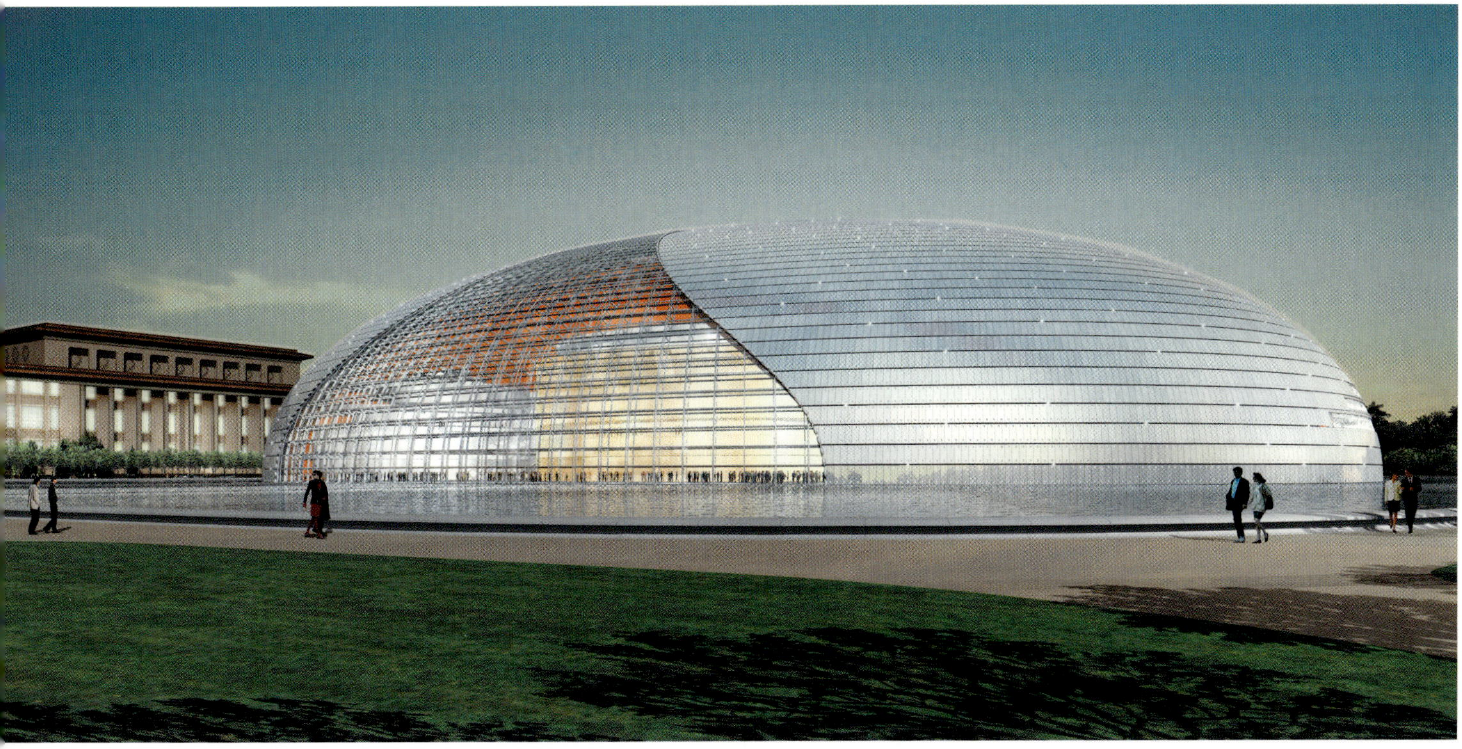

A virtual image below and a construction photograph of the foyer show that Andreu's original concept is closely respected as the structure evolves toward completion. High, generous spaces characterize the interior.

heard quite a few criticisms, some of which are close to be truly insulting. Sometimes the critics make me laugh, for example the fellow who wrote, 'He doesn't have an architect's diploma, he is just an engineer.' Well, I'm sorry if Wright, Le Corbusier and Ando didn't get their diplomas and I did, well then I must be the fool. Aside from that they said that I have no culture. I never pretended to be a specialist of Chinese culture … when the press attacks the person as much or more than the project itself, it becomes very tiring. I do my best to avoid getting involved in this kind of debate because I have to reserve my time

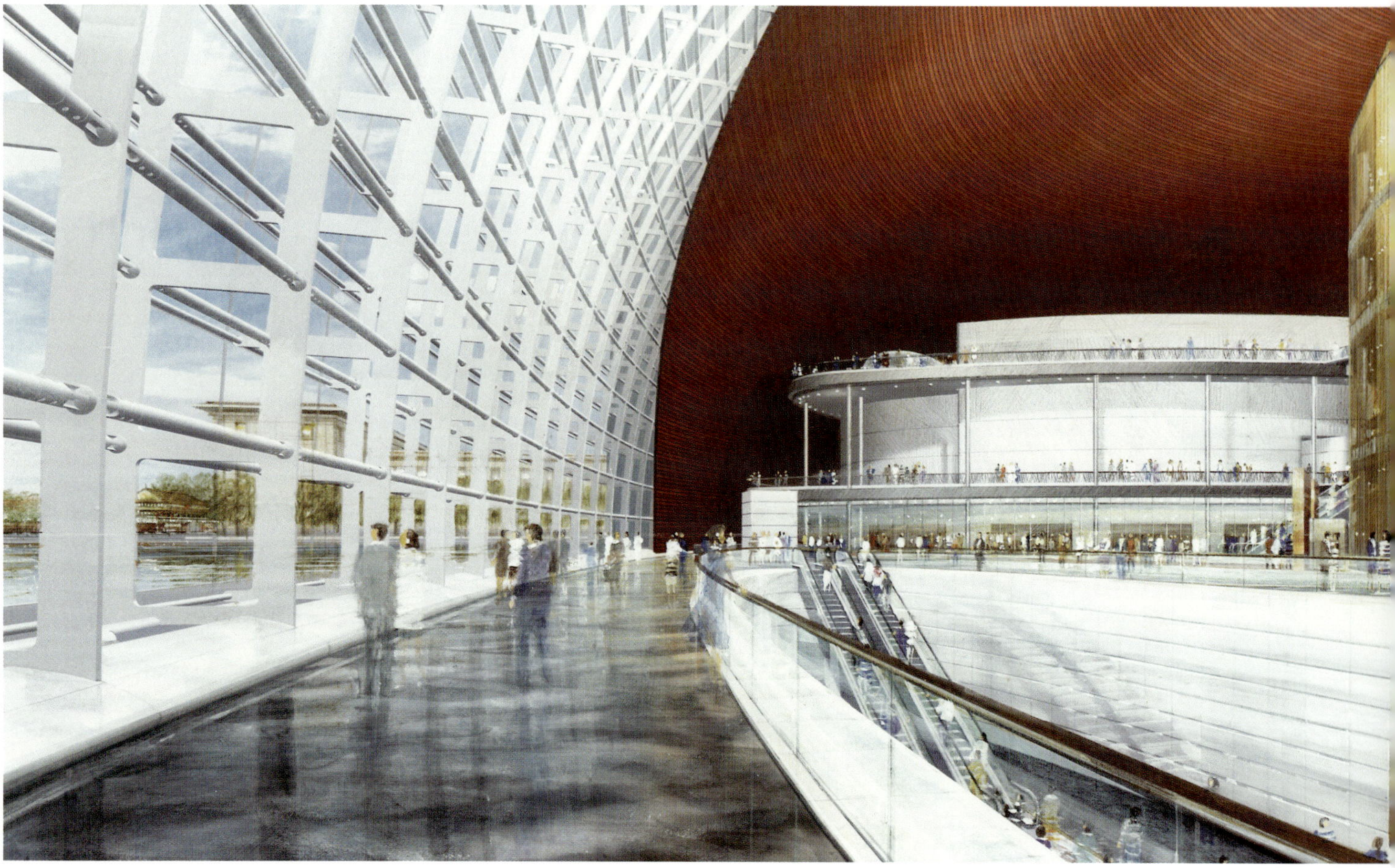

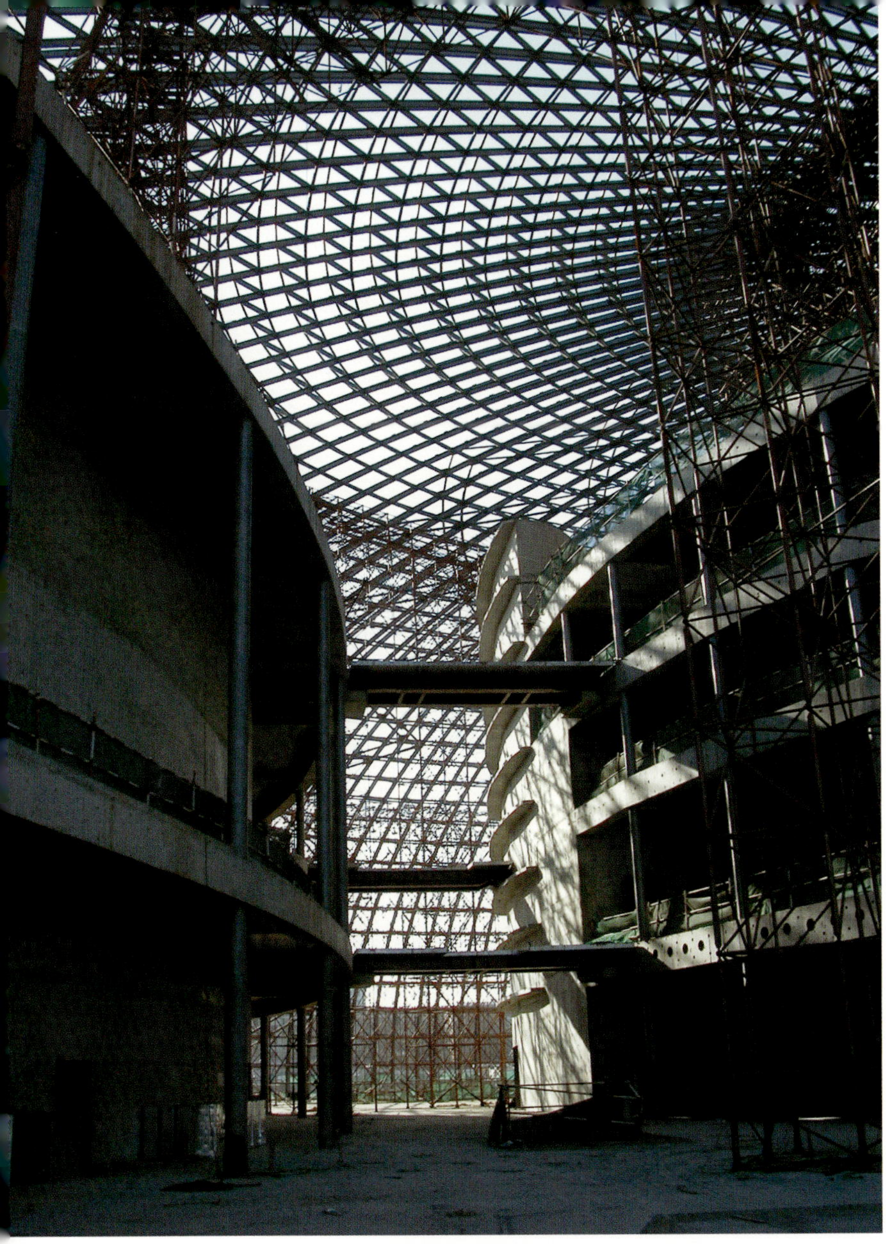

Within, Paul Andreu indulges in the creation of very generous public spaces outside the actual performance spaces. In the halls, broad curves and high ceilings confirm the scale and modernity made apparent by the outer shell.

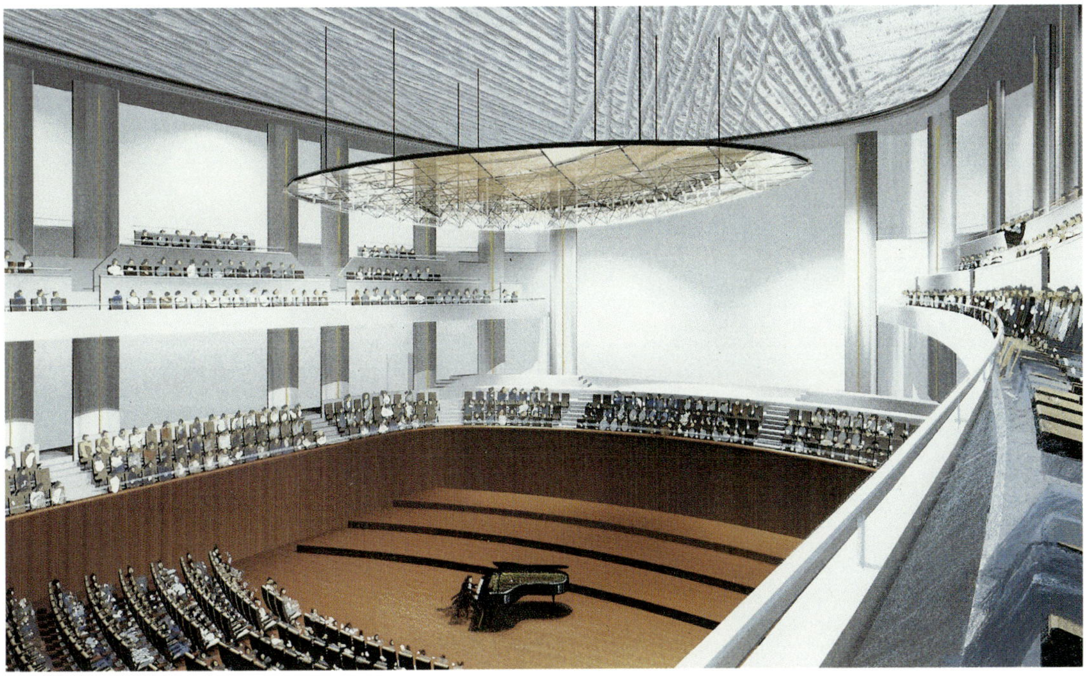

The shell and interior volumes of the Opera under construction. Although the entire shell will not be transparent, these images give an idea of the soaring spaces and clarity of Paul Andreu's architecture.

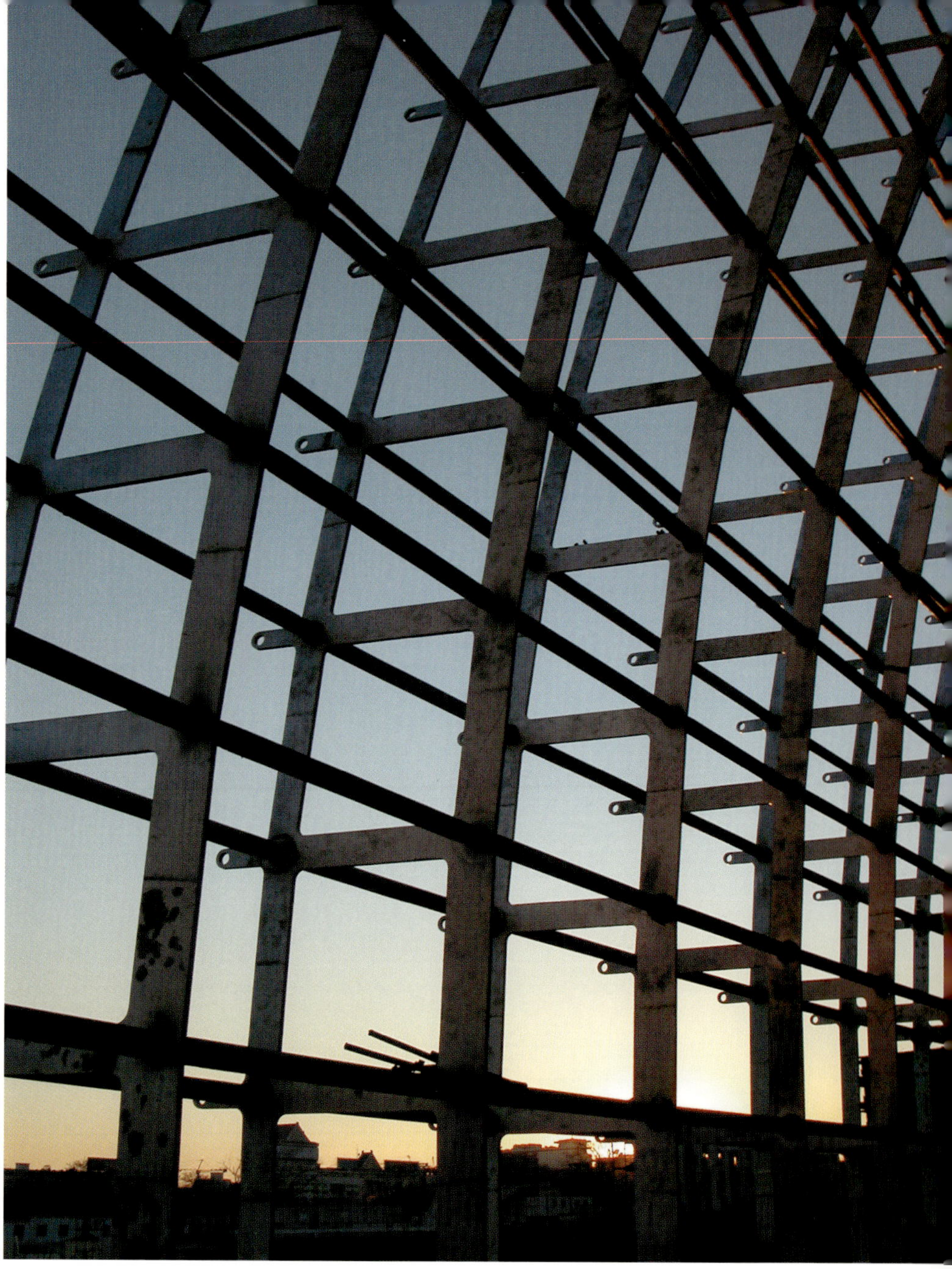

to the project I have been asked to carry out. Sometimes I make a little smoke though … occasionally even some steam." Given its spectacular location and surprising design, this is surely the project by a foreign architect that will mark the Chinese capital the most. Although Andreu relates its downward curving roof to the antithesis of the upward curves of the roofs of the Forbidden City, it is more a contemporary building than it is in any sense influenced by the long history of China. What Western critics sometimes ignore is that the Chinese are not necessarily looking for a watered-down version of their own culture when they select a foreign architect. Rather they are looking for the most advanced and interesting manifestations of international architecture. Anyone can quarrel with this design, just as it is possible to be critical of any building. Chinese architects might have preferred if one of their own number were to be given this prestigious project, but that it not what the government decided. Though Andreu's airports have seen millions of visitors, Roissy and the others are not necessarily places that one associates with a "signature" architect. A monument on the scale of the Beijing Grand National Theater is, and it may well be the building that Andreu is the most remembered for.

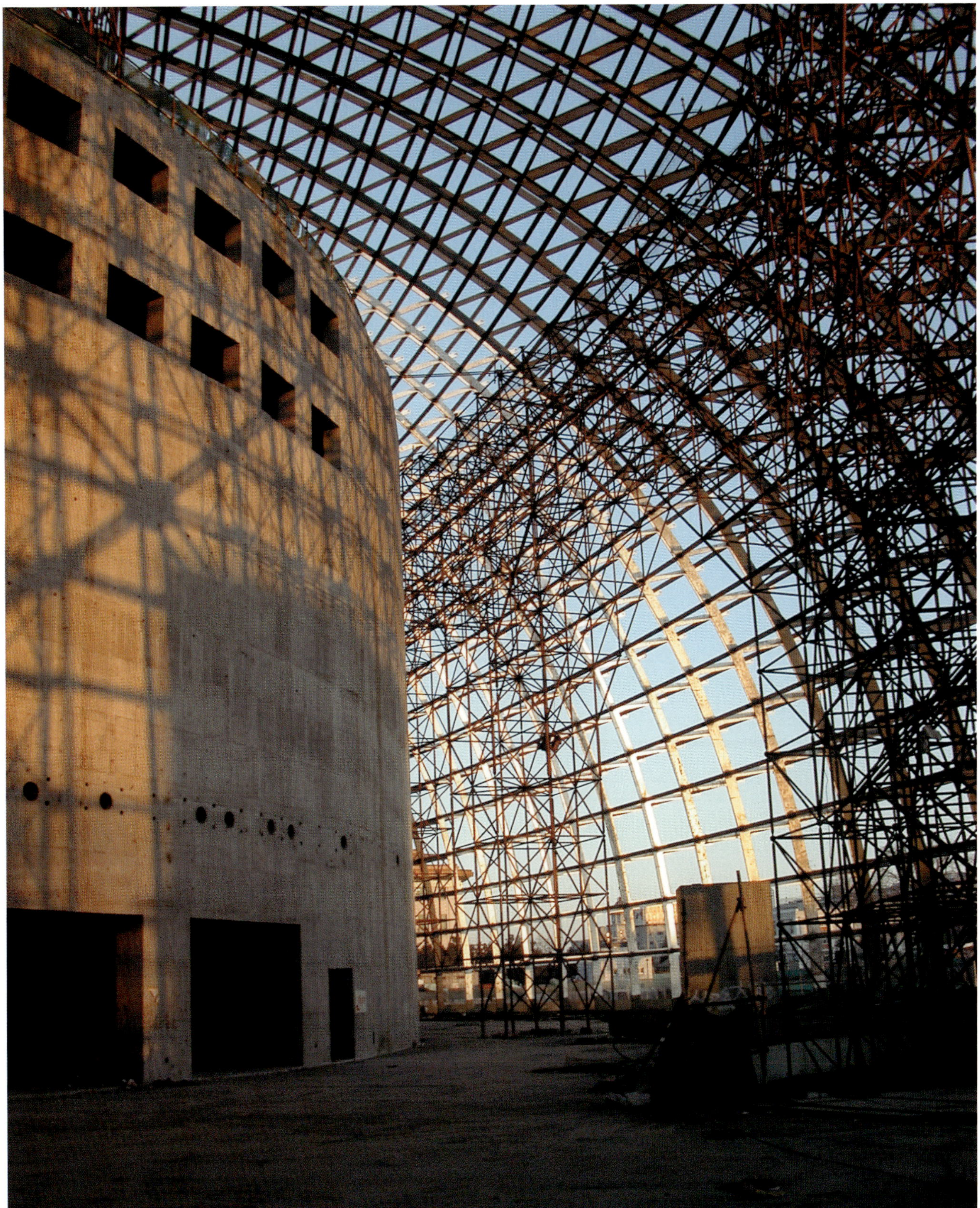

A simply bisected rectangle in the form of a light, arching roof marks the concept of this terminal. Vast dimensions and the possibility of easy expansion are very much in the field of competence of Paul Andreu even if he is based half a world away from this location.

Guangzhou Baiyun Airport Guangzhou

Country: China
Use: Airport
Design: 1998
Surface: 300,000 m^2
Capacity: 30 / 80 million passengers per year

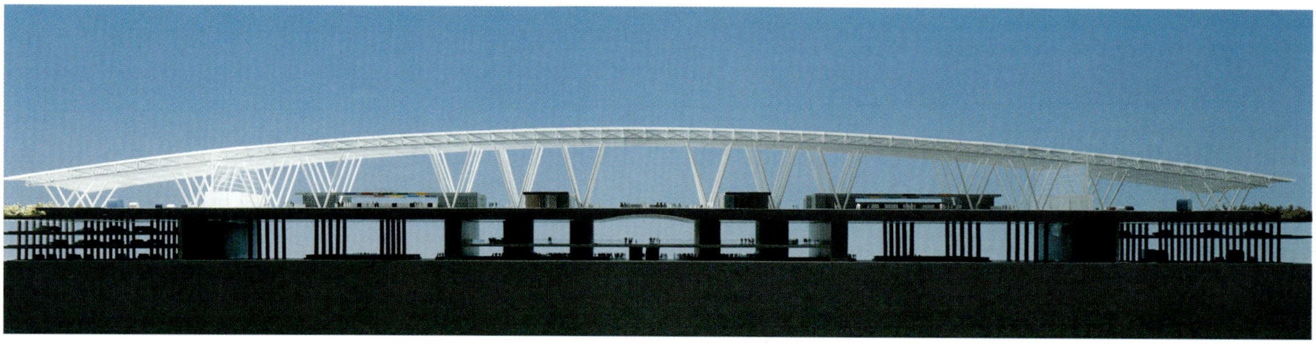

This was Paul Andreu's entry for a 1998 competition that he did not win. It was intended as a high capacity facility (30 million passengers per year) essentially for domestic air travel. The first phase structure would have included about 300,000 square meters of floor area, but future planning required enlargements enabling the airport to reach a capacity of 80 million passengers per year, an indication of the burgeoning Chinese economy and the substantial volume of air traffic. Andreu proposed a two-level structure accessible on two sides from an oval road complex enclosing parking lots, and bus and taxi facilities under planted terraces. In the main axis of the terminal, an underground subway station would point the way toward the future enlargement zones of the airport. Along the secondary axis, a very large-scale shopping center would line the way toward the aircraft. Perhaps the most unusual feature of Andreu's competition entry was his 400-meter by 300-meter translucid roof, with a simple design supported by a "bamboo forest" of thin inclined metal tubes. It might be natural

The extreme simplicity of the basic concept of this facility is obvious in these views showing the light, over-arching canopy roof and the elevated roadways that bring travellers to and from the airport.

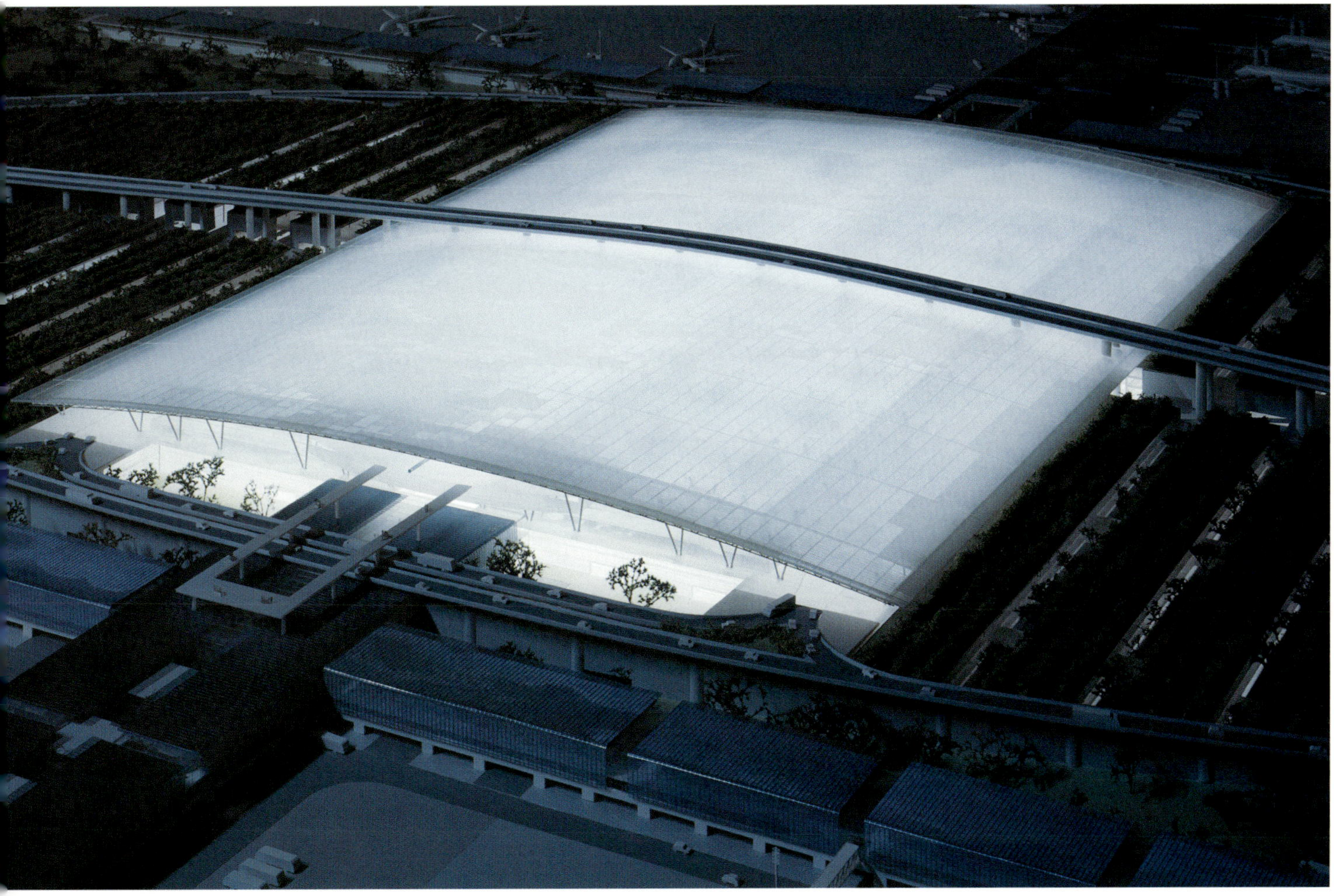

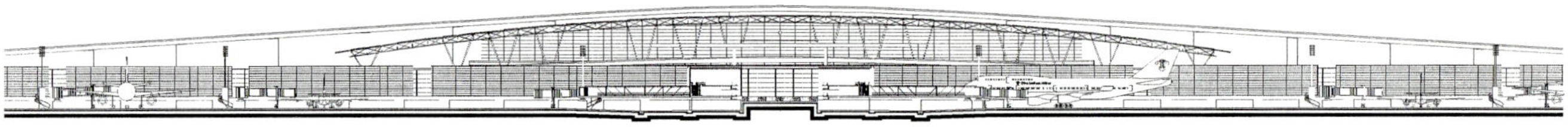

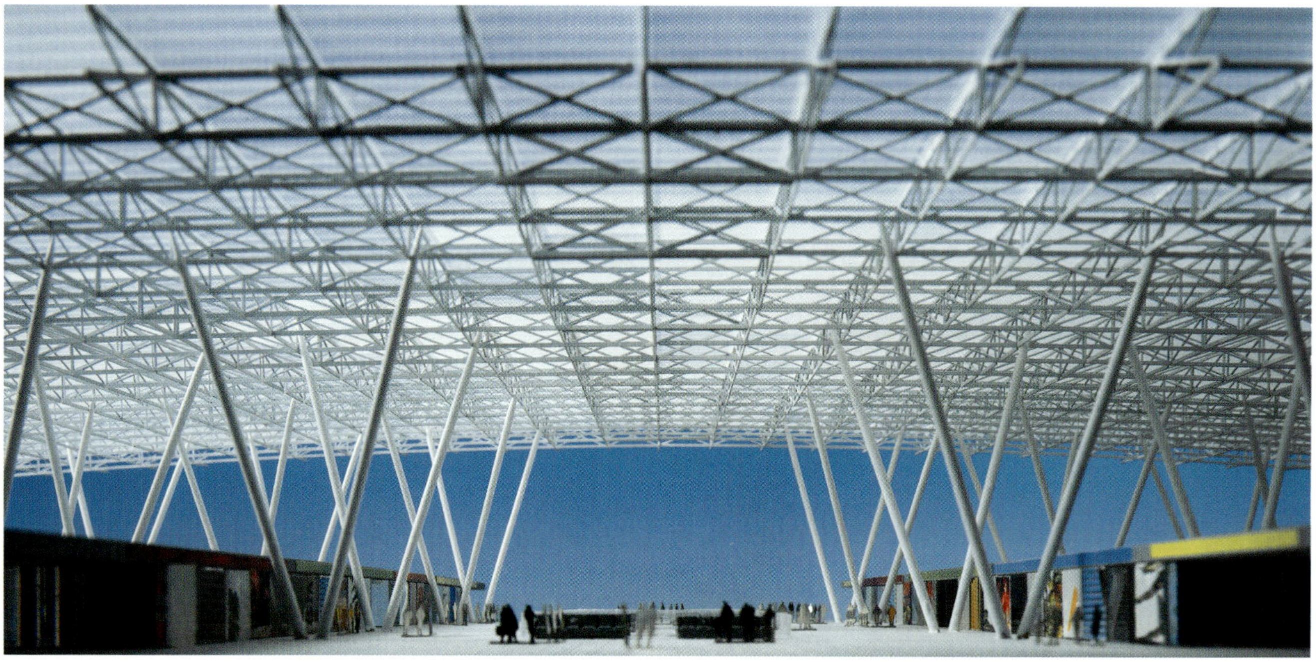

that the Chinese Civil Aviation Authority, in charge of the competition would not award a second major airport to the same architect, yet Andreu's active presence in China is symbolic of his capacity to travel and to bring his message of efficiency and elegant, modern solutions to the other side of the globe. He, like other architects has taken up the challenge of China too because it is a country whose economy demands new large-scale projects at an unheard-of rate. Andreu's extensive experience with airports and other extensive facilities makes him a natural choice over architects who are used to much smaller work.

Situated between the two aircraft areas, the terminal is set in a central green rectangle. Curving approach roads give an eye-like appearance to the aerial view. On the whole, an extremely clear axial division of the complex corresponds to the lightness of the main canopies.

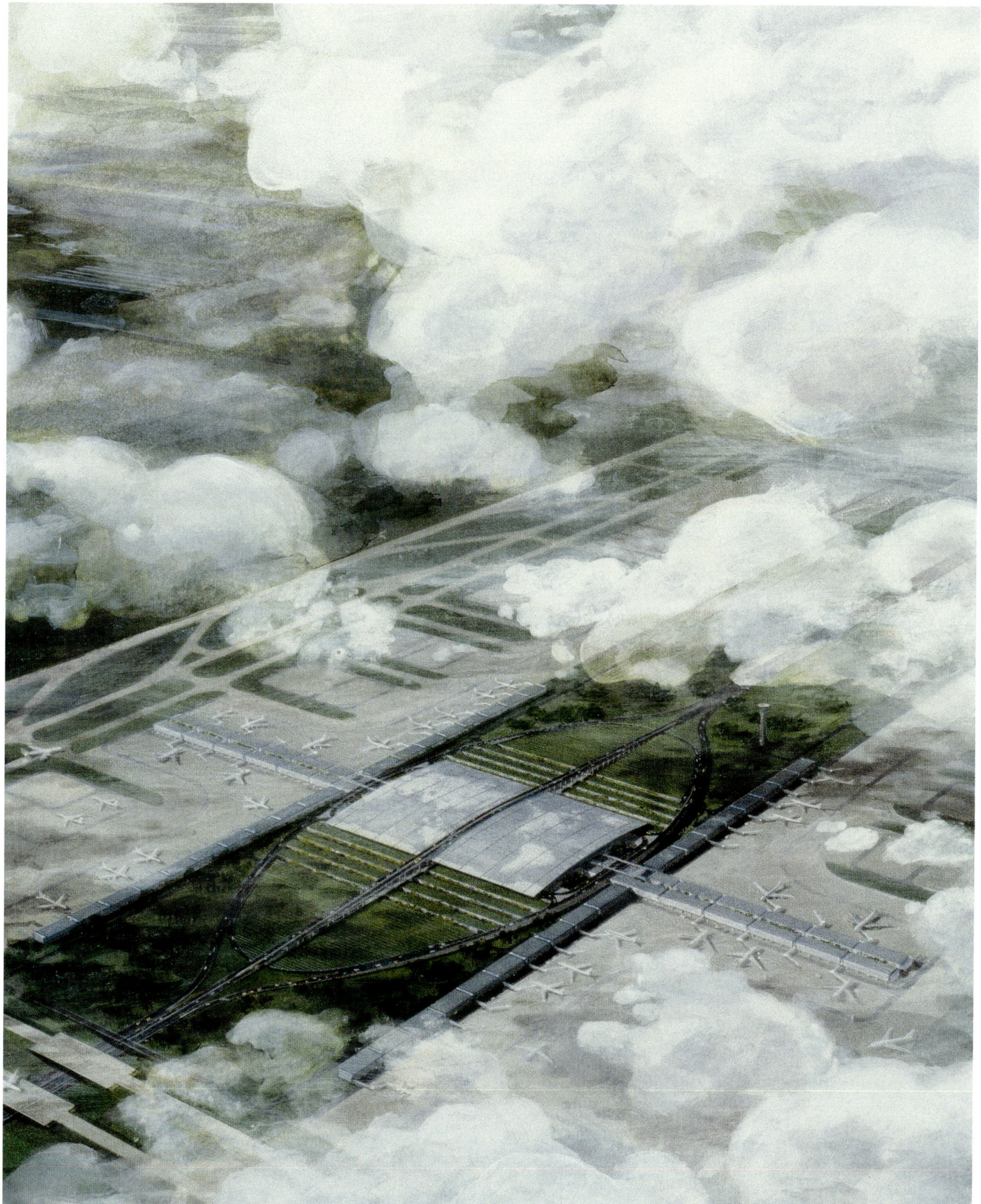

Guangzhou Baiyun Airport

An almost organic, lobed design permits the division of the various functions of this complex along lines that visitors can easily understand. Here as elsewhere, Andreu retains the simple logic of modernism while adding unexpected twists and turns.

Oriental Art Center **Shanghai**

Country: China
Use: Concert hall / theater
Start of project: 2000
Completion: 2004
Surface: 40,000 m^2
Capacity: 1,979 / 1,054 / 330 seats

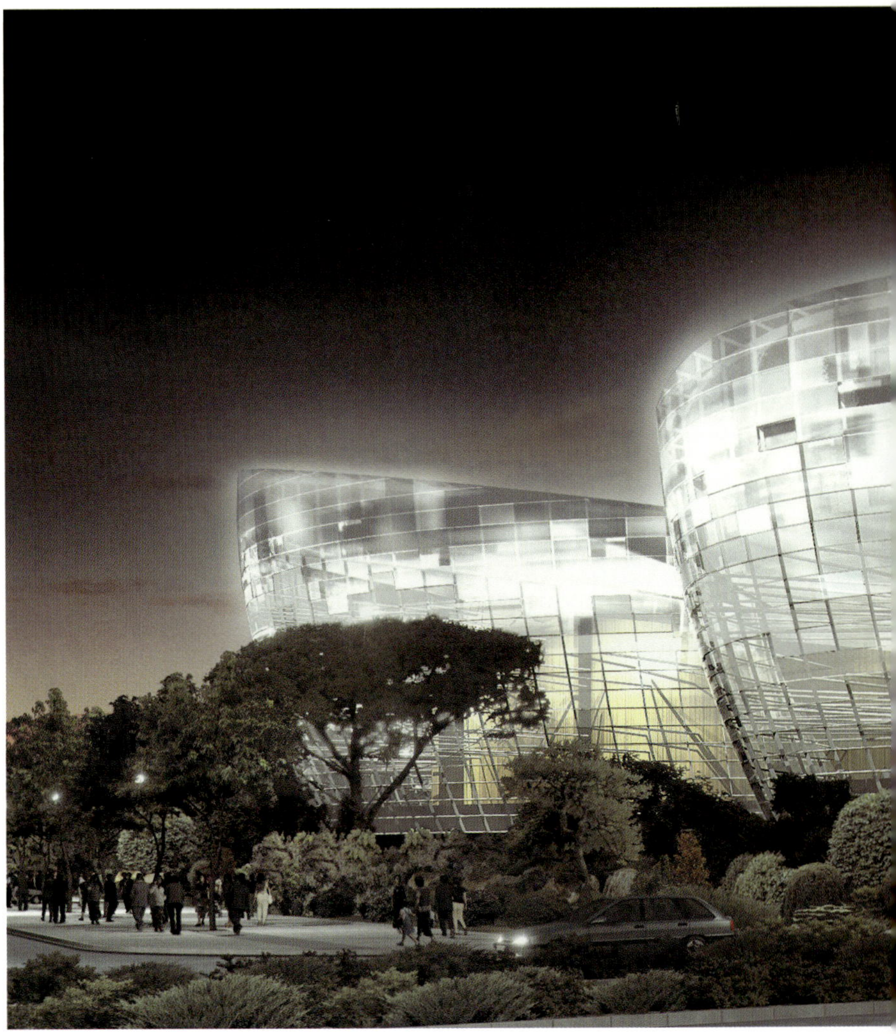

Located on Century Avenue in Shanghai, the Oriental Art Center is a 39,694 square meter facility. It houses a Philharmonic Concert Hall with a capacity of 1,979 seats, a Lyric Theater seating 1,054 and a Chamber Music Hall for 330 persons. The seven-story complex also features ancillary public facilities such as an exhibition hall, music shops, a restaurant, an arts exchange, an arts library and a multimedia and training center. The project includes all the necessary backstage facilities, dressing rooms, rehearsal rooms and lounges.
In his own description for the final phase of the project, Andreu asks a rhetorical question, "What is it?" as though the function of the Art Center would not be readily apparent. "It is, of course," he says, "a place of art, a place for exhibitions and performances. The three interior volumes that rise out of the base in which they are rooted, becoming

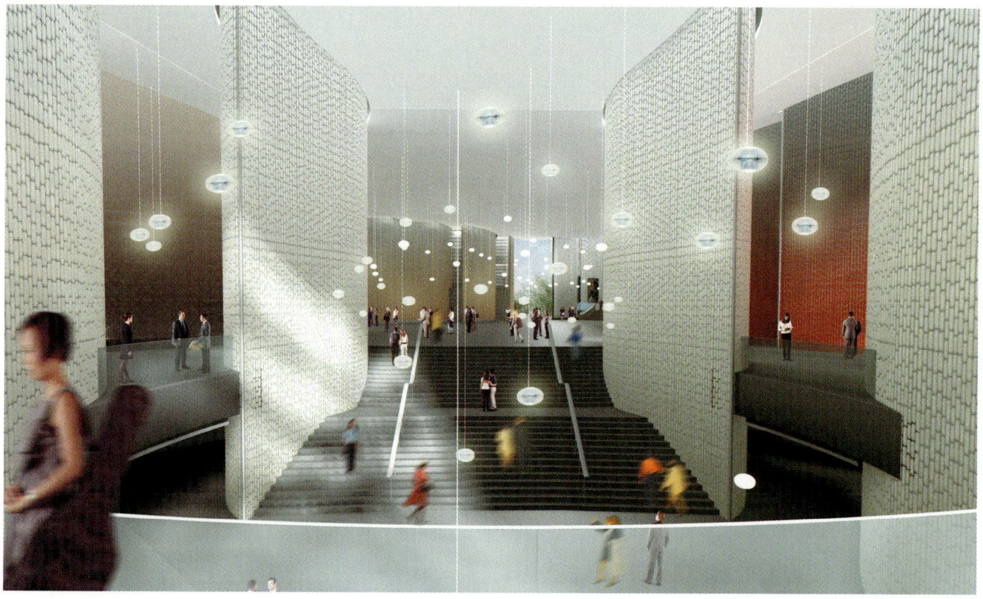

The five-lobed structure rises up in inverted proportions that have an external similarity to the inverted cone employed by Andreu for the latest extension of the Nice-Côte d'Azur Airport. Here, transparency and the setting give a less utilitarian appearance to the architecture.

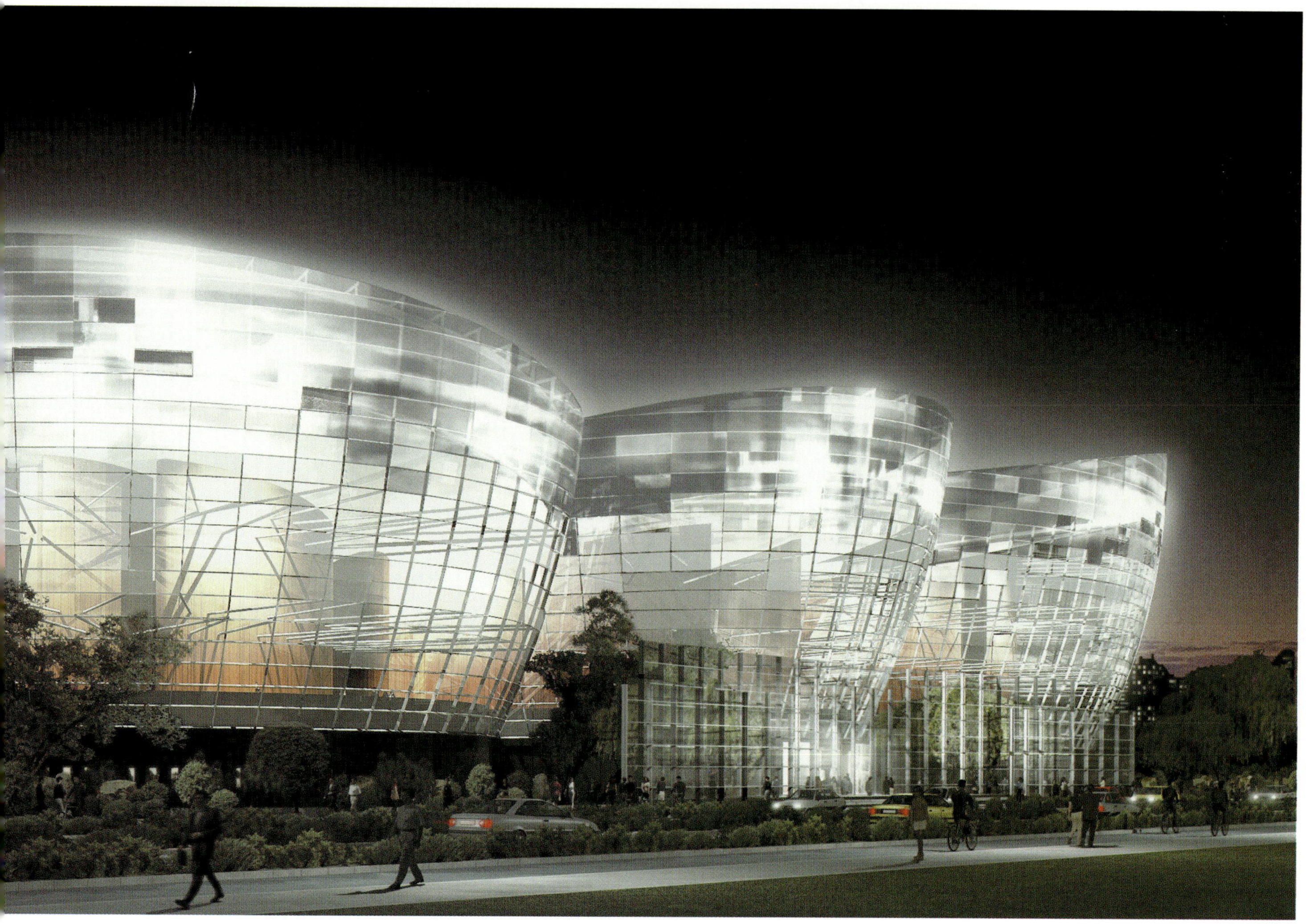

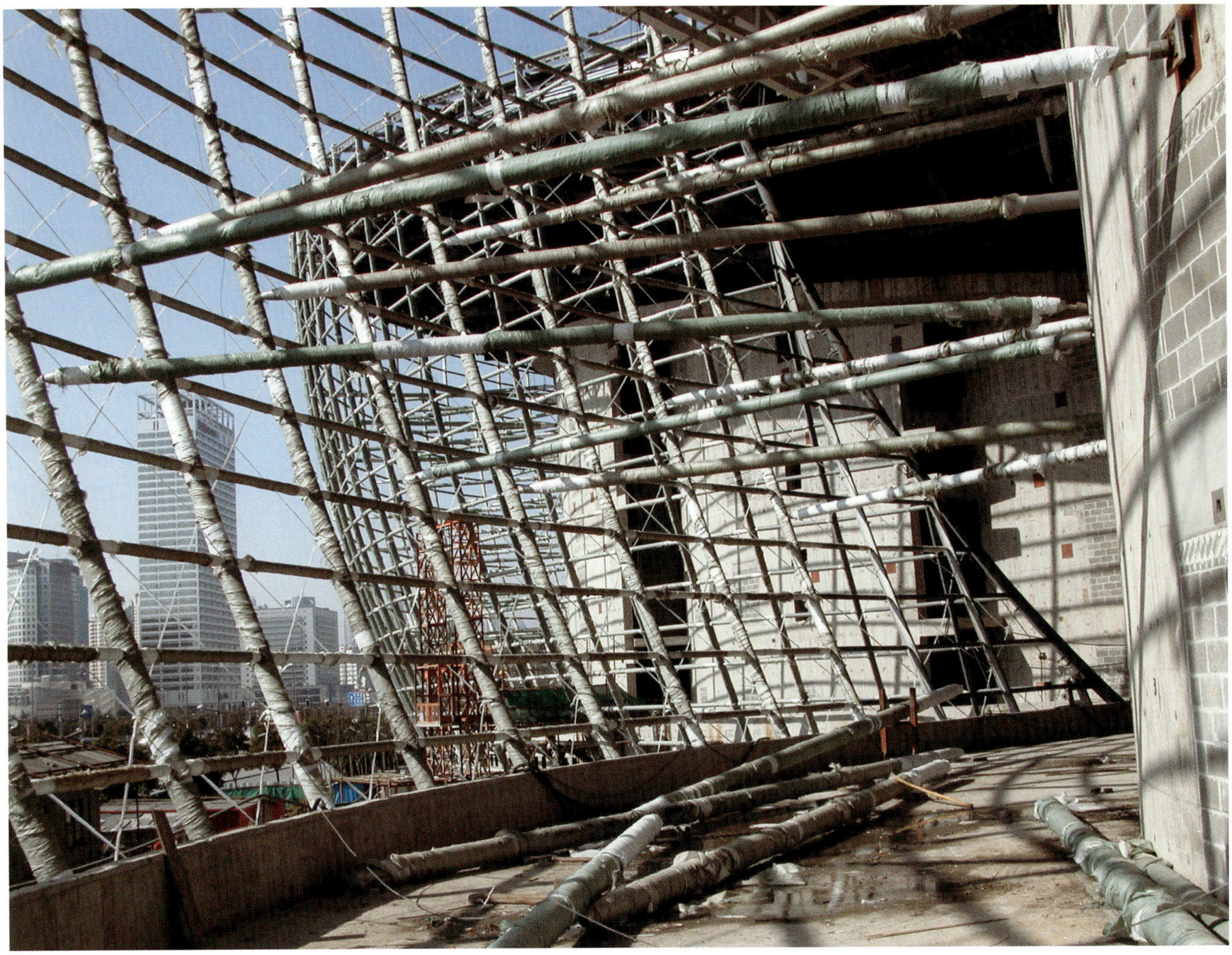

lighter in color as they reach the ceiling, house three auditoriums. They house and protect them as one might protect a place that is precious and fragile. The common space around them, composed as a variation on the twin theme of transparency and curves, comprises an entrance lobby, lounges, and the circulation space and exhibition areas. Functionally and visually, this space links the auditoriums to the city, visible from everywhere, and to the surrounding landscape, the trees and the sky above. What is a performance space? It is the site of an encounter, meticulously prepared yet new and unique each time, a place where artists, public and artworks meet. Everything in the building is designed to make this encounter possible, easy and happy. Seen from this perspective, anything that might have seemed odd in this sculpture set amidst trees in the city center becomes perfectly legible, crystal clear." If Paul Andreu waxes poetic in describing this project, it may be that it is the second major cultural facility that he has designed in China (with the Beijing Grand Theater) and he wants the audience to grasp that he is as much a lyrical architect as a calculating engineer. Somewhat less effusive, his original presentation for the project was also more precise:
"The project is based on the following

The lobed structure permits Andreu to clearly divide the different functions of the complex while giving an overall unity to the architecture. The plan shows clearly how the different volumes are related, facilitating access from the central space. Above, a construction photograph taken in 2004.

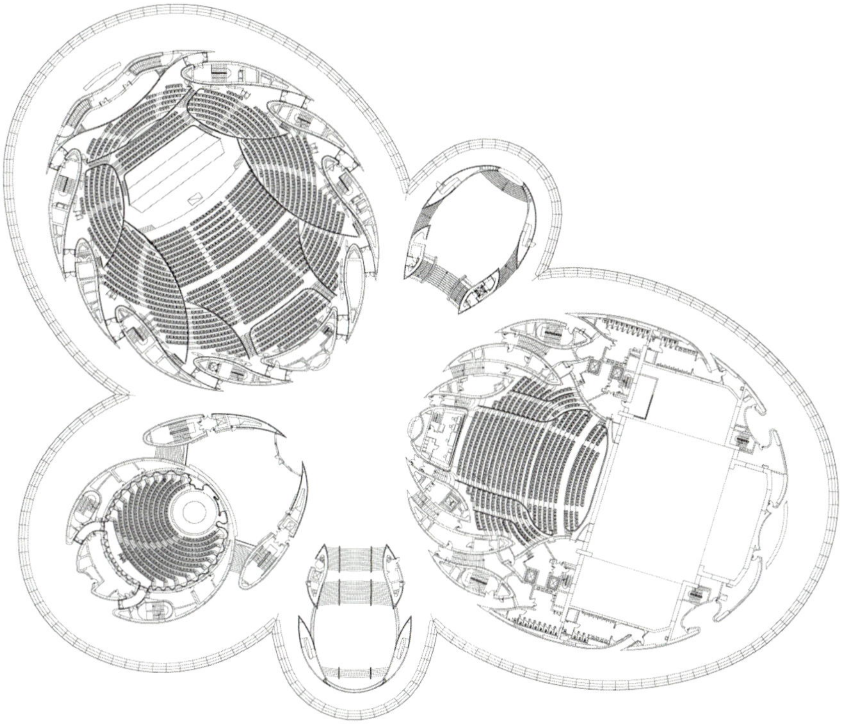

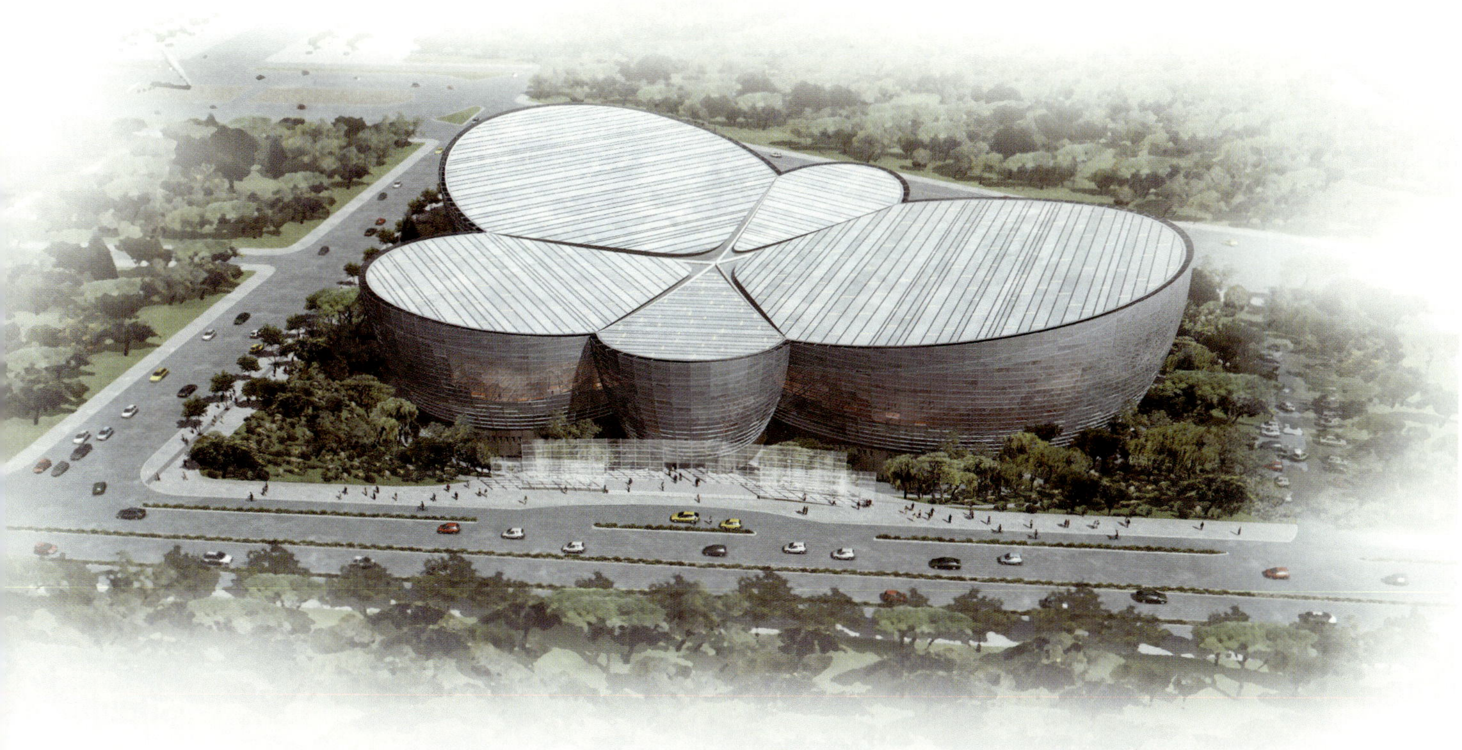

Construction photographs taken in 2004 and a virtual concert hall view emphasize the functional and ultimately light-filled nature of the architecture.

basic principles: 1) The building has a base on which the public spaces will develop; 2) The halls will emerge from the base as trees from the earth; 3) The building should be covered and enclosed by one unique cantilevered roof, linked by curved glass walls to the base; 4) Spaces inside the building are distributed around a central circulation and meeting point. The public space should be open and adaptable in order to increase the potential of use of the building; 5) The performers should be provided with an efficient and agreeable working space; 6) The three performance halls should be different in form and use different materials; 7) The outside walls of the three halls will use enamel ceramic as their main common material; 8) The material of the façades will be a glass

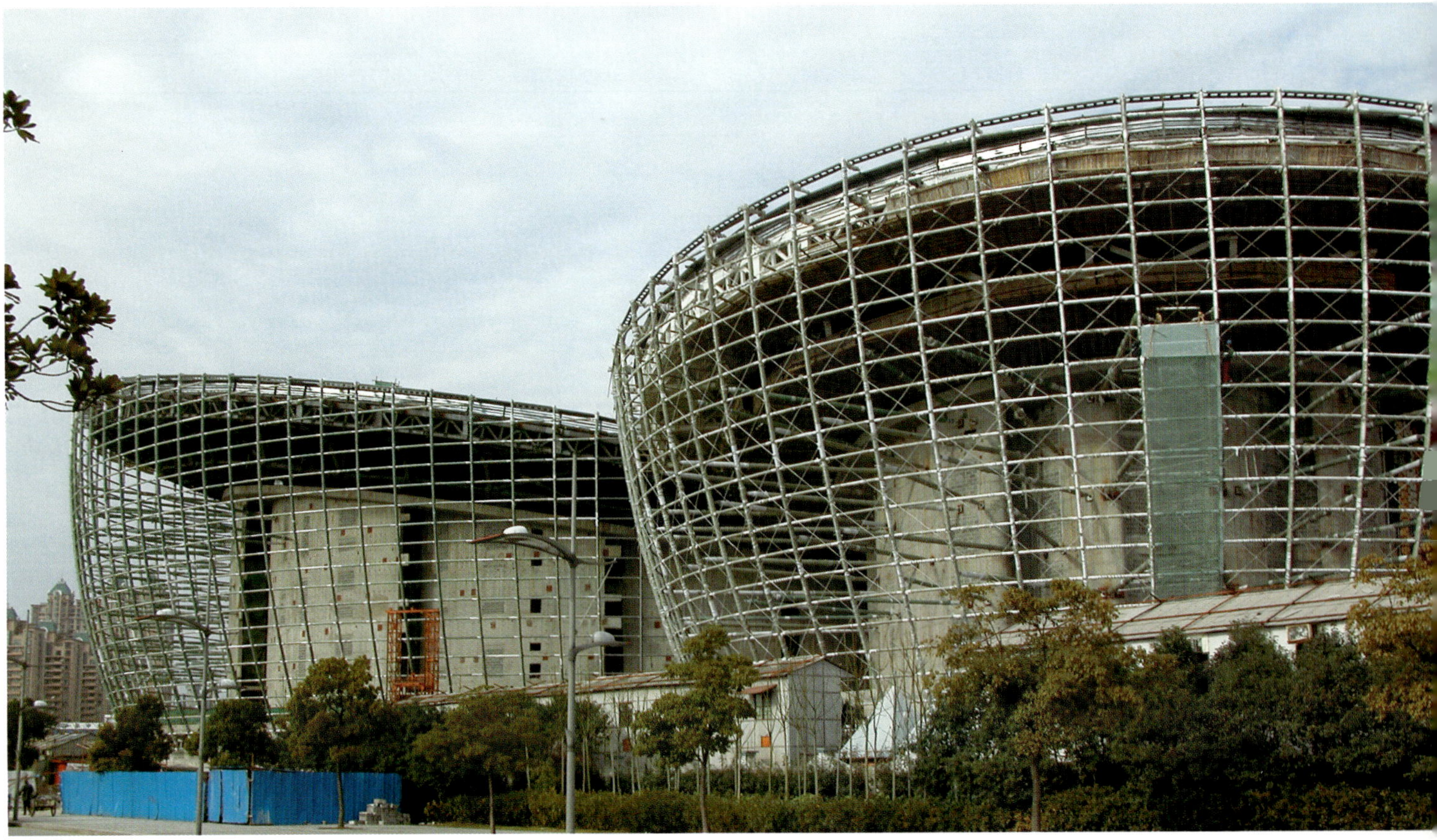

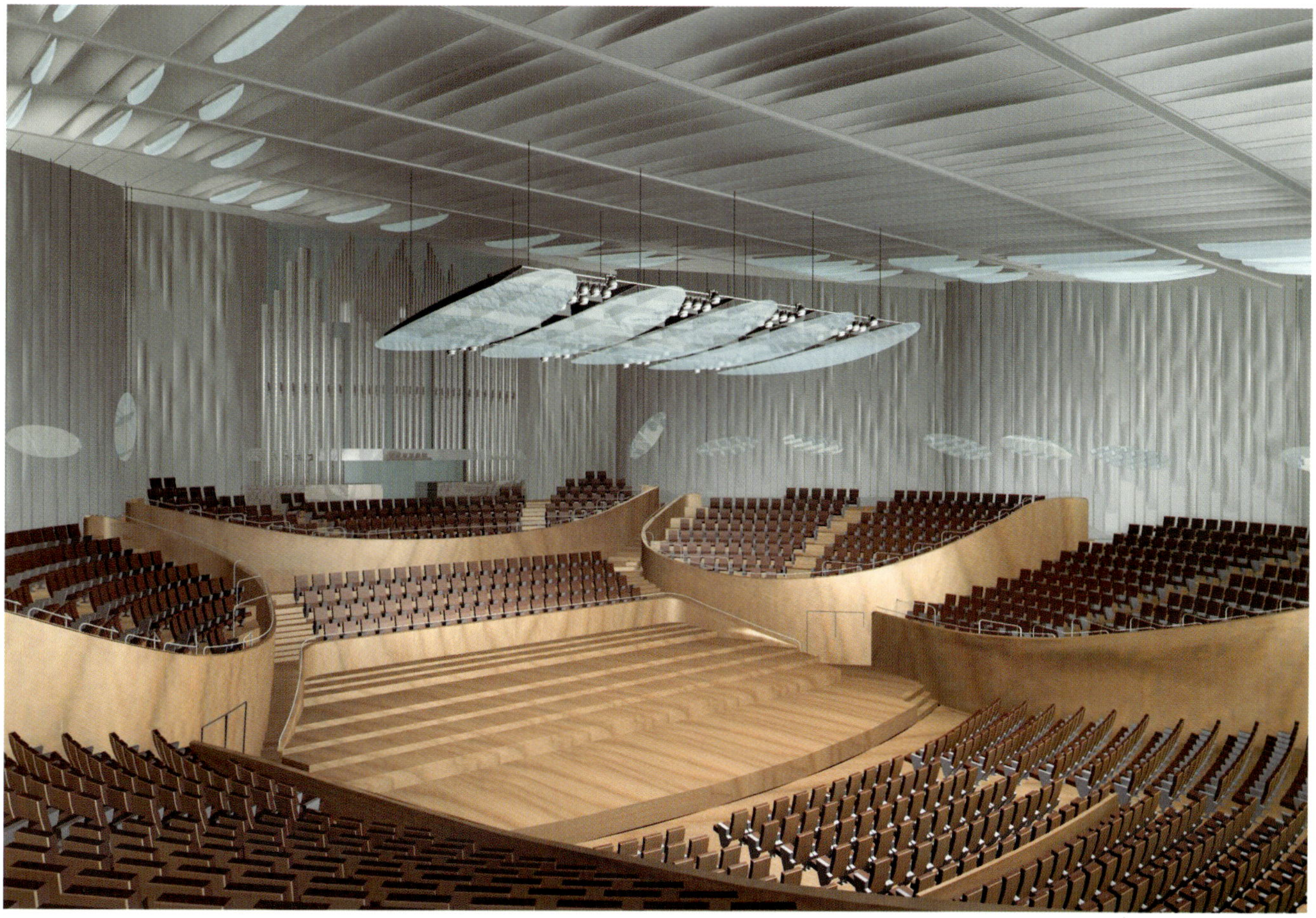

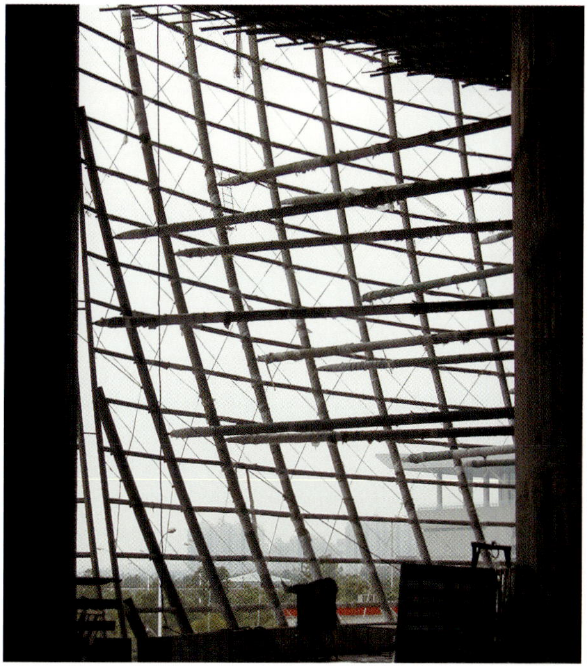

incorporating a perforated metal sheet of variable density; 9) The façades design itself will express innovation, modernity and enhance the public areas; and 10) Although secondary in their functional importance, the public spaces will define the character of the building and its rapport with the spirit of the time." Indeed, if the curving forms that increase in diameter as they rise might bring together the most recent phase of the development of Nice Airport, Andreu here is venturing into new territory. As he points out, many buildings have technical requirements as complex as that of airports. Despite being vast, this Oriental Art Center is smaller than most of Andreu's airport terminals and less complex in terms of factors such as checking-in (ticket counters) or security, less necessary here than near aircraft.

Even more complex than the preceding project, the Guangzhou Science Center also adapts a quasi-organic design, clearly differentiating various volumes. A large natural park setting allows the architect to conceive of his design as an integral part of the site.

Guangzhou Science Center **Guangzhou**

Country: China
Use: Exhibition, entertainment, research, administration
Design: 2003
Competition project
Surface: 120,000 m²

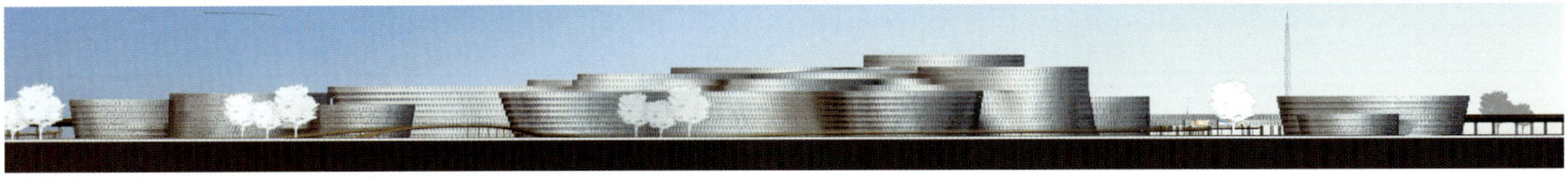

Located in a park in the city formerly known as Canton, this new Science Center is a large structure, measuring 115,000 square meters in area. Surprisingly, more than half this space, 75,000 square meters, is devoted to permanent exhibitions, with another 6,000 square meters set aside for temporary exhibitions. The Center is part of the development zone of the Guangzhou University City, located about 17 kilometers from the city center. The Center itself is on an island and has a site measuring 454,000 square meters with a further 340,000 square meter Eco Park nearby. As Paul Andreu says, "The historical, cultural or physical constraints that might have been imposed by a city-

Virtual images show the volumes of the Guangzhou Science Center from a bird's eye perspective and from ground level. Set between forest and water, the structures are at once unified and varied in their forms.

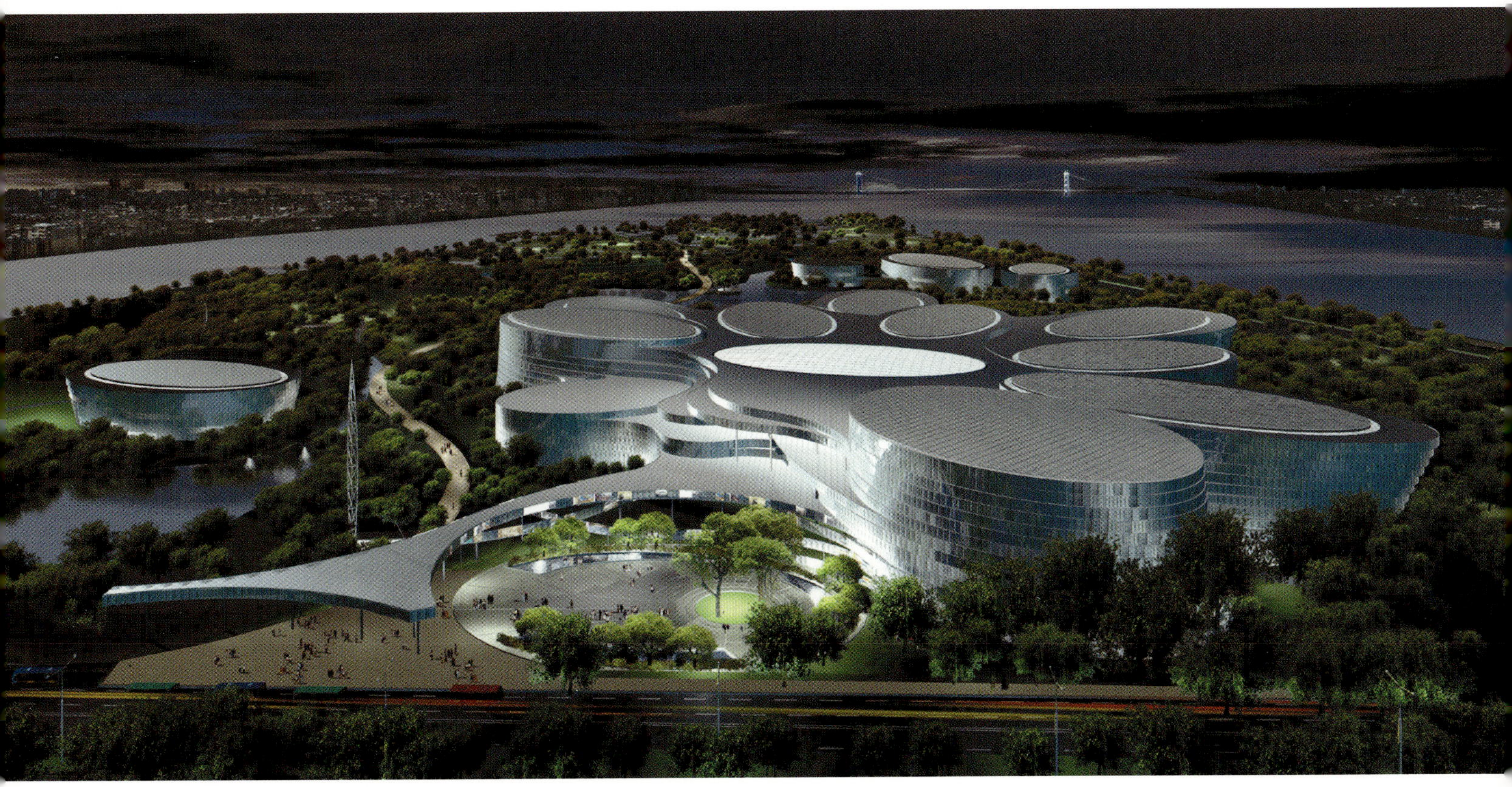

center location have been avoided here. The museum is confronted with nature and must react to it. Of course, it is a natural setting that has been artificially reorganized, but nonetheless, building here is freer and calmer than being in the dense heart of the city." Andreu's interest in science has surely played a role in his concept for this project. He compares science to a language that changes according to our understanding of the world. He correctly observes that early science museums born of a time when it was thought that there might be simple explanations for everything were orderly and majestic buildings. Rather, today, he points to the rapid evolution of scientific understanding and the abandonment, at least for the time being of any attempt to give simple explanations to the complex phenomena of nature. He concludes that a science museum for the new century

The leafed or lobed design of this large complex allows it to integrate its natural setting while maintaining a coherence of overall design and function.

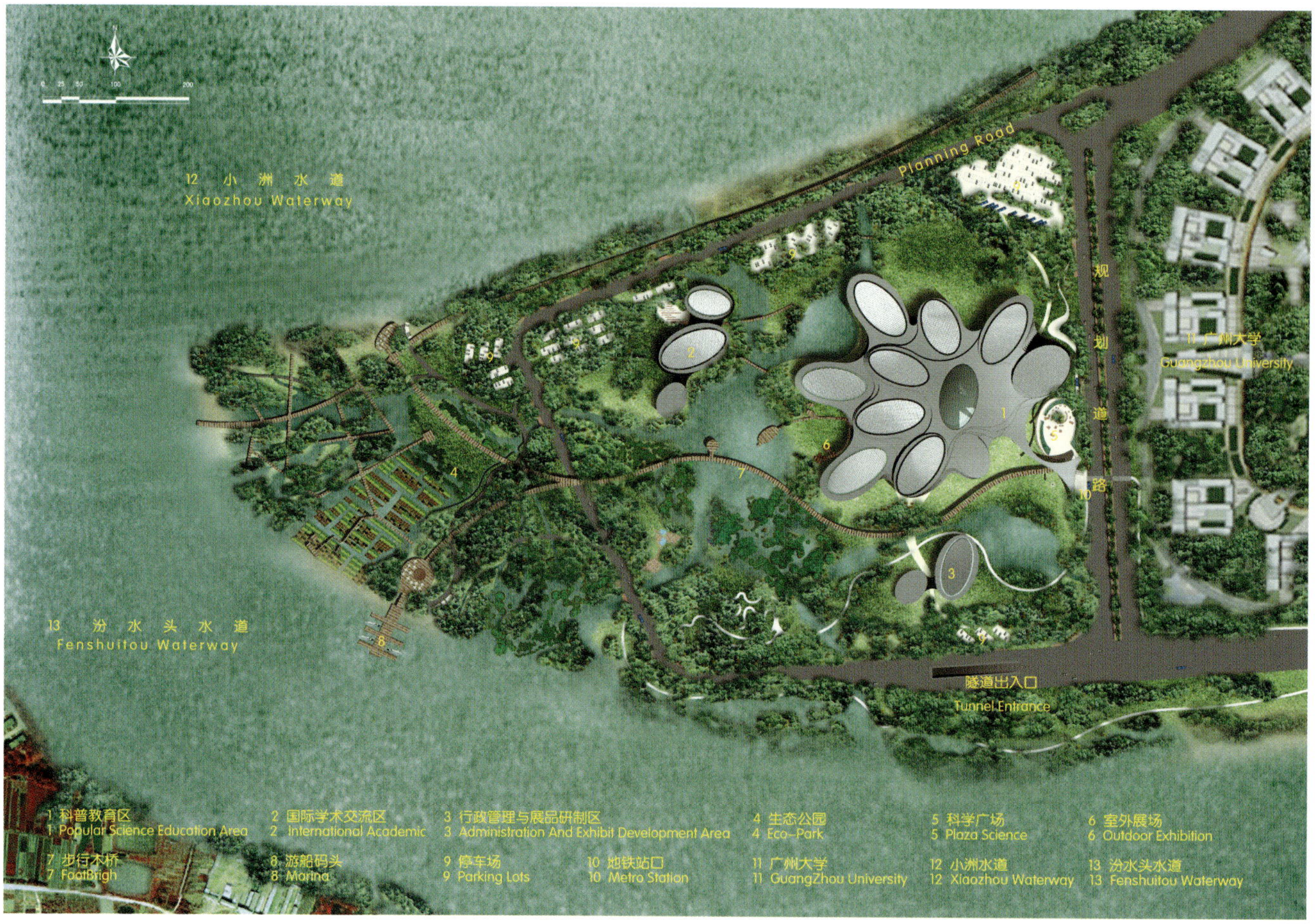

must avoid overt simplification, even in its own design, and provide for the unknown evolutions of the future. Inspiring himself by the meandering curves of the Pearl River but also from his personal views of science, Paul Andreu writes, "In this space at the edge of the water, formed by canals whose inclinations are so slight that their form has become a series of curves, we can let ourselves be guided by natural shapes. The building can become part of nature without making the site completely artificial. The building itself will be a landscape for visitors who see it from the exterior, but above all for those who are

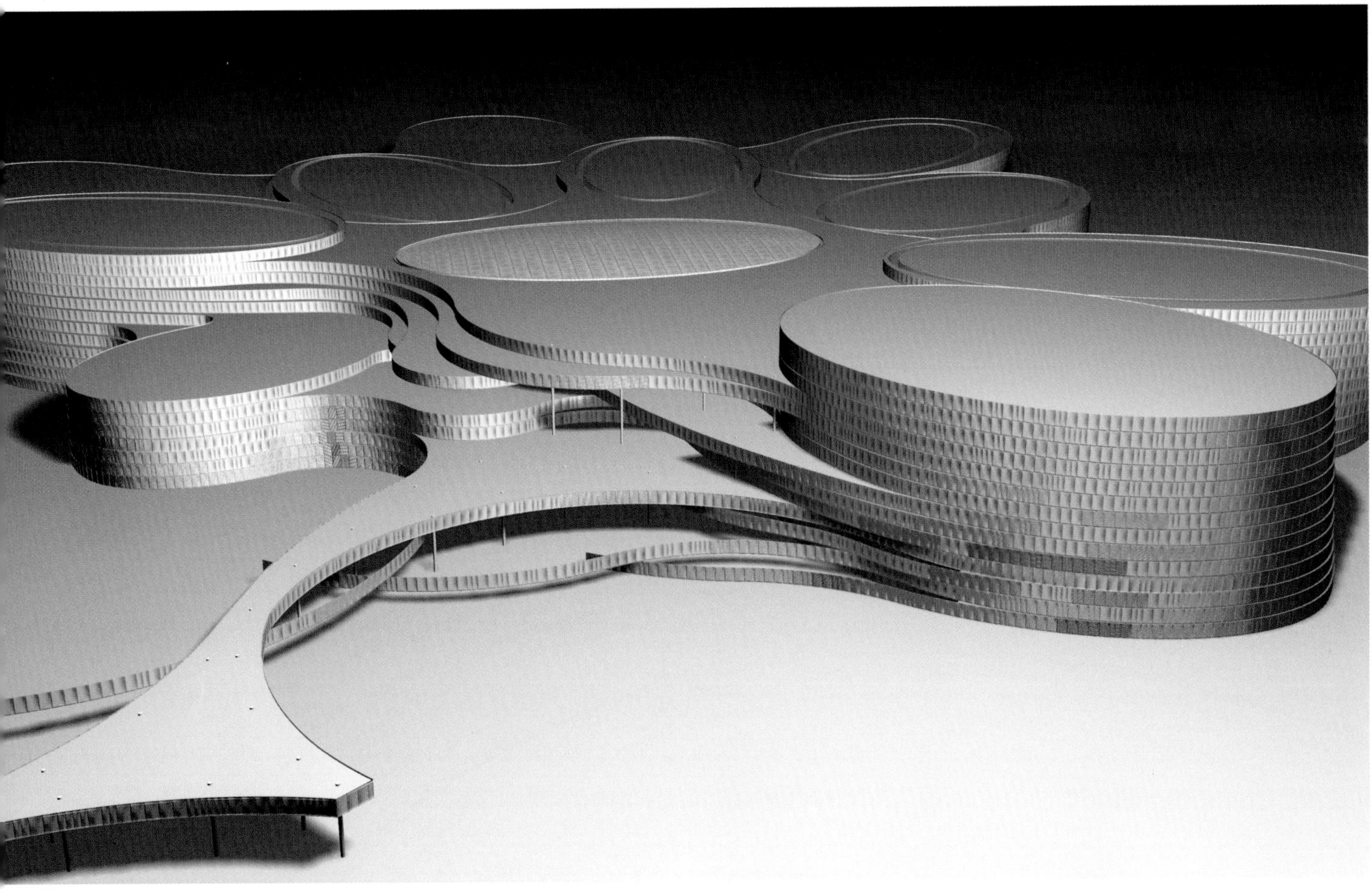

inside: a built form that remains close to nature and analogous to the landscape of science." Aside from the basic exhibition areas, the Center will include an Imax type movie theater and public "laboratory" spaces. A total of 17,000 square meters is devoted to an Academic Exchange Zone including 11,000 square meters of conference rooms. Administrative offices and exhibition development areas account for a further 7,000 square meters. Everything about this science center seems to be at the very large scale of the country itself. With its newly forming ambition to be a major player on world economic and cultural scene, it is encouraging that the authorities look to foreign architects when designing new facilities.

For a new business complex in the Chinese capital, Paul Andreu here reaches a height of his capacity to blend a rather strict geometric base with complex variations on the shapes of the surrounding office towers.

CBD Core Beijing

Country: China
Use: Business and Commercial Center
Design: 2003
Competition project
Surface: 1,300,000 m^2
Capacity: 876,000 m^2 of office space
Towers 250 m – 300 m high

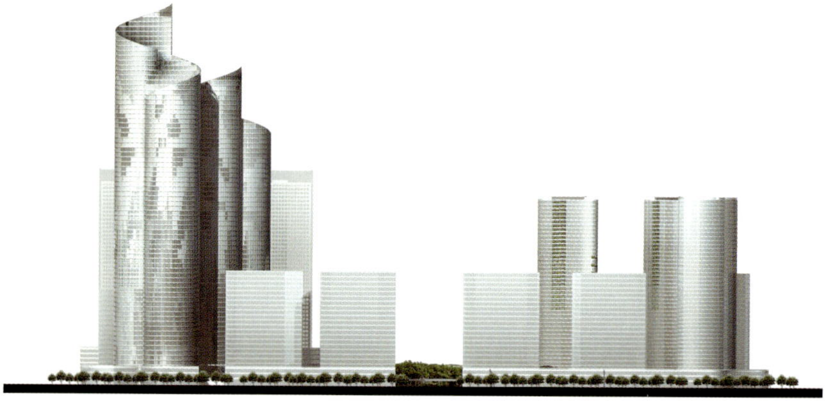

Beijing decided early in the 1990's to build a Central Business District (CBD) about 2 kilometers east of Tien An Men Square, which is to say quite close to Paul Andreu's National Grand Theater. The CBD will cover no less than 4 square kilometers in Beijing's Chaoyang District, where over 60 percent of the city's foreign-funded companies and more than 50 percent of its star hotels are located. 40 office buildings, apartment buildings and other facilities have been built so far in the area. 92 of the 156 large multinational companies that are represented in Beijing, such as Motorola and Samsung, have already set up their representative offices in and near the planned CBD area. The CBD Core is an ambitious development program within the CBD that involves a 30-hectare site and a planned construction area of over a 1,000,000 square meters, at the

As in other projects, Andreu combines a basic geometric form (the circle) with a variety of less strictly defined tower shapes. Although functional efficiency is guaranteed, the overall design maintains a degree of freedom and irregularity that improves on modernist rigor.

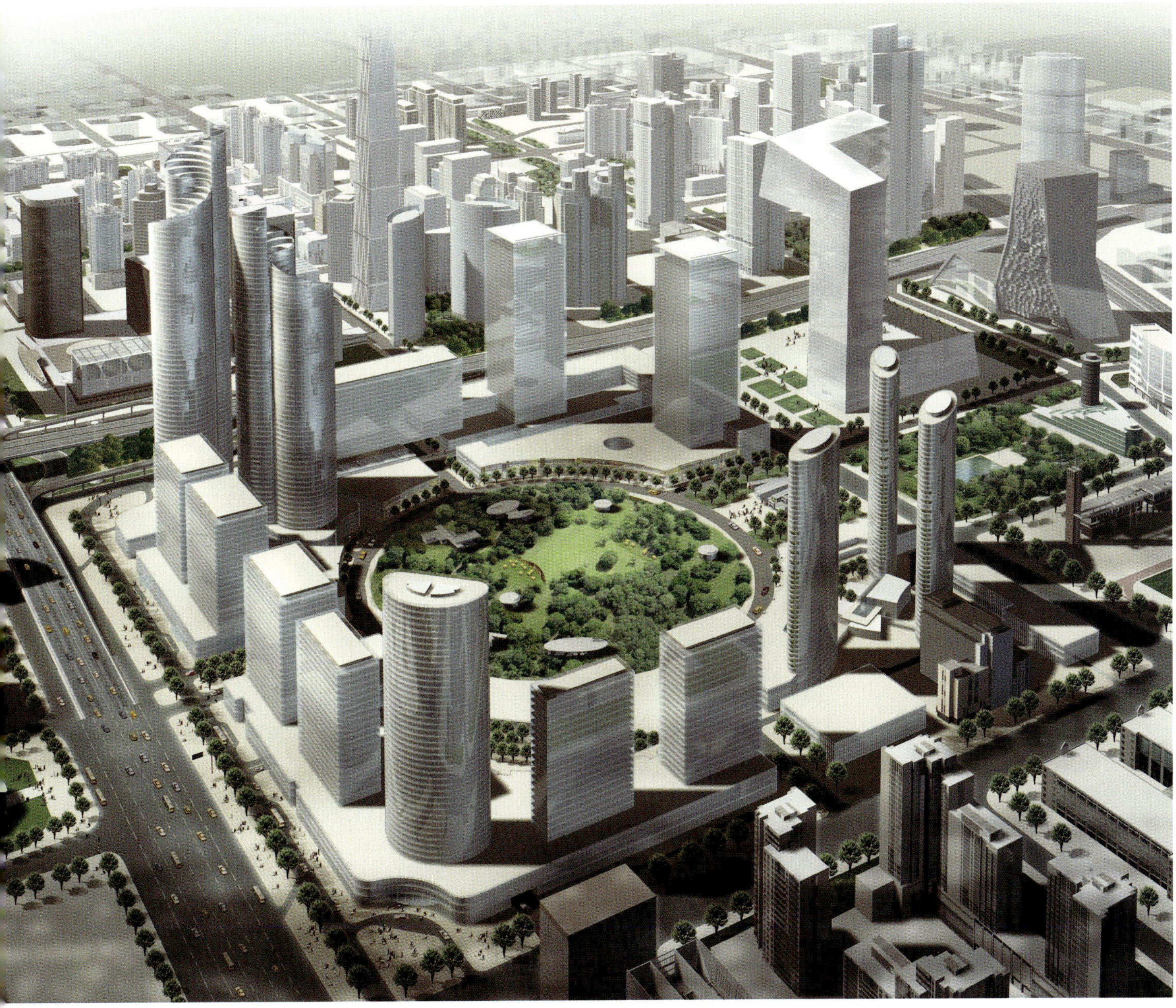

intersection of two major arteries, northeast of the intersection between Chang'an Avenue and the Third Ring East. The CBD Core area will be dotted with modern business facilities including office buildings, hotels, shopping centers and conference and exhibition centers. Paul Andreu participated in an international consultation on the

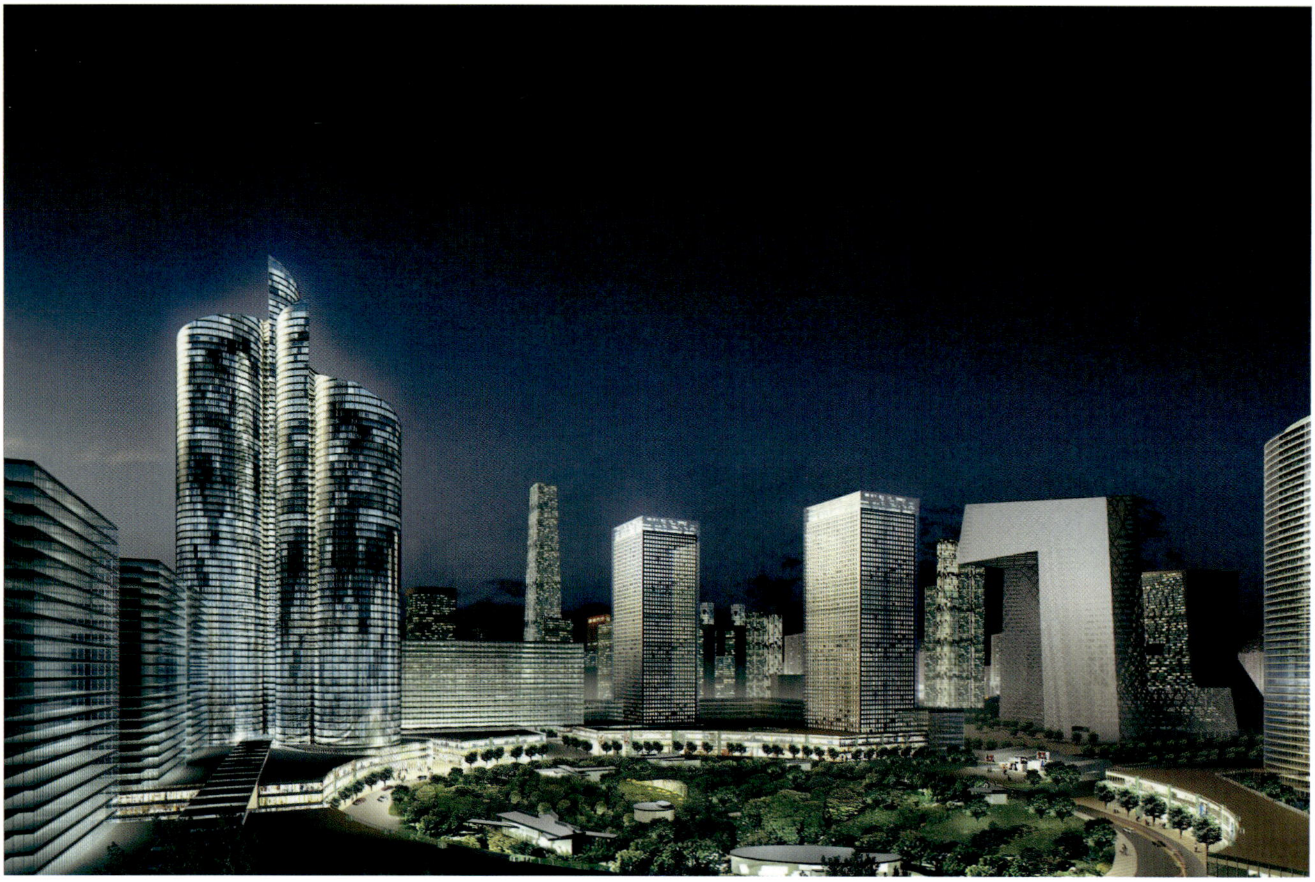

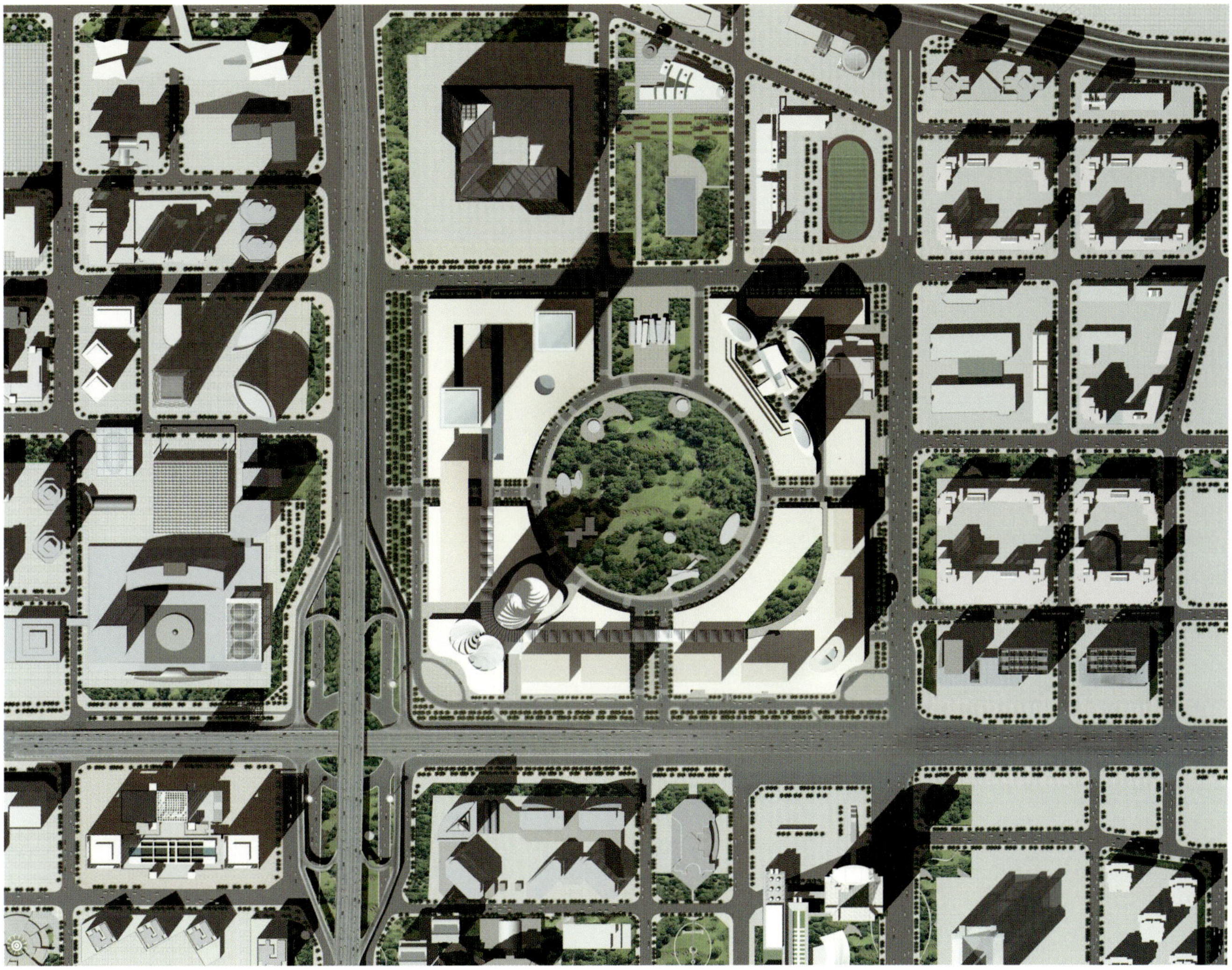

Calling on a geometric design with deep connections to Chinese culture and history, Andreu designed an extremely modern complex that combines open green spaces with high-rise density required in the program.

CBD Core and insisted on three major themes – the site and its day to day life; the functioning of the whole of the CBD and that of the architecture of the entire capital. His plan is laid out around a symmetrically divided central circular garden that clearly recalls elements of Chinese architecture or garden design. He proposes a variety of shapes and sizes of towers and lower volumes around this circle, giving a sense of large-scale spatial organization along the lines of his declared interest in the city. In the face of the haphazard and largely unattractive modern development of Beijing, Paul Andreu offers a more coherent and thoughtful vision.

Project List

Charles-de-Gaulle Airport Terminal 1
Roissy, France, 1967-1974
Completed in 1974

Charles-de-Gaulle
Airport Control Tower
Roissy, France, 1967-1974
Completed in 1974

Charles-de-Gaulle Airport
Main Telephone Office and Climate Controle Building
Roissy, France, 1967-1974
Completed in 1974

Charles-de-Gaulle
Airport Water Tower
Roissy, France, 1967-1974
Completed in 1974

Charles-de-Gaulle Airport
Terminals 2 A and 2 B
Roissy, France, 1972-1982
Completed in 1982

Charles-de-Gaulle Airport
RER Railway Station
Roissy, France, 1972-1976
Completed in 1976

Street Lighting
Roissy, France, 1974
Completed in 1974

EDF Nuclear Reactor
Study made with architects team.
Machine Rooms 900MW C P2
in association with Claude Parent.
Tower for Reactor Type1300MW
France, 1975-1980
Completed in 1980

Cruas Nuclear Center
Nuclear Power Station
Ardèche, France, 1975-1985
Completed in 1985

RER Railway Line A
Study for Châtelet and Gare de Lyon Stations.
Existing Stations: Renovation Studies
Paris, France, 1975

New Abu Dhabi Airport
Study & Supervision
United Arab Emirates, 1975-1982
Completed in 1982

New Doha International Airport
Terminal Study , Qatar, 1976

New Dhaka Airport
Bangladesh, 1976-1979
Completed in 1979

Jakarta Soekarno-Hatta Airport
Study and Supervision
Indonesia, 1977-1985
Phase 1: Completed in 1985
Phase 2: Completed in 1991

Dar-Es-Salaam Airport
New Terminal, Control Tower
Tanzania, 1977-1984
Completed in 1984

Cairo Airport - Terminal 2
Egypt, 1977-1986
Completed in 1986

Air France - Aerial Operations Building
Airport Roissy, France, 1979-1983
Completed in 1983

Nice-Côte d'Azur Airport Terminal 2
France, 1980-1987
Completed in 1987

La Villette Science Museum
Competition
Paris, France, 1981

Finance Ministry
Competition
Paris, France, 1982

Brunei Airport
Extension and Restructuring
of the Terminal
Brunei, 1982
Completed in 1987

Conakry Airport New Terminal
Guinea, 1982-1985
Completed in 1985

Customs Complex Saint-Louis-Bâle
French-Swiss Border, 1983-1989
Completed in 1989

Kuala Lumpur Airport
New Terminal Project
Malaysia, 1984

Grande Arche de la Défense
in association with J.O. Spreckelsen,
competition Winner
La Défense, France, 1984-1989
Completed in 1989

Lahore and New Islamabad Airports
New Terminal Study
Pakistan, 1984

Don Muang Airport
New Terminal Study
Bangkok, Thailand, 1985

Charles-de-Gaulle Airport
Terminal 2 D
Roissy, France, 1985-1989
Completed in 1989

Charles-de-Gaulle Airport
Terminal 2 C
Roissy, France, 1985-1993
Completed in 1993

Channel Tunnel -
French Terminal - Cité Europe
Calais, France, from 1986
Completion 1993 (Cross Channel),
1995 (Cité Europe)

Bercy Bridge - New Upstream Bridge
Competition
Paris, France 1986

Turin Airport
New Terminal, Competition
Italy, 1987

France-Japan Monument
Competition
Japan, 1987

Montpellier Airport Terminal Extension
France, 1987-1989
Completed in 1989

Kansai International Airport
Terminal Concept
Osaka, Japan, 1987
Completed in 1994

Charles-de-Gaulle Airport
Terminal 2 F
Roissy, France 1987-1999
Completed in 1998/1999

Ski Jump – Winter Olympics
Courchevel, France, 1988-1991

Charles-de-Gaulle Memorial
Competition
Porte Maillot, Paris, France, 1988

Renovation of Charlety Stadium
Competition
Paris, France, 1988

Charles-de-Gaulle Airport
TGV-RER Station - Exchange Module
In association with Jean-Marie Duthilleul
Roissy, France, 1988
Completed in 1994

Charles-de-Gaulle Airport
TGV Station - Hotel Sheraton
Roissy, France, 1989
Completed in 1996

French Pavilion
Seville Universal Exposition
Competition by Invitation
Spain, 1989

Bordeaux Mérignac Airport
Terminal 2
France, 1989-1995
Completed in 1996

Paris International
Conference Centre
Competition by Invitation with
Peter Rice & Jean-Michel Wilmotte
France, 1989

New Oslo Airport
Competition
Hurum, Norway, 1989

Orly-West Airport
Terminal Extension, Hall I
France, 1989
Completed in 1993

Sète Contemporary Art Museum
Feasibility Study
France, 1989

Manila Airport -
Domestic Terminal
Philippines, 1990
Completed in 1999

Hiroshima Airport Terminal
Competition
Japan, 1990

Seine Rive Gauche - New Avenue
Study
Paris, France, 1990-1995

New Terminal -
Pointe-à-Pitre Guadeloupe
French West Indies, 1990-1996
Completed in 1996

Port of Marseille and La Joliette CBD
Study
France, 1990

Avenue de France, Rive Gauche
Study
Paris, France, 1990

Toulon Airport, New Terminal
Study
France, 1990

La Défense RER Station
Study with Jean-Michel Wilmotte
France, 1990

Kumihama Golf
Study
Japan, 1991

Paris Exhibition Park
Porte de Versailles
Competition
Paris, France, 1991

Sanya Airport New Terminal
Phoenix, China
China, 1991-1994
Completed in 1994

Santiago de Chile Airport New Passenger Terminal
Competition Winner
Chile, 1991
Completed in 1994

Borobudur Hotel
Jakarta
Study
Indonesia, 1991

Nishinomiya Hotel and Cultural Center
Competition
Japan, 1992

New Athens Airport
Spata
Competition
Greece, 1992

Bridge for the A14 by the Seine
Le Mesnil-le-Roi
Competition
France, 1992

Berlin Schönefeld Airport
Master Plan and New Terminal
Study
Germany, 1992

New Seoul Metropolitan Airport
Competition
Korea, 1992

Manchester Stadium
Competition
England, 1992

Larnaca Airport
Competition Winner
Cyprus, 1992-1993

Harare International Airport
Study
Zimbabwe, 1992-1995

New Doha International Airport
Study
Qatar, 1992-1993

Multipurpose Stadium and Arena
Competition
Melun-Sénart, France, 1993

Atatürk Airport New Terminal
Competition
Istanbul, Turkey, 1993

Osaka Maritime Museum
Japan, 1993-2000
Completed in 2000

Bangkok Airport
Competition
Thailand, 1994

St Denis Grand Stadium
Competition
France, 1994

Douai Exhibition Center
Competition
France, 1994

Eldoret International Airport
Study
Kenya, 1995
Completed in 1996

Tehran International Airport
Iran, 1995
Completion
scheduled for 2004

Multipurpose Stadium
Study
Joyetsu, Japan, 1995

Shanghai Pudong International Airport New Terminal
Competition Winner
Shanghai, China, 1996-1999
Completed in 1999

Abu Dhabi Airport Terminal 2
Competition Winner
Extension to existing Airport
United Arab Emirates (UAE), 1996
Completion scheduled for 2005

Charles-de-Gaulle Airport, Terminal 2 A, New Satellite
Roissy, France, 1996-1999
Completed in 1999

Durban Airport New Terminal
Study
Durban, South Africa, 1997

Nice-Côte d'Azur Airport Extension Terminal 2 - 2nd Module
France, 1997-2002
Completed in 2002

Madrid-Barajas Airport New Terminal
Competition
Spain, 1997

Charles-de-Gaulle Airport - Terminal 2 E
Roissy, France, 1997-2003
Completed in 2003

Shanghai Industrial Museum
Competition
Shanghai, China, 1997

Guangzhou Gymnasium
China, 1998-2001
Completed in 2001

Guangzhou Daily Cultural Plaza Office Tower
Competition
Guangzhou, China, 1998

Guangzhou Baiyun Airport New Terminal
Competition
Guangzhou, China, 1998

Ningbo Airport - New Terminal
Dongshe
Competition
China, 1998

National Grand Theater of China
Opera Hall and Performance Spaces
Beijing, China, 1999
Completion scheduled for 2005

Casablanca Grand Stadium
Project in association with
Mohammed Fikri Benabdallah, Architect
Morocco, 1999
Phased completion

Dubai Airport Terminal 3
Dubai,
United Arab Emirates (UAE), 2000
Completion scheduled for 2005

Oriental Art Center
Concert Hall and Performance Spaces
Shanghai, China, 2000-2004
Completed in 2004

Guangzhou Finance Bureau
Guangzhou, China, 2003

Fort Lauderdale-Hollywood International Airport Terminal 4
Renovation and cost study for the terminal
In association with
Pierre-Michel Delpeuch (ADPi)
Fort Lauderdale, Florida, USA, 2003 - In progress

Guangzhou Science Center
Competition
China, 2003

CBD Core
Competition
Beijing, China, 2003

Publications

Coverage of Recent Projects

2000

- *Femina Hebdo*
  January: Rencontre du 3ème type
- *Le Figaro Magazine*
  January: Un français à Pékin
- *Dialogue*
  January: Buildings of Recreation Theme II
- *Häuser*
  January: Peking Oper à la mode
- *World Architecture China*
  February: Paul Andreu and his Universal Space
- *L'Événement du Jeudi*
  9 February: Paul Andreu se voit confié un nouveau chantier pharaonique: le grand théâtre de Pékin
- *The Independent*
  February: China orders new blackout on the opera house designed by a foreigner
- *World Architecture*
  no. 84, March: Two-part Osaka saga; Andreu unveils stadium Casablanca
- *Archinews*
  March: Paul Andreu : parcours d'un enfant gâté
- *D'Architectures*
  March: Musée Maritime d'Osaka
- *ABC cultural, Espagne*
  March: Paul Andreu y la nueva Opera de Pekin
- *Reportages*
  March: Opéra de Pékin: Ecrin de titane fleur de verre
- *L'Arca International*
  no. 33, March: La resistenza dei sensi/ In Casablanca and Beijing
- *L'Art dans la ville*
  1st Trimester : L'Opéra de Pékin à la mode
- *L'Événement du jeudi*
  30 March to 5 April: Bordeaux, le nouveau vivier de l'architecture française – Opéra de Pékin
- *Opera Now*
  March/April: Back to the future
- *Libération*
  5 April: Opéra de Pékin, que de pépins
- *Le Monde*
  21 April: Controverses autour du projet de l'Opéra de Pékin
- *Sud Ouest*
  April: Pékin: un opéra pas populaire
- *Passenger Terminal*
  April: Middle East calm
- *Elle Décoration*
  April: L'architecte des aéroports atterrit à Pékin
- *Architecture*
  April: Paul Andreu: Osaka Maritime Museum
- *Airport World*
  April/May: Shanghai Airport. The best of both worlds
- *L'Express*
  5 May: Les gagnants de 99
- *L'Express*
  18 May: Transparence place Tiananmen
- *Sinopress / Le Canard Laqué*
  25 May: Opéra à Pékin: la polémique
- *Quotidien de la Clarté*
  7 June: Pourquoi j'ai donné cette forme au NGT de Chine
- *Le Monde*
  19 June: La Chine continue de malmener son patrimoine architectural
- *France Ouest*
  28 June: L'architecte de Roissy pilote l'Opéra de Pékin
- *Télérama*
  5 July: L'urbanisme au bulldozer
- *Le Moniteur*
  14 July: Osaka: Un musée dans le pacifique
- *Le Figaro*
  15 July: Pékin maintient son projet d'opéra futuriste
- *Libération*
  15 et 16 July: Pékin tient à son Opéra
- *Beijing Youth Daily*
  16 July: On the design and the site of the Beijing Opera
- *Libération*
  25 July: Opéra de Pékin: Andreu révise sa copie
- *Le Monde*
  29 July: Paul Andreu a modifié son projet pour l'Opéra de Pékin
- *Architectural Record*
  July: Shanghai-Pudong International Airport
- *China Daily*
  9 August: Review for National Grand Theatre project
- *Libération*
  11 August: Fausse note à Pékin: le projet d'opéra entrouvre un débat politico-esthétique
- *Libération*
  17 August: Feu orange pour l'Opéra de Pékin
- *La Tribune*
  21 August: L'Aéroport de Nice-Côte d'Azur investit un milliard de francs
- *L'Humanité*
  21 August: L'opéra futuriste de Pékin a son ticket

- *Capital*
  August: Opéra de Shanghai
- *City Magazine*
  August: Paul Andreu on National Grand Theatre
- *Southeast Asia Building*
  August: New gymnasium for Guangzhou
- *Nice-Matin*
  13 September: Les grands travaux de l'Aéroport Nice-Côte d'Azur. Sur les ailes du futur
- *Shinkenchiku*
  no. 75, September: Osaka Maritime Museum
- *Domus*
  no. 829, September: Shanghai, the city that exploded
- *Le Monde*
  September: Paul Andreu révise à la baisse son projet d'Opéra à Pékin
- *South China Morning Post*
  September: To build or not to build
- *GA – Global Architecture Japan*
  no. 46, September/October: Osaka Maritime Museum
- *France-Soir*
  10 October: La bande à Bono en piste à Roissy
- *Corse-Matin*
  29 October: Paul Andreu: "L'architecte doit atteindre l'émotion" (Extension de l'aérogare 2 de Nice)
- *Space Hong-Kong*
  no. 22, October:
  The new generation of Museums
  The floating glass-sphere, Osaka Maritime Museum
- *Architectural Digest*
  October: An interview with architect Paul Andreu on the National Grand Theater in China
- *Airways*
  October: Paris Charles-de-Gaulle: Airport of Light
- *AMC*
  no. 110, October: Les grandes surfaces commerciales. Cité Europe
- *Le Figaro*
  Culture, October: Dans les secrets de l'Opéra de Pékin
- *Ming Pao Weekly*
  October: Chinese National Theater – an idea pregnant for 40 years
- *France Soir*
  November: "L'Opéra français" de Pékin déclenche la tempête
- *Space Corée*
  no. 396, November: Paul Andreu, architect, Osaka Maritime Museum
- *South China Morning Post*
  December: Osaka Maritime Museum
- *Murator Plus*
  June: Niezwykly terminal lotniczy , Charles-de-Gaulle Airport

2001

- *L'Arca International*
  no. 38, January: Come una casa del tè, Osaka Maritime Museum
- *Ideat*
  January/February: Paul Andreu, l'homme aux cinquante aérogares
- *Le Journal du Dimanche*
  11 February: Roissy opéré du cœur
- *L'Industria Italiana del Cemento*
  no. 762, February:
  Aeroporto internazionale Shanghai Pudong – China
- *Télérama*
  21 February and 28 March:
  Paul Andreu: Le grand Opéra de Pékin
- *Le Moniteur*
  March: L'aérogare de Roissy fait peau neuve
- *Le Point*
  9 March: L'aéroport d'Osaka prend l'eau
- *D' Architectures*
  April: Shanghai, la modernité sans concession
- *Le Monde*
  4 June: Reprise des travaux de construction de l'Opéra de Pékin
- *Southeast Asia Building*
  May, Passenger Terminal, Shanghai-Pudong International Airport
- *La Nacion*
  13 June: Con novedades y propuestas ineditas
- *Le Moniteur*
  15 June: Complexe omnisports de Guangzhou à Canton, Chine
- *Le Monde*
  19 June: Vers un réveil du chantier de l'Opéra de Pékin
- *Menhir*
  no. 3, July: Museo maritimo de Osaka (Japon)
- *Techniques et architectures*
  August/September: Ciel d'acier, aéroport de Shanghai Pudong (Chine)
- *Asiaweek*
  7 September: Designs on destiny
- *Space Corée*
  no. 406, September: Paul Andreu, Guangzhou Gymnasium

- *Beton, Die Fachzeitschrift für Bau + Technik*
  September: Aérogare 2, Flugobjekt mit Zukunftsplänen
- *Les Echos*
  11 October: Chine, les montagnes lumineuses du complexe omnisports de Canton
- *L'Acier pour construire*
  November: Le Musée Maritime d'Osaka, "Perle du pacifique"
- *A T D, Architecture, Technology and Design*
  November: Guangzhou New Gymnasium, China
- *Colorfulness*
  no. 18, December: Paul Andreu and his airport design
- *L'Express*
  13 December: Paul Andreu
- *South China Morning Post*
  15 December: Theatre go-ahead bursts critics buble
- *China Daily*
  15 December: Work on controversial theatre starts
- *South China Morning Post*
  19 December: Controversial new theatre given go-ahead
- *The China Post*
  20 December: Despite heated debate, China goes ahead with controversial new theatre
- *A T D, Architecture, Technology and Design*
  no. 87, December: Osaka Maritime Museum, Japan
- *Formes et structures*
  March: Musée maritime d'Osaka, Paul Andreu, Architecte.
  Le complexe omnisports de Canton
- *International Architecture Yearbook*
  no. 7, Shanghai-Pudong International Airport
- *Southeast Asia Building*
  December: Gym Tonic, Guangzhou Gymnasium

2002

- *Menhir*
  no. 5, January: Gimnasio de Guangzhou
- *Le Moniteur*
  February: Aéroport de Nice: un cône inversé de verre et d'acier
- *Shanghai Daily*
  22-28 March: Oriental Art Center, Palace of the Arts
- *Aéroports Magazine*
  March: Paul Andreu, architecte ADP: construire des bâtiments aussi peu spécifiques que possible
- *Trendshome*
  March: Opera of Beijing in China by architect Paul Andreu
- *A T D, Architecture, Technology and Design*
  no. 90, March: An airport that grows. Shanghai Pudong International Airport
- *L'Arca International*
  no. 45, March: Il drago trasparente, Guangzhou Gymnasium
- *Interior Design + Construction*
  no. 9, April: An interview with the Master. Talking with Paul Andreu about design
- *La Presse (Canada)*
  19 May: Le nouvel Opéra de Pékin créé par un français
- *iiC l'Industria italiana del Cemento*
  no. 776, May: The museum on the sea
- *A T D, Architecture, Technology and Design*
  no. 93, June: Shanghai Oriental Art Centre
- *L'Arca International*
  no. 171, June: Oriental Art center, Shanghai

2003

- *China Daily*
  27 March: Grand theatre to be completed
- *Casa Brutus (Japan)*
  no. 36, March: Paul Andreu, Maestro of airport design, new architecture in China
- *New Architecture Magazine*
  April: Oriental Art Center of Shanghai – Bouncing Melody
- *Les Echos*
  25 et 26 April: En plein coeur de la capitale, l'Opéra de Paul Andreu s'apprête à recevoir son dôme de verre et d'acier
- *Artein*
  April: Paul Andreu parla del nuovo teatro che sara inaugurato alla fine del

2004

- *Frankfurter Allgemeine Zeitung*
  3 June: Das Pariser Flughafen-Terminal E vor der Eröffnung, Barocke Formen aus Beton, Stahl und Glas
- *Formes et Structures*
  no. 140, June: Roissy Charles-de-Gaulle, Aérogare 2, Terminal E

- *China Daily*
  8 September: Architecture at a juncture
- *Menhir*
  September: Terminal de pasajeros, aeropuerto internacional de Shanghaï-Pudong
- *AMC*
  no. 138, November: Formes complexes. Pékin,Grand Théâtre National de Chine
- *A+U*
  December: National Grand Theater, Paul Andreu, First Prize
- *New Beijing News*
  10 December: The National Grand Theater crowned successfully, The gigantic egg-shaped shell finally closured
- *Libération*
  27 December: Roissy – Pékin sans escale
- *Citizen K International*
  Spring 2004: National Grand Theater of China

Books

- "*La Grande Arche - Carnet de Route*" by Paul Andreu and Hubert Tonka - Editions du Demi Cercle, Paris, 1989.
- "*Metamorphoses of the Circle*" by Serge Salat and Françoise Labbé, Electa Moniteur, 1990.
- "*Carnets de croquis*" by Pascale Blin, A Tempera Editions, 1990.
- "*Paul Andreu. The Non-Linear Metropolis*" by Serge Salat and Françoise Labbé, Seoul Forum Inc., 1991.
- "*Between Silence and Light*" by Serge Salat and Françoise Labbé, Hachette, 1991.
- "*Themes, variations, ruptures*" by Serge Salat et Françoise Labbé, exhibition catalogue Empress Place Museum, Singapure, 1993.
- "*L'aéroport Charles-de-Gaulle, Le Module d'échanges*" by Paul Andreu, Les cahiers de projets d'Aéroports de Paris, 1994.
- "*L'aéroport Charles-de-Gaulle, le Module 2 F*" by Paul Andreu, Les cahiers de projets d'Aéroports de Paris, 1995.
- "*Terminal Transmanche et Cité Europe*" by Paul Andreu, Les cahiers de projets d'Aéroports de Paris, 1995.
- *"Paul Andreu. The Discovery of Universal Space*", L'Arcaedizioni, 1997.
- "*Paul Andreu. Cinquante aérogares*", Les Cahiers de Projets d'Aéroports de Paris, 1998.
- "*J'ai fait beaucoup d'aérogares...Les dessins et les mots*" by Paul Andreu, Editions Descartes & Cie, 1998.
- "*Le Grand Théâtre National de Pékin, comment réussir un opéra, de Charles Garnier à Paul Andreu*" by Gérard Fontaine, Agnès Viénot Editions, 2003.

Biography

Paul Andreu was born on July 10, 1938 in Caudéran in Gironde, France.

Ecole Polytechnique, Paris, 1961
Ponts et Chausées, Paris, Engineer in Chief, 1963
Ecole des Beaux-Arts, Paris, Architect DPLG, 1968.

Officer in the French Legion of Honor.
Grand officer of the French National Order of Merit.
Commander of the French Order of Arts and Letters.
Member of the French Academy of Architecture.
Member of the French National Academy of Air and Space.
Member of the International Academy of Architecture in Sofia.
Member of the French Academy of Technology.

1976
Silver Grand Medal, – J. F. Delarue Prize – awarded by the French Academy of Architecture in recognition of the architectural quality for the whole of Roissy Charles-de-Gaulle Airport.
1977
French National Grand Prize in Architecture.
1981
"Construction's Man of the Year," Engineering News Record, Citation.
1987
President of the Research Group, "Architecture and Exports," focusing on the export of French architectural and engineering ideas, organized by the French Ministry for Infrastructure, Housing, Urban Planning, and Transportation.
1989
Florence Gould Grand Prize, for the whole of his work
1990
1st Category Architecture License, Japan. Special Jury Prize for the best metal construction, awarded for the elevator tower of the Arche de La Défense, Paris.
1994
Laureate of the "Vinci de la construction" awarded by the French Committee of Construction and Beaux-Arts for the whole of his work
1995
April: Nikkei BP Technology Award for technological design work for Kansai International Airport in Osaka, Japan, with: Tsuneharu Hattori, KIA, Ltd.; Renzo Piano of Renzo Piano Building Workshop; Kimiaki Minai, Nikken Sekkei, Ltd.; Takeshi Kido, Japan Airport Consultant, Mr. Obayashi, Mr. Takenaka.
May: Architectural Institute of Japan (AU) Prize for Kansai International Airport, Osaka, Japan, with: Tsuneharu Hattori, KIA, Ltd.; Renzo Piano, Renzo Piano Building Workshop; Kimiaki Minai, Nikken Sekkei, Ltd.; Takeshi Kido, Japan Airport Consultant.
November: British Structural Steel Design Award for the conception of the metal structure for the glass canopy of the TGV RER Train Station at Roissy, with: Hugh Dutton, RFR; Jean-Marie Duthilleul, SNCF; Joe Locke, Watson Steel, Ltd.
Aga Kahn Architecture Award for the integration of the landscape design for Soekarno-Hatta International Airport, Jakarta-Cengareng, Indonesia.
1996
April: First Prize for the Commercial and Entertainment Center Cité Europe in Calais, France, awarded by The International Council of Shopping (I.C.S.C.), in Montreux, Switzerland.
June: Special Prize of the Aeronautical and Astronautical Association of France (A.A.A.F.).
1997
November: Special Award, Commendation, for the three-dimensional structure of the Terminal 2 F at Charles-de-Gaulle Airport, Paris, awarded by The Institution of Structural Engineers, London, with RFR.
1998
December: Competition Prize for the best metal construction, Hall 2 F at Charles-de Gaulle Airport, Paris, awarded by the French Syndicate for Metal Construction.
1999
March: Grand Centenary Medal, awarded by the Aero-Club of France.
2000
September: Honorary Citizenship, bestowed by the City of Guangzhou, China.
2002
March: Special Award, for Osaka Maritime Museum, Japan, awarded by The Institution of Structural Engineers, London, with ARUP.

Paul Andreu's Collaborators

Charles-de-Gaulle Airport Terminal 1
Pierre Prangé, François Prestat, Paul Meyer, Jean-Louis Renucci, Yves Robin, Henri Lazar, Michel Grégoire in collaboration with Joseph Motte for interior design and Adrian Frutiger for typography

Charles-de-Gaulle Airport, Terminal 2 A and B, C and D
Terminal 2 A – B:
Jean-Louis Renucci, François Prestat, Jean-Jacques Baechelen and Jean-Michel Fourcade in collaboration with Joseph Motte for interior design and Adrian Frutiger for typography
Terminal 2 C:
Pierre-Michel Delpeuch and Jean-François Vigouroux in colloboration with Jean-Michel Wilmotte for interior design
Terminal 2 D:
Pierre-Michel Delpeuch, Jean-Michel Fourcade and Jean-François Vigouroux

Charles-de-Gaulle Airport, TGV Station, Hotel
In association with Jean-Marie Duthilleul (SNCF) and Peter Rice (RFR) with Dimitri Georgandelis, Michel Vermeulen, Anne Brison and Hugh Dutton

Charles-de-Gaulle Airport, Hotel Sheraton
Anne Brison.Interior design of the hotel: Andrée Putman

Charles-de-Gaulle Airport Terminal 2 F
Jean-Michel Fourcade, Pierre-Michel Delpeuch, Valérie Chavanne, Hervé Langlais and Gilles Goix

Charles-de-Gaulle Airport Terminal 2 E
Jean-Michel Fourcade, Jean-Paul Back, Anne Brison, Gilles Goix

Nice-Côte d'Azur Airport Terminal 2
Pierre-Michel Delpeuch, Jean-Michel Fourcade, François Prestat and Charles-Jean Schmeltz

Nice Côte d'Azur Airport Terminal 2 Module 2
François Tamisier, Gérard Andreu, Marie-Dominique Ploix, Jean-Pierre Zubléna

Abu Dhabi Airport – Terminal 1
François Prestat and Jean-Claude Flouvat

Jakarta Soekarno-Hatta Airport
Jean-Jacques Baechelen, Jean-Paul Lavit d'Hautefort and Jean-François Vigouroux

Dar-Es-Salaam Airport
Jean-François Vigouroux, Yves Coutant, Pierre Prangé

Cairo Airport, Terminal 2
Pierre Prangé, Michel Grégoire, Jean-François Vigouroux, Anne Brison

Grande Arche, Paris in association with J.O. Spreckelsen, author of the concept, competition winner
Pierre Prangé, Georges Abbo, Laurence Fidelle-Mézière, Jean-Claude Flouvat,

Pascale Gonon, Vincent Jacob, Maurice Kruk, François Tamisier

Cross Channel Terminal, Calais
Pierre-Michel Delpeuch and Dominique Chavanne

Cité Europe Center, Calais
Pierre-Michel Delpeuch and François Tamisier

Kansai International Airport
Concept and specific studies Pierre-Michel Delpeuch and Jean-Michel Fourcade
Architecture: Renzo Piano Building Workshop in association with Nikken Sekkei and Japan Airport Consultant

Ski Jump, 1992 Winter Olympics, Courchevel
Pierre Prangé, Pierre Bourgin, Valérie Latil, Jean-Michel Fourcade

Osaka Maritime Museum
François Tamisier and Massa Bokura

Shanghai Pudong Airport
François Tamisier, Gérard Andreu, Pascale Gonon, Hélène Boitard

Abu Dhabi Airport, Terminal 2
Jean-Paul Back and Jean-François Vigouroux

Guangzhou Gymnasium
François Tamisier, Serge Carillion, Michel Adment, Hervé Langlais

National Grand Theater of China
François Tamisier, Hervé Langlais, Olivia Faury, Mario Flory, Serge Carillion

Guangzhou Baiyun Airport
François Tamisier, Gérard Andreu

Oriental Art Center
Graciela Torre, Michel Adment, Hervé Langlais

CBD Core, Beijing
Hervé Langlais, Mario Flory, Khaled Ben Abdallah, Karim Saad, Carole Rami, Olivia Faury

Guangzhou Science Center
Khaled Ben Abdallah, Hervé Langlais, Carole Rami

and

Patricia Casse

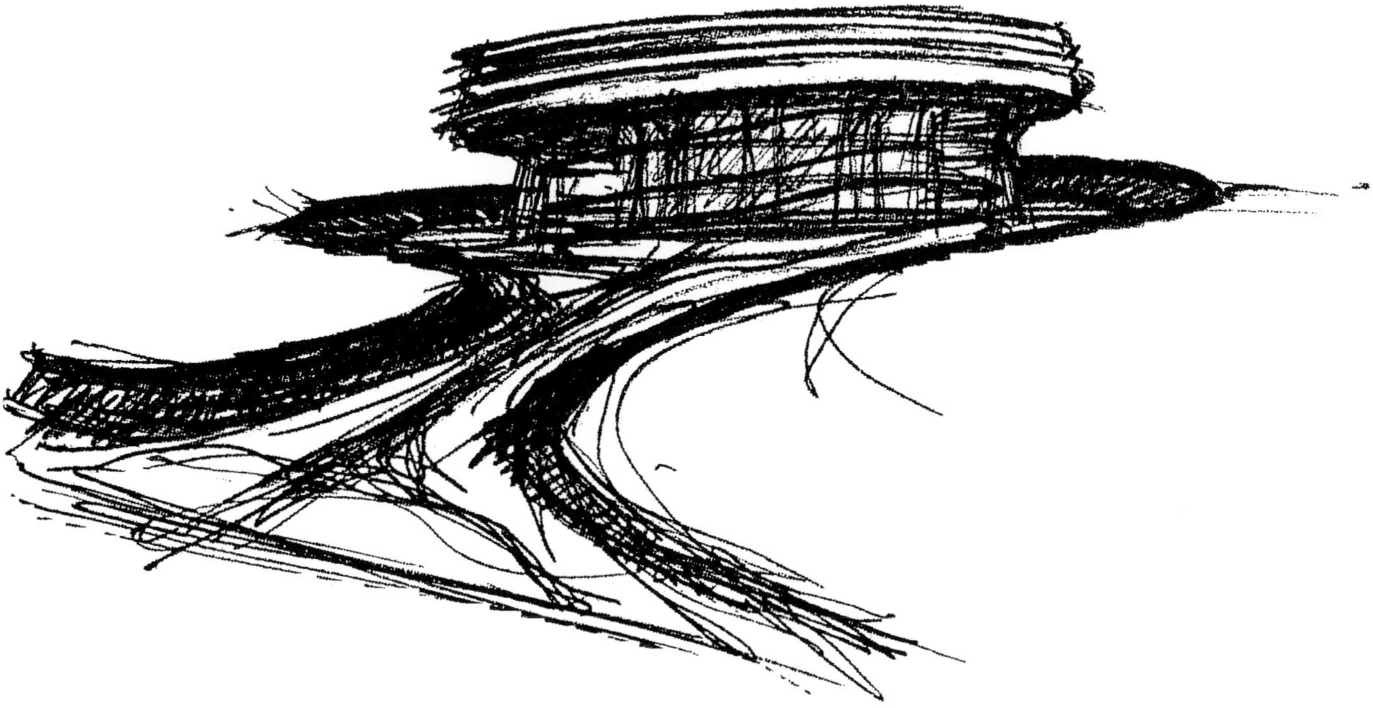

Illustration Credits

All photographic rights © Paul Maurer with the exception of:
Cover p.24-25 © Hervé Langlais
p.21-134-135-136-137-139 © Shinkenchiku-Sha
p.27-163-159 © Li Wen/Point Studio
p.28-31-184-185-186-187-188-189-190-191 © Crystal CG
p.35-47 © ADP
p.44-45-177 © Antoine Buonomo
p.56 ©J.C.Flouvat
p.60-61 © Coulon Lagrange
p.63 © G.Liesse
p.67 © Yori Antar
p.98 © Ph. Da Silva
p.105 © Ph.Kawatetsu. RPBW, Renzo Piano Building Workshop
p.106 Rights reserved
p.133 © Masato Ikuta
p.138 © GA Photographers. Y.Takase
p.140-141 © Tian Pao Huang
p.144-146-168-171 top -172-173-180-182-183 bottom - back cover © Paul Andreu
p.149 © J.L. Fernandez ADP
p.165-169-179 bottom -181 bottom © Axyz
p.166 bottom -170-171 bottom © Antoine Buonomo/Hervé Langlais
p.166 top -167 © Bernard Dragon
p.179 top -183 © ADPI
Back flap © Fred Kihn

The sketches © Paul Andreu